Hitchcock and Humor

Hitchcock and Humor
*Modes of Comedy
in Twelve Defining Films*

WES D. GEHRING

McFarland & Company, Inc., Publishers
Jefferson, North Carolina

ALSO BY WES D. GEHRING AND FROM MCFARLAND

Movie Comedians of the 1950s: Defining a New Era of Big Screen Comedy (2016); *Genre-Busting Dark Comedies of the 1970s: Twelve American Films* (2016); *Chaplin's War Trilogy: An Evolving Lens in Three Dark Comedies, 1918–1947* (2014); *Will Cuppy, American Satirist: A Biography* (2013); *Forties Film Funnymen: The Decade's Great Comedians at Work in the Shadow of War* (2010); *Film Clowns of the Depression: Twelve Defining Comic Performances* (2007); *Joe E. Brown: Film Comedian and Baseball Buffoon* (2006); *Mr. Deeds Goes to Yankee Stadium: Baseball Films in the Capra Tradition* (2004)

Frontispiece: *Top*: The British Film Institute (BFI) ranks *The 39 Steps* (1935) as Hitchcock's greatest English film. Many of the director's pre–American movies were grossly underrated. *The 39 Steps* served as a template for his seminal American film, *North by Northwest* (1959). Though the photos featuring Robert Donat and Madeleine Carroll in this ad appear suitably dramatic, the text adopts a comic tone, reflecting Hitchcock's impish impulse, describing Donat as, "The MAN who put the MAN in RoMANce." **Bottom**: Hitchcock's first, funniest and longest cameo appeared in *Blackmail* (1929). The bratty boy (Johnny Ashby) bothering him would prove to be representative of most Hitchcockian kids to follow.

LIBRARY OF CONGRESS CATALOGUING-IN-PUBLICATION DATA

Names: Gehring, Wes D., author.
Title: Hitchcock and humor : modes of comedy in twelve defining films / Wes D. Gehring.
Description: Jefferson, N.C. : McFarland & Company, Inc., Publishers, 2019. | Includes bibliographical references and index.
Identifiers: LCCN 2019002679 | ISBN 9781476673561 (paperback : acid free paper) ∞
Subjects: LCSH: Hitchcock, Alfred, 1899–1980—Criticism and interpretation. | Comedy films—History and criticism.
Classification: LCC PN1998.3.H58 G43 2019 | DDC 791.4302/33092—dc23
LC record available at https://lccn.loc.gov/2019002679

BRITISH LIBRARY CATALOGUING DATA ARE AVAILABLE

**ISBN (print) 978-1-4766-7356-1
ISBN (ebook) 978-1-4766-3621-4**

© 2019 Wes D. Gehring. All rights reserved

No part of this book may be reproduced or transmitted in any form or by any means, electronic or mechanical, including photocopying or recording, or by any information storage and retrieval system, without permission in writing from the publisher.

The front cover image is from *The Lady Vanishes*, 1938 (Gainsborough Pictures, Gaumont British, United Artists)

Printed in the United States of America

*McFarland & Company, Inc., Publishers
Box 611, Jefferson, North Carolina 28640
www.mcfarlandpub.com*

To Anthony Slide

Table of Contents

Preface and Acknowledgments 1
Prologue: Working Towards *Blackmail* (1929) 3

1. *Blackmail* (1929) 29
2. *The Man Who Knew Too Much* (1934) 45
3. *The 39 Steps* (1935) 61
4. *Secret Agent* (1936) 78
5. *The Lady Vanishes* (1938) 95
6. *Mr. & Mrs. Smith* (1941) 114
7. *Shadow of a Doubt* (1943) 134
8. *Rope* (1948) 153
9. *Strangers on a Train* (1951) 174
10. *Rear Window* (1954) 192
11. *The Trouble with Harry* (1955) 210
12. *North by Northwest* (1959) 225

Epilogue, and Thoughts on *Psycho* (1960) 249
Filmography 255
Chapter Notes 259
Bibliography 270
Index 279

Preface and Acknowledgments

Tom Shone's book, *Woody Allen: A Retrospective* (2015), describes the comedian's *Manhattan Murder Mystery* as "a kind of *Rear Window* [1954] for retirees."

Alfred Hitchcock's methodical use of various comedy genres in his work has yet to receive due credit. Too often anything funny in his films other than black humor has been dismissed as "comic relief." Assorted types of humor, often used simultaneously, have so fueled his films that the movies are often more accurately described as *comic* thrillers. This comedy is so embedded in his films that the term also frequently applies to his antiheroic lead—the *comic* "wrong man." This oversight has worked to my benefit in allowing me to finally showcase Hitchcock's full range of cinematic hijinks, which runs parallel to his mastery of suspense.

However, before addressing this subject, there are many archives and individuals to thank for helping make this book possible. My East Coast research begins with the New York Public Library's main branch at Fifth Avenue and 42nd Street, forever guarded by the lions "Patience" and "Fortitude." At this location, my focus is on the "tombs" section—looking at New York's many seminal dead newspapers on microfilm. The city's Performing Arts Library at Lincoln Center is also a necessary stop, with its period clipping files of film artists and individual pictures.

Previous work on my Robert Benchley book merits noting, since this personality comedian was important to Hitchcock, including the comic actor's appearance in *Foreign Correspondent* (1940). Thus, previous research done at Boston University's Mugar Memorial Library was most helpful, since Benchley's private papers are part of their Special Collections Department.

On the West Coast the Academy of Motion Picture Arts and Sciences' Margaret Herrick Library (Beverly Hills) is also a necessary stop, especially for clipping files. (These holdings, however, often underline the importance of the New York newspapers—all of which are well represented.) Special West Coast film friends (Joe and Maria Pacino, and Tony Slide) were also helpful in my research by way of brainstorming ideas.

At my Ball State University home I must start with a heartfelt thank you to the support of my telecommunications department. And as with all my writing, Janet Warrner supplied invaluable editorial and proofing assistance, with her husband, Ball State history instructor Andy Warrner, being a great sounding board for discussions of periods covered. TCOM office manager Kris Scott was responsible for the computer preparation of the manuscript, as well as additional tasks too numerous to discuss. Ball State emeritus professors David L. Smith and Conrad Lane provided additional valuable discussions about the project. Chris Flook once again was helpful with technology questions. Additional proofing was done by Emma Pynchon. And award-winning filmmaker Bob Mugge always helped keep me on track and forever provided provocative ideas. Plus, BSU's interlibrary loan staff was invaluable: Kerri K. McClellan, Elaine S. Nelson, Jodi L. Sanders, Lisa R. Johnson, Karin Kwiatkowski, Jessie Hatton, and Kyla Hedge.

Finally, a task like this would be impossible without the love and encouragement of my family, especially my daughters Sarah and Emily. With a film professor dad, they have grown into thoughtful movie viewers, too. Be that as it may, acknowledgments could go on forever, so my *profound* apologies for anyone I have missed. Thank you one and all.

Prologue: Working Towards *Blackmail* (1929)

"All my films are dark comedies."—A frequent Alfred Hitchcock comment

A genre which encompasses the visions of Jerry Lewis and Ernst Lubitsch is already in trouble. [Film scholar Jim Leach was encouraging a more ambitious look at multiple comedy genres.] If a genre is defined too loosely, it ceases to be of any value as a critical tool.[1]

As with many books, this text seemed to search me out. For six weeks during the summer of 2017, Turner Classic Movies (TCM) gifted the public with a Hitchcock retrospective of 40-plus films shown in chronological order. Accompanying this movie barrage, the largest single TV tribute afforded a film director, was a free national online course for fans and scholars who wanted to delve deeper into Hitchcock's work. I was lucky enough to be chosen as one of the course commentators. As an author and university film professor of several decades, one cannot write and/or teach without frequently addressing Hitchcock's body of work. Indeed, even for the general public, he is still arguably the most famous "name above the title" director in movie history.

Of course, this was further fueled by two key factors, beyond the groundbreaking quality of Hitchcock's work. First, he hosted the still syndicated popular TV program *Alfred Hitchcock Presents* (1955–1965), which became the *Alfred Hitchcock Hour* in 1963, when its time bracket was expanded from thirty minutes. The suspense anthology's success was anchored in the pudgy director's deadpan ironic opening and closing comments. Indeed, even the iconic beginning of the show oozed sardonic wit, as Hitchcock's substantial shadow filled his fogged glass self-drawn signature profile, accompanied by

Charles Gounod's theme song "Funeral March of a Marionette." Fittingly, like much of Hitchcock's work, Gounod's brief 1872 composition had originally been composed as a darkly comic spoof.

An engaging element of the TV program was that evil often seemed to win in that more censored period ... until Hitchcock's comically macabre closing comments revealed the diabolical had not triumphed. Between TV (with a period defining voice, rivaled only by Rod Serling) and movies, his darkly comic brand of suspense became a cottage industry which even included a monthly publication, *Alfred Hitchcock's Mystery Magazine*. Though he essentially just signed off on the latter, the beginning of most issues aped his TV openings. For example, the August 1960 issue began, in part:

> Dear Readers,
>
> When you read this, I shall be on a trip through the far far East; naturally a trip of mystery and intrigue. If I had desired a different sort of excursion, I would have picked.... Chief Thunder-in-the-Cloud Day Camp ... [Regardless, one] story in this issue, "Crime Doesn't Pay—Enough," may prove most misleading. It is definitely not concerned with management and labor difficulties.
>
> Alfred Hitchcock[2]

The second factor which still makes Hitchcock as well-known as his stars are his brief cameo appearances in most of his pictures. Stories vary on how this got started, such as he was merely filling in for some glorified extra who had not shown up. Yet his first cameo appearance was in *Blackmail* (1929) and involved a bratty child bothering him on the subway. Their interaction is too orchestrated to have been accidental filler. Plus, from the very beginning Hitchcock recognized the importance of self-promotion. Of course, over time the cameos occurred earlier and earlier, since viewers would not plug into the plot until spotting Hitchcock.

Regardless, in my extensive prepping for the TCM tribute, I re-watched, often several times, all the Hitchcock pictures which the course most focused upon—roughly two dozen in number. Naturally, this research also necessitated revisiting a great deal of Hitchcock literature. And what most jumped out at me was the casualness of the comedy references, despite their varied pivotal uses. François Truffaut's game-changing 1967 booklength Hitchcock interview had done its work too well; the deluge of *serious* studies which followed minimized his multifaceted humor.[3] I was reminded of the Jim Leach quote which opens this prologue, especially the portion in which he states: "If a genre is defined too loosely, it ceases to be of any value as a critical tool."

Leach wrote those words some forty-odd years ago, and I have devoted much of my career to breaking down the various genres, or sub-genres of comedy to better understand artists like Hitchcock. Now before one runs from the room yammering something about how analyzing comedy kills it, the process makes more constructive sense than how our often oxymoron-driven comic language prattles on about nonsense: "live recording," "partial cease fire," "true replica," "authentic reproduction," "limited lifetime guarantee," "elevated subway," "original copy," and today's mantra "highly depressed." Socrates' axiom about "the unexamined life is not worth living" does not exclude humor. Indeed, it resulted in dark comedy, since Socrates' provocative questioning of authorities resulted in his being put to death, like a secular Jesus. (Too soon?) Regardless, did TCM's attempt to further explore Hitchcock's oeuvre ruin anyone's viewing experience?

Moreover, like most great auteurs, Hitchcock's filmography embraced numerous genres, besides utilizing various forms of comedy. Usually, the first of his works people think of is the groundbreaking horror film *Psycho* (1960), which popular culture claims impacted society for years, from either making people fearful in the shower, or even reducing the number taken. No doubt deodorant and nightlight sales also increased. Regardless, this movie, coupled with British director Michael Powell's *Peeping Tom* (1960), radically changed how viewers think of horror. Prior to this same year duo, horror was most synonymous with a foreign past, whether it was late 19th century London's Jack the Ripper, or Transylvania's centuries-old vampire Count Dracula.

Psycho and *Peeping Tom* suddenly made horror films just as likely to be about that quiet contemporary American boy living next door. All of this is not to say no previous memorable horror films had existed in a contemporary setting. For instance, one need go no further than writer/producer Val Lewton's remarkable 1940s RKO "B" movies. Plus, horror movies never have stopped periodic forays into the *boogie boogie* past. Still, a shift had occurred in 1960.

Yet, ironically, horror was not really Hitchcock's métier, despite *Psycho*, or later works like *The Birds* (1963) and *Frenzy* (1972). The majority of his best films, at least by traditional definition, which sadly sets humor elements off on that aforementioned trivial comedy compost, are often described as political and/or psychological thrillers. Classic examples would include *The 39 Steps* (1935), *The Lady Vanishes* (1938), *Suspicion* (1941), *Shadow of a Doubt* (1943), *Strangers on a Train* (1951), *Vertigo* (1958, with *Sight & Sound*'s 2012 critics' poll naming it the best film ever made[4]), and *North by Northwest* (1959). However, as this book examines twelve key Hitchcock films, a better description would be "fearful farce," or "wrong man *comedy*." Still, Hitchcock felt all his pictures were dark comedies. To illustrate, *Psycho* spews black humor, such as Norman Bates (Anthony Perkins) observing, "Mother isn't quite herself today"—darn straight; through the magic of taxidermy she is preserved and stuck in the basement. Later Norman explains his mother's temper, "she just goes a little mad sometimes." (Paging Dr. Freud.)

Truffaut once wrote in the historic film journal he helped inaugurate, *Cahiers du Cinéma*:

> Hitchcock revels in being misunderstood, more so because it is on misunderstandings that he has constructed his life.... Hitchcock is a Hitchcockian character; he loathes having to explain himself.[5]

And if truth be told, he often loathed himself. But much of that came later. At first, loads of the loathing was with the world around him, which increased with time. He was a chubby little boy who did not mix well, and Hitchcock's two siblings were enough older that he felt like an only child.

There are two pivotal events from Hitchcock's "constructed" youth which define all that follows. Whether hyperbole or not makes no real difference, since he chose to tell and retell the tales as his own personal Rosetta Stone. The first involves a very young Hitchcock upsetting his father for some minor transgression. William Hitchcock, who seems to have had the temperament of a wet cat, decided to make the punishment memorable. Knowing the local constable, he had his son briefly put behind bars. This trauma, according to Hitchcock, is why his movies tend to portray law enforcement people in a litany of negative ways. The examples would range from *39 Steps*' (1935) dangerously dumb Scottish police inspector, unaware his best friend is a foreign spy, to *Psycho*'s scary stormtrooper-like highway patrolman, who bangs on Marion's (Janet Leigh) car window, after she has fallen asleep on the shoulder of the road.

The second momentous event of young Hitchcock's boyhood was awakening one night and finding his parents gone, though presumably his older siblings, Ellen and William, Jr. (seven and ten years his senior) were at home—a factor not always added to the raconteuring director's chronicles. Regardless, the key takeaway from these two frequently told tales is a factor which quite frankly rules most people's lives at some level—fear. Indeed, it was something upon which the director would build a career.

Plus, Hitchcock was also happy to share other fear factors among his childhood anecdotes, such as the corporal punishment of attending Jesuit Catholic schools. It was not that he was frequently punished—it was the *fear* that weighed upon the youngster. As he later confessed to biographer Charlotte Chandler, "I myself have lived a life in which fear of consequences has always played a part. I was not an impulsive sort."[6] Plus, Hitchcock texts are full of how, after losing his strict father as a mid-teenager, another stressful tradition developed. Each night he was expected to stand at the foot of his mother's bed and essentially give her a report of his day.

This went on for roughly a decade until his marriage to fellow filmmaker Alma Reville sprang him from his mother's home. Setting up a household with Alma, who did not change her name, because she was already professionally established as a film editor and scriptwriter, transferred Hitchcock from one strong woman to another. But she was good for him, because both of them were all about cinema and his movies—especially the early ones, on which they essentially collaborated. As *Los Angeles Times* critic Charles Champlin would later observe of Ms. Reville, "The Hitchcock touch had four hands and two of them were Alma's."[7]

There is an absorbing addendum to Reville's rescue of her husband from a fearfully intimidating parent. That is, Hitchcock's films are well-known for less than flattering, though often entertaining, depictions of mothers, *after* his own mother died during the *Shadow of a Doubt* production. Thus, in *Strangers on a Train*, Bruno's (Robert Walker) mother (Marion Lorne) is definitely the source of his mad hatter genes, while Cary Grant's *North by Northwest* character is saddled with a rather eccentric mother in Jessie Royce Landis. Yet, both men are still most needful of the women. And of course, *Psycho* implies that Bates killed his mother and new husband out of jealousy over her remarrying—and then he ultimately becomes his mother.

Yet, this individual sense of payback hardly stops there. Round little Hitchcock, despite countless variations of fear, not to mention oodles of Catholic guilt, later developed a sometimes mean sense of humor which, ironically, still seemed to be frozen in the mindset of an adolescent boy. It was the exact opposite, say, of fellow filmmaker worrywart Woody Allen, and his comforting "cling to the wreckage" philosophy, as noted in *Annie Hall* (1977):

> I feel that life is divided into the horrible and the miserable. That's the two categories. The horrible are like, I don't know, terminal cases, you know, and blind people, crippled. I don't know how they get through life. It's amazing to me. And the miserable is everybody else. So you should be thankful that you're miserable, because that's very lucky, to be miserable.

Hitchcock it seemed was not feeling "lucky to be miserable." Along those lines, biographer John Russell Taylor mused:

> It is probably not stretching fantasy too far to guess at the first hint of how he latterly delighted to treat the cool, remote-seeming blond heroines of his films in the resentful dreams of a plain, pudgy fourteen-year-old watching some evidently unattainable blond girl near home ... thinking, "If only I had her in my power, just for a few moments...."[8]

Indeed, Donald Spoto's Hitchcock biography documents several such examples. For instance, on *The 39 Steps* (1935), the most farcical and intimate scenes between Richard Donat and Madeleine Carroll, in which the couple find themselves handcuffed together, were scheduled to be shot first. It was a curious production schedule with which to begin, given the importance that these key sequences were to permeate a breezy screwball comedy ambience, and the actors had yet to even meet. However, the first thing the initial morning of the shoot, after introductions, Hitchcock immediately cuffed them together and walked the duo through the extended sequences. However, he was then told some technical problem had occurred and he had to briefly leave, telling Donat and Carroll to just relax. However, Hitchcock failed to uncuff them. Worse yet, he did not return for some time, claiming he had misplaced the key:

> [By then] The actors, of course, were tired, angry, disheveled, uncomfortable, and acutely embarrassed. But Hitchcock was delighted when the rest of the cast and crew found out about his little trick and were shocked. He wanted to know how many people were discussing the manner in which the humiliated couple had coped with details of a decidedly personal nature. "There was no better technician in the business," recalled Jack Whitehead, second-unit cameraman on the film, "but when it came to personal relations, there was certainly a streak of the sadist in him."[9]

Even in Chandler's text on the director, which at times comes across as a template for hagiography, she includes a most telling observation on Hitchcock by screenwriter Charles Bennett. And keep in mind that arguably today's greatest film historian, Anthony Slide, has stated that Bennett's "…contribution to the success of Hitchcock's British films should never be underestimated; he was involved with the director's most famous films … [between 1929 and 1937]: *Blackmail* (1929), *The Man Who Knew Too Much* (1934), *The 39 Steps*, *The Secret Agent* (1936), *Sabotage* (1936), and *Young and Innocent* (1937)."[10] Be that as it may, Chandler's biography briefly quotes Bennett, "Hitch was a very tubby, brilliant man. He was tough to love and easy to hate."[11]

Now before anyone goes *Mommie Dearest* on me, there is a point to the perspective. Bennett's observation could be applied to countless directors, from John Ford to Stanley Kubrick. Indeed, Hitchcock's nastiness to actors even became a brief but major dark comedy point in the recently acclaimed *The Disaster Artist* (2017). But what makes Hitchcock's situation *uniquely different*, and related to the comedy study to follow, is that while the "acclaimed master of suspense" was the consummate filmmaker, countless Hitchcock studies lay crucial thriller/horror arguments at the feet of his cloistered youth—early years which had calcified him socially into a freeze-framed adolescent forever curious about sex but twistedly spooked by sin. For example, playwright and screenwriter Arthur Laurents (1917–2011), who adapted *Rope* (1948) to the screen for Hitchcock, as well as being the companion of a pivotal star in the production (Farley Granger), observed:

> He [Hitchcock] was as intrigued by the varieties of sexual life and conduct as he was the varieties of movie-making methods—in fact, he was like a child who's just discovered sex and thinks it's all very naughty. It was obvious to anyone who worked with him that he had a strong sense of sin … his Victorian Catholic background still affected him deeply. He might have been indirect in dealing with sexual things in his

films but he had a strong instinct for them. He thought everyone was doing something physical and nasty behind every closed door—except himself: he withdrew, he wouldn't be part of it.[12]

So why cannot this enduringly twisted element of his youth also be a window to his varied uses of humor genres—with dark comedy as a base?

This Hitchcock duality (artist/adolescent) was certainly apparent in Truffaut's reconfiguration of film study, via his booklength interview with the serious director, near the close of Hitchcock's career. One moment Truffaut might be asking about the famous *Notorious* (1946) crane shot, and Hitchcock would expound with great technical detail upon the difficulty of making it work. Then suddenly while discussing *To Catch a Thief* (1955) and the subject of romance, Hitchcock's man/boy juxtaposition would surface:

> Definitely, I think the most interesting women, sexually, are the English women.... Sex should not be advertised. An English girl, looking like a school-teacher, is apt to get into a cab with you and, to your surprise, she'll probably pull a man's pants open.[13]

That is a twelve-year-old boy talking—who is 68, and had been telling people for years he had not had sex for decades. And in a funny/sad supplement to that, the man who had gone by the nickname "Hitch" since childhood had also been correcting strangers for nearly as long who mistakenly called him Mr. Hitchcock—"It's just 'Hitch,' no cock." Once again, especially since this was done in nearly any setting, one is dealing with an adolescent's attempt at provocative humor.

When Truffaut brought out another addition of his seminal interview with Hitchcock in 1983, he felt compelled to expand the text with his own additional thoughts on the director, who had died in 1980. The most striking passage to me, in a lengthy addendum, had Truffaut observing:

> ... in *Notorious*, we recognized Hitchcock when [Nazi] Claude Rains timidly goes into his mother's room in the middle of the night [and stands at the foot of her bed] to confess, "Mother, I married an American spy," as if he was a guilty little boy.[14]

Once again Truffaut was breaking new ground in the *serious* study of Hitchcock. I simply propose to take that same artist/adolescent Doppler effect and direct it at various forms of humor.

With that thought in mind, a crucial connection between Hitchcock and humor must be attributed to an author invariably popular with youngsters—Edgar Allan Poe. Such was the case with Hitchcock the boy. How does one resist, especially as a lonely lad aching for escape, Poe's ephemeral scary world—safely enclosed in a book. Plus, one has the added bonus of an author shrouded in as much mystery and moral cobwebs as any of his characters. Just as Hitchcock later made his movie cameos, as a boy I always felt like Poe was lurking somewhere in his stories. (Moreover, and appropriately for a filmmaker, Hitchcock also embraced Poe's short story belief that an entertainment experience should be accomplished in a single setting.)

Hitchcock's love of Poe works on many levels central to the director's later films, including both the use of dark comedy, and his approach to the arts in general. First, though still sadly neglected, Poe was a pioneer in the birth of American dark comedy, as well as providing a template for the first modern detective stories.[15] Indeed, Poe's character C. Auguste Dupin provided the blueprint for Sir Arthur Conan Doyle's Sherlock Holmes, a fact the latter author was the first to admit. Along related lines, one of Hitchcock's favorite Poe stories was "The Murders in the Rue Morgue." While this is frequently mentioned in Hitchcock chronicles, no one seems to have taken the time to read it; just this one tale provides a staggering amount of future links to Hitchcock's later work.

First, and most obviously, one must examine the "Rue Morgue" mix of dark comedy and a murder mystery, with the story showcasing Poe's pioneering detective Dupin. One is immediately in Hitchcockland, though when the filmmaker features a focus sleuth it is invariably of the amateur variety, his signature "wrong man" forced to prove his innocence. Regardless, Poe's tale involves a ghastly double murder which occurs in a house occupied by one Madame L'Espanaye, and her daughter—with neighbors "roused from sleep by a succession of terrific shrieks...."[16] Yet, as the concerned locals rush from room to room and floor to floor, they find no one is about. Not until the fourth level is a suspicious chamber found to be locked from the inside. Upon forced entry the "wildest disorder" greets them:

> the furniture broken and thrown about in all directions.... On a chair lay a razor, besmeared with blood. On the hearth were two or three long and thick tresses of gray human hair, also dabbled with blood, and seeming to have been pulled out by the roots.[17]

Curiously, there was a great deal of money and valuables left but no sign of anyone, living or dead. Moreover, all windows and other entries to the chamber were locked from the inside. Eventually, the strangled corpse (Hitchcock's preferred murder technique) of the daughter was finally found stuffed up the chimney—head downward. Who, or what, could do such an act? And where was the mother? A second search of the house still turned up nothing. Finally, the corpse of Madame L'Espanaye was found outside, at the rear of the building, with her throat slashed so savagely that when authorities attempted to move her, the head dropped off.

So who killed the mother and daughter and then magically escaped a sealed fourth story chamber of horrors? Poe's Dupin eventually deduces (as you do), that the murderer was an escaped ourang-outang (orangutan), who could both survive a long jump from a spring-activated security window, and had always closely watched his master's straight-edge razor shaving. Thus, here was a delightful perverse bit of dark comedy, a wannabe well-groomed creature run amuck, sort of *George of the Jungle* meets *Sweeney Todd*.

This mystery/dark comedy tale also comes with an engrossing back story link to a Hitchcock contemporary tied to the same genres whose detailed art was also strongly influenced by a woman, and who harbored naïve child-like fears sometimes accompanied by juvenile behavior—Will Cuppy (1884–1949).[18] Not surprisingly, despite their often ingratiating manner, such arrested development had resulted in a soured milk taste on humanity for the writer, too. Regardless, Cuppy's day job, though he had reversed life's normal cycle, was nightly writing the *New York Herald Tribune*'s "Mystery and Adventure" book review column, back when Manhattan was densely populated with a fascinating assortment of newspapers. (Still, the *Tribune* was the *Times*' greatest quality rival.) More importantly, he wrote *research*-based humor books which anthropomorphically sideswiped the human race with dark comedy. For example, here is an observation from 1931's *How to Tell Your Friends from the Apes*, a title which almost has a "Rue Morgue" touch to it, as does the quip:

> The Howling Monkey is confined to South America but seems to escape. The back of his head is straight up and down. His howl is caused by a large hyoid bone at the top of the trachea. It can be cured by a simple operation on the neck with an axe.[19]

An offbeat but apt encapsulation of either Cuppy or Poe could be taken from an aside by contemporary *New Yorker* critic Anthony Lane, "[for them] … sleep would be not so much a blessing as a waste of night."[20]

With a certain degree of irony, moreover, for someone with such an entertainingly dark sense of humor, Cuppy's only major bestseller occurred *after* his suicide, *The Decline and Fall of Practically Everything* (1951). The book was even a favorite of both the soon-to-be president, conservative Dwight Eisenhower, and the legendary liberal newscaster Edward R. Murrow. Indeed, on the latter's "normally serious CBS news program *See It Now*, he and a colleague read in turns from … [*The Decline*] until the announcer cracked up."[21]

Cuppy, like Hitchcock and Poe, was something of an enigma. For example, despite the title of his column, he did not particularly like mysteries without dark humor, and his seldom overtly disparaging reviews were often a cover for his own black humor. And while the director liked the genre, is not his mantra of calling all his movies dark comedies really rather similar to Cuppy's viewpoint? However, the writer's direct connection to Hitchcock and Poe's "Rue Morgue" came from Cuppy's inclusion of the story in his 1943 anthology the *World's Great Detective Stories*—the same year as *Shadow of a Doubt*.

Consequently, Cuppy had implicitly "outed" the story as a dark comedy by including it in a volume full of seemingly classic mysteries ... yet mysteries which, when read, were awash with black humor. Moreover, it was also a subtle outing of Cuppy's preference for anthropomorphic dark comedy over mystery, because the anthologized stories also had a predilection for using animals to skewer mankind. For instance, Cuppy's collection also includes Mark Twain's "The Stolen White Elephant." Besides the venerated humorist's mix of humor and horror, Cuppy, and no doubt Hitchcock, would have enjoyed Twain's gleefully misanthropic tone in peppering his tale with news reports about the destruction caused by what is ultimately a runaway pachyderm:

> Elephant arrived here from the south, dispersing a funeral on the way, and diminishing the mourners by two.... I have just learned that nothing of the funeral is now left but ... there is an abundance of material for another ... [and said beast has now] broke up a revival, striking down and damaging many who were on the point of entering upon a better life.[22]

Never had Cuppy so openly shown his dark predisposition, despite the anthology's title, just as Hitchcock had simultaneously done the same thing with *Shadow of a Doubt*, the director's favorite film. While Hitchcock later amusingly noted that the film brought murder and violence "back into the home where it rightfully belongs," none of his other films were ever so viscerally articulate about misanthropy and misogyny—provocative stuff when in countless interviews the director confessed to seeing his murderers as heroes.[23] And as Truffaut observes in his extensive Hitchcock interview/study, "It is obvious Hitchcock is expressing himself in *Shadow of a Doubt* when Joseph Cotten says, "The world is a pigsty...."[24]

This and much more is expanded upon in the later chapter focus on *Shadow of a Doubt*. However, the movie merits two final Prologue postscripts. First, given the proceeding pages' examination of Poe's poor playful orangutan, who just wanted to give a lady a shave, and Cuppy's dark comedy connections to the story, as well as referencing his *How to Tell Your Friends from the Apes*, comes a curious source link to *Shadow of a Doubt*. The film was loosely inspired by the serial killer Earle Leonard Nelson (1897– 1928), who was known as "Gorilla Man." Second, horror and Hitchcock have always been associated with the doppelganger phenomenon, as exemplified by Robert Louis Stevenson's novella *The Strange Case of Dr. Jekyll and Mr. Hyde*.

Like Poe's "Rue Morgue," young Hitchcock was also an extraordinary aficionado of *Jekyll and Hyde*, with the duality being central to many of his good/evil films, especially *Strangers on a Train*. The "Rue Morgue" represents a metaphorical variation of a doppelganger. Poe's brilliant detective would represent the paramount example of *the* logical thinker. Contrast that with the orangutan's pure emotion—capable of anything when upset. The animal's owner had locked him into some small compartment, like an individual might compartmentalize an evil desire or thought. As if retracing animal references in previous pages, Stevenson had even described Mr. Hyde's dark side as "ape-like." How does this connect to Hitchcock? When the director finally becomes untethered towards the end of his life (see the Epilogue), the lonely angry man/child hiding in his darkly comic movies becomes more apparent, like a sudden rack focus (changing focus in a single shot). Biographer James Atlas' description of a Delmore Schwartz poem might have been applied to Hitchcock and his movies:

> ... there was something else [in the poem]—vulnerable, guarded, inaccessible even to himself—that made the poem memorable. It was the presence of the poet's double, the self from which he could never escape. The poem bespoke a loneliness of unfathomable depth. You never get away from who you were.[25]

Even the biographer's description, which Atlas uses for the title of the book from which the quote is drawn sounds Hitchcockian—*The Shadow in the Garden.*[26]

Regardless, after the influence of Poe and Stevenson, sources from which Hitchcock gleaned parts of his dark comedy base, the director was a great fan of American silent comedy, with Keaton and Chaplin being especially important. Moreover, in writing many comedy-related biographies, I have never found another artist who took such interest in the macabre as Hitchcock and Chaplin.[27] Indeed, even *vacations* for the two invariably included stops at prisons, execution sites, and museums of the bizarre. Thus, it should come as no surprise that one of Hitchcock's favorite films was Chaplin's *The Gold Rush* (1925), since the catalyst for the movie was the Donner Party disaster (1846–47). This tragedy involved a group of snowbound American pioneers who resorted to cannibalism to survive.

Chaplin starving in *The Gold Rush* (1925).

Even a comedy team like Laurel & Hardy, here in a scene from *Wrong Again* (1929), can pinball into dark comedy. This sequence is sometimes read as a spoof of Luis Buñuel and Salvador Dalí's surrealistic *Un Chien Andalou* (1928/1929).

Plus, given Hitchcock's tenacious and endless fears, especially as they related to strong women, police, lack of control, pain, death and so on—Keaton's films would have struck a responsive chord.²⁸ Indeed, going from *Cops* (1922) to *College* (1927), Hitchcock would have viewed a smorgasbord of these things—including the tombstone close of both pictures. Moreover, *LIFE* (the humor journal, not the later pictorial) critic Robert Sherwood's take on Keaton's world could double as a projection of Hitchcock's inner demons, "[Keaton has the ability to] impress a weary world with the vitally important fact that life, after all, is a foolishly inconsequential affair."²⁹ Also, given this low self-esteem, Hitchcock would have related to some of the comedian's screen nicknames, from "Zero" (especially popular in Europe), to the more universal "Great Stone Face" (a safety net in not showing emotion).

Fittingly, as these comments suggest, even when discussing Hitchcock and personality comedians, which were a factor in his films (such as *The Lady Vanishes*' Laurel & Hardy-like cricket obsessed duo), the subject dovetails back to dark comedy.³⁰ For example, the young director was also a fan of the Keystone Kops—policemen made to look comically foolish. However, a 1938 *New York Times* interview referencing the Kops has a scenario which would have made Mack Sennett squirm.³¹ Hitchcock is discussing his then latest film *Young and Innocent* (1937, titled *A Girl Was Young* in the United States) and observes:

> In it I have at least partially realized a long-felt desire to take a comic situation and suddenly switch to tragedy—to experiment on the effect of slapstick under fairly sane conditions. I once thought of opening a film with a half-dozen Keystone Kops crawling out of a tunnel, while a thug stands over the exit with a club and hits each one coming out. Wouldn't it be interesting to show a close-up [of the sixth cop] with blood trickling down his face—comedy suddenly turned sober—and then cut to a picture of his family in agony over his misfortune....³²

Interestingly, Mack Sennett made a film not unlike the one Hitchcock describes, *The Fatal Mallet* (1914), only Chaplin is the star. One could say it was a British dark comedy thing, like the Beatles' 1969 song, "Maxwell's Silver Hammer," which made sure people were dead. But that would ignore George Herriman's seminal brick-throwing newspaper cartoon strip, "Krazy Kat," which bridged Hitchcock's move to America.

Regardless, as with the earlier Hitchcock comment/fantasy about what happens when an "English girl" gets into a cab, "...probably [to] pull a man's pants open," his commentary on the Kops has returned to the voice of a twelve-year-old. Yet, here it manages to resonate with some dark comedy truth. The boy/man director might not have been informed about sexuality, yet he had experienced enough fear and frustration via social naïveté that he most certainly knew unforeseen shock—which gets to the heart of dark comedy.³³ And it again underlines black humor as his base, with the interview even being entitled "The Hitchcock Formula."³⁴

In its own way, the director's example is not that far removed from the signature dark comedy transition shock of Arthur Penn's New American Cinema classic, *Bonnie and Clyde* (1967). The sequence in question, of a compound genre film sometimes described with Keystone Kop overtones, involves heist driver C.W. Moss (Michael J. Pollard) parking the getaway car as title characters Warren Beatty and Faye Dunaway rob a bank. However, when the couple come rushing out of the bank, Pollard finds himself wedged in by cars. As he fender bends his way free, our iconic robbers stand flatfooted in mid-street fuming. It is played with broad humor, as if Sennett had shot it. Yet, when Pollard finally breaks out and the threesome start to make their comic delayed escape, a bank teller jumps on the car's running board and a panicked Clyde shoots him in the face at bloody point-blank range. Then, just as Hitchcock had described his example, everything "suddenly turned sober." In addition, this key *Bonnie and Clyde* sequence even offers up a variation on Hitchcock's concluding remarks—"cut to a picture of his family in agony over his misfortune." Penn's film soon cuts to a tearfully upset Clyde, as he also berates C.W. to tears for causing the murder.

Be that as it may, Hitchcock's real life battle between the id and the super-ego often tended to complement his periodic use of a cinematic personality comedy, however small—because as already suggested, he often acted the child (a pivotal component of the clown genre). That would seem to have been the catalyst for his screen cameos, the director's occasional in-joke satires of people he disliked. For instance, Raymond Burr's *Rear Window* murderer was made-up to suggest David O. Selznick. (Chaplin did the same thing in 1936's *Modern Times*, when the film's factory owner purposely resembles the anti–Semitic Henry Ford.) Regardless, the little boy Hitchcock really came out on his first trips to America (1937 and 1938), before wife Alma began monitoring his interviews. For example, *New York World-Telegram* reporter H. Allen Smith, the later bestselling author of such humor books as *Low Man on the Totem Pole* (1941, with the title becoming a national catchphrase) and *Life in a Putty Knife Factory* (1942), interviewed Hitchcock in 1937, producing the most entertaining of profiles. And keep in mind, New York's far left newspaper *PM* called Smith "an interviewer extraordinary, a ruthless exhibitor of inhibitions, a callous collector of taboos."[35] Smith's piece is entitled "Hitchcock Likes to Smash Cups":

> "Lord," said Alfred Hitchcock, fingering a delicate teacup in Club 21, "how I'd love to shatter it. Fling it on the floor. Smash it in a million pieces." Mr. Hitchcock was not mad. He was just feeling good. They had just brought him another American steak— a noble steak full two inches thick and still sizzling. When Mr. Hitchcock feels good he loves to smash teacups.
>
> "People think its peculiar that I like to smash things when I feel good. I always break tea cups after I have a good cup of tea. I can't explain it but it makes me feel fine...."
>
> He was interviewed at the 21 Club because he refused to be interviewed unless he's having at excellent foodstuffs....

> His chief concern when he reached town ... was to try a steak and then he wanted some ice cream.... He has been trying steaks and ice cream ever since—even orders a dish of vanilla for breakfast, and tries it with Brandy poured over it....
>
> [I] find it almost impossible to get him off the subject of eating. "I find contentment from food," he said... "There is as much anticipation in confronting good food as there is in going on holiday, or seeing a good show. There are two kinds of eating—eating to sustain and eating for pleasure. I eat for pleasure."[36]

Whatever movie-related material Smith could extract from Hitchcock might be paraphrased as, "Movies stink compared to the smell of a good steak."[37]

As a food footnote, by the early 1940s Hitchcock had ballooned to over 300 pounds and was in danger of not being insured by Hollywood for health reasons. Ironically, his man/child mentality which fueled this excessive eating *and* drinking (to be addressed later) was the catalyst for one of the director's funniest personality comedy cameos, and easily his most creative. The film was *Lifeboat* (1943), which keys upon the World War II survivors of a ship sunk by a Nazi submarine. In this film for the war effort, Hitchcock challenged himself technologically—to make something cinematic in a confined space. Yet, it seemed to negate his chances for a cameo, since these usually had Hitchcock in the background and/or as a passerby. Thus, short of dog-paddling by somewhere in the North Atlantic, a cameo was a real poser. Finally, the director had an epiphany for what would become his favorite cameo. Having started a "strenuous diet,"

> I decided to immortalize my loss and get my bit part by posing for "before" and "after" pictures. These photographs were used in a newspaper ad for an imaginary drug, Reducto, and the viewers saw them—and me—when [torpedo survivor] William Bendix opened an old newspaper we had put in the boat.[38]

Even then, over a decade before Hitchcock's high profile TV program, innumerable viewers not only noticed the comic cameo—many overweight fans inundated him with letters requesting information about the fictitious Reducto! Regardless, while his personality comedy cameos are fleeting moments in his movies, the director often used the clown comedy genre in more extensive ways, including the *Lady Vanishes* cricket duo (which went on to be a popular comedy team), the lady girdle salesmen (comic Gus McNaughton, billed as himself and Jerry Verno) in Robert Donat's *39 Steps* train compartment, and the twosome of comic character actor Henry Travers and writer/actor Hume Cronyn in *Shadow of a Doubt*—obsessed with crime novels and the perfect murder.

These examples and others will be examined more closely in the subsequent pages. However, it bears noting that besides the previously noted childlike nature, Hitchcock adheres to personality comedy basics. For instance, this genre phenomenon usually follows some sort of team configuration, even if it is no more than Chaplin's little Tramp playing opposite a comically contrasting

Robert Benchley showcases his dark sense of humor in this 1912 public domain drawing from his college days: "Please, mister, have you seen our dog?"

large character. Moreover, the clown genre is also often defined by being antiheroically obsessed with something that makes the characters oblivious to the world about them. The previous illustrations all exhibit such preoccupations—cricket, girdles, and murder mysteries.

The Travers and Cronyn pairing is the most entertaining, both because murder is naturally best integrated into a Hitchcock storyline, and as the duo bumble about discussing the subject, a real murderer (Joseph Cotten) is living in the same household. Also, with the passage of time, the two performers' post–*Shadow* roles have made them more identifiably associated with comedy, from Travers forever being tied to Frank Capra's *It's a Wonderful Life* (1946, as Clarence Odbody, the second-class angel), to Hume Cronyn in *Brewster's Millions* (1985), or the *Cocoon* movies (1985, 1988). Fittingly, Hitchcock was a major fan of arguably the greatest antiheroic print humorist turned character actor of the 1930s and early 1940s—Robert Benchley.

Benchley's essay "Johnny-on-the-Sport" is the seminal description of a buffoon with blinders, included in his inspiringly goofy titled anthology—*From Bed to Worse or Comforting Thoughts About the Bison*:

> If you want to get a good perspective on history in the making, just skim through a collection of news-photographs which have been snapped at those very moments when cataclysmic events were taking place throughout the world. In almost every picture you can discover one guy ... who is looking in exactly the opposite direction

from the excitement, totally oblivious to the fact that the world is shaking beneath his feet. That would be me....[39]

Add all this to the fact that Benchley had a dry dark sense of humor, à la Hitchcock, and it should come as no surprise that the director would cast the humorist in one of his films, *Foreign Correspondent* (1940), allowing him to write his own comic dialogue. Moreover, Benchley was famous for his droll monologue-driven short subjects, such as the Oscar-winning *How to Sleep* (1935). These one and two reelers were a major template for Hitchcock's own later TV monologues.[40] However, a Benchley letter (March 25, 1940) during the production of *Correspondent* puts a pin prick to the auteur legend that all Hitchcock films were forever written and storyboarded to death before production began. After praising Hitchcock as a director, Benchley's letter states, in part:

> The picture isn't written yet, and one of the most important roles isn't cast. It's the same old [wasteful Hollywood] story over again. They're shooting the stuff that's written, and then, when changes in the plot make that obsolete, they shoot it over. We'll be at it until well into May, I'm afraid.[41]

At times, moreover, Hitchcock could even use a more central character as a personality comedian, such as Peter Lorre in 1935's original *The Man Who Knew Too Much*. With his frizzy hair and frequent chasing of women, he is a regular Harpo Marx doubling as a good guy assassin. Another element of clown comedy shtick which he shares with Harpo is that everything strikes him as funny, even if that involves pushing the wrong man off a mountain. (Hitchcock always maintains his dark comedy foundation.) Also like Harpo, frequent movement, even without a woman, through surreal settings, is a given. Thus, at one point in *The Man*, Lorre is chasing a spy through a Swiss chocolate factory, which also happens to be the wacky headquarters for an evil spy ring.

Before moving on to a third comedy genre with which Hitchcock layered his films, a final personality comedy detail merits noting. Throughout his long career the director frequently noted visual imagery was so important that his best pictures were not far removed from silent movies, soundtrack music notwithstanding. However, even when he was not discussing comedy per se, Hitchcock remained so very cognizant of silent comedians late in his career that their films were sometimes used for more generic questions decades later.

For example, in a 1972 interview with the American Film Institute, Hitchcock randomly used a 1923 Chaplin picture to underline his visual image mantra:

> The visual, to me, is a vital element.... I don't think it is studied enough. Go back to the early days. Go back to Chaplin. He once made a short film called *The Pilgrim*. The opening shot was the outside of prison gate. A guard came out and posted a

wanted notice. Next cut: a very tall, thin man coming out of a river, having a swim. He finds that his clothes are missing and have been replaced with a convict's uniform. Next cut: a railroad station, and there coming towards the camera dressed as a parson with the pants too long is Chaplin. Now, there are three pieces of film and look at the amount of story they told. These are the things that I think are so essential....[42]

Though Hitchcock's childhood might have been like a lost ball in high weeds, the third comedy genre he frequently laced into his films was the sexually provocative screwball comedy farce, American style.[43] It is most apparent in his 1930s work, which is appropriate, since screwball comedy was born, in part, as a distraction from that decade's Great Depression. Even today, it is the sort of escapism genre which could have inspired the following riff from novelist Michael Chabon's peppered-with-film-references bestseller, *Wonder Boys* (1995): "...nostalgic addicts who climbed into a movie as into a time machine or a bottle of whiskey and set the dial for 'never come back.'"[44]

Be that as it may, screwball elements frequently surfaced in Hitchcock's films throughout his career—most spectacularly in *North by Northwest* (1959). Indeed, period reviews most often referred to the film as a farcical comedy, or a broad spoof of a thriller. However, for the Prologue's brief overview, a succinct example could come from the director's *39 Steps*, a precursor to *Northwest*. The earlier picture appeared the year after three American films were released which history has loosely designated as a foundation of sorts for screwball comedy: Frank Capra's *It Happened One Night* (February 1934), Howard Hawks' *20th Century* (May 1934), and W.S. Van Dyke's *The Thin Man* (June 1934). The Dashiell Hammett novel from which *The Thin Man* was adapted even offered up a lengthy quote on cannibalism, from *Celebrated Criminal Cases of America*—a text in Hitchcock's extensive library on lawbreakers and/or the macabre.[45]

Capra's *One Night* usually receives the bulk of screwball attention, with regard to the aforementioned trilogy, for two reasons. One, it was the surprise

Chaplin in *The Pilgrim* (1923).

Academy Award winner for Best Picture, as well as becoming the first film to win the five major Oscar categories—Best Picture, Best Director, Best Screenplay (adaptation), Best Actress, and Best Actor. (Even today, only 1975's *One Flew Over the Cuckoo's Nest*, and 1991's *Silence of the Lambs* have replicated the achievement.) Second, *One Night* epitomized the closest thing to a template for the screwball comedy genre which evolved. It was a road picture about a spoiled runaway heiress and her unexpected romance with a reporter who discovers her identity. Of equal importance is its *Taming of the Shrew* slant—she initially dislikes him because he is essentially her keeper (for his newspaper scoop), and the romance can only succeed when her attitude of superiority is brought down a peg.

Besides the Depression, another catalyst for the genre was an American censorship code which had just been enacted. Thus, pictures like *One Night* could only be suggestive to a point—later known as "sex comedies without sex." Titillating situations could be suggested, such as the picture's lead duo, Clark Gable and Claudette Colbert, being forced to pretend they were married, and spending the night in a roadside cabin (a precursor to today's motel)—but nothing could happen.

These screwball components and several more go a long way towards describing major elements of the plot for *The 39 Steps* (see Chapter 3). However, what about that little Hitchcock element of murder? One need only back up to the aforementioned *Thin Man*, which closely follows Hammond's mix of screwball fundamentals and *a murder mystery*. Indeed, the delightfully witty banter and activities of the central couple, Nick and Nora Charles, are directed towards solving a murder. Consequently, given that the Hitchcock picture which preceded *39 Steps*, *The Man Who Knew Too Much* (see Chapter 2), also had screwball elements, a 1935 *New York Times* profile of Hitchcock even stated American journalists expected the director to be a "compound of Dashiell Hammett, Sherlock Holmes and Perry Mason."[46] Moreover, the great critical and commercial success of *The Thin Man* might have contributed to Hitchcock's PR claim that smashing glass relaxed him. The funniest scene in the Hammett adaptation is when star William Powell unwinds on the couch by using an air rifle to shoot up the glass decorations on his Christmas tree. Screen wife Myrna Loy, like Hitchcock's reporter, also finds it an odd way to unwind.

As a final note on screwball comedy, Hitchcock's 1937 *Young and Innocent* also at times is quite similar to *One Night*. Plus, the inclusion of both a romantic rural sequence with the young couple, and their only means of transportation being a funny looking old car (sort of a British version of a Ford Model T, so popular in Laurel & Hardy short subjects), are specific matches with the Capra picture. Still, as a reminder that dark comedy remains Hitchcock's core, *Young and Innocent* was the film in which the director was to have showcased a variation upon the earlier noted gruesome Keystone Kop experiment. According to Hitchcock, however, American censors cut the scene.[47] Still, *Young and Innocent* manages to include many broad Sennett-like digs at the police. This includes two constables made to ride among a cart of pigs while pursuing the film's leading couple and later recycling that silent comedy staple of having the portly cops momentarily become stuck in a doorway as they attempt a quick exit simultaneously.

Before moving to a fourth comedy genre Hitchcock utilizes, one must underscore what should be becoming obvious—Hitchcock's cinematic world is one of compound genres. His thrillers occasionally dip into horror, inevitably have a dark comedy base, and yet are inevitably enriched by interweaving them with another comedy genre. For instance, *The 39 Steps* has just been introduced as exhibiting many screwball comedy tendencies. However, the John Buchan novella from which it has been adapted is an entertainingly straight thriller about secret agent Richard Hannay, without a trace of screwball comedy sexual innuendo. Indeed, there are few women and even less comedy. And it is devoid of the dark comedy world view ballast Hitchcock brings to each of his films. In contrast, it makes the film, especially the latter half, a regular clown shoe parade.

All of these traits lead to the fourth and final comedy genre Hitchcock uses nearly as frequently as his black humor—reaffirmation parody.[48] This is *not* the broad parody of Mel Brooks' *Space Balls* (1987), which is an affectionate undisguised kidding of a sci-fi/fantasy franchise. Brooks' goal is a diverting mind candy laugh fest. In contrast, parodies of reaffirmation are not so obvious. They are frequently confused with the genre being undercut. An excellent example of this is John Landis' 1981 *An American Werewolf in London*, in which transparent parody (as in the use of songs such as "Bad Moon Rising" and "Blue Moon") alternates with shocking horror (graphic violence and painfully realistic werewolf transformation). This produces a fascinating tension (both emotional and cerebral) between genre expectations (in this case, horror—to be scared), and parody that is comic without deflating the characters involved. Returning to Brooks, contrast *American Werewolf* to the more traditional horror spoofing of 1974's *Young Frankenstein*, in which, for instance, Marty Feldman's Igor, with those large misaligned bug eyes and a roving hump on his back, can never be taken seriously.

Consequently, the reaffirmation approach can add a poignancy and/or insight not normally associated with parody. One is truly saddened by the film ending death of David Naughton's werewolf, just as one is with the death of Mr. Memory (Wylie Watson) at the close of the often reaffirmation parody–based *39 Steps*. Moreover, reaffirmation parody brings one closer to the complex/compound randomness of real life—which dovetails into Hitchcock's ever present base of dark comedy and/or death. Moreover, while there is nothing wrong with diverting mind candy, reaffirmation's reality factor brings one closer—makes one relate more—to its characters. That being said, the broadness of the parody in Hitchcock's *The Trouble with Harry* (1955) and *North by Northwest* makes one want to pump the brakes, and think, at times, of the more restrained moments of *Young Frankenstein*, or Gene Wilder's solo *The World's Greatest Lover* (1977, set in Hitchcock's beloved silent era).

Consider each Hitchcock film as yesteryear's traditional "hall tree," back in the days when men wore hats—the days in which the director's films were made. This vertical broom handle in the hall, with its various hooks for hats and other outside apparel, represents the genre being subtextually spoofed in a reaffirmation parody. For instance, whether a Hitchcock film is initially seen as a thriller or horror film, all the basic components of that genre should be on display. Thus, even while a reaffirmation parody is working towards a sardonic subterfuge the film begins by first being true to its target genre. This is sometimes referred to as "creative criticism."[49] In other words, by creating any sort of parody, however muted, this exercise in spoofing is actually educational. Ironically, in teaching a genre class, sometimes one can even better define a given type of film via parody.

Regardless, each time Hitchcock incorporates another genre into his picture, it is like placing a hat on his metaphorical hall tree base. Since black humor is almost a given in his work, and he has a penchant for adding farce and/or personality comedians who wander in and out of his discombobulated narrative, the hall tree begins to be decked out quickly. Moreover, while any movie is a time capsule of when it was made, Hitchcock had a talent for either immersing his films in a then current cinematic movement or anticipating an emerging trend—"more hats."

Consequently, Hitchcock's film beginnings made him a student of the dark fatalism of 1920s German Expressionism. In the 1930s he was more than a little influenced by American screwball comedy to the point of actually directing a darkly conventional example of the format—1941's *Mr. and Mrs. Smith*. In the 1940s and early 1950s, with pictures like *Shadow of a Doubt* (1943) and *Strangers on a Train* (1951), he first preempts and then rides the crest of film noir—without really abandoning the various nuances of what came before. Hitchcock was a regular intellectual juggler of various genres which he incorporated into his compound genre reaffirmation parodies— which were initially just passed off as a simple mainstream Hitchcock thriller or horror film.

Be that as it may, a teenage Hitchcock was adrift about a career, though he mixed some training in mechanical draftsmanship with a drawing class at London University. However, this bookish, self-consciously heavy youngster was forced into the job market by the sudden 1915 death of his father. He found work at London's Henley Telegraph and Cable Company. Between his weight and helping support his widowed mother, young Hitchcock escaped the horrors of World War I (1914–1918), though Germany's periodic shelling of the city fed his fears of life's sudden moments of chaos. This and a dead-end job possibly fueled his obsession with American films, and later those from the European continent, especially Germany.

As with every budding filmmaker of the time, D.W. Griffith's *Birth of a Nation* (1915) had a huge influence on him, as did such comedians as Buster Keaton and Chaplin. Between the editing of Griffith, which would eventually have Hitchcock creating his actors' performances through the cutting, and the pioneering dark comedy of Keaton, Hitchcock had two of his early filmmaking fundamentals. Mix this with his continuous voracious reading of the macabre, be it the classic Poe or true-life crime, and he seemed to be unintentionally prepping for his future film career. Plus, the tendency to control both an actor and an audience via formalist devices (self-conscious filmmaking signatures, such as editing, a moving camera, provocative uses of sound…) was given a further boost by being transferred to Henley's advertising department.

By 1920 Hitchcock was ready to take a stab at filmmaking. And it would entail working for his favorite national cinema—American's Paramount pictures had opened a production company in London. One should add that between the weather and class system's snobbish preferences for the theatre, British cinema was then in a bad place. For example, as late as 1929, a West End (Britain's Broadway) hit play, *Rope* (which Hitchcock would adapt to the screen in 1948), had fun trashing pictures:

> RUPERT: I once went to a picture and saw Mary Pickford.
> RAGLAN: Oh, how did you like her?
> RUPERT: Oh, I don't know, like all *these* [films], you know…
> LEILA: What was she in, anyway?
> RUPERT: I can't quite recall. "The Something Something," I think. Or something like that. (Pause) Something very like it, anyway.
> LEILA: I don't believe you ever went.
> BRANDON: I never knew you were a fan like this, Leila. I simply abhor the things myself.
> LEILA: What—on moral grounds?
> BRANDON: Oh, no. They simply make me go to sleep. And all those places [theatre] are so infernally stuffy….[50]

Indeed, in later years Hitchcock would sometimes credit his most famous observation upon this English elitism. That is, in early career, after feeling that some British actors behaved as if they were merely slumming in his films, he was purported to have said, "All actors were cattle." Whenever questioned upon this, he would dryly correct the observation to variations along the lines: "No, I said they should be treated like cattle." Though amusing, and possibly an early catalyst for such a biting comment, between his general misanthropy and formalistic filmmaking, the comments were essentially dead on. For example, in Truffaut's 1967 query on the subject, Hitchcock fundamentally said performers should be treated as props:

> ... the chief requisite for an actor is the ability to do nothing well.... He should be willing to be utilized and wholly integrated into the picture by the director and the camera....[51]

Regardless, Hitchcock had a meteoric movie beginning. His artistic talents enabled him to find a movie industry niche in 1920 by creating silent film inter-titles. And barely past the mid-decade mark, he had directed Britain's greatest film up until that time—*The Lodger* (1926/released 1927, a modern variation on "Jack the Ripper"). Though a talented hard worker, willing to take on and master any production task, he would not have been able to accomplish these things without the help of assistant director Alma Reville, who had also become his wife by this time. In fact, when he first entered the industry, she outranked him as a veteran editor. Alma would always be an integral part of his career, whether her name was noted in the credits or not. But they would make British cinema history with *Blackmail* (1929).

Though Hitchcock and Reville continued to work together and separately during the rest of the 1920s, a certain creative malaise had engulfed their pictures until *Blackmail*. However, this film would both receive international attention as Britain's first sound film (validation for their often struggling industry) and put Hitchcock on the cinematic map. First, the *New York Herald Tribune*'s review opens by fully fleshing out the period frustration of British cinema for recognition—making the picture a cause célèbre now forgotten by cinema history:

> "Blackmail" is the English talking picture which caused the London critics of the cinema to grow more than belligerent. If Americans, they proclaimed challengingly, couldn't see its vast merits, it would be final proof that they were opposed to the British importations on nationalist or economic reasons rather than artistic growth. Fortunately, there turns out to be no reason for the chip on their shoulder... "Blackmail" ... is highly credible work, and there is no reason to believe that any of the local reviewers will deny it.[52]

Nearly simultaneously, the *New York American* was corroborating "Hitchcock's significance:

> Alfred Hitchcock, who directed "Blackmail.".. is now the acknowledged ace of directors in that country ... he has turned out what is determined to be one of the most perfect specimens of the talking picture art produced abroad.[53]

Before proceeding with this methodical examination of Hitchcock's multi-faceted use of comedy genres, one must return to the director's pivotal Prologue opening observation, "All my films are dark comedies." This is both the central humor genre Hitchcock uses, and is tied directly to his most famous story-driven device—the "MacGuffin." That is, in simple language, always a rarity in film study, a "MacGuffin" jumpstarts and drives a Hitchcock story by creating something seemingly important but which by the film's close does not really matter, such as the stolen money in *Psycho* (1960). Fittingly, one might describe Hitchcock's MacGuffin as a comedy sketch which would have been at home in a period British music hall. The routine of this narrative driver is set on a Scottish *train*—naturally. A passenger notices a goofy-looking package in the overhead luggage rack:

> FIRST MAN: What is that?
> SECOND MAN: It's a MacGuffin.
> FIRST MAN: What's that?
> SECOND MAN: It's a contrivance for catching lions in the Scottish Highlands.
> FIRST MAN: But the Scottish Highlands don't have any lions!
> SECOND MAN: Well, then, I guess that's no MacGuffin![54]

While one can obviously embrace this comically insightful guide to the director's pictures, this is where the tip stops in Hitchcock literature. As Yankee manager Casey Stengel was fond of saying, "You can look it up." *No one has made the natural leap to dark comedy and a theatre of the absurd primer like Waiting for Godot* (1953). That is, early in Samuel Beckett's play, and other works of existential ilk, a character or more is given the quasi-MacGuffin idea that God and/or something else of extreme importance is to surface by the story's conclusion. These invariably amusing figures, usually inspired by primal comic characters, then invariably both charm the viewer and give them a reason to watch a rather illogical story (Hitchcock's modus operandi), in which the big finish never occurs. This serious though seemingly logical tie of the MacGuffin to dark comedy hits all the genre's basics, from absurdity to death, and fits Hitchcock's misanthropic nature. Modern black humor is all about the minutiae/MacGuffins to which one is drawn in order to not think about the inevitable "big sleep."

Keep in mind that this study does not suggest that the director who dressed like an English undertaker studiously examined all the basics of the comedy genres he utilized in his films (with the possible Brillo pad beauty of black humor). Like most great artists, he was instinctually drawn to them. However, that should not diminish, as is invariably the case, all these humor genres to what is minimized as "comic relief."

Consequently, with these comedy guidelines in place, this study will focus on twelve Hitchcock pictures which seem to best showcase this humor: *Blackmail* (1929), *The Man Who Knew Too Much* (1934), *39 Steps* (1935), *Secret Agent* (1936), *The Lady Vanishes* (1938), *Mr. and Mrs. Smith* (1941), *Shadow of a Doubt* (1943), *Rope* (1948), *Strangers on a Train* (1951), *Rear Window* (1954), *The Trouble with Harry* (1955), and *North by Northwest* (1959). Plus, with the Epilogue briefly examining *Psycho*, as well as references scattered throughout the text, the reader will actually be receiving a Hitchcock's "baker's dozen." As the list documents, the book attempts to join the current revisionist celebration of his British period. For example, in Peter Ackroyd's excellent recent biography of Hitchcock, here is how he describes the two versions of *The Man Who Knew Too Much* (1934, 1956), "The American product is more technically assured and more carefully executed, while the English version is funnier, faster and lighter."[55]

Regardless, now on to the most definite of dark comedies—*Blackmail*.

1

Blackmail (1929)

"What an awful way to kill a man," observes a *Blackmail* bit player. "With a *knife!* Now a good stiff whack over the 'ead with a brick is one thing—there's something *British* about that!"

Ah, what a fascinating dark comedy suggestion—that each country has its own special way of offing someone. One can see it now, a brick snuggled between Britain's Union Jack flag and John Bull—their equivalent to our Uncle Sam. Its casual utterance is also a most succinct summary of dark comedy's three themes—man as beast/killer, the constant presence of death, and the absurdity of signing off on killing if the proper weapon/object is used.[1] However, what is most satisfying is that after the Prologue's multi-faceted examination of the various genres of comedy which Hitchcock uses to help stitch his movies together, *the* picture that establishes him so fully embraces how he saw *all* his work—as examples of black humor.

Interestingly, as a positive *New York Evening World* review noted, *Blackmail*'s "story is simply told," with a PR attached subtitle of sorts, which sets a chauvinistic tone not out of keeping with the director's often misogynist nature.[2] The unofficial marketing subtitle is "The Story of a Foolish Girl"—who allows herself to be picked up by a young man and goes to his lodgings.[3] A rape is attempted and the heroine (Anny Ondra) manages to defend herself by stabbing the attacker (Cyril Ritchard) inside his curtained bed. The viewer only manages to see her arm desperately come through the drapery and grab a bread knife from a bedside table plate holding what appears to be a previous night's snack.

Ondra's character, ironically named in the play Alice *White*, has a dinner and a movie date with her longtime detective boyfriend (John Longden). Upset that he has been late, she initiates an argument at their regular restaurant, hoping, it seems, to have him leave so she can meet an admirer (her future attacker) who had apparently slipped her a note days before, "I'll be

"The Story of a Foolish Girl" newspaper ad for *Blackmail* (1929), during its initial New York run.

here on Tuesday at 6:30. Will you?" Her quarrel works. Longden's detective leaves, though not before seeing her go off with Ritchard's seemingly romantic interloper, who, fittingly, turns out to be an *artist*—already a stereotyped cad long before Hitchcock admired Chaplin's *The Kid* (1921, in which an artist abandons a pregnant Edna Purviance). Alice's original plan was to have Ritchard's character (simply billed as "The Artist") walk her home. However,

1. Blackmail *(1929)*

he entices her to come to his boardinghouse studio. The title card observation which precipitates the action becomes a basic Hitchcock component—dialogue telegraphing dark comedy, "I think a girl knows instinctually when she can trust a man."

Paintings, of which Hitchcock became an avid collector, often play a role in his films, be it the museum portrait with which the 1958 *Vertigo* heroine (Kim Novak) seems obsessed, or the 1959 *North by Northwest* art auction Cary Grant uses for protection. However, seldom, with the possible exception of *The Picture of Dorian Gray* (1945), has a painting so central to a storyline been so linked to dark comedy as it is in *Blackmail*. (Indeed, this is the first film in which Hitchcock uses a famous location as one of his auteur components—the near finale is at the British Museum of Art).

Regardless, the *Blackmail* portrait is that of sneering jester pointing at the viewer with a knowingly contemptuous smile. Hitchcock potently uses the image no fewer than seven times in the movie. Like a dark comedy appendage, the painting never seems to go away. (There is no mention of it in the Charles

Hitchcock (seated) observes on the set of *Blackmail* (1929) as film personnel work on details.

Bennett play from which it is adapted.⁴) One could also see the jester as a surrogate for Hitchcock, since it represents his position and the figure is sometimes shot in such a manner that it seems to break the fourth wall—suggesting a direct address from the director. Hitchcock as jester also plays to his love of the doppelganger effect.

The jester first appears when the couple enter the artist's flat, and it startles Alice. The painting is on an easel near his bed—his latest work. One should add that a jester is arguably history's first icon of dark comedy. That is, unlike modern comic figures, be it a Johnny Carson or a Jon Stewart who provokes insightful laughter, the original court jesters were figures to be laughed at. Though they might perform simple amusing actions, their primary source of humor was their oddity, be it hypokyphosis (sometimes called a humpback), dwarfism, a minority rare to that part of the ancient world, mental illness, or other difference.

In time, however, these jesters took on the mantle of the "wise fool," and were not necessarily suffering from some form of human deformity. They were still to be laughed at, yet occasionally a barbed hint of satire might be safely directed at the audience—because, were they not *fools*? This is the nuance to be found in the expression of Hitchcock's *Blackmail* painting. The pointing jester seems to be saying to the girl, "You're the fool; wait and see." The periodic reappearance of the painted jester throughout the film documents the influence of German Expressionism in Hitchcock's work. Of course, he often camouflaged it by way of various genres. Here the *dark comedy* clown showcases a central theme of the German movement—an inability to escape life's shadowing fatalism.

In the film, however, the portrait is a fledging icebreaker for the couple, and Alice is encouraged to make an attempt at a drawing. Her small canvas drawing of a girl's face is simplistic but not without a certain childlike charm, with the artist then providing a minimalistic but sensual body. Alice rather gets into what is for her a "game" and they both sign their names. She then notices a ballerina-like tutu, worn by one of his models, and she ponders what it would be like to don it herself. He encourages her, and while she initially declines, after a drink she decides to put it on. While she changes behind a screen, the artist sits at his piano, and in seeming Noel Coward period fashion sings a popular 1920s song, "Miss Up-to-Date." He cannot see her behind the partition and the audience can—essentially a split-screen effect. With several undergarments remaining on, her change is only mildly provocative, though the *New York Evening World* observed, "This scene is what we used to call daring, and probably still do."⁵ Regardless, the song demonstrates another dark comedy given—music at cross purposes with the scene, such as the marching band coming down a street as a coffin is being removed from a church in *Harold and Maude* (1971). Though the *Blackmail* example is not

1. Blackmail (1929)   33

as dramatic as that—the artist hardly means it as harmless background music for a woman/child naïvely playing at being a model for him, "Miss Up-to-Date" suggests an amoral Jazz Age flapper in search of fun.

All the artwork-connected patter, the drink, and the change into the modeling costume are not in the original play. In Bennett's stage production, the back and forth between the two has none of this playful interaction. It is reduced to a conversation between the two which showcases a highly nervous young lady increasingly aware of the fact that she has made a mistake, with the stage notes on Ritchard's character defining him as much more of a predator.

Ultimately, she comes out and this soon results in the artist forcing a kiss on her. She rebels and returns to the curtained off area to change and leave, but he has tossed her clothes, hanging over the partition, behind him—forcing Alice to retrieve them. Then he makes his sexual attack—which is shot with his shadow actually representing the artist assailant, not unlike the silhouette of the title character in F.W. Murnau's *Nosferatu* (1922) attacking another young victim as a vampire.

Forced behind the curtain bed, the artist attempts to rape her as her hand desperately reaches through the curtained drapery for something to make the attack stop. The sequence takes long enough to unfold that the rape has possibly begun, when her hand chances upon a nightstand bread knife. (The curtained bed does not allow the viewer to see the attack.) Regardless, a knife is a phallic symbol, and in a perverse way, as she uses it in her defense, a sort of double rape is occurring. Moreover, in dark comedy, sex and death have long been associated as a loss of control—a sense of life's chaos.

Once Alice has killed the painter and emerges from the curtained bed, the chauvinistic Hitchcock has achieved what will become one of his ongoing themes. That is, by making his blonde movie heroine much more flirtatious than in the play, he has essentially increased her sense of guilt over both coming up to the studio and the resulting death in her defense. And once more cue the jester painting; Alice prepares to leave the studio by gathering her randomly tossed clothing—which has been tossed over the painting. As she picks up her clothes, the clown gives her another, even more biting, "Gotcha" moment. There is that fatalism sinking in: this was going to happen no matter what the sort of foreplay was going to be. But the shock of the jester image has her lashing out at it and tearing the painting.

Though Alice has the forethought to paint over her name on the canvas on which she has collaborated with the painter, she leaves her gloves at the scene. While executing a careful exit, she is seen by an acquaintance of the painter who has been badgering him for money, a figure known only as Tracy (Donald Calthrop). He will become the blackmailer, as well as collecting the highest critical praise. For example, *Variety* called his "performance the standard ... as the rat crook. He looks like it."[6]

While the play has Alice's parents (who run a tobacco shop) worried sick about her, only to give her a hard time over coming home at dawn, Hitchcock has her managing to get home without discovery. And more creatively, he adds several cinematic tricks to underline the girl's shock and shame over what has happened. He has her wandering the London streets all night, with electric advertisements mocking her at every turn—all of which accent Hitchcock's black humor humiliation of Alice. For example, a play is just letting out and the theatre marquee is announcing "A New Comedy"—which one could interpret as "Hello Dark Comedy."

Next, she sees a flashing ironic sign for:

Gordon's Gin Gordon's London gin White for Purity

As previously noted, actress Anny Ondra's name in the play is "White," and the extended period it takes her to subdue the artist all but makes it a rape. And if her innocent but broken spirit were not enough, the hit play had made a major point that she was saving herself for her future husband.[7] And in a striking contrast, the play's artist has a black humor philosophy anticipating the philosophy of a character in Woody Allen's dark comedy *Crimes and Misdemeanors* (1989): in a godless world, "The whole matter [of guilt] is a manner of conscience ... *that* needn't bother you much."[8] The spirit of this dialogue is replicated in the film. And the listless walk is the chaos which envelopes all dark comedy characters eventually—never to leave.

The final electric sign that Alice observes in her wandering London walk shows further disintegration of her mindset. Instead of ironic metaphors tied to "new comedy," or "purity," the girl sees giant advertising hands shaking a bright cocktail shaker, evoking a pivotal scene in Chaplin's *The Idle Class* (1921). Yet, almost immediately Hitchcock has transformed the sign into a stabbing hand that will not stop. However, most Hitchcock texts miss an early creative use of sight and sound, a variation of which receives great historic praise in his later *39 Steps* (1935).

The sequence in question involves Alice's random observation during her walk of a sleeping tramp's dead-like outstretched arm, and it vividly reminds her of what she has come from. She seems to let out a piercing scream. And while yes, a scream does occur, Hitchcock has made a sound cut into the next sequence, and the wail one is really hearing is that of the artist's landlady discovering his dead body. The famous *39 Steps* variation upon the scene has one more boardinghouse woman finding another corpse, and as she begins an anticipated shriek, Hitchcock does a sound cut to the following scene and one hears the searing sound of a train whistle from the locomotive on which a stereotypical Hitchcock "wrong man" is escaping.

The acclaimed use of sound for which *Blackmail* is best known occurs later in the story, after Alice has managed to slip unseen into the combination tobacco store/apartment in which she lives with her parents and brother. However, before that occurs, it is time for the jester painting to put in another disquieting appearance. The film cuts to Alice's boyfriend detective at the crime scene. He picks up a glove resembling one of hers. And then he has the double whammy shock of seeing almost simultaneously the jester and the dead artist—whom he recognizes as the man Alice had left with the night before. Realizing that she has both killed the victim and possibly cuckolded him, his gaze again inadvertently returns to the pointing jester. He feels mocked and made to play the fool himself. Still, he loyally takes the glove with him.

Next, one sees Alice successfully returning home unseen. She is barely in bed pretending to be asleep when her mother comes to wake her. This barely in bed gag before the authority figure comes in first thing in the morning is now an old bit of comedy business. An early example occurs in Chaplin's *Pay Day* (1922) and involves a wife. (This will be expanded upon shortly.) As a variation on the scoffing jester, the first thing Alice sees upon getting out of bed is a large framed picture of her boyfriend in his former beat officer's uniform. Hitchcock, ever the *do it visually* filmmaker, has told the viewer everything about the several lines devoted to it in the play. That is, instead of verbiage devoted to their long courtship, this photo of a young uniformed patrolman says everything at a glance.

After Alice changes to go downstairs for breakfast, the casual shop/home setting has a gossiping neighbor come in and begin discussing the murder which opens the chapter. As she babbles on about the darkly comic un–British etiquette of killing someone with a knife, Hitchcock both slowly turns down the volume of her prattling and garbles the content except for the periodically most distinctive word "knife." Alice's fixation on the term increasingly agitates the young woman. When her father asks her to cut some bread for breakfast the next utterance of *the* word causes the knife to fly out of her hand. Her father gently admonishes Alice to be more careful, with his choice of words oozing black humor irony: "You might have cut someone with that." Though Hitchcock clearly meant the "knife" scene to be a clever pioneering use of sound, it can also be "read" as a darkly comic take on the state of early talking pictures—in which primitive equipment and stationary mikes could reduce a bit of dialogue to fluctuating sound levels, gibberish sounds, and random burst of verbal clarity.

Aware that something is bothering her daughter, the mother asks if Alice has "had another row with Frank" (the boyfriend). This introduces what will become a Hitchcock norm—happy couples and/or their prospects are a rarity in his films. This even involves Hitchcock films with more farcical, à la screwball comedy, elements. For example, despite the sexually charged image of a train going through a tunnel at the close of *North by Northwest*, how long is it going to be before Cary Grant's character starts wondering/asking Eva Marie Saint how many other James Mason–like villains she slept with in her former life as a secret agent?

Even the seemingly simpatico ending to 1955's *To Catch a Thief* has Grace Kelly casually remarking to Cary Grant that Mother will be living with them. And these are the most upbeat conclusions. As befitting a dark comedy, the finale for *Blackmail* is much more bleak for the couple, as opposed to the play from which it was adapted. However, one must first return to our narrative.

Alice's detective suitor, with whom she seems to frequently argue (not to mention her part in a secret liaison which turns deadly), comes directly from the crime scene to her parents' shop. However, before the duo can have any time to really hash out what happened, a surprise blackmailer makes his presence known—the aforementioned Tracy drops in at the shop, too. And he does not have to go into much detail to make his point, since he has the other glove Alice left behind. Calthrop's Tracy also establishes what will become yet another Hitchcock given—the likable villain.

Though seedier than most, Tracy's trampish manner elicits a reluctant smile, and his comments often provoke comic replies. For example, he immediately requests the best cigar in the shop. Alice's father must climb to a top shelf to obtain the obviously seldom requested premium stuff. When Tracy observes, "They look good." The owner replies, "They ought to; I've had them for years!" Naturally, Alice's Frank will end up paying for the cigar. Then Tracy suggests that an arrangement might best be discussed over breakfast, and the young woman prepares one, while her mother walks out—upset over Tracy's gall. But not unlike the random surfacing of *It*, the deadly clown (Pennywise) in the 1990 adaptation of Stephen King's novel, the jester painting once again appears.

However, Tracy is unaware of the development, because Hitchcock has cut to Scotland Yard and the victim's landlady on the screen. While Tracy is happily whistling "The Best Things in Life Are Free," she is going through mugshot photographs. Ironically, this time the painting's presence among the evidence startles the viewer more than the little old lady calmly looking for a match to the man who had been bothering her late tenant for money. Thus, while Tracy is unmindful of the threatening clown, the painting again proves prophetic, for the blackmailer has a record and becomes the number one suspect in the artist's death. Like a bad penny, the painting keeps turning up unexpectedly.

Moreover, once again the music does not reinforce the visual. That is, thinking he has it made, Tracy continues happily whistling "The Best Things in Life Are Free." At the same time Frank is taking a call from Scotland Yard linking the blackmailer to the killing. Tracy attempts to bargain, but Frank sees this as the perfect solution—an individual with a record had been seen near the victim's flat. This resolution becomes all the more perfect when Tracy makes a run for it, after realizing a paddy wagon has already been dispatched. The chase will take them to the aforementioned British Museum. The *New York Sun* stated, "The museum proves itself one of the most effective backgrounds for melodrama that any director has yet discovered."[9] Plus, at a time when people did not travel extensively, Hitchcock's beginning use of famous backdrops was an added plus—with *Variety* noting, "[It] should be quite interesting to those who go to pictures over here [in the United States and] have heard of the British Museum."[10] It also represents an ironically callous example of dark comedy—why not mix a little murder with your travelogue?

As an addendum to the *New York Sun*'s reference to *Blackmail* as a "melodrama," in pre-1960s criticism, before dark comedy moved to the center stage, "melodrama" was code for black humor—if the action thriller had comic overtones. In my research on pioneering examples of the genre by Charlie Chaplin, Buster Keaton, and Ernest Lubitsch's *To Be or Not to Be* (1942), "melodrama" or "comic melodrama" often emerged as critics' precursor phrase for "dark comedy."[11]

Regardless, as Tracy attempts to escape through the museum, Hitchcock cuts to an agitated Alice at home—she cannot let an innocent man take the blame for the killing, even if he is a nefarious type with a record. Once again, though his character comes courtesy of the play, is this an anticipation of Hitchcock's well-known "wrong man" twist? For what it is worth, the director does make Tracy a more sympathetic character than one's impression from the play. For a later parallel, Calthrop's Tracy might be compared to scene-stealing character actor Harry Dean Stanton (1926–2017), both in appearance and performance. For instance, *New York Times* film critic Vincent Canby's description of Stanton's work would apply to Calthrop in *Blackmail*, "[He is] able to make everything he does seem immediately authentic."[12]

As Alice stews at home, Hitchcock cuts back to the museum chase, including the movie's most evocatively unforgettable scenes. It is a long shot of tiny Tracy climbing down a rope past an Egyptian-like giant mask (presumably a *death* mask—more black humor) of a woman whose eyes seem to be watching him. Again, Hitchcock is using art to drive a dark comedy narrative. However, unlike the black humor themes of death and of man as beast, associated with the taunting jester painting, the faint smile of this mammoth museum figure speaks to dark comedy's absurdity theme—the little man versus the weight of history.

And this sense of the bizarre has multiple levels. First there is the museum's prodigious inner space and the gigantic head watching Tracy's figure descend into what—life's metaphorical abyss? Is this not the bottom line for dark comedy—the existential insignificance of man? Second, after getting over this breathtaking visualization of absurdity, it is cartoon funny. An immense mask of antiquity watches a decidedly more minor human gasp in a building dedicated to artifacts of the end—art to the enigma of death. Third, though without the knowing sneer of the jester, the huge death mask completes the painting's macabre message—only the viewer is not quite done with either the story or the jester.

The chase continues and there is yet another haunting image inside the museum—an overhead shot of a series of never ending circular card catalogs in the reading room. It is another striking nod to German Expressionism, which reduces the individual to geometric patterns, while, in this case, documenting man's obsession with recording things to keep busy until that *Waiting for Godot* end, killing time until it kills you. It could also be called a long delayed form cut from *Blackmail*'s beginning—a spinning disk whose abstraction eventually turns into a fast moving paddy wagon wheel, the reason Frank was late for his date with Alice.

Eventually, the chase for Tracy ends on the museum dome when the title character falls to his death. Alice is in the clear. But like a character from Hitchcock's beloved Poe, Alice cannot live with herself. She writes out a confessional note to Frank:

> I am going to give myself up. I cannot bear the thought of that man being accused of something I have done.

When she goes to Scotland Yard, Frank is not yet back from the British Museum. On arrival she asks the police clerk on duty, an acquaintance by way of her boyfriend, if she can see the commissioner. Once again, a dark comedy component kicks in. The genre loves nothing better than to ironically demonstrate humanity's obtuseness by having a guilty party honestly answering a serious question put to them by the general public. Thus, the clerk tells her she has to fill out some forms, and teasingly asks, "I suppose you're going to tell him who did it, miss?" And he chuckles at her straightforward reply, "Yes."

By the time Alice is ushered into the commissioner's office, Frank has arrived and attempts to stop her. However, just as she starts to say, "I know who did it," the phone rings and the chief waves her off for Frank to handle. As he takes Alice out, the show of dimwittedness continues. The guard asks him, "Well, did she tell you who did it?" Now it is Frank's turn to say, "Yes." And his colleague laughly replies, "You want to look out, you'll be losing your job, my boy!" Of course, the added bonus for Hitchcock, as noted in the Prologue, is being able to make policemen look foolish—another Hitchcock auteur element.

As Alice and Frank begin to leave Scotland Yard, the Jester painting as character manages to deliver two final dark comedy blows. First, as the couple's forced laughter to the guard's joke occurs, Hitchcock cuts to the sudden, almost demonic image of the jester pointing at her. For the viewer, it is an editing shock, and as Hitchcock cuts back to her it suggests this cruel clown image of guilt will forever be seared into her brain. However, the filmmaker again cuts to the jester in a moving shot—revealing both that the painting exists in real space and is being moved to an evidence room, and that Hitchcock has also manipulated the viewer, as he will do so often in the future. Of more importance, however, is another cut to Alice, which could be interpreted as the broader horror that this now forever links her future to Frank.

While the detective had implicated himself in the killing by hiding the glove, his position in law enforcement could probably make that go away. But her fragile nature suggests, if he so desired, she is still culpable for the killing. Consequently, Alice will always be *bonded* to him. Bondage, both literal and metaphorical, will also be a future given in the Hitchcock oeuvre. And the final image of the dark comedy canvas, as it is being carried down that Scotland Yard hallway, also underscores that fact, as well as providing another dour dig at the police.

That is, both the viewer and the couple can now also see another canvas behind said jester—the mildly erotic drawing Alice had done with the artist. Thus, while the case appears closed, what sloppy work Britain's finest law enforcement agency has applied to the investigation, especially with one of the two signatures on the canvas being blackened out.

One cannot find a serious Hitchcock source that does not anchor its *Blackmail* examination in his displeasure with the close, in which the couple simply walk away. It is like an academic version of tossing out free t-shirts at a ball game. The most cited source is from François Truffaut's book length Hitchcock interview, in which the director states that he would have preferred that the girl be arrested by her detective boyfriend, who then

> ... would have had to do the same thing to her that we saw at the beginning: handcuffs [more bondage], booking at the police station and so on.... But the producers claimed it was too depressing.[13]

With all due respect to Hitchcock, this ongoing incantation merits a darkly comic revisionist discussion. The producers got it right. The ending as it stands is much more depressing. Alice will be in mental anguish for the rest of her life. Indeed, the theme of marriage as a sort of bondage is something that even becomes a significant component in the majority of the director's future films, such as the catalyst for the murder Jimmy Stewart's character uncovers in *Rear Window* (1954).

Alice was already having issues with Frank before the killing, or she never would have gone up to the artist's studio. And her mother, as previously cited, has noted their frequent fights. Plus, Frank's uniformed picture as a street cop, which Hitchcock so effectively used by placing it on Alice's bedroom wall, can also be "read" differently from its initial chapter reference. Instead of a long love story, one might ask, "Why are they not yet married?" Short of someday becoming the police commissioner, Frank's position as a detective is the top of the line, and his longtime girlfriend is still *living at home*. And most obviously, it was an attempted rape, and while nearly a century ago, when society was even more chauvinistic in its thinking about a young woman "asking for it," the same era was also skittish about convicting a woman of murder—especially with just cause.

An even greater puzzle to me, however, with regard to the close, is the misinformation about the ending of the original source material from which the film was adapted. The key reference for this would seem to be Donald Spoto's often very insightful *The Dark Side of Genius: The Life of Alfred Hitchcock*.[14] For example, other Hitchcock authors, such as David Sterritt, have piggybacked Spoto and recycled a falsehood—that the director "'fashioned an adaptation 'even darker than [playwright] Bennett's original; in Spoto's words....'"[15]

Nothing could be further from the truth. Bennett's close to his *Blackmail* is practically the equivalent of skipping down a flowery path alongside a white picket fence. And the girl neither has to die nor take the blame. Thanks to the late artist's doctor, the detective work of Alice's brother, who also just barely keeps Alice from confessing, and Bennett resorting to help from the deus ex machina one hears from Frank (Herold) in the play:

Blackmail's (1929) stuck-with-each-other couple, Anny Ondra and John Longden.

[The artist's] ... doctor went to Scotland Yard tonight ... because they were after *you* [to Tracy], a police surgeon was sent down to the mortuary at once.... Did you think he was murdered? My God! ... Why the wound wasn't deep enough to have killed. He died ... of HEART FAILURE!... brought on by over excitement. His heart's been weak for months so the doctor says.... He was about to have his supper when something ... happened to upset him. He had a seizure ... the bread knife was in his hand ... he fell.... ON THE KNIFE! He managed to crawl to the bed where he died a few minutes later of ... heart failure.[16]

Thus, far from being Hitchcock's tortured couple, the play ends with the detective taking Alice "in his arms ... affectionately ... she nestles up to him" and he says, "'You poor kid.'"[17] Let the diabetes begin.

Ironically, however, Hitchcock might have used Bennett's too-good-to-be-true ending for dark comedy purposes. That is, on occasion, black humor can use a fantasy-like happy ending as an ironic commentary on seemingly more mainstream movie genres. An excellent pre–1960s example would be W.C. Fields' *It's a Gift* (1934). Obviously the genre most readily associated with the movie is personality comedy. Yet, most clown persona figures work in a compound comedy arrangement relevant to the funny figure.[18] For example, Bob Hope's go-to connection was usually parody, such as *My Favorite Brunette* (1947, spoofing film noir), or *Paleface* (1948, the Western). And Will Rogers had a direct link to populism, especially with his John Ford collaborations such as *Judge Priest* (1934) and *Steamboat 'Round the Bend* (1935).

For Fields, it was forever dark comedy, whether he was in his huckster persona, as in *Poppy* (1936), or the fifth columnist henpecked husband of *The Bank Dick* (1940), or the aforementioned *It's a Gift*. Jumping to the post–1960s validation of black humor, the overly upbeat endings of *Catch-22* (1970) or *Brazil* (1985) are really defecations on rosy endings. Consequently, Hitchcock could actually have used Bennett's *Blackmail* close for his own twisted black humor designs.

Blackmail is, however, somewhat unusual among the Hitchcock movies to be examined for this text. In most cases, the director adopts and embellishes a type of comedy, or comedy sub-genre, to help move along what is more generally seen as a thriller and/or horror film. But in this case, I would posit that the movie is simply best labeled a dark comedy first and foremost. This has great significance, because for all practical purposes, *Blackmail* puts Hitchcock on the international movie map. And it gives greater evidence to the Hitchcock mantra that for him at least, all his movies are dark comedies.

The text has also noted a number of Hitchcock auteur basics essentially used for the first time, from the extended comic cameo on the tube/subway with the bratty kid, to a famous place finale. One of his auteur tendencies, never fully underscored (at least to me) in Hitchcock literature, however, is to depict relationships as either unhappy or at least pointed in that direction, enabling him to better facilitate his use of dark comedy. This is certainly true of *Blackmail*, with the radical changes he made to the play's conclusion. Personally, I label it the "Buster Keaton factor," both because it was also a predilection of the American comedian so admired by the British director, and because the former artist's glory days were ending just as the latter's career was taking off. Of course, maybe part of it is just that they both so utilized trains (often for black humor) in their work, and also that my most recent book was on Keaton.

Paradoxically, Hitchcock's provocative uses of sound (often for dark comedy purposes) could almost qualify as an unofficial auteur trait. That is, while this movie started off as a silent film and he was *forced* to be technically creative, as the following pages will chronicle, the director often enjoyed challenging himself on subsequent pictures with a difficult technological task. However, with regard to the silent/sound beginning of *Blackmail*, this has always been a rather thorny issue with me. While the film definitely started as a silent, stories on how it became Britain's first sound film vary. For example, most tales chronicle how the movie was essentially done as a silent, yet producers told Hitchcock they might have access to sound equipment before the film was completed—thus, *Blackmail* could then be tweaked into a pioneering sound picture. This would necessitate added reshooting and the incorporation of dialogue and sound effects.

However, other accounts have Hitchcock anticipating the likelihood of it going to sound all along and planning accordingly. This seems logical, since it would have allowed him time to devise his creative sound sequences, such as the one involving the repeated use of the word "knife." But all accounts give Hitchcock kudos for how he managed to save the day when the thick accent of his Polish-born heroine (Anny Ondra) was solved by having British actress Joan Barry stand just off-camera and speak her lines. (British cinema was not yet capable of traditional dubbing.)

My complaint is one cannot have it both ways. If Hitchcock saw it becoming a sound picture all along, why would he have a heroine, as talented as she was, whose voice would not be acceptable, especially as that of a British shop girl? Indeed, when the film was released there were even some minor complaints that Barry's obviously trained English verbalization was not that of a lower class British teenager.

Another qualifier found in *Blackmail* and future films to be addressed later in the text is Hitchcock's periodic complaint about producers sabotaging his attempts for a darker conclusion to a picture. Yet, Hitchcock was a huge Poe fan, and that writer often used a dark comedy close that caught the viewer off guard (as was the director's M.O.) by a simple, safe gotcha explanation. For example, in Poe's "Premature Burial" (my scariest nightmare as a child), he takes the reader through all the horrors this would entail for the victim. *But the conclusion reveals that a traveler has been forced to randomly catch a ride on a small inland ship carrying what, for today, would be labeled sod. In falling asleep amid the cargo, he has dreamed of a "Premature Burial."*[19]

What makes this a bit more hypocritical is that as a young man Hitchcock wrote a few short stories, one of which survives via its publication in a magazine for a company in which he then worked. Called "Gas," it is entertainingly Poe-like, already complete with Hitchcock's decidedly dark comedy misogynistic nature. He would later describe it thus:

> [It is] about an unfortunate young Englishwoman who goes to Paris and is kidnapped by a gang of cut throats, robbed [raped], and then tossed into the Seine. At the end of the story, we learn that she has dreamed it all under anesthetic at the dentist's office.[20]

It is obviously a variation of Poe's "Premature Burial." This is not to say the artist does not have the right to choose whatever ending s/he desires. Yet, whenever I hear of this director making a complaint of that nature, it chips away at his alleged Poe foundation, not to mention his similar early adventures in short story writing.

Be that as it may, Hitchcock also peppered *Blackmail* with little dark comedy footnotes. For instance, while it goes by very quickly, in one shot of the unscrupulous painter, the director manages to have a shadow fall over his upper lip which ever so briefly makes him seem like a Mack Sennett stereotypical villain with the indispensable mustache. And when Alice and Frank meet for their aborted dinner, the movie the couple had planned to see is a crime picture—which she belittles by saying she has seen every London film worth attending. Thus, Hitchcock is mocking himself along the same lines as those actors he despised for treating movies like slumming. Moreover, the heroine is taunting her boyfriend's profession.

There is also another innovative sound item Hitchcock uses which goes by many viewers, and when noted it can be defined in two ways. Alice is working in the family shop the morning after the killing when her detective boyfriend enters. She is fearful that he might know, and the director's use of sound at this moment is described by Hitchcock author George Perry in a *boogie boogie* manner: "The clang of the shop bell reverberates like the knell of judgement day."[21] In contrast, my response is a campy dark comedy "reading" in the same overwritten style of Perry. Given these Hitchcock comic embellishments, they merely underline *Blackmail* as a dark comedy.

Given the historic status of Hitchcock's film, it is not surprising the reviews were solid, even if peppered with some surprising nays. In the *New York Times*' "London Film Notes," critic Ernest Marshall quoted Field Marshal Sir George Milne exhorting filmmakers and executives to "carry the British film industry into every corner of this very great empire" and reported, "Claim is advanced that 'Blackmail' is the 'best talk-film yet,' and that it will 'give a shock to the Americans.'"[22]

The *New York Telegram* said, "'BLACKMAIL' is expertly made, and entertaining first rate entertainment," while the *New York Herald Tribune* praised the movie as "a highly credible work."[23] The *New York Evening World* considered *Blackmail* had captured

... the atmosphere of London, seems to be well reproduced and the tale is smoothly wrought ... [and the best acting is by villain Calthrop who has] extensive experience on the legitimate [stage and] gives a portrayal that reminds one of Lionel Barrymore's [natural] technique.[24]

The *New York World* critic stated:

I have seen "Blackmail" ... and it may as well be stated here and now that so far as this part of the American public is concerned a most favorable impression has been made.[25]

Some other *Blackmail* reviews, though not negative, were less enthusiastic than the film's initial high praise. Maybe this was best summarized by *Variety*:

As admittedly best in England of any all-English all-talkie to date, "Blackmail" for America ranks in the class as a fair program [average] picture.[26]

While the *New York Sun* was not without some aforementioned praise for *Blackmail*, its first paragraph still seconded the *New York Times*' verdict: "In spite of all the advance hurrahing by English newspapers, the film is only a program picture, not a road show."[27]

Be that as it may, coming full circle back to *Blackmail* as a dark comedy, *Variety*'s period review actually projects dark comedy into Alice and Frank's future:

With the assumed murderer out of the way, the heavy [brutish] lover takes his girl by the hand, and telling her to shut up, or something like that, probably marries her, to be ever after watchful of her knife hand.[28]

2

The Man Who Knew Too Much (1934)

> The *London Observer* "[is] very happy about this film. It seems to me because of its very recklessness, its frank refusal to deal in subtleties, to be the most promising work that Hitchcock has produced since *Blackmail*."[1]

Though *Blackmail* put Hitchcock on the map, a memorable critical and commercial hit does not necessarily mean the artist and/or the studio knows exactly how to get back to that place. Such was the case with both the director and British International Pictures. After breaking with the production company, Hitchcock would observe, "'I hate this sort of stuff' on the set of [the independent film] *Waltzes from Vienna*, a musical about Johann Strauss the Younger, of all things, that he rashly took on during a jobless period in 1933."[2] While Hitchcock always felt he knew where he was going artistically, the multiple collaborations beginning in 1934 with Michael Balcon (for Gaumont-British Pictures) and writer Charles Bennett were not without their influence. This trio, starting with *The Man Who Knew Too Much*, would usher in the golden age of Hitchcock's British pictures. As previously noted, film historian Anthony Slide said in an essay on *The 39 Steps* (1935), the follow-up to *The Man*, "Charles Bennett's contribution to the success of Hitchcock's British films should never be underestimated...."[3] (Balcon's gift was to help make productions happen and give Hitchcock creative freedom.)

I make the point because of an inspired insight by *New Yorker* critic Anthony Lane in an article on the director, "In Love with Fear," arguably the best single essay about Hitchcock:

> Hitchcock is the only great director who mastered those elusive hybrids, the romantic comedy and the comedy thriller. In each instance, he sees that the comedy is not something you apply like lipstick, to brighten the tone, but something that is already there—luminous natural coloring thrills, a blush in the very notion of romance.[4]

How does this phenomenon connect with Bennett? Hitchcock's compounding of these genres becomes more apparent when Bennett comes on board. This is not to say he was *the* factor, but he was certainly an element. However, of equal importance, as noted in the Prologue, was America's 1934 birthing of a new brand of farce known as "screwball comedy."[5] *It Happened One Night* (1934) was a monster hit, and was often coupled with a variation on the genre, Dashiell Hammett's *The Thin Man* (1934), which threw in a murder case, and whose best sequels paralleled Hitchcock's unique British period. Indeed, period critics sometimes mentioned Hitchcock and Hammett together, and years later there was even a short attempt at collaboration.

Before noting the opening parallels with screwball comedy, one should note that unlike the out and out dark comedy of *Blackmail*, *The Man* is a film densely populated with several genres, besides being a thriller. It is almost as if Hitchcock is presenting a smorgasbord of types—most comic. With regard to screwball comedy, the genre deals with wealthy people at play in la-de-da settings. Consequently, *The Man* opens with a series of travel brochures before

In *The Man Who Knew Too Much* Edna Best flirts in the arms of another man (Pierre Fresnay), as her off-camera husband uses an unwinding yarn gag borrowed from Chaplin's *City Lights* (1931) for farcical revenge.

2. The Man Who Knew Too Much (1934)

placing the story in the Swiss vacation resort of St. Moritz (The Hitchcocks had honeymooned in St. Moritz and always attempted to return on their anniversaries.)

The sexual mores of the screwball couple are decidedly casual, especially for the time. Hitchcock's couple, Bob and Jill Lawrence (Leslie Banks and Edna Best) play this to the hilt. Between witty banter and comic differences, Jill flirts constantly with a casual new friend, Louis (Pierre Fresnay). At one point, with her husband looking on, she romantically cuddles in Louis' arms, calling him "my love," and then casually informs her husband, "I'm just going off with another man." She then suggests to Bob, "You go to bed early with Betty" (Nova Pilbeam,

Nick (William Powell) and Nora Charles (Myrna Loy) from the first *Thin Man* (1934).

their 14-year-old daughter). This would be a provocative comment even today. Her husband pretends to cry. One is also immediately reminded of the indifferent sexual repartee of the *Thin Man*'s married couple.

> NORA: "You got types?"
> NICK: "Only you darling—lanky brunettes with wicked jaws."
> NORA: "And how about the redhead you wandered off with at the Quinns' last night?"
> NICK: "That's silly. She just wanted to show me French etchings."[6]

Like Bob and Jill, Nick and Nora are relatively young, wealthy, and seemingly on a permanent "holiday," which would later serve as a fitting title for a 1938 example of the genre.

Paradoxically, to paraphrase Hitchcock, he "...liked to put ordinary people in extraordinary situations." And while the latter portion of this formula kicks in with the kidnapping of Bob and Jill's daughter, *The Man* couple were definitely not a common duo. They were more perfectly at home in another phrase used to describe the screwball genre—"caviar comedy."[7] Plus, even with the kidnapping of their daughter, they are continental cool. Granted, the mother faints, but Jill collapses like she merely has a mild case of the "vapors" in a bad production of a Tennessee Williams play. As the father of *two* daughters, my response would have been much more manic.

Plus, dogs abound in screwball comedy—usually for some set purpose in the film, before they up and disappear. Of course, Nick and Nora's pooch does not cause anything as dramatic as Betty's canine ruining Louis' ski jump—*more fun among the rich*—before it just vanishes from Hitchcock's story, too, as was often the case with Nick and Nora's dog, Asta. In addition to the pooch, screwball comedies are adrift with spoiled rich kids, or near adults. For example, Betty is neither bothered by letting her dog ruin Louis' ski jump, or later distracting her mother during a skeet shoot competition—again hardly a regular activity for the average population, let alone during the Depression. Interestingly, however, Hollywood's period poster child for *screwball* was Carole Lombard, a known excellent skeet shooter in real life—regularly beating future husband Clark Gable.[8]

Moreover, as in a screwball comedy, Bob and Jill merely seem *unnaturally* blasé about Betty's action—or about life in general. It anticipates a scene in *My Man Godfrey* (1936), when Lombard's screen father (Eugene Pallette) is told the family's scavenger hunt gathering is like an asylum, and he flippantly replies, "All you need is an empty room and the right kind of people." Still, no doubt at Hitchcock's insistence—because he was decidedly not into children—Jill does offer the general advice, after Betty has cost her the skeet shooting competition: "Let that be a lesson to you; never have any children."

As a footnote to Hitchcock and kids, the director makes a W.C. Fields-like confession in a 1937 *New York Times* article:

> Babies unnerve me when they won't cry to order. Somehow I fight back the inherent desire to stick a pin in them and nowadays I have tumbled on the most successful ruse. I get the attendant mother to walk away from her child on the set, which results in the most satisfactory howls![9]

Naturally, *The Man* does have Betty getting kidnapped, which will be addressed shortly. However, I might have been tempted to follow the example of the 1910 O. Henry short story, "The Ransom of Red Chief." This is the tale in which another spoiled child is kidnapped from a wealthy family. But the boy's bratty behavior drives the ne'er-do-wells to distraction. Ultimately, the kidnappers are the ones to pay the ransom to get rid of the mollycoddled kid. Actually, there is a tie, of sorts, here with *The Man*; even before Peter Lorre's wonderfully wicked Abbott has her kidnapped, he makes a friendly gesture to humor the pampered Betty, who he thinks might still be upset over causing the ski jumping accident which knocks down Louis and most of the principals, including Lorre, like Mack Sennett dominos. Lorre's consideration involves offering the girl the chance to play with his toy-like chiming pocket watch as a distraction. However, she refuses with the crack, "I'm not a baby!"

2. The Man Who Knew Too Much (1934)

Yet, her action contributed to her mother losing the shooting match. Thus, Betty is ill-mannered with her kidnappers even before the event occurs. Yet, it is a significant bit for several reasons, beyond further establishing her as a scamp, and feeding the picture's dark comedy, as in, who cares if she is kidnapped? First, it connects Lorre with the chiming watch for a poignant ending sequence. Second, this stubby figure with the large, mesmerizing eyes responds with laughter which meshes with critic David Thomson's description of him as pushing "portraits of delicate deranged kindness ... to the point of frantic malice."[10] Yet, this merely contributed to making him a pioneering Hitchcock norm—the disturbingly likable villain.

Third, a point that will be expanded upon shortly, it surprisingly introduces Lorre as a darkly comic twisted personality, beyond the compulsory needs of a thriller villain. His performance is nuanced here in comic manner just as layered as his unnerving psychotic child murderer in Fritz Lang's *M* (1931). For now, just think of Lorre's *The Man* character as a live action variation of the painted jester in *Blackmail* (see Chapter One).

Regardless, *The Man* is like a Russian nesting doll—containing enough comedy genres that it turns an early Hitchcock comment about comedy on its proverbial ear. For example, here is the director's take on the subject as summed up by a *New York Times* writer in 1938:

> Next to reality, Hitchcock places his accent, he admits, on comic relief. Comedy, strangely enough, he argues, makes a film more dramatic. On the screen it takes the place of an intermission in the theatre. It relieves tension that threatens to become unbearable; it eases the mind for the next tense situation; it fends off a threatening anti-climax.[11]

First, if this were a football game, Hitchcock has immediately started off with the misdirection play. Hitchcock and "reality"? That is like saying, "John Ford and jump cuts."[12] A least during his British period (through the 1930s), it would have been closer to the truth for Hitchcock to imply he emphasized the dramatic in order to avoid unsustainable saturation comedy, which many filmmakers then felt an audience inadequate to handle.

If this sounds like I am over overemphasizing Hitchcock's use of comedy genres in *The Man*, one only has to continue the film's narrative. After continental lover Louis (who turns out to be a British spy) is shot while dancing with Jill at a St. Moritz nightclub, in the most casually elegant murder on record, he imparts to her some secret agent information dearly wanted by the British home office. Naturally, Bob and Jill's brat is kidnapped to keep them from sharing said information. But once our British variation on a screwball comedy is interrupted by this seemingly sober stuff, it is on to another comedy genre.

Since Bob and Jill will not cooperate with authorities for fear of losing a losable daughter, the husband and a close family friend named Clive (Hugh Wakefield), a delightfully vacuous fellow, decide to rescue the daughter.

Instantly, viewers are ushered into personality comedian land. But before his characters become Sherlock Holmes and Watson meet Laurel & Hardy, Hitchcock decides to give poor Clive the proper half-baked, bonkers build-up. The director cuts to Clive playing with an electric toy train set he had once given to Betty. He mildly complains to Jill that her daughter has never seemed to play with it, as he continues on his hands and knees to be obsessed with the toy choo-choo. Jill, sounding a bit like the source from which Betty got her rude behavior, tells the antiheroic Clive he never gave Betty a chance to play with it—which immediately morphs Clive into little bad boy mode, like Stan Laurel on the verge of tears.[13]

As noted in the Prologue, Hitchcock, especially in his British pictures, enjoyed giving his stories supporting comedy teams. Bob and Clive are among the most amusing Hitchcock duos when they are back in London. All Bob and Clive have to go by is a clue left by deceased agent Louis: "Wrapping, G-Barber, Make Contact A. Hall, March 21st." With this note, the duo follow most of the basic traits associated with personality comedians.[14] To start with, each has an easily definable persona, which especially follows the traits of most comedy teams. At its most quintessential level, this means one (Bob) will dominate his dense companion, rather like Bing Crosby always putting Bob Hope in comic harm's way during the "Road Pictures."

Second, as the "Road" teamings suggest, there is usually travel or an ongoing set of new locations to visit. This enables the clowns to exhaust everything funny in one spot, before moving on to a new setting with comical potential, such as Pee-wee Herman (Paul Reubens) going on the road to get back his stolen bike in *Pee-wee's Big Adventure* (1985). The humor bonus of such gallivanting comes from placing comic figures in a setting that is particularly incongruous to their persona and/or the reason for their exploring—such as Pee-wee searching the Alamo for his bike.

Consequently, for Bob and Clive, the clue has revealed that "Wrapping" is a district in East London, with Dickensian docks near the Thames. Rather an upscale area today, it is anything but in the movie. A sign sets the comic tone immediately. But it is unlike the electric Piccadilly Circus marquee and advertisement lights which set a black humor mood as *Blackmail*'s Alice wanders about the city after the stabbing. In contrast, the portion of the clue "Wrapping, G-Barber" (which is still as vague as many addresses remain in Britain and Ireland) is that of the dentist George Barber (Henry Oscar). But his sign, which Hitchcock cuts to in a broadly comic close-up, is a massive set of wooden choppers that would be suitable for George Washington's Mount Rushmore mouth. These molars are laugh-out-loud funny, as if Bob and Clive have stumbled upon the teeth of some extinct sea monster, or being near the Thames, maybe the dentist doubles as a wood carver who creates figureheads for ships designed to scare sharks.

2. The Man Who Knew Too Much (1934)

Third, personality comedies constantly reinforce the childlike nature of the figures. Thus, the duo have stumbled upon the apparent secret hiding place of these allegedly nefarious spies—and it turns out to be a dentist's office with a sign guaranteed to scare little children and small animals. What is more, it is located near a window like that of a toy shop. So despite being on a mission of life and death, the mindless Clive is suddenly enamored by a model ship behind glass.

Fourth, while not all clowns are part of a team, most operate in a team-like situation, even if it is as simple as Charlie Chaplin's "Little Fellow" having a nemesis the size of Paul Bunyan. However, having Bob and Clive as an official duo works on three levels. First, it spoofs Britain's iconically brilliant Sherlock Holmes and his sweet ignoramus sidekick Watson. Second, this would have especially appealed to Hitchcock, since he strongly disliked those final page wrap-ups in which everything is solved by Sherlock's amazing cerebellum. Third, it also allowed Hitchcock to pay credit to the American silent comedians he so greatly admired, with Bob and Clive sometimes even compared to Laurel & Hardy by film critics.[15]

The fourth and most important reason for teaming Bob and Clive is that it allows Bob to use, or more correctly misuse, Clive for both sleuthing and silliness. Indeed, Hitchcock goes at it with such broad humor one might call it *silly sleuthing*. Thus, Clive becomes Bob's canary in the metaphorical coal mine that is the dentist's office. Bob even emphasizes his casual comedy cruelty by first asking to see Clive's teeth before sending him off on his wacky reconnaissance mission. After seeing Clive's perfect pearly white molars, Bob nonchalantly says, "Seems a pity," meaning taking a tooth for the team. (Red Skelton will lose a tooth in a similar comedic sequence from 1947's *A Southern Yankee*, arguably his best film.) Of course, Clive takes his assignment without question, and soon is without a tooth and holding a cloth to his mouth.

Before Bob plays patient, he quietly tells Clive to "keep his mouth shut." Again, there is dark humor in his observation. That is, he is saying both, "Don't talk, you idiot, and blow our cover," and "keep your trap shut because your bleeding gums are disgusting." So much for appreciating his puppy dog sidekick's sacrifice. One is reminded of a Preston Sturges screwball comedy line from 1942's *Palm Beach Story*: "Chivalry is not only dead, it's decomposing."

While Bob's dental turn starts with him as a crumb of an action hero, it also turns to broad comedy. Sitting in the dentist's chair, he must kill more time until Lorre arrives and goes to a back room—guaranteeing that this *is* the hideout. But when a suspicious dentist decides to use laughing gas to "knock out" his doubtful patient, Bob turns the tables and manages to gas the doctor. One gets a guilty chuckle from the scene, for who has not fantasized about taking just that sort of action in one of civilization's legal torture chambers—the dentist's office. Once the doctor is subdued, Bob quickly changes places, puts on a dentist's lab coat, and obscures the surprise victim's face with a towel, just as Lorre passes through to the back room office.

Hitchcock has claimed he had first planned to use a barbershop for the scene, in order to justify a setting in which employing a towel to obscure a face would be natural. However, just prior to shooting he had seen a similar sequence in 1932's *I Am a Fugitive from a Chain Gang*.[16] This comes from François Truffaut's book length interview with Hitchcock, thirty-plus years after the fact.[17] However, I believe the director was really thinking of 1932's *Scarface*. Both are crime movies starring Paul Muni, include barbershop towel sequences, and were released the same year. I have four reasons for this hypothesis. First, a dentist's office lends itself more to the *everyone can relate to* setting of fear which was *so* important to Hitchcock. Second, the director saw the world in dark comedy, even sadistic terms, and a dentist's office fulfills that promise much more than a barbershop.

Third, personality comedy is densely populated with such sequences. Almost every major screen comedian has essayed such a scene at sometime, including the early duo Hitchcock enjoyed, Laurel & Hardy—*Leave 'Em Laughing* (1928). Indeed, among Bob Hope's non–Road pictures, it is often cited that his two top grossing pictures were *Paleface* (1948), and its sequel *Son of Paleface*—with his title characters both being dentists.[18] Fourth, without trying to be a tease, the final and most telling reason will be addressed shortly, because it is closely tied to some significant parallels between the closes of *The Man* and *Scarface*—parallels surprisingly never noted before, and which best belong to the upcoming portion of the chapter devoted to Lorre.

Returning to personality comedy's love of incongruous settings, Bob and Clive's gumshoe work takes them to, of all places, a sun worshipping chapel. When Clive asks, "what are they?" Bob deadpans, "They probably have nothing on." Yet, this zany cult set-up anticipates Conrad Veidt's serene séance cult facility in Red Skelton's later comedy star-making *Whistling in the Dark* (1941)—a spoof of thrilllers.[19] *The Man*'s kooky congregation is being led by tall, gaunt Cicely Oates, only known in the story as Lorre's close companion, Nurse Agnes.

Bob and Clive, attempting to fit in, make an entertainingly bad job of it, as they mumble their way through a sun worshipping hymn. They then broaden the humor by playing a child-like musical game which a young Hitchcock quite possibly did during Catholic school mass. Bob and Clive attempt to orchestrate a plan by lightly singing subsequent possibilities. However, the comic topper to their cult visit is when a knowing Nurse Agnes has poor dumb Clive step forward to be hypnotized. Agnes is most severe in appearance, bringing to mind the period comic line about America's recent

2. The Man Who Knew Too Much (1934)

President, Calvin Coolidge—"He appears to have been weaned on a dill pickle." However, despite this sober façade, her request of the already vacant-looking Clive usually results in laughter from my college students: "Your mind is becoming quite blank." That is its natural state. One cannot help thinking of Stan Laurel's definition of the mental capabilities of Stan & Ollie, "Two minds without a single thought."

Again, as could be expected of an amusing cult/church finale, it ends in a slapstick chair-throwing finale befitting the personality comedian genre. During the Truffaut interview, Hitchcock had credited his 1956 remake of *The Man* as superior.[20] Yet, in an interview for *Film News* from Criterion's 2013 Bonus Feature DVD reissuing of the film, the director had credited the first version with being "more spontaneous," à la the flying chairs sequence—and though it had "less logic," the director added, "logic is dull."[21]

This soundtrack commentary quote is seminal, not only for 1935's *The Man*, but for most of Hitchcock's British pictures during that decade. Sometimes the added bells and whistles he had after his 1940s move to America slow down the pacing and lessen the humor of the latter slick pictures. This is certainly true of the overlong, sluggish 1956 remake, with the all-American Jimmy Stewart giving an angry and rare flat performance. And the latter picture has nothing to match the scavenging creativity of Hitchcock in Britain's threadbare industry *and* the presence of Lorre.

During the fight, the final part of the note, beginning with "Contact A. Hall..." nails down the time and place for the attempted assassination of the foreign diplomat—Britain's celebrated Albert Hall, yet another Hitchcock use of a famous location. Lorre's gang includes the assassin who had defeated Jill at the beginning of the film's Swiss skeet shooting competition. The plan is to have him shoot the visiting emissary during an Albert Hall performance, just at the moment when the clash of symbols will cover the sound of his gun.

Bob succeeds in phoning Jill the information before being captured following the chair fight. Bob's attempt to find his kidnapped daughter had made him linger, while Clive contrives to exit the fight and essentially the film—his entertaining half-wittedness having served its purpose. However, Jill will thwart the assassination with an Albert Hall scream just as she spots the shooter—which startles the gunman enough that his shot merely wounds the target. The point acts as a transition, bringing in yet another genre, which still dovetails back into dark comedy and Lorre's greatest moments.

Prior to the failed attempt, Lorre had calmly told Bob, in that spellbinding way of the character Europe called "the walking overcoat" and America had christened "the man with the peculiar grin":

> You know, with a man with a heart there can be nothing sweeter than a touching scene such as a man saying goodbye to his child for the last time.

Yet, as period theatre historian Wilhelm Kosch has described him, "[Lorre is] an episode of the fantastic, the farcical in human being [form], a macabre humor."[22] Thus, Lorre's earlier but chilling statement might have been uttered in a classroom discussion of the human comedy. This is reinforced by earlier comments by Lorre which mix the same philosophical attitude with dark comedy. For example, at one point, upon leaving the hideaway, he instructs a gang member to tell Bob and the bratty daughter:

> Tell them they may soon be leaving us. Leaving us for a long, long journey. How is it that Shakespeare says, "From which no traveler returns." Great poet.

The unearthly comment, delivered in such an elegantly lackadaisical manner by Lorre's small, otherworldly, moon-faced, bubble-eyed figure, is nothing less than bewitching. As in his first American film, *Mad Love* (1935), which appeared shortly after *The Man*, Lorre's objectively less than positive figure created the following response from the *New York Times* critic: "[Lorre is] gripped in his characteristic mood of wistful frustration," even if that *wistfulness* embraces dark comedy's base—death.[23]

The phrase "wistful frustration" is also the consummate phrase to describe Lorre's character after Bob and Clive have nearly exposed *The Man* spy ring. Lorre uncharacteristically strikes Bob, only to smile contritely and say, "Sorry, please forgive me." Here is another bit of dark comedy—absurdity. The "walking overcoat" figure then thoughtfully offers the hero a cigarette from an extravagant case, only to have the straightforward but rather boring Bob ask, "Are they poison?" To this Lorre responds with the child-like laughter of the "spontaneous" nature of which Hitchcock would speak so winningly decades later. Lorre's almost tittering hysterics are as if to say, "Don't you realize we are merely *playing* at sort of a cloak and dagger *game*?" (He could also recycle Hitchcock's constant mantra, "It's only a movie.") One half expects Lorre to pat Bob on the head and say, "Don't worry about yourself." Yes, Lorre is something of an enigma, but he is an enigma who intuitively anticipates Chaplin's later world weary truism, "In the end everything is a joke." (Lorre's darkly comic persona would not be out of place in *Waiting for Godot*.)

And speaking of Chaplin, the comedian and Lorre became immediate friends, when the latter went to Hollywood later in 1935—bonding over comedy. Stephen Youngkin's definitive biography of Lorre shares the two artists' primary topic of conversation upon their first meeting:

> [Lorre felt] Chaplin, who had played a hapless private in [the dark comedy] *Shoulder Arms*, would share his enthusiasm for Jaroslav Hasek's *The Good Soldier Schweik*, Lorre told him he held an option on the novel and one day hoped to portray [the wise fool] soft-headed *batman* [officer's personal servant] in a film version of the World War I comedy.[24]

2. The Man Who Knew Too Much (1934)

Thus, *the* Lorre biographer actually suggests that the actor's primary mindset in 1935 was that of a sneaky man/child personality comedian, never mind that Hitchcock's film was supposed to be a thriller. Moreover, Youngkin states the actor infused more than a few of his best film roles with this comic character.[25] Plus, Lorre and Hitchcock immediately hit it off on *The Man* (despite the actor's limited English), in part because they shared a love of darkly comic pranks and of the genre in general. Thus, formalist Hitchcock, according to Lorre biographer Youngkin, allowed the comic-oriented actor "an unusual degree of creative freedom ... a rare [Hitchcock] confession...," something the director later also granted Robert Benchley in *Foreign Correspondent*.[26]

Be that as it may, it is now time to address the point of *Scarface* being *the* film which influenced Hitchcock more than *I Am a Fugitive*. My hypothesis goes much beyond whether a barbershop or a dentist's office location was to be used; it embraces a much broader scope of *The Man*. And this starts with tacking yet another genre upon Hitchcock's picture—but one which dovetails back to dark comedy. In many American circles Hitchcock's picture was perceived as a *gangster* film. For instance, while *Variety* called it "built along gangster lines," the *New York Daily News* peppered its review with comments like, "The battle outside the gangster's quarters is thrillingly done," the *New York Herald Tribune* likened it, at times, to *Little Caesar* (1930), and the *New York Sun* was the most thorough of all in its gangster dissection:

> Gaumont British [Studio] went American, flamboyantly American, in "The Man Who Knew Too Much." This very English studio has turned out a gangster film chockful of machine guns, kidnapping, and smiling assassins; and it has made a monstrously good job of it.... They may perhaps have manufactured "The Man Who Knew Too Much" just to prove they could ... whatever the reason, the direction is more American than English in building of suspense ... "The Man Who Knew Too Much" may startle Hollywood out of its customary smugness.... These English studios are treading at our heels.[27]

The reference to "may startle Hollywood out of its customary smugness" refers, in part, to *The Man* riding the still successful wave of gangster films made possible by sound—particularly the pioneering trilogy *Little Caesar*, *Public Enemy* (1931), and *Scarface* (1932).

So now a loose connection has been made between Hitchcock's film and gangster films, à la *Scarface*. But what is the broader connection, and how does the dark comedy link occur? First, in Robin Wood's groundbreaking study of Howard Hawks, who directed *Scarface*, Wood categories the director's films by genre. But he opens the chapter on Hawks' comedies, which include such classics as *Bringing Up Baby* (1938) and *His Girl Friday* (1940), thus:

> It may seem perverse to approach the comedies via a gangster film.... But *Scarface* belongs with the comedies ... [Lorre and *Scarface*'s title character, Paul Muni] perform monstrous violent actions which the films never condone, yet ... retain the audience's sympathy to the end ... [Lorre, like Muni] presents his gang wars as kids' games played with real bullets. A sardonic, macabre humor is seldom absent, and some of the outrages are treated as uninhibited farce ... [Lorre, like Muni] is funny and touching because he is an overgrown child, emotionally arrested at an early stage.... He dies when he loses his essential innocence....[28]

Second, to further cement the coupling of these two absurd man/child figures, some parallel plot points need to be mapped out. The most important person in Muni's world is his sister (Ann Dvorak), with whom an incestuous relationship was implied until the censors demanded cuts be made. The pivotal person in Lorre's life is his aforementioned Nurse Agnes, though he seems to have no needs to be taken care of unless they are sexual. However, between his childlike nature and her being older, it could very well be a brother-sister or son-mother twosome—which would match Hitchcock's fascination with atypical sexual relationships and his own unusual mother complex.

Everything changes for Abbott (Peter Lorre) with the death of Nurse Agnes (Cicely Oates).

2. The Man Who Knew Too Much (1934)

Third, besides the given that both Lorre and Muni have distinctive scars (hence the nickname of the infamous period gangster Al Capone), each of the women is fiercely loyal, and as long as they are alive both of these child-like "gangsters" find life rather like a diversion. Indeed, Lorre is particularly prone to laughter—both ironic and innocent—such as being the first to appreciate the unraveling scarf yarn joke Bob plays upon promiscuous Jill as she dances with the other man/spy at the film's opening. (This comic bit cannot help but remind one of Chaplin's unraveling yarn sequence with 1931's *City Lights*' blind girl.)

Four, the final shootout, which even seemed to impress the *Hollywood Reporter* critic, who otherwise gave *The Man* one of its rare pans, has several previously unnoted parallels with *Scarface*.[29] When this sequence is addressed, contemporary discussion normally *only* belabors how it was inspired by a real London shoot-out prior to World War I—the January 1911 "Battle of Sidney Street." (It was also the first such gun battle caught on film in Britain.) Even some American period reviewers felt compelled to reference the event, such as the *New York World-Telegram*.[30] What had made it especially memorable for the time was that special arrangements had to be made to get weapons for the normally unarmed bobbies (London policemen), and that the British army was also involved.

All this is well and good but it neglects to detail what occurred inside the hideout. As with *Scarface*, Hitchcock's retreat has been made into a fortress of steel—something seldom seen, if ever, in other period gangster films. More importantly, though hopelessly outnumbered, the child-like Lorre and Muni treat this dilemma like just another play day adventure—*until* the two women die. Abruptly, it is no longer a game. Then Lorre, just as Wood chronicles Muni—"...dies when he loses his essential innocence ... [and it is] eventually pathetic."[31] Muni is shot attempting to run, and Lorre is gunned down hiding behind a door, ironically given away by his aforementioned toy-like watch playing a lullaby.

Moreover, just as there were no farcical or screwball elements in the H.C. McNeile *Bulldog Drummond* novels which inspired *The Man*, there were no women involved at the "Battle of Sidney Street." Indeed, Jill's character is actually the central figure at the film's close, bringing the picture full circle back to its beginnings. That is, her kidnapped daughter's attempted escape places Betty on the roof of the hideout during the near conclusion of the fray—pursued by the failed assassin Ramon (Frank Vosper), to whom Jill had lost the film-opening St. Mortiz skeet shooting contest. And there is one of those delayed dark comedy moments which Hitchcock was fond of adding for his own pleasure. That is, since audiences normally viewed a film only once and obviously did not collect films/DVDs for repetitive home scrutiny, no period audience could enjoy the earlier, now comically ironic, dialogue exchange:

JILL: We must have another battle one day, shall we?
RAMON: I shall live for that moment.

Well, actually Ramon will *die* for that moment, when Jill's shot blows him off the roof, after the police sharpshooter does not want to risk the shot for fear of hitting Betty. (More dark comedy; mom is not afraid of killing her kid.)

There is also a delayed dark comic moment here, however, for which the Hitchcock fan will *not* necessitate repeated viewings. That is, when the director places someone in a dangerously high place, a villain like Ramon is going to die, or even a victim like Kim Novak's character in *Vertigo* (1958). One might couple this same phenomenon to Hitchcock's overhead shots. When this happens, bad things are also to happen, as for example, when *The Man* siege is just beginning, with massing policemen. There are two almost back-to-back overhead movie shots, when authorities with increasing clout arrive. After each visit, there are more dead policemen. Moreover, further into the violent encirclement, two police sharpshooters commandeer a pretty young girl's second story bedroom, to allow for a better firing placement. The viewer sees their activities from above, and after their almost obligatory Hitchcock dialogue about one preferring the warmth of her bed over his wife's, that policeman dies.

One might say this is hardly dark humor. But the macabre-loving Hitchcock is obviously telegraphing these moments, especially as in the latter case, this forever fearful strictly raised Catholic Gothic director can also couple it with alleged retribution for sinful thoughts. As perverse as this might sound, I place these same Hitchcock moments with the black humor response that hits me when, during a war film, some poor soldier shows anyone a picture of his girl back home. The fellow will be toast in five minutes.

The overhead shot merits another comment. Besides the story-based meaning for a Hitchcock film, there is a sense of God-like control inherent here, not just for this director but for all artists. (It is just that the filmmaker's shot can literally showcase a godly view.) But while most creative people turn to art to fashion a sense of the rational that does not exist in the chaotic world, Hitchcock brings *no* relief. Disorder can also happen here, to anyone, at any time. While hardly alone, Hitchcock is not a kind artistic god. Beyond the talk show patter of "actors should be treated like cattle," he is a more darkly comic master:

> When he was working on *Sabotage* [more death from on high], Hitchcock used to joke with the writer Peter Viertel about his audiences as "the moron masses," but in the film itself the phrase is given to an American admirer of the Nazis.[32]

One is reminded of another variation on this theme in Carol Reed's sometimes Hitchcock-like *The Third Man* (1949), with Orson Welles' question to Joseph Cotten from atop a giant Ferris wheel. The actor inquired, in part, "If

I offered you 20,000 pounds for every dot that stopped [person far below that died], would you really, old man [not take it]?"

While *Blackmail* (see Chapter One) plays as much as a dark comedy as a thriller, thus far *The Man* has distinctly mixed its thriller dark comedy base with the fundamental elements of screwball comedy periodically morphing into the essentials of personality comedy. Indeed, some reviews, such as that in *Variety*, actually felt there should have been "more comedy by [pea-brained Hugh] Wakefield and some of the minor characters."[33] Regardless, given these measured comedy inroads attached to *The Man*, their cumulative effect has been to usher in one final comedy genre—a parody of reaffirmation. This is a nontraditional burlesque of a given genre mixing the serious and the comic. In fact, the films are usually self-referential, deconstructing the genre even before the critics. For instance, an example already noted—but applied to Lorre as a darkly comic personality comedian only playing at being a villain—is when Bob asks him if the cigarette being offered him is poisoned. One would not ask that in a straight thriller. That is why Lorre gets such a big laugh out of it. Like an example of direct address, it further connects him to the audience—another reason to better enjoy the villain.

In *The 39 Steps* (1935), Richard Hannay (Richard Donat) agrees to take home the sexy Annabella Smith (Lucie Mannheim) from a riot at the London Palladium, because she claims to be in danger. Back at his flat, when she starts to explain her dilemma, he tells her it sounds more like a spy story—which it is (self-referential parody)! With *The Man*, one of the reasons the film is not tightly close to the *Bulldog Drummond* stories which inspired it is that the title character in the novels is a professional adventurer.[34] Thus, amateurs Bob and Jill do not know the action adventure rules and can spoofingly stumble along, as well as add a farcical element, à la *The Thin Man*. Still, this is not a broad parody, à la Mel Brooks' oeuvre. In fact, in most Hitchcock cases, the viewer is not even thinking along any parody lines ... except for maybe *The Trouble with Harry* (1955) and *North by Northwest* (1959).

The beauty of the reaffirmation parody is that it produces a fascinating tension between genre expectations (in this case the straight thriller) and a parody which is comic without deflating the characters involved. Consequently, in a broad burlesque no one dies. In contrast, the reaffirmation version adds a poignancy not normally associated with parody. One is truly saddened by Lorre's death via his musical watch giving him away, or "Mr. Memory's" conscientious professionalism sealing his fate at *The 39 Steps*' close. Since many or most viewers would *not* see the subtextual spoofing involved here, Hitchcock could enjoy yet another variation on his darkly private inside jokes.

All this is not to say that Hitchcock systematically mapped out all of the details of these various distinctive definable comedy genres visible in *The*

Man. Much of it, no doubt, was just the intuitiveness of any great artist. However, it more than demonstrates that the pieces of humor which surface so consistently and casually in Hitchcock's films are much more than mere random distractions. Indeed, the director's brew is most broad. He links a British variation on upper class screwball comedy with low brow personality clowns, all the while maintaining his dark humor base filtered through his early German Expressionism into a thriller ... which eventually piggybacks on the comparably influenced period popularity of American gangster films. Plus, the latter genre, particularly as showcased in *Scarface*, also showcases black humor and the influence of German Expressionism. In fact, one could argue that an element of Hitchcock's English films is comparable to the works of Britain's recent Nobel Prize winner for literature—Kazuo Ishiguro. A *New York Times* description of his fiction certainly has some parallels with 1930s Hitchcock:

> He has obsessively returned to ... mortality and the porous nature of time ... [He] stands out for his inventive subversion of ... genres, his acute sense of place and his masterful passing of the British class system.[35]

The next several chapters will further underline this malaise which masquerades behind a new version of the *comic* thriller. And the subject of class is still a largely neglected factor in Hitchcock's eventual move to America. However, until then, there are several additional British classics to explore which exploit his humor as much as a thriller designation.

3

The 39 Steps (1935)

> Not since "The Thin Man" [1934] ... has there been such an excellent amalgamation of humor and melodrama or, for that matter, a more thoroughly entertaining ... film than "The 39 Steps"—*New York World-Telegram* (September 14, 1935)[1]

At the risk of pushing all the chips to the center of the table, under the cover of American screwball comedy, Hitchcock also has placed elements of his fondness for German Expressionism into a mainstream movie. This was also the case in *The Man Who Knew Too Much* (1935), just by saying six words: "the painted jester and Peter Lorre," the iconic man from *M* (1931). (For more on these Hitchcock links to this German movement, see periodic asides in the Prologue and the preceding chapters.) However, the American genre masks *Steps* even more.[2]

This was definitely not a movie in which Hitchcock placed his spine in a blind trust. And to his credit, *Steps* reviews, starting with the chapter's opening quote, backed him by often keying upon farce over the film's thriller façade. For instance, the *Hollywood Reporter* opined:

> [Robert Donat] is humorously buffeted about, backwards and forwards ... [especially when Madeleine Carroll is] handcuffed to Donat to prevent his escape. An amusing sequence follows when Donat makes a getaway, dragging the furious girl after him, and the two are obliged to put up together for the night at the inn.[3]

The *London Times* called it a "comedy thriller," with Donat and Carroll knowing "how to get the last ounce of excitement from an adventure approached humorously.[4] The *London Cinema Quarterly* said the original novel "has been thoroughly modernized and a light romantic element introduced."[5] The *BFI [British Film Institute] Monthly Bulletin* reported, "...the comedy rises naturally even from the most dramatic sequences, and the romance between Hannay [Donat] and Pamela [Carroll]...."[6]

The *New York Post* critic declared, "Donat does an excellent job as the debonair Londoner whose unsolicited predicament never quite downs his sense of humor. It is a gay and warming performance [and] Carroll is likewise [comically] admirable...."[7] Indeed, the *Post* went so far as to suggest that *Steps*' comedy might necessitate redefining spy stories.[8] Later in the year a *London Observer* profile of Hitchcock provided further screwball fodder. First, it also connected the director to *Thin Man* author Dashiel Hammett, whose novel helped spawn the genre the year before. And second, it provided arguably the most screwball of all Hitchcock print interviews, something often done for PR purposes by anyone remotely connected to this genre. Though a brief toned down variation of what follows occurred later in a New York interview (see the Prologue), this much longer and more unhinged session even hints at his antics helping get actors in a screwball mode:

> Me [Hitchcock] breaking tea cups [from above], I always do it when I'm feeling good. That was a teapot once! [He seems to be referencing broken crockery on the floor below.] I like to get up to a high rostrum with a camera, and tip the tray over. Or push cups over the edge of a platform. Or just open my hand and let the whole thing drop. Wouldn't you?.... [The befuddled interviewer below admits "that the game had its possibilities...."]
>
> You must let me have my fun ... all I'm concerned with is to get the characters developed and the story clearly told ... surely you don't begrudge me a bit of fun between scenes?
>
> ["He ended reproachfully, kicking a sugar basin to the floor."][9]

Naturally, Hitchcock is having fun with the reporter. But after doing two books on screwball comedy, I find the director is shifting a public display of the genre to a new gear. Just imagine the image of the then nearly 250 pound Hitchcock on something like a camera crane raining down studio china from a godly height on the interviewer. One is reminded of Salvador Dali (1904–1989) throwing himself down stairsteps for attention ... as a child. Regardless, his zany activity could both inspire screwball performers, and actually be a sequence in a film essaying elements of that genre. One might title it "Welcome to the Three Ring Circus"—actor, film, and director.

Fittingly, moreover, another screwball comedy component found in *Steps* reviews involves an impromptu political speech Donat makes during a brief respite of dodging the police and spies. Yet, first one must back up the narrative bus to see how Donat has come to this particular comic complication. Once briefly sketched, it will seem most familiar to any cinema fan, because it represents the basic template for what viewers now think of as a Hitchcock picture—an everyman falsely accused of a crime and forced to prove his innocence.

Donat's character is a Canadian in London who has gone to another of Hitchcock's famous film settings, the city's Palladium, for a night's entertainment. As noted in the previous chapter, a beautiful mysterious lady (Lucie Mannheim) asks him to take her home because she is in danger. Donat's Hannay agrees, prophetically responding with a casual dark comedy observation only Hitchcock can enjoy at that moment, "It's your funeral"—since she will stagger into Donat's room *the following morning* with a knife in her back, warning him to clear out, or he will be next.

His flight will take him to Scotland, thanks to a map Mannheim's character gives him before dying. It is during this time that he slips into a union hall and is mistaken for the featured speaker—a point which is not immediately obvious to him. So how does this come full circle back to screwball comedy? In America's approach to farce, the key players doubled as the clowns, instead of the supporting actors. This has already been demonstrated in the previous chapter when Leslie Banks, as Bob Lawrence, spends a considerable amount of time with his idiot friend Clive (Hugh Wakefield), attempting to discover what has become of his daughter in *The Man*.

Solo or as a couple, a pivotal example of American screwball stars doing the heavy comedy lifting occurs in the previously cited *It Happened One Night* (1934), a film *Steps* often resembles. The former film's lead actors, Clark Gable and Claudette Colbert, are periodically forced to play the clowns. This is best demonstrated when the duo pretends to be an amusingly bantering married couple—forced to spend the night together in a 1930's motor lodge. Donat and Carroll replicate a variation of the same sequence, too, which will be addressed shortly. However, the featured couple need not play the clowns together. Consequently, the *Steps* scene which generated the most period critical acclaim was when Donat's Hannay must comically wing a speech at a union gathering. This is best articulated by the period *BFI [British Film Institute] Monthly Bulletin*:

> ... the high spot in the film is the political meeting where Hannay, taking refuge from persons who join the audience, [is] mistaken for a political speaker from London and faced with an audience about whom he knows nothing, improvises a speech which suits the political occasion....[10]

In America, the same *Steps* scene is especially singled out by *New York Sun* critic Eileen Creelman:

> The shrewd comedy of the picture is dryly delightful. Hannay, fleeing desperately ... runs through an open door. Then warmly welcomed, he finds himself taken for a visiting orator. Bewildered but quite up to the occasion, he addresses a large political meeting with tremendous success.[11]

The sequence effectively works on several levels. First, it follows the screwball formula of further elevating a featured player for greater viewer identification via comedy. Moreover, the genre is often "implosive," meaning the couple frequently come from different classes, with the blue collar figure frequently having a greater grasp on reality/survival. This is the case with Gable and Colbert; he is a reporter and she is a runaway heiress. ("Implosive" meant more during the 1930s Depression—everyone had to pull together.) This also perfectly plays to Hitchcock's goal—which really starts with *Steps*—that the central male be an everyman. And as a viewer, who does not want to identify with an inventive everyman? Moreover, Carroll initially comes across as upper class, à la Colbert.

Second, the sequence also works as a visceral black humor attack on political crowds—which plays to two Hitchcock givens. One is the director's belief that all his pictures are fundamentally dark comedies. And two, despite the genial comments just made about the efficient everyman Hannay, the fact that Donat's speech is the hit of the evening, despite his not knowing what he is talking about, embraces the director's private view of the masses as morons. Be that as it may, the director's love of Chaplin, and Hitchcock's pioneering use of sound (see Chapter One's discussion of the repeated application of the word "knife" in *Blackmail*), one wonders if Hitchcock thought of *City Lights'* (1931) opening during Hannay's talk.

That is, Chaplin starts *City Lights* with a political speech that actually works on three levels. Two are anchored in Chaplin using only distorted sounds for two speakers. It is a public unveiling of a multiple-figure monument. First, it is funny because the gibberish mocks the poor sound quality of early talkies. Second, it is amusing because local civic pronouncements are notoriously dull. In fact, the person that introduces Hitchcock's Hannay might just as well have been speaking gobbledygook, because he mumbles with such a lack of enthusiasm that he may very well have been bringing out Donat's character. Of course, Chaplin pulls a third send-up of officialdom squared when the last speech ends with the unveiling of a monument entitled "Peace and Prosperity"—it's now the Depression and a Tramp named Charlie underlines the fact by lying asleep in the lap of the Prosperity figure.

Returning to Hitchcock's *Steps* and screwball basics, neither the director nor the genre has much respect for relationships. As previously noted, the genre essentially spoofs romance. Couples might ultimately end up together, yet there is neither a promise of longevity nor much happiness if they stay together. Indeed, one saw that immediately in *The Man*. Had bratty Betty not gotten kidnapped, Bob and Jill would have been splitsville before the end of the first reel.

That being said, as formerly chronicled, *The Man* and especially *Steps* showcase a great deal of witty banter and sexual innuendo. *Steps* is at its best along these lines in the sequence in which Donat and Carroll, as the *Hollywood Reporter* delicately described it, "are obligated to put up together for the night at an inn."[12] What more conservative period publications avoided noting was that the couple were handcuffed together at bedtime, having had to register as man and wife. Wet and cold, when Carroll flirts with removing a silk stocking, Donat casually observes, "Take it off. I don't mind."

The provocative silk stocking sequence between Donat and Carroll.

When Carroll takes him up on this suggestion, it necessitates that one of his handcuffed hands must limply brush along the length of her leg. And when it is time to turn in, she refuses to get onto the double bed with him —which would have been forbidden by the American censorship code. However, he responds firmly, "Where I lie, you will [too]." And a more liberal England allows the clothed couple to lie down together. Though she has warmed to Donat's character, Carroll still has her reservations, which encourages him to spin a yarn about his family's alleged long history of crime. They are so gloriously infamous that Madame Tussaud's wax museum would be in a quandary about which grisly crime section would best suit the clan.

Paradoxically, this manages to put Carroll's Pamela to sleep, thus eliminating any sexy scenarios that would have bothered the more liberal British censors. (In the comparable situation from *It Happened One Night*, Gable and Colbert are not only relegated to single beds—a blanket on a rope separates them.) Interestingly, however, even though the British version starts more provocatively, Hitchcock manages to still get across his philosophy that few couples are ever content. That is, like an old married couple, while Donat seems primed for romance, his talk has put Carroll to sleep.

Hitchcock underlines this *what may have been* scene by closing with the camera moving to a lit candle on a nearby table—a symbol the director used for passion back when he created arty titles for silent cinema.[13] However, Hitchcock's coup de grace for the future happiness of this ever more seemingly romantic, though feisty, couple closes the picture. The duo are seen from behind at the London Palladium, where the film began. Hannay and Pamela's hands are searching for each other's until they clasp together. But before diabetes sets in, one notices that the aforementioned handcuffs are still hanging from Hannay's wrist. It is an ending worthy of how Keaton, a Hitchcock favorite who also favored dark comedy, closes *College* (1927). One moves through a series of dissolves, going from newlyweds to harried parents to bitterly bickering senior citizens to two tombstones.

Again, how is this pertinent to screwball comedy? It is a genre one might divide into two frequently unhappy camps. The first could be defined as "stalker-like." This is best defined by *Bringing Up Baby* (1938), in which Katharine Hepburn just wears down Cary Grant. When it was remade as *What's Up, Doc?* (1972), heroine Barbra Streisand articulated it perfectly to her romantic prey, Ryan O'Neal, "You can't fight a tidal wave." The second variety is sometimes referenced as "the comedy of remarriage."[14] Thus, the film begins with a divorce and/or separation, and works its way back to a recoupling which frequently seems to have landmines doubling as the sidewalk to that new home. This description superbly describes Hitchcock's total embrace of the genre in 1941's *Mr. and Mrs. Smith*, with Carole Lombard and Robert Montgomery. And it loosely applies to *Steps*, because while Donat and Carroll do not start out as married—they are definitely at odds with each other. The rest of the movie works towards bringing them together.

Regardless, screwball comedy's basic questioning of a happy and/or monogamous relationship—can you say farce?—plays to a Hitchcock given. When discussing the genre, this is regularly demonstrated by displaying a myriad of dispirited supporting twosomes—maybe the all time topper being 1981's *Arthur*. Well, *Steps*' examples blow by that mark. And it begins immediately with the film's Palladium opening. Headliner "Mr. Memory" is introduced as an act in which he answers questions shouted from the audience. Several inquiries promptly follow, before "Mr. Memory" can say word one, such as, "Where's my old man ...?" Finally, the Master of Ceremonies steps in and provides the guidelines that the questions need to be serious. Then the proceedings begin, briefly following the regulations until someone asks who was the last English heavyweight champion of the world. Again, matrimonial broadsides immediately follow, such as "My old woman" and "Henry the [wife beheading] VIII."

Moving on to the following morning and Donat's *wrong man* with a murdered Mata Hari in his bed, Donat must get by the two killers who have staked out his apartment. Though it is early morning, fortuitously (an ongoing given for Hannay) a milkman comes in the front door. Our hero starts out with the truth but it is too early for spy stories; there is milk to deliver. However, it is never too early for a juicy story of adultery ... I mean farce. Hannay inadvertently sets the table flawlessly by asking this young man, no less, "You married?" And bingo, he is gifted with the quintessential response for a provocative setup, "Don't rub it in."

Prior to this the milkman has been a blank sheet. One does not know if his house is on fire, or he has won the lottery. However, he lights up like a winning slot machine when Hannay resorts to farcical fiction, telling him he spent the night with a lady ... only her brother and husband are now waiting outside. The milkman smilingly asks him why he did not say so earlier, and offers to help. Moreover, when a grateful Hannay offers to pay for the assistance (of exchanging clothes), the working man smilingly declines, saying, "You'd do the same for me." And Donat manages to get by these metaphorical spy wickets. However, it is only a matter of time before his dead house guest is discovered, and the police and enemy spies will be tracking him.

Be that as it may, Hitchcock continues to comically skewer marriages. That is, the viewer next sees Hannay in a train compartment, presumably in London's Victoria Station, anxiously waiting to depart for Scotland. He shares the cramped quarters with a clergyman and two women's undergarment salesmen—another variation of Hitchcock's affinity for comedy twosomes, such as *The Man*'s Bob and Clive, or the cricket obsessed British duo in *The Lady Vanishes* (1938, see the Prologue). Now, while poor Donat is working on a stroke, Hitchcock suddenly seems to call time-out and marriage again takes it on the chin. The salesmen begin to talk shop, and when an old style girdle is displayed, his commercial competitor spontaneously retorts, "Brrr, my wife!"

The sequence quickly loses the embarrassed clergyman, yet the two prattle on, such as one salesman exhibiting a new decidedly more alluring girdle and his friend requesting he bring it back filled with a young lady. Yet, this seeming comic break in the action is really Hitchcock switching gears back to his blank humor base—a little reconnaissance work in what drives all his films. That is, news of the murder has by now made the papers. However, when the twosome discuss the murder, it is only along the lines of entertaining gossip, driven, in their eyes, by immoral behavior. There is no compassion for the victim.

All this immediately takes one back to dark comedy 101. That is, death has easily manifested "man as beast" characteristics in them. Plus, their ability to not only move seamlessly from commerce to killing while maintaining the same nonchalant manner denotes an inherent callous *absurdity* in the world. The clergyman originally in the compartment, though he leaves early, would seem to represent the young Hitchcock ... the loner off to the side watching and conflicted with Catholic guilt. This brings to mind how passionate director Guillermo del Toro is about exploring *Psycho*'s (1960) shower scene as another insight to Hitchcock's Catholic sense of guilt.[15] It necessitates poor Marion's (Janet Leigh) death for unmarried sex—the metaphorical cleansing of the water still cannot wash away her sin. If one were to somehow embrace this *absurd*—more dark comedy—take on sin, ideally these two salesmen would suffer a much worse fate. Moreover, to further flesh out this black humor aside, keep in mind that the genre is frequently driven by the inherent absurdity of institutions like the Catholic Church, or organized religion in general.

The *Steps* compartment sequence reminds me of the *Chinatown* (1974) nursing home moment, when Jack Nicholson asks the director at the establishment whether they accept Jewish residents. Of course, the answer is no. The question did not advance the narrative; the nursing home visit served another purpose in the story. Yet, this throwaway line encapsulated the whole ugly world of *Chinatown*. Thus, never let Hitchcock, or any cinema critic, pass off moments like this scene in *Steps* as only comic relief. Yes, that can be one component, but it is never the only ingredient in a Hitchcock picture. Plus, as casually as any of this director's comedy may unfold, it invariably follows the formula of various forms of funny.

That being said, film history best remembers the train compartment segment for its famous sound edit. Hitchcock has briefly cut away to Hannay's cleaning lady finding the dead body, and as she throws her head back to scream, the viewer first hears the train whistle squeal of the next shot. Donat's runaway is just coming out of a dream, and for a moment one wonders if his thoughts race to the whole situation just being a nightmare. Regardless, there is more dark comedy to be noted when comparing Hannay to the salesmen. Hitchcock speaks of his wrong man as being the everyman but ironically the salesmen no doubt better fulfill that phrase. This is because Donat has neither taken advantage of the sexy spy who had invited herself to his flat, nor later the handcuffed sleeping partner (Carroll) who eventually becomes his ally.

However, one can now use Carroll as a farce-like narrative transition point, because soon the authorities are onto Donat. And as he attempts to flee on the train, which Hitchcock so frequently and effectively uses as a smothering sealed entrapment—a moving jail if you will—he chances to see Carroll alone in another compartment. Making it up as he goes along, an actor without a script, he takes a chance and rushes in and gives her a passionate kiss, like a long lost lover. He then quickly tells her in the most abbreviated of explanations his plight. But when the authorities arrive, she turns him in and the train is stopped—providing the viewer with two more signature Hitchcock moments. First, the train has stopped at another famous spot—Scotland's Forth Bridge (to be chalked up alongside the earlier London Palladium). And second, Hannay manages to escape/hide by dangerously clinging to one of the bridge's giant girders, with Hitchcock providing yet another view downward from a great height.

Despite closing the train sequence with such an alarming perspective, Carroll's earlier pushing Donat away from his unwanted embrace metaphorically plays to screwball comedy's aforementioned description as a genre of "remarriage." For notwithstanding another of Donat's haphazard bits of luck on the run, Carrol will later become a random roommate and more during their flight—however one might question the post-film chances of the relationship.

Another aspect of screwball comedy surfaces in Hannay's flight across Scotland. Why Scotland? The murdered woman in his flat had previously told him of a professor/contact there. Also, the evil spy mastermind can be identified by the missing top joint of a pinkie finger. Then, after her death, he had taken a map of Scotland from her hand, with a marked destination. (For Hitchcock's ongoing sense of dark humor, the most boldly marked nearby location on said map is the actual city of "Killin.") How does geography play into the screwball template? This comedy genre has a love-hate relationship with the countryside. The landscape is often beautiful but the people there are eccentric and/or mean spirited.

To demonstrate, the screwball genre paralleled American painting's Regionalist movement. The most prominent artist of the school, Grant Wood (1891–1942), provides a quick Rosetta Stone to this screwball dichotomy. His portrait *American Gothic* (1930), a pitchfork-toting man and a woman who may be his daughter, is arguably the most spoofed painting in American pop culture. It oozes small town/rural narrow mindedness. This has been given added resonance in recent years by the revelation that Wood was a closeted homosexual. Yet, his landscapes are colorful salutes to the rolling hills of his Iowa home.

Consequently, while Donat is pursued across the stark unspoiled Scottish moors, the geography might showcase his vulnerability. Like a lone John Ford cowboy in Monument Valley, it still remains an engrossing atmospheric backdrop. Interestingly, like the "Regionalists," the European art scene also had only recently discovered the country showcased by the "Scottish Colorists." For the text's purposes, the most pertinent artist from the movement would be Francis Cadell (1883–1937), with one of his key paintings being *Iona, Looking North* (circa late 1910s). Hitchcock, being both a collector and director frequently using art, à la *Blackmail*'s (1929) painted jester, like an evil "Lubitsch Touch," would no doubt have known this painting of a rugged shore—especially given its anglicized name when translated from the Gaelic, *Icolmkill, Looking North*.

Regardless, unlike Cary Grant's *The Awful Truth* (1937) screwball spoof of Gary Cooper's eccentric small town rube in *Mr. Deeds Goes to Town* (1936), Donat will come up against the vicious crofter (English tenant farmer) John Laurie in *Steps*' Scottish outback. It is not obvious initially, like the savage dog/boy that comes out of a nasty small-town nowhere to bite Fredric March in the screwball classic *Nothing Sacred* (1937). However, Laurie will sell out Donat the following day, after our "wrong man" has stayed for a night's lodging. The crofter and his wife (Peggy Ashcraft) are a May-December relationship that bring to mind Wood's *American Gothic*, which most people think is a husband and wife—not a father and daughter. Indeed, when Hannay first meets them, he asks the crofter if she is his daughter.

However, while *The New York Times*' underrated critic Andre Sennwald called Laurie "the treacherous Scot," Ashcraft is most sympathetic—grasping almost immediately Donat's plight by his fleeting glances at a newspaper story on the innocent man's escape.[16] The preference of the city to the country is also accented by Ashcraft and Donat's bonding conversation over the wonders of her original Edinburgh home and his London adventures—places she tells him her husband finds evil. Even before Laurie discovers Donat's dilemma, he is jealous of a romance, and on the odd pretense of locking the barn (no one locked barns in the 1930s), the crofter goes outside to voyeuristically spy on the two through a window. Naturally, he misconstrues the couple's animated conversation about Donat being in danger. And after she has helped Hannay to escape, the Crofter demonstrates off-camera how bad Hitchcock relationships can get—the farmer beats his child bride. One cannot help but think of her eventual demise being like the closing madness of *The Wind*'s (1928) isolated Lillian Gish.

Be that as it may, Hitchcock's quick's pacing has Hannay once again on the run, with a sustained return to screwball comedy land, which is also known for its mix of verbal wit and physical humor. Thus, as he once again escapes the police on the Scottish moors, several stumble and fall like so many Keystone Kops as they attempt to cross a shallow stream in pursuit. The Kops reference is pertinent here, since the viewer will soon lose sight of these comic uniformed men, which is precisely how Mack Senett closed many Keystone chases—police falling into some body of water.

In stark contrast to the crofter's decidedly non-screwball cottage, Hannay next finds himself back in an urban setting. He arrives at the previously noted professor's house during a cocktail party. Ah, one is now in the true bastion of screwball comedy. The upper class drinking features Professor Jordan (Godfrey Tearle), representing a profession frequently skewered at the time as essentially frivolous, as was education in general. For example, during the Depression Will Rogers would say, "Maybe ain't ain't correct but I notice that lots of folks who ain't usin' ain't, ain't eatin'." While Jordan is not an absentminded professor, à la Grant in *Bringing Up Baby*, or Jimmy Stewart in *Vivacious Lady* (both 1938), he is decidedly cordial, and when Jordan sends away the police, Donat begins to relax—big mistake.

Hannay explains his tale and when he gets to the part about the mastermind missing a pinkie digit, one gets a shock comparable to discovering who the culprit is in *After the Thin Man* (1936)—Jimmy Stewart. Except Hitchcock gets both a dark comedy laugh, and the perfect set-up. That is, as Donat notes this signature trait, Jordan makes like show and tell and holds up the flawed hand like a parlor trick. Doubling down on this dark comedy moment, he then proceeds to shoot Donat with the casualness of Paul Henreid asking Bette Davis in *Now, Voyager* (1942), "Shall we have a cigarette on it?"

This sudden mix of screwball and dark comedy acts like a one-two punch, yet as the scene ends one wonders how things will proceed with a dead Donat. But a bit more black humor comes to the rescue—the crofter's wife has saved Hannay again. It seems that the dusky coat of her husband's she had thrust upon the escaping Hannay, to be less visible on the moor, had contained a bullet-stopping hymn book. Paradoxically, while Hitchcock's organized religion can be mean spirited and/or deadly, more *absurdity* bubbles to the top— its accoutrements, like hymnals, can serve more practical purposes.

Donat ends up at the nearest police station and seems to be believed by the local sheriff (Frank Cellier). But it turns out the head constable had only been humoring him, since his best friend is actually the professor, and the sheriff is only waiting for plainclothes men to arrive and take Donat off his hands. But Hannay's character flirts with *reaffirmation parody* yet again with another getaway—bursting through the police station's large front windows, just as he is being handcuffed. This type of parody is joined at the hip with the seemingly non-stop fortuitous things which come his way, such as fading into a Salvation Army parade which just happens to be passing by.

The remainder of the movie is as comic as it is a thriller, from Hannay's aforementioned ad-libbed political speech, to his adventures in farce handcuffed to Carroll. Plus, there are simply innumerable comic bits lightly folded in. For example, from the film's beginning Donat has been a wellspring of dry quips, such as when his soon-to-be-knifed spy tells him she has no country, and he cracks, "Born in a balloon, huh?" This continues to the conclusion, including a definite Hitchcock *trashing the law* touch, when the couple and their captors, prior to yet another escape, are stalled by a flock of sheep. Hannay breezily observes, "A whole flock of detectives."

The latter portion of the film, however, remains largely anchored in farce and/or broad comedy team shtick, substantially assisted by the handcuffs. Besides already noted high profile examples, such as the removal of Pamela's stockings, there are several other visual bits. For instance, when the duo first escape, the cuffs get hung up on a bridge guard rail and the couple have to twist themselves about to get untangled. Plus, early in their "attachment," distrustful Carroll is not with the program, and Donat is comically dragging her along like a reluctant pooch on a leash.

Conversely, when Carroll manages to get out of the cuffs and the bed, after Hannay has fallen asleep, she makes for freedom. But from the upstairs balcony she overhears the enemy agents at the front desk asking questions—that is the catalyst for finally believing in Donat. Thus, she returns to their room and sweetly looks at him sleeping. As if to make up for the trouble she has caused him, she then tucks a blanket around him. However, she is still a proper woman, so she attempts to retire on a glorified pew-like bench at the foot of the bed. However, Scottish inns, especially of the pre-war era, are chillingly drafty, and she is cold. Consequently, in an amusingly realistic bit of humor, she gets up and takes the blanket back from Donat.

The next morning, Donat and Carroll, unhooked and now a team, find themselves back at the London Palladium. Approaching the ending, the tale becomes more serious and slides back to the ever present dark comedy. Indeed, one even gets this transition telegraphed in the theatre's marquee lighting. Just as Anny Ondra, wandering the dark London streets after the *Blackmail* killing, sees the ironic theatre sign "New Comedy" (dark comedy), *Steps*' bright Palladium sign has a subtitle which fatalistically describes the bookend time period of the movie—"CRAZY MONTH." Moreover, the lettering is twisted to the unbalanced world of German Expressionism and black humor.

Once inside, "Mr. Memory" is back on the bill, or maybe he has never left. And the tune Hannay has periodically been obsessed with humming but frustrated over its origins finally comes to him; it is the entertainer's theme song. Thus, like the innocuous melody Peter Lorre's child murderer had whistled in *M*, the film which so impressed Hitchcock and the world, one harmless song eventually leads Donat to the connection between "Mr. Memory" and the picture's MacGuffin—"the 39 Steps." The Professor is at the theatre, too, in a box seat, waiting until after the program to obtain the secret the headliner has learned.

However, Hannay has only now put this all together. And as the police are about to arrest him at the Palladium, he desperately calls out to "Mr. Memory," "What are the '39 Steps'?" For our poor entertainer, who has been duped into memorizing a government secret as yet another mind game, it *fatalistically* means his doom. This German Expressionism and dark comedy component—like a clockwork orange (part machine, part man)—compels him to answer any audience question. Thus, the professor, from his theatre perch, is forced to shoot "Mr. Memory." However, unlike the wannabe theatre box assassin from *The Man*, he is successful. Yet, this will also result in his being soon shot and killed on stage in an attempt to flee.

3. The 39 Steps (1935)

In this theatrical play within a play close, the last bit of darkly comic fatalism belongs to "Mr. Memory." He does not die immediately, as if he must professionally answer Donat's question completely before passing. Moreover, once his aircraft engine design MacGuffin has been fully recited, he still must add his act's signature closing comment to the questioner, "Am I right, sir!" Only after Donat provides this approval can he die. The funny/sad poignancy of "Mr. Memory" is yet another link to *Scarface*. Paul Muni's dumb but professional little secretary, who is compelled with dark comedy diligence to take phone messages, even during gun battles, also pays the ultimate price. Regardless, the nature of *Steps*' theatrical nature and its wrong man theme flirts with Oscar Wilde's black humor derailing of Shakespeare, "All the world is a stage and the play is badly cast."

Hence, returning to Hitchcock's inescapable black humor base, beyond earlier examples, which are so often intertwined with German Expressionism, there is an initial *Steps* touch which is reminiscent of *Blackmail*'s use of the painting of the pointing jester. The multiple screen showcasings of the clown begins with a prophetic "statement" of fatalistically appalling things to come, with each subsequent view of the painting being an escalating taunt. In *Steps*, shortly after Donat's own prophetic "It's your funeral" comment to the woman spy who asks to come home with him, the two enter his flat. Near the door there is, on a wall-hugging table, a statue. The art piece is a male figure pointing towards a large window to their left. Moreover, the apartment has a morgue-like feeling to it, with sheets covering the furniture. The following morning the same window is open, with the curtains ominously blowing inward towards the pointing figure. And Donat's lovely mysterious guest has been fatally stabbed—obviously death has come through the window. Or was the previous night's first sight of the figure a warning to clear out, just as Anny Ondra's first sight of the painted pointing jester was a warning for her to get out, too? Of course, human beings tend to be either oblivious to the world around them, or let warnings slide off them like Teflon.

Regardless, there is no suggestion that the seemingly classic Greek statue reproduction has the sneer of the pointing jester, since the viewer's perspective does not reveal the figure's face. However, in the final analysis, both works of art, just like Hitchcock's filmography itself, suggest the same "and so it goes" Vonnegut mantra. That is, we use these mainstream forms of entertainment, be they books, films, or decorative artwork—to numbly mask the ultimate abyss which is the human comedy as it "hides" in plain sight. That the statue is obviously a copy from antiquity merely underscores it has always been this way.

Before addressing the critical response of what is now considered Hitchcock's greatest British film, the source from which it was adapted, John Buchan's novella, *The Thirty-Nine Steps* (1915; Hitchcock's film used the numeral in the title) merits discussion. Most Hitchcock sources suggest that the director and screenwriter changed so much, such as adding the farcical elements with Donat and Carroll, that in considering the film, one can essentially ignore the novella—since it is largely a secret agent story involving Major General Sir Richard Hannay, with hardly a woman in sight. For some, this is further justified by the fact that there were many other Hannay mystery stories along the same lines. Yet, this does a disservice not only to the book in general but to the comedy and comedy potential to be found in Buchan's original text. Plus, signature scenes in the film often have at least a foothold in the novella. For example, the movie's most praised sequence in 1935 reviews was Donat's off the cuff speech.

Hannay must also give a talk in Buchan's text. Though he knows about it ahead of time, his situation is similar to Donat's plight. Sir Richard amusingly confesses to the reader, "I tried to think of something to say ... but my mind was dry as a stone."[17] And though the novella does not gift us with his speech, it would not have played well in print anyway. Since the movie sequence is predicated upon Donat's masterful performance, the viewer is watching his brain work at high speed to succeed. That being said, Sir Richard is quite capable of an engagingly funny description of the preceding speaker:

> I never heard anything like it. He didn't begin to know how to talk. He had about a bushel of notes from which he read, and when he let go of them he fell into one prolonged stutter. Every now and then he remembered a phrase ... straightened his back and gave it off like [the celebrated but self-absorbed actor] Henry Irving.... It was the most appalling rat....[18]

Other pivotal Hitchcock scenes which had a least a toehold in the novella include a spy (although male) knifed to death at Sir Richard's home, an escape under the guise of being a milkman, an adventure which also takes a month, an attempted capture involving a plane, the kidding of the police, and a touch of dark comedy. The skeleton of Buchan's book is far from being a thorough outline for the director's adaption. Yet, I am still somewhat reminded of how Howard Hawks turned *The Front Page* (1931) comedy/drama into the 1940 screwball farce *His Girl Friday* (1940) simply by casting a woman (Rosalind Russell) into what had been a male part. There is something of that in Hitchcock's picture, except the major transformation comes about by *adding* Carroll as a woman companion.

Be that as it may, one must understand Hitchcock's natural pleasure with the tale. During his youth, the Sir Richard stories were a popular series that the future director might have known. And besides Buchan inadvertently also playing to Hitchcock's kidding of the cops, there were other components the filmmaker would have enjoyed. For example, besides the director's fondness for fine wines and food, to the detriment of periodically hamstringing his health, he also enjoyed discussing the subject. And Buchan's book is peppered with such interludes. For example:

> I never ate a meal with greater relish, for I had had nothing all day but railway sandwiches [which train loving Hitchcock would be aware of]. Sir Walter did me proud, for we drank a good champagne and had some uncommon fine port afterwards. It made me almost hysterical to be sitting there ... [Next] we went to his study for coffee.[19]

Maybe the topper, however, to the Hitchcock-Buchan link over *Steps* is a statement the novelist wrote about the book that essentially summarizes a pivotal view the director felt about most of his films: "[The] incidents defy the probability and march just inside the borders of the possible."[20] For example, at the beginning of Hitchcock's adaptation foreign agents manage to murder his lovely spy of a houseguest but leave Donat's character untouched. Yet, the following morning they lie in wait outside his flat to kill him. If the agents were so sure Hannay had learned something, why did they not kill him at the same time as the spy? Oh, of course, one would then not have had a movie.

Regardless, as the chapter opening comedy focused film reviews suggest, *Steps* was a major critical and commercial success. Indeed, one gets a sense of both the praise and the implied comedy in the *New York World-Telegram* review:

> ... it is not only ten times better than the average spy story but it actually has very little to do with spies—which is the reason I hesitate to classify it as such.[21]

Besides the comedy factor, the acclaim usually keyed upon Hitchcock as the above-the-title star. Thus, the *New York Times*' critique opened thus, "Alfred Hitchcock, the gifted English screen director, has made one of the fascinating pictures of the year."[22] *Variety*'s appraisal backs up Hitchcock's often stated comment that *Steps* was what really made America's film capital take notice; despite the aforementioned so-so comments from the *Hollywood Reporter*, *Variety* opined,

> Hitchcock, probably the best native director in England, has had a relatively easy time putting over a picture that is bound to appeal to the general run of picturegoers throughout the world.[23]

However, the title of the *London Observer*'s review was the most succinct in stating the director had arrived: "A Genius of the Films: Alfred Hitchcock and His Work."[24]

During the 1930s *The Lady Vanishes* (1938) was sometimes considered Hitchcock's best British picture, because the filmmaker won the New York Film Critics' Best Director Award, which was a relatively rare competitive victory for him. His mainstream popularity worked against such honors.

Regardless, at the end of the 20th century, the British Film Institute (BFI) picked their top 100 native pictures, and while *The Lady Vanishes* logged in at the reputable 35th placement, *The 39 Steps* came in at number four, following only Carol Reed's *The Third Man* (1949), and two David Leon productions, *Brief Encounter* (1945) and *Lawrence of Arabia* (1962).[25]

All this is not to say *Steps* was not considered as at the top of the heap during the 1930s, from Hollywood beginning to court Hitchcock, to American radio adaptations by Lux Radio Theatre (1937, hosted by Cecil B. DeMille), to a 1938 version by Orson Welles' Mercury Theatre (though the latter version's focus was on the novel). While Welles is on record as being especially fond of this Hitchcock film, his ego probably made the novella more attractive since the focus is entirely on Hannay. In contrast, light comedian Robert Montgomery—whom Hitchcock would later direct in the screwball comedy *Mr. and Mrs. Smith*—was teamed with Ida Lupino in the more farcical Lux Theatre radio adaptation.

As a final point for the strong methodical comedy headwinds attached to *The 39 Steps*, one need go no further than two examples, one from the period, and another of a relatively contemporary nature. The first is Bob Hope's affectionately excellent parody of the movie in *My Favorite Blonde* (1942), something seldom acknowledged but oh so much better than Mel Brooks' one note spoof *High Anxiety* (1977), which awkwardly throws together signature Hitchcock scenes from his whole filmography for mixed results. Plus, as noted earlier, since the original *Steps* also works as a reaffirmation parody, it makes a broader spoof more difficult to

This poster for *The 39 Steps* teases, "romance or handcuffs, which will it be?"

accomplish. However, Hope pulls it off by keying just on the Hitchcock original, as well as using basic burlesquing principles, such as direct carryovers from the comic target—such as Carroll again being cast as the leading lady. Moreover, what says Hitchcock more directly than Hope's title—*My Favorite Blonde*?

The more recent comedy homage to *Steps* comes with the critical and commercial Broadway hit play of the same name during 2008–2009, after a comparable success in Britain. Four actors frantically play the story's 100-plus characters, and the action is non-stop fun, with a generously witty peppering of other Hitchcock references. Thus, the director's original was equal parts humor with thrills, and with the passage of time the comedy has been in the ascendency.

During the approaches war years, in which politics will be more front and center in Hitchcock's films (see the following chapter, Winston Churchill made his famous comment about trying to understand Soviet Union dictator Joseph Stalin—"…a riddle wrapped in a mystery inside of an enigma." Yet, Churchill might just as well have been speaking about Hitchcock.

4

Secret Agent (1936)

> [Lorre] chases women around like Harpo Marx and licks his chops over the prospect of a good, clean murder—*New York Post* (June 13, 1936)[1]

While critics often reference a Hitchcock film as a "melodramatic thriller," and the director was most apt to call his films "dark comedies," *Secret Agent* just begs to be called a hybrid comedy. Indeed, short of Hitchcock's out and out screwball comedy, *Mr. and Mrs. Smith* (1941), *Secret Agent* has to be overwhelmingly ranked as a comedy first. The *New York America's* period review might have best described this situation: "The fable [*Secret Agent*] is pretty well given over to the development of the romance and the eerie comedy of Mr. Lorre...."[2] So where to start, with personality comedy, romantic/screwball comedy, or cumulative black humor? The *New York American's* closing paragraph most decidedly points one towards personality comedy: "...the outstanding performance is that of Peter Lorre in the rich character role of a sinister jokester role with a bulging eye for the girls."[3]

Flash forward over 50 years to a BFI (British Film Institute) tribute to Lorre's career and the personality comedy interpretation is further underlined.[4] For example, critic Michael Newton's 2014 *London Guardian* article described Lorre's *Secret Agent* thus:

> [Both] ... killer and clown, Hispanic Peter Lorre finds the murder business ludicrously comic.... He played best with a great foil, his ridiculous relish for excess up against [co-star] John Gielgud's elegant Home Counties restraint....[5]

Consequently, one has a basic personality comedian trait—the tendency for the screen clown to be teamed (if only for one movie) with a contrasting type. Moreover, this also matches Hitchcock's tendency to pepper his pictures with comic twosomes, either in support or the lead.

Indeed, Newton's article also compared Lorre's *The Man Who Knew Too Much* (1934) teaming with the rather colorless Leslie Banks:

Lorre cannot help but [comically] steal each scene; he's a physically present actor, often, you feel, surrounded as he is by the pallid English, the only one in the room with a body.[6]

Another *London Guardian* article, also from 2014, had Philip French even crediting Lorre with besting Gielgud in *Secret Agent*: "he gave a brilliantly comic performance that somewhat showed up stilted co-star John Gielgud."[7]

Regardless, Newton's *London Guardian* piece further fleshed out the Lorre ongoing shtick/persona, which is another trait of the personality comedian, first addressed in Chapter Two. Consequently, besides the round face, bulging eyes, and small stature (five foot two), Newton perceptively added:

> Lorre looked like a sleazy baby, his face registering every passing petulance, ready to drop from a hopeful grin down to a sulk ... he seems haunted, shiftless; he moves between an uncanny calm and fits of restless mania.[8]

Newton's preceding observation suggests another basic personality comedian component—being the underdog. Yet, while the standard screen clown links his persona to another comedy genre, such as Will Rogers' pictures compounded by the good will of populism, or Bob Hope joining his personality comedy to parody, Lorre's connection is usually with dark comedy. Thus, in the meat of Lorre's career, his underdog status did not translate to a happy ending.

However, in his two Hitchcock pictures he is granted a poignancy which even his friend and fan Charlie Chaplin would have admired. In Chapter Two's examination of *The Man Who Knew Too Much*, he is gunned down behind a door when his child-like musical pocket watch gives away his hiding place. His death scene in *Secret Agent* is more nuanced. It occurs the one time he lets down his guard and does not immediately play amusing assassin. Having survived a massive train wreck, his target is fatally injured but shoots Lorre before he dies.

An often Harpo-like Lorre in *Secret Agent* (1936).

Even on the set, comic Lorre (right) commands one's attention, with Hitchcock (center) and John Gielgud.

The moving culmination to Lorre's death scene comes in his last words even as he still stands. Throughout the film when not on screen he is known with comic affection as "The General" or "The Hairless Mexican," though he is neither a general nor a bald Mexican. Yet, whenever he meets someone new he introduces himself with a mile-long name and an amusingly curious somberness, which invariably elicits a smile or a laugh from the viewer, "I am General Pompellio Montezuma De La Vilia De Conde De La Rue." Indeed, sometimes it is milked for more humor. For example, after one such introduction a character asks, "Ah, do you mind if I call you Charlie?" A flabbergasted Lorre replies, "Yes, I mind!"

In view of the fact, it is astonishingly affecting at the close when Lorre must deliver his elaborate introduction one final time before dying ... with its seriousness now most fitting. It is rather like *The 39 Steps*' "Mr. Memory" needing to finish his final answer *and* formal stage sign-off, before dying. Ironically, however, I am reminded of the line Mandy Patinkin repeats throughout *The Princess Bride* (1987), "My name is Inigo Montoya. You killed my father. Prepare to die!" Both introductions by Lorre and Patinkin have

4. Secret Agent (1936)

the same comedy by repetition tactic going on, but culminate in completely different ways.

Before further elaboration on Lorre's comic touch and the other comedy genre layers of the *Secret Agent*, a brief story synopsis is due. Set during the third year of World War I (1916), a British captain (Gielgud) comes home on leave to find his newspaper obituary and a foreign office appeal to accept a secret mission. With dry wit, Gielgud replies that he must love his country, because he "just died for it." The commander, known only as "R" (a bit of Kafkaesque absurdity?), tells him his mission is to go to Switzerland to liquidate a foreign agent about to leave for Turkey in order to create trouble in the Middle East. Gielgud's new identity is Richard Ashenden, and he will be assisted in this assassination assignment by Lorre's character and by a surprise wife (Madeleine Carroll), both of whom are already on their way to neutral Switzerland. This is yet another screenplay collaboration between Hitchcock and Charles Bennett, adapted from stories by W. Somerset Maugham, from his 1928 book, *Ashenden: or The British Agent*.

Previous Hitchcock studies have been dismissive of the influence of Maugham's stories, which are loosely based upon the author's experiences during the conflict. Indeed, even their acknowledgment is compromised by only casually crediting "some stories" or "two stories"—without even noting titles. But as with similar offhand allusions to other Hitchcock source material in the text, this chapter will demonstrate Maugham's tales were mined for several key adaptation points. Plus, they were not, as is often implied, a random collection of short stories. Instead, the tales are often linked by return visits from characters, beyond being anchored by Maugham's autobiographic character, surrogate secret agent Richard Ashenden. A comparison could be made with Christopher Isherwood's *Goodbye to Berlin* (1939), which doubles as a collection of boardinghouse short stories with pivotal character intertwined throughout the book.

For the record, the *four* Maugham short stories pivotal to Hitchcock's adaptation are "The Hairless Mexican," "The Dark Woman," "The Greek," and "The Traitor." As the first title obviously suggests, "The Hairless Mexican" was the most beneficial in trolling for colorful details for the film. However, Ashenden's teaming with the "Hairless Mexican" for their secret mission also stretches through "The Dark Woman" and "The Greek."

In Maugham's writing the description of the "Hairless Mexican" is that of a bigger man who actually is bald—though he wears wigs. Thus, Hitchcock has ratcheted up the comic factor by casting the small Lorre with a toned down Harpo-like curly do.[9] And Lorre's *Secret Agent* ethnic background is otherworldly, fittingly like the men from Marx.

Otherwise, Maugham's and Hitchcock's figure is like Harpo with a voice—living to chase girls, quick to laugh, a child-like wave of ever changing emotions which always dovetail into humor, a wise fool seemingly capable of anything, never without a sharp instrument, iconoclastic yet with a youngster's loyalty and generosity, and—despite his looks—a funny/sad sense of dignity. Maugham's Ashenden could be describing either character:

> ... he was a rarity to be considered with delight. He was a purple patch on two legs. Notwithstanding his wig [Harpo wore obvious wigs] and his hairless big face, he had undoubtedly an air; he was absurd, but he did not give you the impression that he was a man to be trifled with. His self-complacency was magnificent.[10]

A pocket definition of the character from Maugham also rings true: "He was ... ridiculous, but you could not take your eyes from him."[11]

The beauty of having an original source is that one can further flesh out a film's character as well as why a director might be so attracted to a certain figure. For example, Maugham's "The Dark Woman" reveals that the Hairless Mexican, like Hitchcock, likes reading detective stories and planning perfect murders. Plus, all of this is presented in an incongruously chattering little boy manner—a bonus, because this is a dark comedy component which is Hitchcock's bulwark. However, the long "Dark Woman" passage which will most grip the Hitchcock aficionado could easily have come from the novel *Strangers on a Train*, or the director's 1951 adaptation. That is, Maugham's "The Dark Woman" is a succinct template for that future perfect crisscross murder. "The Hairless Mexican," in the excitable voice so like Lorre's *Secret Agent* character, explains, in part:

> "If your murder is as ingenious as you think, the only means you have of proving the murderer's guilt is by the discoveries of motives.... If there is no motive the most damming evidence will be inconclusive.... But if he were a total stranger you would never for a moment be suspected.[12]

Maugham also provides "The Hairless Mexican" with another trait which immediately reminds one of *Strangers on a Train*, as well as another manner Hitchcock often employed for cinematic kills—strangulation. That is, when "The Hairless Mexican" and Ashenden are crossing a national border by train, the latter figure suggests he briefly take the other's gun and knife. Ashenden explains he has a diplomatic passport, and the customs authorities would be less likely to search him. "The Hairless Mexican" agrees. But when Ashenden asks if there are any other weapons to volunteer, his eccentric partner offers a darkly comic reply, "My hands but those I daresay the custom officials will not make trouble about."[13]

While "The Hairless Mexican" is amusing in Maugham's stories, Hitchcock embellishes the part while expanding upon the inherent dark comedy. For example, once in Switzerland, Ashenden and this eccentric partner are to meet a contact at a village church. Upon entering the abbey, the double agent church organist seems stuck on a constant ominous chord. Further explanation finds their church connection dead at the organ. While Gielgud's Ashenden is bothered by the murder, Lorre comically mimes the slitting of a throat, while he professionally admires the murderer's craftsmanship.

Also, the dark comedy genre's trio of themes are at work: death, man as beast (both the murderer and Lorre's response), and absurdity—the minister and/or organist dead at the keyboard in a somewhat upright position, as if he were touched by being allowed to play his own dirge. Moreover, black humor relishes attacking establishment institutions, like religion, a franchise which offers a crutch in a chaotic world—invest up-front in a "layaway" program which only kicks in after death, to a place on no map. Oh, and the five star ratings cannot be verified. Regardless, Lorre's blasé response to the killing demonstrates another quintessential dark comedy fundamental—the ongoing callous nature of death. However, this time the seemingly unfeeling response one-ups Kurt Vonnegut's later *Slaughterhouse-Five* (1969) mantra for indifference—"and so it goes." That is, instead of detachment, Lorre finds it amusing.

Lorre further trumps the same existentialist lesson of Abert Camus' *The Stranger* (1946), in which the most lackadaisical of killers is executed not so much for the act but rather for not being able to demonstrate remorse. In contrast, Gielgud and Lorre eventually find the individual thought to be their target, and the Mexican pushes the individual off the mountain. But almost immediately a British coded telegram reveals this is "the wrong man." Gielgud's Ashenden is stunned, but Lorre's character cannot contain his laughter at the absurdity of it all. (While the response of the Mexican is not revealed in Maugham's "The Greek," this is the tale in which the execution is by a knifing.)

This is a good point, therefore, to examine the influence of Maugham's fourth tale, "The Traitor," on Hitchcock's film. The director has, moreover, done some rearranging of the tales and tweaking of the facts. For example, in Maugham's "The Traitor," Ashenden is on another mission, and though the destination is again Switzerland, he is working solo. However, Hitchcock makes the tale a continuation of the first operation, and brings back the Mexican. Plus, "the wrong man" murder is made more darkly comic. However, Maugham's "The Traitor" still provides much fodder for Hitchcock's final film, from Ashenden having strong childhood memories of the organ at which the dead double agent turns up, as well as a reconfiguration of a couple at the inn.

However, before addressing the significant influenc of "The Traitor" on Hitchcock's adaptation, Maugham includes musings by Ashenden that reveal basic dark comedy elements on how one might compartmentalize killing. These are things to which the director would have related, not to mention Hitchcock feeling everyone was capable of murder:

> He was traveling with a brand-new passport ... under a borrowed name, and this gave him an agreeable sense of owning a new personality. He was often slightly tired of himself and it diverted him for a while to be merely a creature of R's facile invention. The experience he had just enjoyed [mixing a potential assassination with a vacation setting] appealed to his acute sense of the absurd. R ... had not seen the fun of it ... you must be able to look at yourself from the outside and be at the same time spectator and actor ... in the comedy of life.[14]

In a much briefer dark comedy aside Ashenden later drily added, however, that with killing, of course, too much "introspection" could be "unhealthy ... [and] unenglish."[15]

Like an efficient traveler, Hitchcock the artist packs a tight suitcase in effectively incorporating this final Maugham story, "The Traitor," into his adaptation. In the director's *Secret Agent*, the aforementioned "wrong man" who is killed is a most likeable Englishman, living in neutral Switzerland out of devotion to his wife. That is, his protection is based on her being German, and with World War I raging, Britain's abhorrence towards all things German would have made an English life untenable. The sympathetic couple have a bull terrier that doubles as their child, and the pooch seems to have an almost telepathic connection to the husband. Given that Ashenden and the Mexican are certain the Englishman is the target, they lure him into a mountain hiking expedition, with the dog left at the lodge. The canine becomes increasingly agitated as he senses his master is in danger. Thus, instead of Ashenden only sensing the Mexican has knifed the "wrong man" in "The Greek," it becomes a high profile off-camera scene in Hitchcock's film, with Gielgud uncomfortably present, soon to be topped by how much the murdering mistake amuses Lorre's character.

In addition, the dark comedy is not only heightened by the unconventional execution—just pushing a spy off a mountain—but also by Lorre's laughter. Hitchcock has again utilized sound for a special effect. But this is not a thriller application, such as *The 39 Steps* sound cut of the cleaning lady's almost scream turning into a train whistle. *The Secret Agent*'s employment of sound is for a macabre cartoon-like death. That is, at the precise moment the victim is being pushed off the cliff, a sound cut to the next scene is that of his dog making a mournful whine which could double for the woo-wind noise of Wile E. Coyote falling off yet another precipice.

Hitchcock's *Secret Agent* is further bathed in black humor because his "wrong man" inadvertent "skydiver" is a sweet innocent old man, while Maugham's comparable figure, though also likable, is a spy. Moreover, while his dog's telltale cry coincides with the traitor presumably being executed someplace else, Ashenden, or a partner, does not have to play executor.

Consequently, with all these ties and more between *Secret Agent* and Maugham, why have these stories been so brushed off for decades? Already this text, as well as other research I have done, often reveals that scholars (so called) do not go to the original sources, or they simply accept a countlessly repeated claim that some document was so reworked one need not bother with it. Of course, to Hitchcock's credit, the screwball comedy blueprint, which was so masterfully dropped over the Maugham model, and was then tweaked with dark personality comedy, marinated in black humor, no doubt also contributed to the "stories" being disenfranchised. Thus, Maugham would have been entitled to think his original work had been corroded inside, like a bad battery.

Regardless, Hitchcock's misdirection use of screwball comedy begins with recasting the director's prototype blonde, Madeleine Carroll, back from the pioneering *39 Steps*. Moreover, her antics are even more appropriate for the genre. That is, this time she is a dingy society type (a given for the genre) who enters the spy game as casually as screwball Carole Lombard goes on a *My Man Godfrey* (1936) scavenger hunt the same year as *Secret Agent*. Carroll will act as a cover/pretend wife to Gielgud's Ashenden. A positive review from the all-important *Variety* indirectly suggested screwball comedy-like silliness was at work, at least with her role:

> Carroll [is] somewhat straining on the credulity. British intelligence service couldn't have been as bright as it was cracked up to be if it picked 'em as dumb as she is made to behave. The film has her philandering at the game of espionage and out of sheer ineptitude pulling one of the major coups of the service.[16]

The *New York Times*' generally positive review, however, managed to reframe her hijinks as merely consistent with the whole cast taking a rather zany perspective for a purported thriller, with loopy winning out over logical:

> practically every member of the cast turns out to be a spy.... After this terrific effort of the imagination it will not be hard to think of Miss Carroll as a dilettante who has joined the Intelligence Service for a thrill ... to play the wife of Gielgud for espionage reasons, falls in love with him while being pursued by Mr. [Robert] Young.[17]

The reference to Carroll falling in love with Gielgud from the preceding quote is not exactly correct—that is a situation more likely in a romantic comedy. Shortly after the couple and laughing boy Lorre realize the wrong man was killed, Carroll confesses to Gielgud, "I fell in love with you at first sight." That "first sight" component is one of its key differences with romantic comedy—accenting the illogical nature of the genre, versus the slow maturation towards romantic comedy love.

In reality, no sane person falls in love at first sight, unless s/he has been drinking. For instance, in the classic screwball comedy, *Bringing Up Baby* (1938), the mad as a hatter Katharine Hepburn has barely met Cary Grant before she causes an accident which dirties his suit. Yet, she immediately observes, "If he gets some [clean] clothes, he'll go away. And he's the only man I've ever loved!" A kismet moment is not required for screwball comedy

Secret Agent (1936) often plays more like a European screwball comedy, with Robert Young as Carroll's flirtatious shadow.

but when it occurs, it underscores the genre's preposterous world, or as Charles Ruggles tells Grant in *Bringing Up Baby*, "I don't like to say so, sir, at the moment, sir, but everybody knows you're crazy."

Of course, when Gielgud first meets Carroll at the Swiss hotel suite the foreign office has assigned them, one might question any kismet scenario—since she is allowing another guest (Robert Young) to flirt outrageously with her. Plus, Gielgud's initially flustered stiffness, often a screwball given, especially when the heroine is daft squared, is perfectly understandable, since his boss, "R," has minimized mentioning an assigned "wife."

Moreover, a less censorship-prone Britain has heightened the farcical bewilderment of Gielgud by having Carroll entertaining Young while she is in a bubble bath, and Young is right there nibbling grapes. One half expects Gielgud's Ashenden to mouth one of period comedian W.C. Fields' signature expressions of exasperation, which perfectly fits this scene—"Shades of Bacchus!" And then add on a little shaking like a car with cheap gasoline after you turn the engine off.

Regardless, before Carroll's Elsa and Ashenden can get into some typical screwball comedy banter—instant love never negates that given—one has Lorre's Mexican (sometimes also referenced as "The General") be a surrogate angry male. Yet, he is not complaining about this typical farcical three-way but rather the fact that "R" did *not* assign a cover wife for him. Lorre goes into the first of his many comic fits, sputtering lines like, "He gets beautiful girl!" and "She was issued!"

While Lorre's conniption completely steals the scene, as he so often does much of the movie, one can examine the action along two comedy genre lines. First, it would be correct to state his General has interjected, as previously cited, an element of Lorre's twisted personality comedian. However, a second explanation dovetails one right back to screwball comedy. The genre is peppered with quirky little foreign men often of no set nationality that wander through a storyline in an incensed and/or eccentric manner. Classic examples would include Mischa Auer's Oscar nominated Carlos the monkey man in *My Man Godfrey*, Mary Astor's indecipherable pet-like lover Toto (Sig Amo) in *The Palm Beach Story* (1942), and the confused mystic Prahka "in the bowl" Lasa (Richard Libertini) in the Steve Martin/Lily Tomlin *All of Me* (1984).

Be that as it may, after Lorre's meltdown, Gielgud and Carroll have a physical *Nothing Sacred* (1937)–like slapping match, which screwball comedy study sometimes calls "romance by ordeal." So much for her later love at first sight statement. One wonders what the outcome might have been had she initially hated him. Regardless, consistent to Hitchcock's ongoing question as to whether couples are ever happy or stay happy, the comic rough patch concludes with the line, "Married life has begun."

As in *The Thin Man* series, when things could get dangerous, Ashenden, like Nick (William Powell), leaves wife Nora (Myrna Loy) behind to kill the traitor, or what is called a "wet operation" in intelligence circles. The previous night at a gambling nightclub (more screwball escapist high life), Gielgud and Lorre think they have their man, as the story skates between farce and comic intrigue. The General has to throw another comic fit, however, to get their suspect to go hiking in the mountains the next day—this wrong man had had other plans. Once the deed is put into action, Lorre and Gielgud linger behind as they ascend the mountain, discussing both death and their target. Then the soon-to-be victim adds a bit of Hitchcock's core dark humor by calling back and ironically asking, "what are you waiting for?"

Consequently, as at the beginning of the film, with farce and Lorre's merry macabre comedian playing off each other, one now has a mix of Ashenden and The General as a perverse comedy team, and a journey into black humor will culminate with the cartoon sound of what proves to be the wrong man falling off the mountain, courtesy of a push by someone Europe called

"The Walking Overcoat." ("The Walking Overcoat" image also brings to mind the strains of surrealism in Nikolai Gogol's 1842 absurdist story "The Overcoat"—in which the ghost of a pestered man haunts St. Petersburg stealing coats after the theft of his own signature overcoat led to his death.)

Regardless, up until this point in the film, one has frequently seen Robert Young's character, Marvin, really putting the romantic rush on Carroll's Elsa, whether Gielgud's Ashenden is present or not. Marvin might not seem to let up for two reasons. First, as in any farce, Elsa enjoys the attention (not unlike Edna Best's flirtatious lead in *The Man Who Knew Too Much*, 1935, see Chapter 2). Second, and again playing the screwball farce card, Marvin initially seems to be one of those characters who thinks he could charm a nun out of her habit. It is more likely, however, that two other factors are at play. Hitchcock, like Ernest Lubitsch (whose influence on the Englishman is too often neglected), is a director for which love is always implied to be temporary. This is in marked contrast to 1930s American screwball farce, in which permanent love is the ultimate assumption. Consequently, Young's Marvin is arguably simply being the proverbial "continental lover."

However, this multifaceted comedic *Secret Agent* is billed as a thriller, and with a considerable amount of time having already elapsed without an enemy spy surfacing, one begins to second guess Young's presence. For example, one could draw an analogy with whatever your favorite sporting event might be. That is, if the favored team, which one could label Ashenden and company, cannot put away (defeat) the competition after a reasonable period of time, anything is possible. In the case of the *Secret Agent*, Young increasingly seems to most likely be the competition (enemy).

The viewer's suspicions seem confirmed when both Young and Carroll plan to leave Switzerland at the same time. Marvin's destination is allegedly Greece, while Elsa just wants an exit to anywhere. The death of a "wrong man" which so amused The General has greatly upset her. She is learning the lesson that innocence itself is dangerous—making Elsa more vulnerable to an approaching risk, as she attempts to shed her silly screwball secret agent play. The mistaken death has upset Ashenden, too. But he and The General will see the assignment through, and have already left to follow up a lead. A screwball heroine does not attempt to change a potential partner (which is the opposite in romantic comedy, à la "you make me want to be a better person"). Consequently, she leaves Ashenden a note and just decides to leave ... eventually asking Marvin to take her with him. After all, despite her love at first sight comment to Ashenden, she has spent more time sexually toying with Marvin. *But* when she offers herself to him, he becomes serious for the first time in the picture. Moreover, he even attempts to talk her out of it—this from a man who had recently told her, "Look what you're passing up, a [lusty] caveman with a college education."

However, at the 11th hour Marvin reluctantly agrees to Elsa joining him on a train really meant for Turkey, the Central Power gateway to the Middle East, where he will attempt to disrupt Allied actions in this remote theatre of the war. While this is just beginning to unfold between Elsa and Marvin, Ashenden and The General's latest covert mission has released the emergency brake on logic and anticipates a turn worthy of the later dark comedy, *Willy Wonka and the Chocolate Factory* (1971). That is, while nasty enemy agents had used a dentist's office for their hideout in *The Man Who Knew Too Much* (when Lorre was a likable bad guy), in *Secret Agent* a Swiss chocolate factory is the sanctuary for enemy operations. (Evidently, one can assume the war has jettisoned dental hygiene concerns by the enemy.)

Like an episode from *I Love Lucy*, Lorre spots a suspicious-looking chocolate assembly line character placing a note in one of the candy containers. Immediately, Lorre makes like the Road Runner and bolts to a circular staircase as he attempts to follow it as the factory belt takes the boxed message to the second floor. He even seems to be moving faster than his aforementioned film introduction, when he looked like Harpo Marx chasing a young woman.

Lorre is not able to get to the note but the brief message is revealed to the viewer, "Two English spies here. Phone police anonymously." For a bit of dark comedy irony, just as Lorre and Gielgud are finally making some progress, Hitchcock cuts back to Elsa writing her own aforementioned note about not being able to "do this job." The brief edit allows some sinister types to close in on Lorre and Gielgud as the director cuts back to the factory. Of course, the setting also represents classic picaresque personality comedy, as the mismatched English spy duo find themselves in a rather incongruous setting for their line of work—a chocolate company.

Moreover, one can intensify on the incongruity factor, since comic twosomes are supposed to be a funny contrast (à la fat and skinny), and never have Gielgud and Lorre been so entertainingly clashing in appearance, like Sherlock Holmes teaming with a "Harpo" now wearing a loud checkered coat. Things become more precarious, and just as the police start to arrive, Lorre performs a variation on one of his comic persona traits; he feigns a goofy fainting spell. This allows Gielgud to push a factory emergency button and bedlam follows. With the police simultaneously arriving, Hitchcock then actually reverses a Keystone Kop chase by having the exiting chocolate workers push the police back.

Naturally, our odd couple will escape, fulfilling both plot necessities, and allowing Hitchcock to exercise one of his own auteur traits, making law enforcement characters once again look foolish. Plus, Sennett often used a chase to signal a short subject ending, and even though Hitchcock has tweaked the process, that is what essentially happens here as Lorre and Gielgud run to safety through a surrealistically bizarre empty factory. Before making their escape, however, a factory contact has alerted them to the fact that Young's Marvin is the mystery agent. Plus, when they call the hotel and discover Carroll and Young have left for the station, though she has yet to beg Marvin to take her with him, "Sherlock and Harpo" think she has been the first to crack his identity, with Gielgud observing, "She's three jumps ahead of us all the time."

Consequently, Lorre and Gielgud rush for the station to catch Carroll and Young's train. Despite immediately being caught in a tight spot by a guard stopping them at a crowded boarding gate, Hitchcock takes the time to spoof a trope of action adventure films. Even in 1936, it was a cliché for the hero to slip someone a tip in order to obtain entry to a restricted area. Thus, Lorre gives the gatekeeper some money to get by, and as he and Gielgud move forward the guard still blocks them. Lorre is entertainingly upset. Still, maybe there has been a misunderstanding or not enough cash has been exchanged. Hitchcock then milks the gag by having Lorre further grease the security guy's palm. Now a more confident duo attempt to get by, only to be stopped again.

One can almost see the steam coming out of Lorre's ears. This is doubly entertaining because despite both his amusing appearance and antics, he enjoys killing people ... and now he is being stopped by some bottom of the-totem-pole flunky. In addition, Hitchcock piles on a bit more absurdity by having Lorre go into his fit mode again, and attempt to find the station master and complain that his guards do not accept bribes! Lorre's "logic" here is that he is entitled because he is *The General* (italics mine).

Regardless, before Lorre gets far, the mob at the gate push through and almost immediately Gielgud spots Carroll (only in the movies). Again, she wants no more killing, as he and Lorre have figured out the train Young will really be on is set for Constantinople. Though Gielgud tells her to wait for him, she is determined to go with him. What he does not know is that now her new personal mission is to stop the killing ... even if Young is the enemy. In fact, it is during these closing minutes of the film that Hitchcock employs another of his signature creative uses of sound. As Carroll walks down the corridor the train wheels seem to be saying: "He [Gielgud] mustn't, he mustn't, he mustn't [kill Young]."

Once on the train Gielgud, Lorre, and Carroll work their way toward a compartment. But at a border checkpoint they can see three men hanging in the distance; Gielgud's Ashenden, in true gallows humor, remarks: "Look, that's a pretty sight." A comical Neanderthal-like enemy soldier then asks where he is from, and Ashenden says America (the United States was not yet in World War I). The dumb trooper is much taken with America, as symbolized by Chicago, with Hitchcock seemingly anachronistically kidding the United States' association with the international success of its 1930s gangster films. (See Chapter 2 for more period allusions to American gangster films in Hitchcock pictures.)

As has been a constant in *Secret Agent*, Hitchcock can never just stop at one even veiled gag. Indeed, he often follows black humor with something more broadly comic. For example, the dark comedy antics of Lorre when the dead church organist is discovered are quickly followed by Gielgud and the pint-sized assassin hiding in the church steeple when the ringing of the bell drives then into an amusing dance of deafness. Thus, after the reference to the hanging men and reducing America to a land of gangsters, the soldier asks Ashenden where in America he is from. Filmmaker Hitchcock seems to spoof his whole production by having Ashenden respond "Hollywood." Then, true to filmland's rule of threes in setting up a joke, Hitchcock has his trooper seriously ask if Hollywood is in America, and after a comic beat for all that implies, such as does La La Land really exist, Ashenden responds, "Yes."

Shortly after this, a surprised Young spots Carroll in the train corridor, with Gielgud and Lorre making themselves scarce in their compartment. Despite Young's earlier promise to take Carroll along, he thought he had ditched her at the station by claiming he was departing on a different train, before wandering off to allegedly obtain cigarettes. Now distrustful of Elsa, he leads her at gunpoint to his compartment—though she manages to convince him that Ashenden and The General are not on the train. They banter a bit before British planes suddenly attempt to bomb the train. He has instinctively covered her for protection, despite just having told her all his flirting had merely been a show.

After the planes have passed, the two remain in a provocative embrace and he remarks, with a touch of comic absurdity, that it was "very funny" that a German spy would protect a British lady (spy) from British bombs. But then he cannot resist and he gives her a hard forced kiss. Big mistake. While his guard is down, Lorre and Gielgud have rushed the compartment.

With Young having pocketed his gun, his two adversaries finally seem ready for an execution. Moreover, Ashenden's inner struggles with this assignment are given a reprieve by Lorre. Snapping his knife open, he orders Ashenden and Elsa from the compartment, and with his succinct sense of dark humor observes, "You [Gielgud] go with her, our conference [my killing of Young] will be very short." However, Carroll stops the proceedings by grabbing Young's gun from his pocket in order to stop the killing, despite its ramifications. How this would have played out remains a mystery, because another English plane successfully bombs the train. The screen momentarily goes black, before revealing a harrowing wreck.

Returning to the train compartment, Young appears in fatal condition buried under debris, when two hands slowly appear in an attempt to strangle him. With the audience thinking it is Lorre, the camera then reveals it is Gielgud ... who passes out, seemingly as injured as Young. A prone, dazed Lorre takes this all in and produces his flask. Then, as the *Hollywood Reporter* observes, he "offered ... [Young] a drink ... as the only decent thing...."[18] But in the tradition of Hitchcock's dark comedy base, morality equals absurdity, and Young somehow produces a gun and shoots Lorre, before dying himself. As noted earlier, the closing compartment scene then belongs to the funny little Mexican General, who somehow manages to stand and repeat his signature introduction, as if he is now meeting an ephemeral figure of death seen only by himself. Plus, having seen this atypical sober Lorre perspective periodically throughout the film, almost like a photograph, one is reminded of writer Fleur Jaeggy's comment on a fixed image, like *Blackmail*'s (see Chapter 1) painting of Jester, "It's the unknown. It's the abyss."[19]

This sorrowful picture of Lorre's exit is the movie's money shot, and *Secret Agent* should have closed there. However, Hitchcock then artistically stumbles by tacking on a montage of Allied victories in the Middle East, followed by a scene back in London with a postcard to "R" stating "never again" from Gielgud and Carroll. Finally the couple themselves happily stare into the camera for a direct address close. The *New York Times* correctly described this discombobulated close as "shots of ... [a] disconnected, meaningless kind which Hollywood discarded years ago...."[20] And the *Hollywood Reporter* simply said the add-ons should "be cut," while still titling their review: "Gaumont 'Secret Agent' Will Repeat Success of '39 Steps.'"[21]

With the exception of *Blackmail*, thus far in the text, Hitchcock films have been using multiple "by the book" comedy genres to create compound thrillers. Again, with *Secret Agent* he has created a picture which is legitimately at a tipping point as whether to be called a comedy or a thriller. Even his uses of parody are just as likely to be broad, versus the often under the radar reaffirmation burlesques mentioned earlier in the text. After *Blackmail*, with the exception of Hitchcock's *Mr. & Mrs. Smith* (1941), *The Trouble with Harry* (1955), and *North by Northwest*, (1959), *Secret Agent* is the director's most out and out comedy.

The pivotal point for this switch comes with the nuanced performance of Lorre. Yes, some period viewers could still find him chilling. But with his Harpo-like introduction, he colors the most potentially macabre situations, such as finding the dead organist, with a wry sense of dark comedy. And as the chapter-opening excerpts from several 1930s reviews documented, this phenomenon was being recognized then, too. It is also arguably Lorre's first and most successful gentle burlesquing of his disturbing *M* (1931) persona. In *Secret Agent* Lorre controls the laugh. But by the time of Bob Hope's 1947 film noir parody, *My Favorite Brunette*, Lorre's knife-wielding killer is the joke.

4. Secret Agent (1936)

For all the screwball antics of *Secret Agent*, with the witty banter between farce's perennial threesome (Gielgud, Carroll, and Young), the *New Republic*'s pioneering critic Otis Ferguson fathomed the film's salient characteristics:

> Best of all is Peter Lorre's study of the assassin as artist. As satyr, humorist and lethal snake, he shows as always, a complete feeling for the real juice of situations and the best way of distilling this through voice, carriage, motion. He is one of the true characters of the theatre, having mastered loose oddities and disfigurements until the total is a style, childlike, beautiful, unfathomably wicked ... [introduced here by a] scream, the horrified servant girl running up [the stairs], then back to the door and Secret Agent Peter in hot and sly pursuit—a perfect entrance.[22]

The *New York Tribune* seconded this by stating Lorre "overshadowed" the others, and then added, "one regrets that Mr. Hitchcock did not throw away the disconnected ... romantic passages and give Mr. Lorre more to do."[23] The *New York Daily News* called Lorre's performance a "hypnotic study," while the *Hollywood Reporter* said "it should stand out in the year's performances."[24]

A bewitching Lorre is fittingly at the center of this still, with a plot description that might have doubled for *The Thin Man*, if Nick and Nora had ever left America.

Because Hitchcock allowed Lorre a great deal of freedom, *Secret Agent* is gifted with a subtle difference of dark comedy which uniquely linked farce and suspense. It is reminiscent of author/critic Jonathan Lethem's comments on Anna Kavan's novel *Ice* (1967), another work like *Secret Agent*, not fully recognized at the time: "...as in Kafka, Poe and Ishiguro's 'The Unconsoled,' [humanity's] essential disturbance resides in the inextricable interplay between inner and outer worlds."[25]

Regardless, a final addendum for *Secret Agent* might bring one back to yet another darkly comic gangster film reference. Yet, this case involves a future classic of the genre—*Bonnie and Clyde* (1967). Hitchcock scholars Eric Rohmer and Claude Chabrol discussed how the first half of *Secret Agent* is broadly comic before turning more serious, or what I would call darkly comic.[26] Ironically, they struggle with the arc, yet this artistic transition is at the heart of *Bonnie and Clyde*, even though any remaining 1960s remnants of the censorship code did not require retribution. Moreover, each film's central figures, *Secret Agent*'s Lorre, and *Bonnie and Clyde*'s Warren Beatty and Faye Dunaway, have showcased a new unexpected element of comparisons— only to immediately be "rewarded" with violent deaths. In addition, both pictures, despite their obvious compound genre natures, are ultimately best "read" as dark comedies. Consequently, the closing deaths of these figures whom viewers have come to embrace, despite their past acts of violence, illustrate yet again one of dark comedy's three key themes—life's inherent absurdity, as well as the absurdity of audiences becoming so emotionally connected to such antiheroes. But such is the nature of dark comedy.

5

The Lady Vanishes (1938)

> Hitchcock ... has more fun with the people on that [*Lady Vanishes*] train than a barrel of monkeys.... It's as much comedy as straight plot ... [It is] done with relish and droll good humor, planted not only in dialogue and perfect delivery but in the concept of type and situation[1]—Otis Ferguson, *New Republic* (October 19, 1938)

The previous chapter on *Secret Agent* (1936) ultimately described it as a "hybrid comedy." That "reading" is also true of *The Lady Vanishes*, with Otis Ferguson, then America's leading film critic, emphasizing just that point in the above excerpt from his review. (His tragic death during World War II cut short a brilliant young career.) However, he was not going out on a limb with his comic verdict. Just as the last chapter opens with critical commentary keying on the comic nature of *Secret Agent* (1936), period reviews for *Vanishes* also consistently focused strongly on its comedy. The *New York Times* said:

> If it were not so brilliant a melodrama [period comedy code for black humor], we should class it as a brilliant comedy ... when your sides are not aching from laughter your brain is throbbing in its attempts to outguess the director. Hitch [only] occasionally relents with his rib-tickling ... [The team of] Caldicott and Charters—or Naughton Wayne and Basil Radford—whose running temperature about "how England is doing [in cricket]" makes the most hilarious running gag of the year.[2]

The *New York Post* seconded this by describing *Vanishes* with having "extraordinary humorous asides ... [and] it can match the best of the comedies with its subtle characterization of the two cricket-loving Englishman."[3] The *New York Herald Tribune* essentially recycled the *Post*'s praise of this Laurel & Hardy–like duo, before adding that the actors playing the team "Naunton Wayne and Basil Radford ... would have made any film worth seeing by themselves."[4]

What is more, the *Vanishes* significance of Charters (Basil Radford) and Caldicott (Naunton Wayne) has only grown through the years. In Hitchcock historian Leonard Leff's 2007 documentary, *Mystery Train: Hitchcock and*

The Lady Vanishes, he states that the twosome "quietly steal the movie."[5] And in Philip French's 2012 *London Guardian* article about the film, "My Favourite Hitchcock," he describes its "mesmerizing plot, perfect casting and the greatest comic duo in British cinema...."[6]

With all this praise, one is tempted to repeat the ongoing Paul Newman and Robert Redford mantra from *Butch Cassidy and The Sundance Kid* (1969, with regard to an unshakable posse), "Who are those guys?" Though not part of the Ethel Lina White 1936 novel, *The Wheel Spins*, from which *Vanishes* was adapted, this first time teaming of Radford and Wayne was a random exercise in brilliant casting. Both had been successful solo British stage and screen character actors throughout the 1920s and 1930s, with the more heavyset Radford (also distinguished by a World War I saber scar on his right cheek) having even appeared in Hitchcock's 1937 *Young and Innocent*. Though Radford and Wayne would still occasionally later appear in solo parts, their future fame and fortune would be tied to frequent reteamings in several films on British Broadcasting Corporation (BBC) radio, and early BBC television. Their best follow-up pairing would be in Carol Reed's more serious variation on *Vanishes—Night Train* (1940). Two partial reviews of this film, which focus on this sometime team, actually provide better descriptions of their basic shtick in Hitchcock's film. Thus, *Variety* opined:

> Made by the same British studio that turned out "Lady Vanishes," the film "Night Train" makes similar use of Basil Radford and Naunton Wayne as two tourist Englishmen with a ludicrous interest in cricket.[7]

A more succinct observation in the *New York Times*' review of *Night Train* zeroes in on another pivotal component of their shared personality comedian persona, "Basil Radford and Naunton Wayne's tourists are as British as suet pudding."[8]

All things considered, however, there is no greater way to underline that *Vanishes* is a *comic* thriller, than to compare it to *Night Train*. The comic relief of Charters & Caldicott comes relatively late in this film, and is not comically interwoven throughout the picture as Hitchcock does so masterfully in *Vanishes*. Moreover, Charters & Caldicott are amusingly brighter in *Night Train*. But consistency always tops random funny bits, or one soon loses personality comedian status. Thus, the team's most diverting *Night Train* routine has Charter suddenly able to read German. Moreover, he is reading Hitler's *Mein Kamp* (*My Struggle*), and the following exchange occurs:

> CHARTER: I believe they give a copy to all the [German] bridal couples over here. [It was a required purchase, making Hitler a fortune.]
> CALDICOTT: Why I don't think it's that sort of book, old man.

Funny but not their sort of shtick. It should have been given to anther character, like Rex Harrison's egotistically cold character. This observation leads

5. The Lady Vanishes *(1938)*

to another seminal reason *Vanishes* is a comic thriller, and *Night Train* is not. The latter film's romantic couple do *not* take part in the comedy, which was the new development in 1930s farce, à la the American screwball comedy.

Regardless, a brief *Vanishes* plot should now be pulled from one's pocket to both better understand how this Hitchcock headscratcher can also double as a multiple genre comedy mix of personality and screwball comedy—with Charters & Caldicott essential to every facet of this funny puzzle. Consequently, like so many 1930s Hollywood films, such as the Marx Brothers' *Duck Soup* (1933), which exists in the imaginary country of Fredonia, Hitchcock's cast is stuck in some pretend postage stamp-sized inn called Gasthof Petrus, in the tiny land of Bandrika. It is one of the world's "few undiscovered corners," sort of like Frank Capra's Shangri-la from the previous year's *Last Horizon* (1937), but with minimal signs of intelligence.

However, Bandrika does allow for unlimited comedy, especially a comic madhouse gibberish language, so central to the comedy of the upper class Charters & Caldicott—who cannot fathom why no one speaks English, or lives for cricket. This also slides into a basic screwball comedy component of *Vanishes*, in which a supporting character (here an innkeeper) both provides indecipherable gobbledygook, as well as simply embellishing the screwball ambiance. (See previous chapter.) Regardless, Bandrika, like Shangri-la, does have snowy mountain accessibility problems.

The film's train passengers (what else in the world of Hitchcock?) have been delayed by an avalanche, with the picture's leading lady, Margaret Lockwood's Iris, affectionately enjoying comically correcting the innkeeper's mangling of the word "avalanche." She is there with two friends on a final fun outing before she will basically be stuck in an unhappy marriage (a Hitchcock given) with a "blue-blooded cheque chaser," not so very far from the planned blueprint for Claudette Colbert in *It Happened One Night* (1934, see last chapter).

The British passengers also include a couple committing adultery, Cecil Parker's Mr. Todhunter, and his companion, the lovely Linden Travers, traveling as Mrs. Todhunter. She, however, is gradually coming to realize Parker's promise of a real marriage is about as real as the fictitious Bandrika turning up in a geography class. While cheating is fundamental to farce, America's period screwball variation on the phenomenon would not have been allowed to be so open about it. Indeed, early 1930s American censorship was a partial catalyst for birthing screwball comedy.

Another pivotal delayed British train passenger is Michael Redgrave's Gilbert Redman—a struggling folklorist and musicologist. Besides being Margaret Lockwood's eventual love interest, his quasi-profession could be called that of a professor—a frequent male activity in screwball comedy, such as Cary Grant's paleontologist in *Bringing Up Baby* (1938). Being an academic, especially during the Great Depression, was viewed by many Americans neither as a real job, nor even as a meaningful activity. Part of this was anchored in a time when people were struggling to stay alive and found studying the past secondary to putting food on the table.

This often provided three key screwball comedy plot points at work in *Vanishes*. First, such study usually necessitated demonstrating an unusual activity which was easily transformed into something funny. Thus, Redgrave has three native Bandrikan citizens performing a comically convoluted vanishing folk dance as he transcribes it. Naturally, this is occurring during the evening in his room at the local inn, just above Lockwood's lodging. Naturally, she complains to the manager, "Someone upstairs is playing musical chairs with an elephant." Yet, when the desk clerk/manager goes upstairs to complain, Redgrave's Gilbert responds with typical urbane wit to the county yokel:

> You dare to call it a noise. Ancient music with which your peasant ancestors celebrated every wedding for countless generations. They danced when your father married your mother ... supposing you were born in wedlock, which I doubt...."

(In 1935 Fred Astaire and Ginger Rogers' *Top Hat*, which was considered "screwball comedy set to song and dance" by the producer who teamed them, Pandro S. Berman, had the duo meeting along the lines of Redgrave and Lockwood. Astaire is dancing in a hotel room just above the suite of a sleeping Rogers and she also reads him the riot act. Given that Hitchcock saw every American film he could, *Top Hat* would have been hard to miss. After 1935's *Mutiny on the Bounty*, it was Hollywood's top grossing picture of the year.)

The second screwball professorial plot point (Redgrave's study of historical subjects) connects him with the past and death. And while Gilbert seems lively enough, it gradually comes out that he is at loose ends, and feeling himself rather valueless. In contrast, the screwball heroine's purpose in the genre is often to liven up the dead-end existence of the male. Lockwood's Iris does just that when he becomes her only ally in the search for the lady that vanishes. Though a possible murder might seem an extreme screwball rejuvenating factor, it is at the heart of some genre examples, such as two from its most celebrated heroine—Carole Lombard.[9] Homicide was central to both her *The Princess Comes Across* (1936) and *True Confession* (1937).

Third, while the goal of the screwball comedy is often to rescue the professorial male from either a pointless existence, or the threat of such a reality, remnants of that existence often help drive the plot. For example, the comically endless search for the missing brontosaurus bone in *Bringing Up Baby*. Thus, *Vanishes'* missing secret code/MacGuffin is part of a musical number known only by the most unlikely of spies—Dame May Whitty's delightful little old lady/nanny Miss Froy ("it rhymes with joy"), the film's title character.

5. The Lady Vanishes *(1938)*

Consequently, near the picture's close, when things get dicey for all concerned, what better character to share the musical code with, should something happen to the delightfully mellifluous old maid secret agent, than Gilbert's musicologist. Comically, after surviving a shoot-out and a lengthy trip back to London's Foreign Office, he forgets the tune! But luckily, the most resilient of senior spies also survives, and all ends well.

Consequently, how do the seminal personality comedians Charters & Caldicott fit into *Vanishes*' densely populated compound of genres, with an accent on various forms of comedy? The duo are intertwined among a group of travelers initially stuck at a random Bandrika inn, before Hitchcock chronicles their trip home on a crowded train traveling from what one presumes to be the Alps. Ironically, the viewer's focus is on a character who receives very little time in either the printed pages (adapted from Ethel Lina White's 1936 novel *The Wheel Spins*) or Hitchcock's film—the aforementioned Miss Froy. Appropriately, given the nanny's largely off-screen presence, the Miss Froy description from the novel by her eventual rescuer, Iris Care (Henderson in the film) is fittingly fuzzy:

> ... middle-aged [actually mid–60s], with a huddle of small indefinite features, and vague coloring. Someone drew a face and then rubbed it nearly out again. Her curly hair was faded and her skin was bleached to oatmeal. She was not sufficiently a caricature to suggest a stage spinster. Even her tweed suit and matching hat were not too dowdy, although lacking distinctive note.[10]

The novel and film are very much about, and satirical of, late 1930s Britain. And no one better fulfills that stereotype than Hitchcock's use of Charters & Caldicott—not even Miss Froy.

However, why is Whitty's Froy largely missing in action, and how does Lockwood's Iris end up being her liberator? In the novel Froy is simply a nanny who has witnessed something that is seemingly insignificant but which has serious political repercussions—important enough to be kidnapped and murdered. In the adaptation, Whitty is the most unlikely of spies, with her cover being that of a nanny in the quasi-medieval pretend kingdom of Bandrika. Cinematic Froy's secret is simply the proverbial MacGuffin that drives the narrative of *The Lady Vanishes*.

Be that as it may, one needs to momentarily back up the train before playing "Where's Whitty?" This is relevant, since Hitchcock takes a leisurely half-hour to even get his troupe on the train, let alone lose Miss Froy. And once again, the nanny takes a backseat to the Laurel & Hardy–like personality comedy antics of Charters & Caldicott, and the budding screwball comedy tendencies of Redgrave and Lockwood.[11] Moreover, the zany slapstick tendencies which operate as the norm in this goofy little international inn are reminiscent of that most unconventional of households in Frank Capra's *You*

The Lady Vanishes' (1938) title character Miss Froy (Dame May Whitty, left), with Margaret Lockwood and Michael Redgrave.

Can't Take It with You (1938), an Oscar-winning Best Picture stuck somewhere between screwball comedy and populism. Though released several months before *Vanishes*, it had earlier been an award-winning Broadway play.

However, first things first—Charters & Caldicott. Given the overcrowded public house, this pleasantly proper duo have been lucky to book the maid's attic room for the night. The low ceilings and exposed beams provide them with a basic personality comedian setting—a laughter laboratory for bumping heads and general slapstick in a confined space. They are comically indignant. To paraphrase a Mark Twain comment when nettled—"why, it's un–American; it's unBritish; it's French." In this case it is Bandrikan.

Given such a slight, they are just tucking into bed together, when the room's attractive maid comes in unannounced to get some clothing. Once again, they are upset by such an impropriety. Given that this is Hitchcock, one might want to play the gay card to ratchet up the situation's indelicacy. After all, this is a norm for the director. Examples include *Rebecca's* (1940) seemingly lesbian housekeeper, the perceptible gay lovers of *Rope* (1948), and Bruno's (Robert Walker's) attraction to Guy (Farley Granger) in *Strangers on a Train* (1951). Indeed, Hitchcock even liked to cast gay performers, because in that sadly closeted era, he felt they were better "actors"—since society's narrow-mindedness forced them to "act" 24/7.

Be that as it may, Laurel & Hardy slept together all of the time in such movies as *Berth Marks, They Go Boom* (both 1929), *Brats* (1930), *Laughing Gravy* (1931), *Babes in Toyland, The Live Ghost* (both 1934), and so on, with no such suggestion.[12] Indeed, it merely represented another fundamental element of personality comedy—a childlike nature. Moreover, like Laurel & Hardy, Charters & Caldicott are inseparable playmates. This is also best demonstrated throughout the film by their boyish obsession with cricket. And this segues to much of the film's satirical subtext about the political climate in Europe at the time *Vanishes* opened—shortly before English Prime Minister Neville Chamberlain's acts of 1938 appeasement to Hitler.

Consequently, with Britain on the verge of war, Charters & Caldicott are constantly making comments about cricket that are seemingly more applicable to the coming world war, such as, "[It's a] time of crisis," or "[You] can't be in England and not know the score." The only goal of these two boys/men is to get back to England for a major cricket match. Later on the train the duo avoid getting involved in helping find the kidnapped nanny, when everyone else on the train, except Lockwood, claims she never existed. They know otherwise, and such non-action can be "read" as a political metaphor for appeasement. Plus, Hitchcock cannot avoid attaching some childhood bathroom humor to the duo when, briefly, Miss Froy seems to have been found. Caldicott casually observes, "The bolt must have jammed [on the door in the toilet, and locked her in]."

However, before the boarding of the train and the losing of Miss Froy, the screwball elements introduced at the inn need to be further expanded upon. Thus, after Lockwood's Iris has made the musical hullabaloo introduction to Redgrave's Gilbert, the latter character is tossed out of his room. As farcical revenge to Iris, Gilbert arrives at her room prepared to share her bed. In fact, though dressed, the couple both briefly occupy said four-poster— which would not have been allowed in America—paralleling the same handcuffed bedtime twosome in *The 39 Steps* (see Chapter 3).

The gangly Redgrave, however, makes it more palatable by his almost slapstick movement and the joy it brings him to upset Iris. Keep in mind that screwball comedy is a marriage of visual humor and verbal wit, since many of its signature directors came from silent comedy. For instance, major screwball director Leo McCarey, who won a Best Director Oscar for a pivotal example of the genre, *The Awful Truth* (1937), teamed and molded Laurel & Hardy during the silent era.[13] And the aforementioned Capra, who won the Best Director Oscar for *It Happened One Night*, helped create the persona of major silent comedian Harry Langdon. Consequently, while the coming of sound films brought countless wordsmiths from the East, screwball comedies were still usually directed by filmmakers schooled in physical humor.

Thus, couple Redgrave's non-stop movement with such verbal slapstick as asking her which side of the bed she prefers sleeping on—which he answers with rapid-fired absurd repartee when she is caught speechless, "Then I'll sleep in the middle." Finally, when she finds her voice and again threatens to call the manager, he parries with straight farce, "[Then] I'll only tell everyone you invited me here." As with *The 39 Steps*, one could apply the aforementioned subtitle of Stanley Cavell's book on screwball comedy, *Pursuits of Happiness: The Hollywood Comedy of Remarriage*, to what follows this fight. After a rocky start, though Redgrave and Lockwood are not married, the movie spends the rest of the time molding them into a couple.[14]

Before further discussion of *Vanishes*' screwball roots, two frequent mistakes in Hitchcock literature merit correcting. First, some texts on the director suggest, "He got two young writers, Frank Launder and Sidney Gilliatt, to put the screenplay together for him from a novel by Ethel White...."[15] In point of fact, during 1937 Hitchcock was "at loose ends for a script, [and] he reached for a project already developed...."[16] However, this is not to say Hitchcock did not extensively assist in reworking the script, especially as it applied to Charters & Caldicott, as well as a more action oriented conclusion. But said writers deserve their due. Second, the novel has routinely been said to have had no farcical elements. Yet, in what has become a continually sad revelation in these pages, many "historians" do not seem have returned to the original sources and *read* them. When this will change, I would guess ... right after never.

Granted, *The Wheel Spins* is not farce per se but many of the elements are clearly there. And the funny/sad commentary on this particular lack of research would have only necessitated reading a *few* opening pages of the novel. On just the second page of White's book (though numbered 6), the thoughts of an already established "semi-Society girl—vain selfish, and useless" (as so many screwball heroines were) relates recent event which would do any farcical woman lead indulgently proud—though maybe a bit blunt for censorship oriented America:

> On vacation, matrimonial boundaries became pleasantly blurred. Surrounded by a mixed bag of vague married couples, it was a sharp shock to Iris when one of the women ... suddenly developed a belated sense of propriety, and accused her of stealing a husband ... her sense of justice was outraged. She had merely tolerated a neglected male, who seemed a spare part in the dislocated domestic machine. It was not her fault that he had lost his head.[17]

The novel's Iris also has screwball's biting wit. For instance, at one point before departure she randomly finds herself stuck seated beside a fellow traveler suddenly showing Iris a picture of her naked baby, Gabriel. The woman chatters about the family having named him after the Archangel. Now apprised of this information, Iris immediately responds with the crack, "How sweet. Did he send a mug?"[18]

Regardless, the night before the exit from Hitchcock's inn, a pivotal yet odd sequence of dark comedy occurs which seems like a refugee from a Warner Bros cartoon. It is the viewer's first foreshadowing of ominous goofy things to come. However, at the same time it is such a ludicrous bit of black humor that it is all one can think of ... other than it being an obvious parody of the German Expressionism that so influenced Hitchcock. Curiously, a troubadour is serenading the senior nanny below her balcony. And as he sings the shadow of a pair of hands slowly comes into the film frame to strangle him, à la the silhouette of Dracula that seems to seduce the young maiden in F.W. Murnau's 1922 *Nosferatu*—a film and filmmaker greatly admired by Hitchcock. Unknown to viewers at the time, the tune is the message this sweetly frumpy spy is to carry back to London's foreign service. However, at the time it seems like pure absurdity.

This entertainingly mad bit of black humor brings one back to the Hitchcock constant of dark comedy. In this case, all the genre's three themes are tied together—absurdity, the presence of death, and man as beast. Indeed, however Hitchcock came into contact with White's novel, its early homage to black humor sounds like misanthropic Hitchcock should also have received a byline:

> Here, under the limitless blue, people seemed so small—their passions so paltry. They were merely incidental to the grave. One met them and parted from them, without regrets.... You talk of ordinary citizens. No one is ordinary but a bag of his special prejudices ... [And when Iris comes to from a sunstroke, the mob] stared down at her with indifferent apathy, as though she were some street spectacle—a dying animal or a man in a fit. There was not a trace of compassion in their blank faces, no glint of curiosity in their dull gaze. In their complete detachment they seemed devoid of the instincts of human humanity.[19]

This Hitchcock dark world view would become all the more apparent in his American films, particularly in *Shadow of a Doubt* (1943), *Rope* (1948), and *Strangers on a Train* (1951), all forthcoming chapters.

Regardless, it is time to board the train and really begin this comic mystery. Moreover, unlike Agatha Christie's extremely popular 1932 novel, *Murder on the Orient Express*, Hitchcock's 1938 adaptation of *The Wheel Spins* has given the viewer a leisurely comic character study prologue to one's cinematic traveling companions for the rest of his mystery. And as opposed to Iris' aforementioned sunstroke from the novel, in the film she has suffered a near concussion from a falling flower planter, meant for Miss Froy. (This also gives it a more cartoon screwball tone.) Though assumed to be an accident at the time, this attempted attack on the nanny is appropriately coupled with Miss Froy actually being a spy in Hitchcock's film.

Ironically, the snotty Iris (needing to be brought down a peg or two à la screwball comedy) had earlier found Miss Froy to be something of an agreeable bore before the journey began (thus the young woman's previously vague description of her). Yet, the nanny is the only passenger who demonstrates any compassion/care for her after the "accident," as they depart. Iris has remained somewhat lightheaded after being struck on the head, and Miss Froy, consistent with her cover as a nanny, has become something of an unofficial guardian—including taking her to tea. Fittingly, even here, thanks to Charters & Caldicott, the humor continues, as the childish duo must reluctantly give up the sugar cubes to Miss Froy—with which they were diagramming a cricket play!

Iris' sunstroke in the novel, which becomes a blow to the head in Hitchcock's film, is a pivotal plot point. That is, after tea Iris still feels a bit dizzy, and Miss Froy suggests the young woman take a nap once they are back in their train compartment. Paradoxically, given all that Iris will soon do for the nanny, Lockwood's character complies both for health reasons and to escape Miss Froy's incessant chatter. Yet, after Iris awakens, there is no Miss Froy, and all the other passengers deny she ever existed. And consistent with Hitchcock's habit of having an affable villain, Paul Lukas' Dr. Hartz suggests her head injury has made her simply imagine the existence of the nanny.

Over roughly the next hour, therefore, with person after person denying the existence of Dame May Whitty's Miss Froy, and then essentially questioning Iris' sanity, one could say Lockwood's figure nearly goes through Elizabeth Kübler-Ross' five stages of death. First comes her shocked *denial* that everyone could say Miss Froy never existed, including their dining car waiter. Naturally Iris soon becomes *angry*. However, after Lukas' ever so courtly Dr. Hartz reasonably introduces his medical hypothesis, about mental side effects from her injury, Lockwood's Iris self-consciously flirts with stage four, *bargaining*. That is, given that both Iris and a threatening collection of passengers are seemingly acting like the heroine needs to rest at some vague sanitarium, Iris must weigh this crusade for Miss Froy against her own safety. Naturally, this leads to phase four, *depression*. Luckily, however, for her, and especially for Miss Froy, she never fully embraces the final juncture of *acceptance*— though it is closer to occurring in the novel. The saving grace in the film is that farcical fellow Redgrave. In the novel Iris' romantic interest is not really a presence until she has boarded the train, and he eventually comes across as more of a caring brother than a lover. But Redgrave's Gilbert is a much stronger character, who is granted increased story time, as well as being a sardonic three-dimensional farcical character.

Keep in mind, of all the subgenres of comedy—screwball, romantic, personality, parody, populism, and dark—screwball is the closest to black humor.[20] That might best be demonstrated by simply noting the title of yet

5. The Lady Vanishes (1938)

another classic screwball comedy that stars Carole Lombard—*Nothing Sacred* (1937). This is underlined here by the fact that farcical dialogue, as has already been demonstrated by both Iris and Gilbert, becomes even more cutting by Redgrave when he joins forces with Lockwood.

Plus, it need not even apply to the mystery of Where's Miss Froy? For example, the urbane villain, Lukas' Dr. Hartz, is on the train with a seriously injured patient (wrapped up like a mummy), a patient initially attended to by a nun. Moreover, Dr. Hartz is also a well-known surgeon, who has recently performed a brain operation on a prominent member of Britain's government. Thus, register Redgrave's cheeky small talk upon first meeting Lukas' character:

> GILBERT: You flew over to England the other day and operated on one of our cabinet ministers.
> DR. HARTZ: Oh yes.
> GILBERT: Tell me; did you find anything?

As noted before, *Vanishes* came out shortly before England's prime minister's final act of appeasement to Hitler. Charters & Caldicott's initial refusal to assist Iris was a metaphor for just that sort of isolationism—Britain in a state of denial, or as the title of a 1940 book by a very young John F. Kennedy so aptly put it—*While England Slept* (a publication of his senior Harvard thesis).

That being said, unlike Charters & Caldicott, Gilbert was, as the saying goes, a man at home with all the lights on—just as he recognized the fear/incompetency of 1938 British leadership, one knew that with him as Iris' only ally, Miss Froy was going to be found. Charters & Caldicott's head-in-the-sand perspective, or as Stan Laurel's aforementioned mantra for Stan & Ollie's persona phrased it, was "two minds without a single thought." Plus, being so obsessed with cricket not only made them child-like, it also played well to those personality comedians with half a brain—so seemingly impervious to the truth that they would use any minutiae to distract them from reality. These were the type of people, my father once said, who would rearrange deck chairs on a sinking ship.

The beauty of these diverse personalities brings one full circle back to Hitchcock's core comedy sub-genre—black humor. It also answers a question in funny 101: "Does comedy always need its pound of flesh?" Dark comedy does. Plus, as an addendum to the aforementioned distracting minutiae, one need not even be as delightfully dense as the Laurel & Hardy–like Charters & Caldicott. The following year Jean Renoir applies the same misdirection to the allegedly wise hosting marquis (Marcel Dalio) in 1939's *The Rules of the Game*. That is, as Europe totters on the verge of World War II and the collapse of the old order, the marquis is too obsessed with his ever growing collection of oversized mechanical toy musical figures—with their rigidity also being a metaphor for his class' inability to change and/or even see the approaching apocalypse. Secular humanist Renoir treats the marquis with generous sympathy, yet the figure clearly does not know how much he does not know. One wants to photoshop the image of Edward Munch's *The Scream* behind him.

Regardless, this just underlies the seriousness of the times. And it goes beyond implied meanings in fictional films. For example, a late 1938 *Hollywood Reporter* article titled "Chamberlain on [Frying] Pan for Censoring Clips" stated, in part:

> Government censoring of newsreels containing political angles regarded as opposed to England's foreign policy comes up for debate again in the house of commons, and the opposition will demand that the Chamberlain party go on record with hands-off policy on future clips.[21]

Ironically, by the time the film came out (1938) and a paperback of *The Wheel Spins* was reissued, one could drop all the drivel about the pretend kingdom of Bandrika and double-agent nannies—the cover featured a train and a *Nazi* soldier—though the locomotive received more jacket space.[22]

With all this somber heavy lifting going on in the background, Hitchcock then uses pivotal scenes from his simultaneous running of screwball and personality comedy components in *Vanishes* for a black humor coup de grace keying upon absurdity. What is more, he accents this absurdity factor by sequences one might have seen in a period British music hall. Let us first start with Charters & Caldicott. Though they had not initially spoken up for Iris, for fear of missing their cricket match, eventually the Laurel & Hardy-like duo come through. One might best define this dependability from an observation by Kurt Vonnegut from his 1976 novel *Slapstick*, which is dedicated to the team:

> The fundamental joke with Laurel & Hardy, it seems to me, was that they did their best with every test. They never failed to bargain in good faith with their destinies, and were screamingly adorable and funny on that account.[23]

Regardless, as Charters & Caldicott sit in their train compartment, the latter teammate twice remarks, people "don't vanish in thin air," and both times Charters answers with an observation that smacks of what was then called a "Dumb Dora" response, à la George Burns & Gracie Allen. That is, Gracie would answer a reasonable George question with a logical reply ... from a different dimension. Thus, when Caldicott twice makes his "vanish in thin air" argument, Charters' comebacks, in those days of Britain's world empire, is that such disappearances can be done by way of the Eastern "Indian rope trick"—the late 19th century magic routine in which a rope is made to levitate from a basket and the performer, or an assistant, can seemingly climb it until s/he disappears. With different variations, the individual eventually climbs down.

5. The Lady Vanishes *(1938)* 107

Like Charters & Caldicott, the sometime team of Bob Hope and Bing Crosby would not only reference the magic bit years later in *Road to Bali* (1952), their modification would naturally involve sometimes producing a pretty young woman. Regardless, Charters & Caldicott would ultimately find their way to helping Iris, and consequently metaphorically recognize the foreign political threat facing Great Britain. Indeed, in one of Hitchcock's additions to the original novel, both comedians would be most obliging at the near close in helping the found Miss Froy to escape.

The second *Vanishes* music hall–like routine which plays with absurdity involves Redgrave and Lockwood actually finding props for a real act whose title includes the phrase "Vanishing Lady"—which therefore has Hitchcock juggling three comedy subgenres with the couple. First, by this late point in *Vanishes*, Redgrave and Lockwood have evolved into a true screwball comedy couple determined to find Miss Froy. Second, their comic actions in the train's storage car as they look for Miss Froy have them acting like personality comedians. Third, one of the passengers involved in the nanny's kidnapping is a magician, and these are the props the screwball couple stumble upon. But the fact that the performer's act's title involves the film's storyline, the "Vanishing Lady," slips both the sequence and the film into reaffirmation parody.

This more sophisticated form of burlesque is often self-referential, deconstructing the genre even before the critics. Instead of leaving it to the audience to stumble through thriller clichés, Redgrave and Lockwood essentially discuss *Vanishes*' plot via the music hall materials they have discovered. What is more, their actions actually dovetail back into personality comedy. That is, first they inadvertently begin to play with the props, such as the telephone booth-like box in which one is seemingly made to disappear. And second, when they are discovered by the villainess performer and a fight ensues, it doubles as an impromptu comic show.

Besides being funny, Hitchcock pays homage to a similar accidental performance by *the* personality comedian, Charlie Chaplin, in his *The Circus* (1928). Near the beginning of this picture Chaplin's Tramp bungles his way into a magic act already in progress. In both films the tricks of the sorcerer's trade are engagingly displayed, from a false bottomed box enabling people to disappear, to the various animals hidden away. These included bunnies in a top hat, to pigeons exiting from every prop in sight. And for once, Hitchcock uses his editing for humor over horror. For example, as the fight continues the director periodically cuts back to how three cute rabbits in a hat are responding to all this comic mayhem. The quintessential fight editing has the trio slowly withdraw out of sight into the depth of their haberdashery hideaway.

One could also "read" this unspooling of a Chaplinesque sequence as just more self-referential commentary, one step removed from Hitchcock. After all, film movement is also just an illusion called "persistence of vision"—

still images projected at 24 frames a second create the impression of motion. One is reminded of the fact that in Ingmar Bergman's *The Magician* (1958), an account of a 19th-century hypnotist-magician, the Swedish director self-consciously showcases a 20th century movie projector in his film to link the similar trickery of diverse artists.

Regardless, it also bears noting that Hitchcock's *Vanishes* was not just impacted by the director's love of Chaplin's comedy. As previously noted, the British director was very taken by the comedian's *A Woman of Paris* (1923). One visual metaphor Chaplin created in that film was to use a quick cut of a locomotive's moving iron wheels to mean the passage of time. Though Hitchcock did not limit himself to this device, it was the first and most frequent device he used for that purpose.

Be that as it may, what happened to Miss Froy? As a spy transferring a secret European alliance, the vague powers that be, for this was the picture's MacGuffin, were out to kill her. And this plot was largely orchestrated by Lukas' agreeable Dr. Hartz. His mummified "patient" was to be replaced by Miss Froy, once she was abducted during Iris' nap. Of course, the fact that a whole train full of passengers either could be depended upon to be bribed, or were indifferent enough to almost let this happen—save for Iris—shows Hitchcock's talent for telling a tale despite drop-kicking logic out the window.

The rescue is helped, in part, by the member of Lukas' crew disguised as a nun (Catherine Lacey). And despite or because of Hitchcock's strict Catholic upbringing, the director as naughty little boy comically surfaces here. One of the comic clues leading to the nature of the abduction is Iris' observation that the nun is wearing high heels. Moreover, shortly after this Hitchcock provokes a mildly provocative laugh at the comic incongruity of Lukas coming into his compartment when the nun is fixing her makeup. However, Lacey's character had no idea that murder was involved, and helps orchestrate the rescue.

However, once the liberation has occurred, Hitchcock's desired action finish is implemented (shades of the close to *The Man Who Knew Too Much*). Though the train has reached its next stop, the famous surgeon Dr. Hartz uses his influence to have the train car with Miss Froy and company attached to another engine, in order for it to be removed to a remote location and taken by storm. By this time, even the children/men, cricket-obsessed Basil Radford and Naunton Wayne, have come around, despite Hitchcock historian George Perry affectionately describing them as the "silly ass roles of Charters and Caldicott."[24] Paradoxically, the fact that the duo both enter into the gun battle *and* are good at it even manages to add more humor where one would not expect it.

While even this British Laurel & Hardy have finally realized the foolishness of their metaphorical isolationism, Cecil Parker's adulter passenger

5. The Lady Vanishes (1938)

Mr. Hunter—a barrister no less—then makes the blindly funny declaration, "They can't possibly do anything to us; we're British subjects." This quickly turns to dark comedy, as he exits the besieged train car under cover of a quasi-white flag (waving his handkerchief) and is shot dead. If such a naïve comment seems a stretch for dark comedy's forte of going from humor to smack-in-the-face death, note the black humor in a straight *New York Times* article which paralleled the British premier of *Vanishes*. Titled "Nazis Now Drive to Complete Their [anti–Semitic] Programs," and written by the newspaper's Berlin correspondent, it stated, in part:

> ... it appears to have been the general assumption of ... the British government that the ... [Nazis'] program, after all, was only a party platform for election purposes and that now that.... Hitler had achieved undoubted success ... he would be willing to settle down, lead a quiet life and perhaps go fishing ... the British Foreign Secretary, it is believed here, considered Herr Hitler a second Gandhi, whom he would tame, and Prime Minister Neville Chamberlain is thought to have considered Herr Hitler a British labor leader whom he could dress up in knee breeches and take before the King.[25]

As a footnote to Parker's aforementioned adultery lawyer whose naïveté (veiled isolationism) leads to his death, several Hitchcock texts make much of the fact that his companion (Linden Travers) is the only woman in the cast whom Hitchcock seems to have photographed to further enhance her beauty.

Sadly, this yet again reveals more Hitchcock "historians" not familiar with White's original novel. Throughout the text Travers' character is described as nothing short of a "statuesque beauty," with Miss Froy so taken with a "profile ... like a beautiful statue," that she comically expresses an almost lesbian-like wish to see her silhouette one more time——"Oh, lady, please turn your head."[26] Indeed at another point in the novel the lovely Travers gets such praise that other women were equally drawn to her:

> Wherever she went, she attracted notice and she also excited feminine envy by her special atmosphere of romance. Apparently, she had everything that a woman could want—beauty, poise, exquisite clothes....[27]

Hitchcock's heightened treatment of Travers certainly demonstrated his close scrutiny of the novel, as well as demonstrating another aspect of farce—the fact that Lukas' character is a cad, who reneges upon his promise to make her the new Mrs. Todhunter. Unfortunately, the tightly told cinematic tale did not allow space for Hitchcock to have Travers' already married character articulate a petty comment in the spirit of this quote from the novel: "The passionate adventure had not matured according to its promise. It taught her that a professional man did not differ so greatly from a tradesman in essentials and that they looked much the same before shaving and without their collars."[28]

The lovely Linden Travers (center right) with, from left to right, Michael Redgrave, Margaret Lockwood, and Paul Lukas.

Besides once again demonstrating White's ability to play at being farcical, another aspect of the novel that Hitchcock would no doubt have been drawn to was the book's frequent cinematic references. Occurring so frequently, White's movie allusions almost act like self-referential parody, as if one is deconstructing a screen treatment before one is even written. For instance, examples ranged from short references, a man looking like "Mickey Mouse," or a couple resembling "film stars," to lines that could have been taken from a script—"The electric lights were set in clumsy wrought-iron chandeliers, which suggested a Hollywood set for a medieval castle."[29]

White's casual, sometimes even wickedly biting use of movie-related writing had one thinking of novelist Michael Chabon's later superlative use of what I will call "cinema speak" in his brilliant *Wonder Boys*, also adapted into a first-class but underrated film.[30] Regardless, *The Wheel Spins* movie notation which has one most thinking of Hitchcock was nothing short of a decoded interpretation of the director. He loved train travel and movies nearly from the time of film's inception. What follows is an interaction between Iris

5. The Lady Vanishes *(1938)*

and Miss Froy that makes a lovely connection between these two Hitchcock loves as the nanny's love of exploring:

> IRIS: "Why do you like it?"
> MISS FROY: "Because it's travel. We're moving. Everything is moving. Iris also had the impression that the whole [train] scene was flickering like an early motion picture."[31]

Moreover, in a more subliminal manner, one might further hypothesize about Hitchcock and life by way of the multiplicity of White's title—*The Wheel Spins*. One's first thought is of trains and travel. Yet, the title also suggests the roulette wheels of the director's much beloved sophisticated, farcical world of Saint Moritz—in which to spin the whirling wheel is a metaphor for the fatalism of his also beloved German Expressionism and dark comedy—the randomness of life itself.

Before coming full circle by incorporating more of *Vanishes*' period *comic* critical praise, which opened this chapter, one must offer a closing sample of the film's concluding humor which makes a final bow to the various comedy sub-genres ever present in the text. For example, even Miss Froy secures a brief *personality comedy* moment. In a closing gun battle that allows her to slip away, Hitchcock's footage of this normally tottering old lady spy running away, filmed from behind, would have had her beating Jessie Owens of the prior Berlin-based Olympics (1936). It is cartoonishly funny.

Plus, the film-stealing personality comedians of Charters & Caldicott must end on a standard Laurel & Hardy close of frustration—since that has been their archetype throughout. Thus, when they finally get back to London for their all-consuming cricket match extravaganza, abysmal weather (after all it is Britain) has cancelled the event. And returning to screwball comedy, which always mocks love, and frequently ends by dodging a marriage ceremony, à la the close of *It Happened One Night*, and arguably most inspiringly with *Arthur*, the ending does not disappoint. Lockwood's Iris ducks the designated husband-to-be at the London station and grabs the genre's typical type—Redgrave's Gilbert. And parody gets the final showcase, with Miss Froy ending this suspect spy film by playing her MacGuffin ditty on a rather unusual foreign office piece of furniture—a piano. One really has not come that far from the silliness of a shadow strangulation serenade, exterminated incongruously in German Expressionism style, early in the picture. It is again cartoonishly funny.

Be that as it may, to return to some final comic-tinged critical praise for *Vanishes*, one knows it has to be an amusingly remarkable film when the usually hard to please *New York Times* manages to produce not one, not two, but three positive critiques. A previously noted *Times* kudos appeared December 26, 1938 (see note 2), but there were also twin Christmas hosannas from the previous day. Both are comic focused, but one keys more on the film, while the second feasts on Hitchcock as personality comedian. Thus, the former observes:

> ... there is no let-up to his new film [*Vanishes*]. And it is much funnier than his others ... [It has] a contrapuntal comic rhythm to ... [it].[32]

Even the review title summarizes the tone—"Chips Off the Yule Log: The Season Ends on a Merry Note."[33]

The other Christmas 1938 *New York Times* focus treats the quality of *Vanishes* as a given and keys upon Hitchcock as the self-promoting comic personality comedian previously noted as the champion of broken crockery. He self-deprecatingly plays upon his size at the picture's London opening. Given that the event was being televised, he even manages to anticipate his later comic American mix of the small screen visual (by his shadow walking into his signature silhouette), and with his dry wit. The article is vague about the director's comic use of his physique on this pioneering use of the TV medium but Hitchcock embellishes it in his droll commentary:

> ... he told us that it was the custom, owing to his unusual size, to provide him with two seats for his own at every premiere. [But the] Problem tonight was how to occupy two seats, one on either side of an aisle.[34]

Other period reviews of *Vanishes* which could not refrain from highlighting the humor might begin with the *New York Sun*:

> The picture is amusing from the start, with the English director chuckling as loud as anyone at certain types of his countrymen, the Britishers who hold cricket more important than anything else, even a possible murder.[35]

The *New York World-Telegram* sounded like a comic pep rally for *Vanishes*:

> A Hitchcock film is usually something to see but when he turns out one as ... impishly humorous, breath-taking and vigorous as this one, it becomes not only your pleasure but your duty as a movie-goer to see it. It is Hitchcock at his best.[36]

That closing comment of "Hitchcock at his best" is very important to the thesis of this study, since this period review is smothered with praise for the director's *comedy*. Plus, this was the culmination of his British career—with the producer who would soon bring him to America, David *Gone with the Wind* Selznick, being so taken with the film that he wrote, in part, to the director, "Thanks for your kind mention of me on the radio. [I] saw 'Lady Vanishes' last night and I love you...."[37] Needless to say, this *comic* thriller was what put Hitchcock over the top in America. And again, to return to one of the *New York Times* reviews, the director, as already cited in several of these period critiques, was often treated as if he himself was a personality comedian, "...having given you fair warning, we still defy you to outguess that rotund spider, Hitch. The man is diabolical; his film is devilishly clever."[38]

5. The Lady Vanishes *(1938)*

What is so often forgotten is that this sort of picture is what best defines Hitchcock. Or, as the contemporary *London Guardian* stated, "[*Vanishes* is] challenged only in the master's oeuvre by *North by Northwest* [1959] for the title of best comedy thriller ever made."[39] Modern Hitchcock scholar Julia Johnson best put this dual genre in perspective, as well as elevating the director's British films by noting:

> Hitchcock's last important and most acclaimed British film, *The Lady Vanishes*, in many ways epitomizes his British films, which are simpler and less pretentious than his later American ones. Few Hitchcock films have had such an enthusiastic critical reception as *The Lady Vanishes*, which is ... certainly one of his most ingenious and entertaining.[40]

After killing time in Britain on a minor work, *Jamaica Inn* (1939), it was on to America.

6

Mr. and Mrs. Smith (1941)

> "I'm warning you [estranged husband Robert Montgomery], I'm killing you in cold blood sometime, someday when your back is turned. I'll stab you"—Carole Lombard, near the close of *Mr. and Mrs. Smith*

Ever since forever, *Mr. and Mrs. Smith*, Alfred Hitchcock's first set-in-America film, has been treated like an aberration in the director's filmography—seen simply as a mere screwball/farce past its heyday, and seemingly so at odds with today's Hitchcock's auteur image of suspense and horror. One can hear some condescending cinema snob flippantly observing, "Well, even Edward Hopper [whose paintings the director admired] had Monday mornings." Nothing could be further from the truth. Remember, as the previous *Lady Vanishes* chapter chronicled, several critics struggled to decide with which term to accent its "comic thriller" description. For example, The *New York Times* had said of the latter picture, "If it were not such a brilliant melodrama, we should class it as a brilliant comedy ... [with audience] aching from laughter."[1] And the *New York Post* said, "...its extraordinary humorous asides ... can match the best of the comedies...."[2]

In fact, it could be argued that *Smith*, which wrapped up production in late 1940, was a film one might have expected from Hitchcock soon after *Vanishes*. Except now the finger on the scale was weighted more towards a decidedly darker screwball comedy, as the opening threat by Lombard's Mrs. Smith suggests. In point of fact, *New York World-Telegram* critic William Boehnel essentially says, in part, just that in his *Smith* review:

> [This is a] frisky, scampish, gleeful comedy ... about that brand of guerilla warfare known as marriage.... But Hitch never lets it descend to the crazy level. Instead, he introduces us to people who are drawn from life, so that its comedy springs from [real, even edgy] characters ... [Some might] feel that Hitch should stick to mysteries. A plague on them![3]

6. Mr. and Mrs. Smith *(1941)*

Late in Hitchcock's career he added to this *Smith* disconnect when he told François Truffaut, in the younger director's groundbreaking book-length interview with the old master, that the film was merely "done as a friendly gesture to Carole Lombard ... and she asked whether I'd do a picture with her. In a weak moment, I accepted...."[4] However, as important as that text can be, it is often peppered with misstatements. For example, as early as 1983, Donald Spoto's Hitchcock biography reveals, with regard to *Smith*:

> The RKO archives tell a different story, however. It was true that he wanted very much to work with Lombard. But it is also true that he was wild about this particular idea. "I wanted to direct a typical American comedy about typical Americans," he said the first week of shooting.[5]

As the author of nearly two dozen biographies, I believe all interviews with a focus subject and their working contemporaries are important. Yet, when the sessions are done late in the artist's life, as was the case with the Truffaut/Hitchcock collaboration, one can often summarize such an interview with a paraphrasing of the old axiom, "It might not have occurred exactly in that manner, but that is the way I choose to remember it." Or, sometimes a tale has been told so many times through the years that it has simplify calcified into the "truth." Interviews and other documents from the time are where the true accuracies lie.

Interestingly, both Hitchcock and Lombard were fans of each other *prior* to the director's move to America. (His family's first temporary home in the states was a Bel-Air rental owned by the actress, and the two artists immediately bonded over their affinity towards spicy humor, practical jokes, and gossip.) Even more importantly, appropriately enough, as one of Lombard's earliest biographers noted, she had "enjoyed" Hitchcock's British films for years, "but in all of them she detected an adroitness for humor that was the match for his bag of suspense tricks."[6] This was even clearer by the time of my 2003 Lombard biography.[7]

A qualifier to all this was that Hitchcock's first two American films were *Rebecca* (1940), the year's hauntingly somber Oscar-winning Best Picture, and *Foreign Correspondent* (1940), the entertaining but overly patriotic for Hitchcock World War II warning to America. This is not to say that either picture was without several select Hitchcock showpieces, especially the latter, yet there are distracting side stories to both films. If one assumes the auteur perspective, then the former picture belongs to non-stop memo-machine producer David O. Selznick, whose meticulously controlling posture had also resulted in the previous year's Best Picture—*Gone with the Wind* (1939).

Foreign Correspondent is back on more solid Hitchcock comic spy thriller footing with additional room for humor. For example, as previously cited, Hitchcock even had the picture's first "foreign correspondent" played by one of America's best-known print humorists and screen personality comedians of the time, Robert Benchley. Indeed, Hitchcock even allowed the comic author/funny man to write his own dialogue for the drunken part. Be that as it may, this is still on a decidedly more serious spy thriller setting than *The 39 Steps* (1935), or *Vanishes*, for two reasons. First, by the time *Foreign Correspondent* and *Rebecca* had been released, World War II had begun in Europe. And Hitchcock, like Charlie Chaplin during World War I, was receiving a great deal of criticism for cowardice about not being back in England and assuming a more direct involvement with the war.

In truth, Hitchcock was possibly even garnering more condemnation. Of course, no one had expected the obese director to take up arms, as was the case with the younger Chaplin. However, the timing of Hitchcock's English exit and his initial American activity was different than the creator of the Tramp. That is, when World War I started (1914), Chaplin had already lived on and off in America for several years. Moreover, the comedian had immediately become involved in an extended war bond tour which raised over a billion dollars in today's money.[8]

Conversely, Hitchcock's departure for the world's film capital, with all the production bells and whistles to which he so desperately wanted access, occurred in 1939, just months before the war started in Europe. Plus, instead of then being involved in some conflict-related expatriate activity for England, he was mired in a drawn-out period of preproduction inactivity on the adaptation of a best-selling British novel—*Rebecca*. Worse, yet unlike many artists in Hollywood's British colony, he also did not return to England as soon as his contracted-for work was completed. For instance, *Gone with the Wind* co-star Leslie Howard went back at the war's outbreak and was later tragically killed (1943) when the Nazis appear to have shot down his plane while the actor was on a mission for the government—Germany thought Winston Churchill was onboard.

Moreover, budding Hollywood heartthrob and *Rebecca* co-star Laurence Olivier volunteered for the Royal Air Force and eventually found himself in the Fleet Air Arm of the Royal Navy. Moreover, as an indirect nationalistic contribution to the war effort, Olivier then produced, directed, and starred in an adaptation of *Henry V* (1944/1945), which would win a special Academy Award. (The film industries of most major countries involved in World War II were producing movies celebrating their nation's past. Ironically, even as Germany's Third Reich was collapsing in 1945, some troops were being diverted for a patriotic film production!)

Thus, the conclusion to *Foreign Correspondent* took flag waving to a seriousness atypical for a Hitchcock picture. That is, in the Edward R. Murrow-like CBS finale broadcast by title character Joel McCrea, the actor comes close to breaking cinema's fourth wall in his "the lights of Europe are going out" alert to America. Though never approaching the controversial conclusion for peace of Chaplin's *The Great Dictator* (1940) a few months later, in which the comedian literally stepped out of character to deliver his peace message, Hitchcock's windup did not fit the director's oeuvre.

All things considered, therefore, after *Rebecca* and then after *Correspondent*'s jingoistic conclusion, it should come as no surprise that Hitchcock was anxious to make a farce. This should be especially obvious, since he had left England essentially riding the wave of his hit critical and commercial quasi-comedy *The Lady Vanishes*, which the *London Mercury* possibly best described as a "comedy-melodrama."[9] Lombard was also anxious to return to screwball comedy.[10] She had been the 1930s poster child for the genre. After several early years in film, including a silent era slapstick stint with Mack Sennett, she finally became a major star in Howard Hawks' pioneering example of the genre—*Twentieth Century* (1934). This film, Frank Capra's *It Happened One Night* and W.S. Van Dyke's adaptation of Dashiell Hammett's novel *The Thin Man* (both 1934) are together considered the foundation of screwball comedy.

Pivotal to her stardom, and pertinent to Lombard's later work with Hitchcock, was the reason Hawks cast her—he based it on the private person. He saw her "at a party with a couple of drinks in her and she was hilarious and uninhibited and just what the part needed."[11] Hawks thought of her as a poor actress but a great personality—"marvelous gal, crazy as a bedbug.... If she could just be herself, she'd be great for the part."[12] Hawks' goal was simply to find a personality free spirited enough to match the over-the-top acting power of the celebrated John Barrymore, America's favorite ham actor, her co-star.

Hawks was as good as his word, because when the rehearsals started, Lombard was intimidated by Barrymore, and her "acting" was just not working out. Finally, the director took her for a walk:

HAWKS: "What would you do if someone said such and such to you?"
LOMBARD: "I'd kick him in the balls." (The beautiful actress' salty language had given her the Hollywood nickname of "Profane Angel.")
HAWKS: "Well, he [Barrymore] said something like that to you—why don't you kick him?"[13]

Although stunned by the freedom Hawks was sanctioning, Lombard finally grasped his nonacting directive and the subsequent shoot proved to be a comedy success.

This "be yourself" mission was not entirely new to Lombard; she had received similar advice from Sennett. Channeling her inner zaniness, she went on to do many other important screwball comedies, with her Oscar nominated *My Man Godfrey* (1936) performance being arguably her quintessential oddball. Fittingly, her *Godfrey* co-star William Powell, that rare combination of close friend/ex-husband, continued with the same "be yourself"

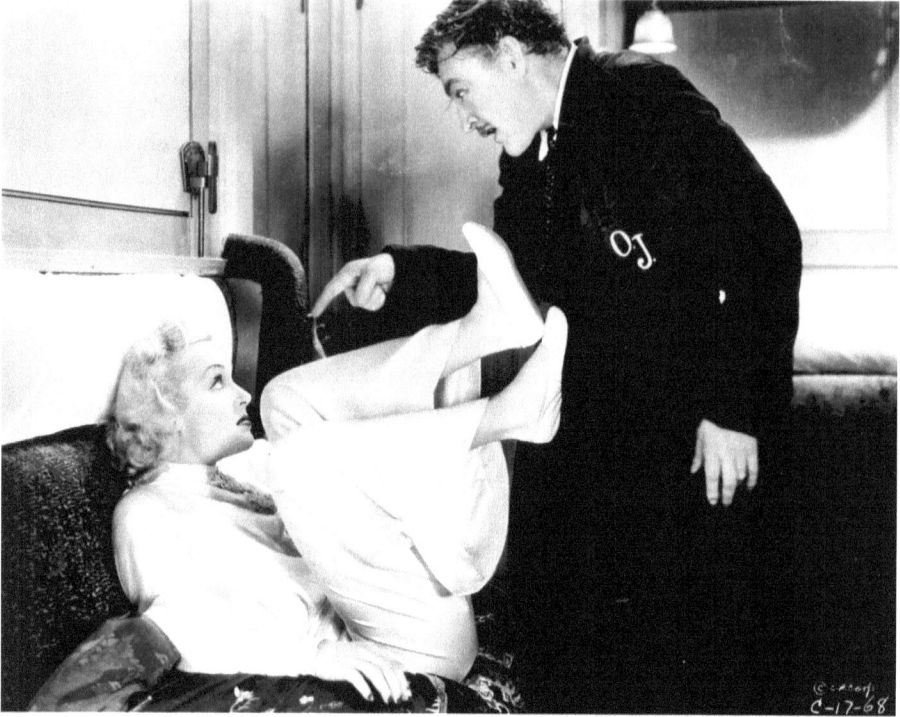

Carole Lombard being herself against John Barrymore in *Twentieth Century* (1934).

mantra. Indeed, Powell's up-close awareness of her off-the-wall identity was central to her getting the part. Again, this is a key subtextual component to her role in Hitchcock's *Smith*, which will be addressed shortly.

By 1938, Lombard was officially crowned queen of the eccentrics by the cover article in America's uncommonly popular mainstream magazine, *LIFE* (not to be confused with the earlier similarly titled satirical journal)—"A Loud Cheer for the Screwball Girl."[14] The essay brought the premise that Lombard equals screwball back to the foreground of the discussion:

> To act the part of a murderess ... an actress does not need to kill anyone.... Similarly the world's No. 1 attractive neurotic might well in her private life be as placid as a Holstein cow at twilight. This point however cannot be proved by the character or career of Carole Lombard. Her personal behavior is certainly as kaleidoscopic as that of the characters she impersonates and her career would supply first-rate material for either [a] case history or screenplay.[15]

At this point, Lombard became interested in more serious roles, both for versatility's sake and to beef up her resume to enter the competition for Hollywood's coveted woman's role of the decade—*Gone with the Wind*'s

6. Mr. and Mrs. Smith *(1941)*

Scarlett O'Hara. Ironically, Lombard's lover and future husband, Clark Gable, would eventually but reluctantly play the picture's other seminal part—Rhett Butler. Lombard, besides being a good sport about losing the role of Scarlett, was largely responsible for Gable co-starring. The 1930s' number one male lead, known as "The King," was paradoxically modest, and was insecure in period pieces. Moreover, he rightly felt what would become a nearly four-hour epic blockbuster hit essentially keyed upon Scarlett. Yet, it is now unimaginable without the balance he brought to the film.

Coming full circle back to Hitchcock and Lombard's *Smith*, the actress was then under contract to, and friends with, the producer of *Wind* and *Rebecca*, Selznick. Moreover, between not getting the role of Scarlett, and finding her fans were not embracing the actress' serious roles—maybe Hawks had been right about her being a personality—she was ready to return to screwball comedy. Under contract to RKO, it was easy to get Hitchcock on loan out from Selznick. Plus, both Hitchcock and Lombard loved the black comedy edged screwball script for *Smith*. And top it off with the director being fond of his leading lady:

> I liked her [Lombard] very much. She had a bawdy sense of humor and used the language men use with each other. I'd never heard a woman speak that way. She was a forceful personality, stronger, I felt, than Gable.[16]

Hitchcock's inner suppressed Catholic child must have found it difficult to contain himself. A specific example might best describe this phenomenon. Hitchcock's little boy toilet humor found great satisfaction when *Psycho* (1960) became the first mainstream American film to prominently feature a privy. Consequently, imagine the boyish glee the director must have experienced when he heard Lombard's frequent description of her remodeled bathroom, after her 1939 marriage to Gable—"…the most elegant shithouse in the San Fernando Valley."[17]

Since another attraction of America for the Hitchcocks was escaping the British class system, they would also have been drawn to the casual, unpretentious ways of Lombard and the murder mystery-reading Gable. Plus, for a man who had already been introducing himself for years as "'Hitch, no cock," the director no doubt enjoyed Lombard frequently kidding Gable, arguably the number one male sex symbol in the Western world, as "a lousy lay." Besides speaking to Hitchcock's comment about Lombard being the more forceful personality, one is reminded of the response Gable once gave when asked what his epitaph should be, "He was lucky and he knew it."

Regardless, when the voracious script-reading Lombard had finally found her screwball comeback property in *Smith*, if anything, Hitchcock was even more pleased with it. Why? One can only speculate, especially since the director later downplayed the picture as a favor to his obsessive type—a beautiful blonde.

However, while Lombard no doubt saw the script as simply something in her wheelhouse, Hitchcock quite possibly recognized that a Lombard screwball comedy was often darker than the normal example of the genre. And this script, though sometimes criticized for being rather a thin storyline, was ripe for the dark comedy base the director claimed all his pictures possessed.

Before addressing this point, the chapter merits an ever so slight tutorial on how screwball comedy is the closest to dark comedy in the humor genre pecking order. The most basic template for laughter is personality comedy. And while there is nothing to keep the clown sub-genre from going black humor rogue, à la Charlie Chaplin's *Monsieur Verdoux* (1947), one is usually talking mainstream laughter here. Romantic comedy by its very nature is excused, with only the occasional bittersweet picture, such as Woody Allen's *Annie Hall* (1977). Populism is wired for second chances and often sweetly sideswipes fantasy, as in *It's a Wonderful Life* (1946). And parody only *affectionately* kids genres and auteurs, as in Mel Brooks' uneven spoof of Hitchcock in *High Anxiety* (1977). Of course, any of these types could jump the tracks and go dark—but that would be the exception.

Now, this brings one back to farce/screwball comedy, in which not even love is venerated. That is best summarized in the title of a key example of the genre—*Nothing Sacred*, also a Lombard hit. The message, that "love fades," is sometimes also showcased by satellite couples, such as the adulterous duo in *The Lady Vanishes*. Regardless, yes, one ends up with a seemingly loving couple, but there is no guarantee it will last. For instance, it is often predicated upon the notion of opposites attract, such as the genre's Depression

Lombard's March 29, 1939, wedding day to Clark Gable. Hitchcock and his wife, Alma Reville, moved to the United States that year, and the couples became close until Carole's tragic 1942 death.

era circumstance of "implosion"—the duo coming from different classes. Yet, realistically, how long are unique deviations going to remain "cute?" Hitchcock showcased it best at the close of *The 39 Steps* (see Chapter 3), when the aforementioned mismatched couple are shot from behind as they attempt to hold hands ... yet a pair of handcuffs still hang from Richard Donat's wrist.

While most American takes on the genre have tried for an eternal bliss scenario, such has rarely been the case in Europe, as exemplified by *The 39 Steps* or an Oscar Wilde axiom which could serve as the continental coda for the genre, "One should always be in love. That is the reason one should never marry." Consistent with that, Lombard's screwball comedies generally telegraph that romance will be fleeting. Indeed, *Twentieth Century* does not even feature real intimacy—Barrymore's egomaniacal Broadway producer is too much in love with himself and putting on hit plays by conning anyone, including the slapstick-kicking blue collar Lombard. It is more of a boxing match taking place in a Hitchcock setting, a train—America's then famous transcontinental express, the *Twentieth Century*.

Moreover, one cannot mention Lombard and screwball pugilism without zeroing in on the signature scene from *Nothing Sacred*. The questionable duo of Lombard and Fredric March find themselves in a sequence in which her co-star finds it necessary to physically rough her up, with Lombard begging, "Just let me hit you once." However, the episode concludes with him feeling it necessary to knock her out, and a finale necessitating a fake suicide. And with violence as a given in her screwball comedies, murders, as in *The Thin Man* series, are also sometimes sandwiched in. For instance, in her popular *The Princess Comes Across* (1936), Lombard plays a Brooklyn-born showgirl trying to jumpstart a movie career. Deciding this in Europe, she reinvents herself as a Swedish princess (allowing her an extended spoof of Greta Garbo). The trick produces a movie contract. However, on her ocean liner return to the States a murder subplot occurs with the death of a passenger who had been blackmailing Lombard's wannabe film actress. The love interest with Fred MacMurray is assisted by all these complications, not unlike what occurs in *The 39 Steps* or *The Lady Vanishes*. What will happen to the romance when the exciting teamwork fueled by a crime disappears? The reviews even sounded like those accorded these Hitchcock films. For example, the *New York American* described *The Princess Comes Across* as "...delightful and exceptional film fare ... filled with fun, humor and spiked with thrills."[18]

The following year Lombard again teamed with MacMurray on another critical and commercial hit screwball comedy titled *True Confessions* (1937). As with *The Princess Comes Across*, the skewering of romance mixes murder and merriment. In *True Confession*, Lombard plays the wife of a defense lawyer (MacMurray) so honest that he can find few clients he trusts. In contrast, Lombard's character, in screwball fashion, is just the opposite—a congenital liar. With no money coming in, she is forced to take a secretarial job with a wealthy businessman. When he makes a pass at her, she walks out. Returning later for her hat and coat, she finds the boss murdered. She soon becomes the prime suspect. Deciding to go with her natural flair for lying, she hatches a whopper, claiming she murdered her boss when he attempted to take advantage of her. The beauty of the plan is that it also provides her husband with his big chance to win a high-profile acquittal and make his career. Besides mixing comedy and suspense, the picture apes both a screwball and Hitchcock component—making a satirical target of the law.

New York Daily News reviewer Kate Cameron noted that Lombard both "...proves once more that she is one of the greatest comediennes," as well as giving a classic "tongue-in-cheek" performance.[19] (The "cheek" reference was a punning celebration of Lombard's *True Confession* tendency to roll her tongue around in her mouth just prior to telling a tall tale). However, during the production there was also another public suggestion that there was little separation between the *anything goes* Lombard persona and the person herself. *Time* magazine reported that some Missouri tourists interrupted the shooting of a *True Confession* scene. The actress cut loose with language so blue that a "distraught assistant director scurried up waving his arms: 'Please, Miss Lombard, please! Remember there are ladies present.'"[20]

All of this brings one to Lombard's most continental-like screwball picture, prior to her posthumous Ernst Lubitsch directed *To Be or Not to Be* (1942). However, while *Smith* is still very much an American example of the genre, which had been Hitchcock's goal, between both the darker world view to be found in the director's and Lombard's previous pictures, American audiences were to be in for a more earnest example of the genre. In fact, very early in the picture, Lombard's character, three years into her screen marriage, asks husband Robert Montgomery, "If you had it all to do over again would you have married me?" His slow answer "No," because he wants to respect her litany of marriage rules, starting with absolute honesty, actually embraces the "love fades" question almost immediately. Interestingly, Lombard manages to live with that answer— a most un–American response for the genre in 1941. However, another development soon puts her at war with him.

The movie opens with a very messy outer area of a New York apartment bedroom suite, including piles of trays with unwashed dishes, and an unhappy, pajama-clad, disheveled Montgomery playing solitaire, smoking and looking tired and disgruntled. The viewer next sees Lombard, or what one assumes to be the actress. She is rolling about in the master bed, completely covered. A maid then knocks on the suite's outer door with breakfast, and we suddenly get a peek of her eyes under the covers. Montgomery takes the tray in and sets it by the bed. She turns away. He manages to close the bedroom door and hide behind the loveseat before Lombard pops up in bed.

Through the hired help one learns that this siege has lasted three days, and the couple's record covered eight days. Regardless, Montgomery slowly surfaces from behind the small sofa and thankfully Lombard smiles. He rushes over, they embrace, and the audience learns what has occurred—one of her rules: "You are not allowed to leave the bedroom after a quarrel until you have made up." As they warm to each other, and he gently observes most men cannot stay away from the office so long, they reminisce about past holdouts. He mentions two previous examples of six days. But she corrects him, saying the time periods were each five and a half days—one included the weekend at the Yale game, and the second was over Christmas.

These revelations produce several darkly comic concerns. First, what provoked these holdouts, including this recent eight day record. Second, causes are never revealed. This implies the incidents were over something relatively trivial, and at normally upbeat times, Christmas and a major sporting event (back when Yale was a major football power). Third, it is also suggested she was the catalyst for *all* of them, which is soon borne out by a reference to her rule number seven (never explained). Fourth, the opening impasse has already established that this is a normal scenario for their marriage.

In fact, one could add a fifth point with regard to time restrictions. It is soon demonstrated that there are no clock constraints with regard to what is fair game for upsetting Lombard, with regard to their marriage. To illustrate, as their early morning conversation continues, Montgomery carefully proposes that her time span might be too broad, "Like that trip I took to Paris the year I graduated from college. I was only 21." But she quickly interjects she forgave him ... over something which is clearly implied was both before they met, and was another incident seemingly so minor it also did not merit further explanation.

The woman is clearly mad as a hatter. And most consequential to this movie, there is a wild card triggering device present producing a darkly comic tension rarely if ever seen in *any* screwball comedy. What is this component? Loony Lombard has another regular ritual she brings to this screen marriage. (Paging Mr. Hitchcock.). Lombard loves to shave Montgomery with an old school straight edge razor as often as possible—but especially after they have had a fight. Mrs. Smith does not think his barber shaves him closely enough. And as the opening quote suggests, this is a woman that threatens to kill him on a regular basis. In fact, shortly after scraping him down after their eight day standoff, there is nearly another fight. But Montgomery's use of the phrase "You're my little girl" seems to calm her down.

Consequently, one is essentially dealing with an unstable, child-like little Miss Sweeney Todd. This is not exactly a comforting domestic barbershop scenario. True, there is no bouncing head shaft to a meat pie basement. But one always has sequels. Moreover, keep in mind, most screwball heroines from the period, especially Lombard's only rival for her crown of eccentricity, Irene Dunne, only assumed a madcap manner as needed—in a controlled manner.[21] This is best exemplified by a Dunne picture whose title says it all—*Theodora Goes Wild* (1936). Lombard and her persona are bipolar 24/7.

Now before one thinks this author is stretching this scenario, remember that one of Hitchcock's greatest influences is Edgar Allan Poe's "The Murder in the Rue Morgue" (see the Prologue's extensive examination of the short story). So what is the climax conclusion to the tale—a head is offed by a straight edge razor?

Moreover, one need not even remove Montgomery's noodle. Does the man have a dodgy heart? How could one not, living with this certifiable kook. She might just hold the blade to his throat and extend the boundaries of the genre to making his ticker shut down. Hitchcock would actually use that plot in a later episode of his television show—"The Return of Verge Likens," first broadcast October 5, 1964.[22] Peter Fonda's character avenges his father's death by pretending to be a new assistant barber—causing the lathered up, unsuspecting murderer to have a heart attack as the young man hauntingly describes just how he will slit his throat.

Okay, so *Smith* is still a screwball comedy, but this kind of thing is what makes the genre so provocatively close to dark comedy. How great a leap is it from a ha-ha screwball world to that of existentialistic black humor—in which a certain knowledge of what is right or wrong is missing? True, screwball comedy generally plays it more broadly for the diverting easy laugh. Yet, it is often not unlike the amusing killing time factor to be found in a Theatre of the Absurd production like *Waiting for Godot* (1953). In fact, one of the ways Montgomery calms the volatile Lombard is to tell her, "I'm used to you." Does this not approach Kurt Vonnegut's "And so it goes" mantra? That is, one's ongoing acceptance of an ever increasingly sick world? Plus, as already noted, many screwball comedies, especially those of Lombard, already come equipped with a murder sub-plot.

In the Prologue, I posited that a systematic examination of Hitchcock's far from random use of humor was like merely pulling a tablecloth off. A systematic comedy surface has always been there. However, in jerking away the cloth, one must yell, "Voilà." Why could one not now use the same analogy on Hitchcock's frequent focus in the American phase of his career—his entertaining but darker brand of black humor applied to *the study of crazy*? For example, Joseph Cotten's *widow*-shopping Bluebeard "Uncle Charlie" in *Shadow of a Doubt* (1943, see chapter 7)—first cousin to Charlie Chaplin's *Monsieur Verdoux* (1947), the real-life Leopold and Loeb experiment in murder which inspired *Rope* (1948, see Chapter 8), the delightfully deranged Bruno (Robert Walker) in *Strangers on a Train* (1951, see Chapter 9), and the

6. Mr. and Mrs. Smith *(1941)*

pièce de resistance Norman Bates (Anthony Perkins) of *Psycho* (1960, see the Epilogue), which even closes with a clinical diagnosis drawn from another true story.

The beauty of the neglected *Smith* is that it so perfectly bridges the England to America bookends of Hitchcock's career. The film is both a variation of sorts on his British farcical comic thrillers, and a masterfully disguised peek at the darkness to come. No wonder the director was even more pleased than Lombard about the script she had found. And all this is not to say the American Hitchcock did not continue to systematically use his complete comedy palette, such as the director's extraordinary reworking of his British masterpiece, *The 39 Steps*, in *North by Northwest* (1959).

The allure of researching and analyzing history is rather a wonderful time machine experience. However, as biographer Paul Murray Kendall has written, one engaged in the process can never be assured of the "absolute truth," and what s/he must aim for is telling the "best truth" possible.[23] Thus, why do Hitchcock's American films, as a group, seem to be so systematically darker? One might posit several things, from how the horrors of World War II further clouded his world view (as they did so dramatically with George Stevens' films), to simply the frustrations of age. Certainly, the latter explanation could be linked with the director's 1960s Tippi Hedren scandals, which are seemingly and disturbingly surfacing on the screen in *Vertigo* (1958).

Yet, I would go with the centuries-old William of Ockham "Occam's razor" hypothesis. Indeed, it rather sounds like something out of *Smith*. It proposes that with a question involving a myriad of explanations, usually the simplest one is the most likely. Thus, as the Prologue demonstrated, Hitchcock's rather twisted childhood had molded him into a darkly comic contrarian, with a weakness for cruel jokes. Consequently, the through-line of his work from England to America was not that he had changed but rather his ever growing status/control merely allowed him to reveal more of his eclipse of the moon personality.

That being said, however, his serious view of America often seemed like a variation of a previously noted observation—that innocence is itself a danger because it is so malleable. The text has more than established Hitchcock's misanthropic view of humanity, regardless of what continent he called home. And, if possible, his view of mankind having a jackrabbit attention span seemed especially true of America at a time when its often naïve new status as a world power was usurping the longtime British Empire. That being said, the American Hitchcock reminds me of a recent *New Yorker* view of Susan Sontag's deadly sense of seriousness, "[It] was a flashing machete to swing at the thriving vegetation of American philistinism."[24]

Be that as it may, a return to *Smith* reveals several further neglected Hitchcock auteur traits. First, after Montgomery has briefly escaped, via going to work, what the *New York Times* described as his "... squabbling Punch and Judy [marriage]," he finds a funny little man (Charles Halton) waiting for him at his law office.[25] It seems because of a recent discovery of a boundary error between Idaho and Nevada, the site of the Smiths' wedding, they are no longer legally married. Montgomery's David could not be happier. He has been granted one of Hitchcock's fortuitous twists—his desire for a second chance do-over, with regard to his union with Lombard's Ann, has been granted.

However, in a truly continental and Hitchcock view of marriage draining love from a relationship, Montgomery has his secretary call *former* wife Lombard on the phone. As David is doing this, he prints her maiden name in his calendar book—"Miss Krausheimer." He makes a date with her for an evening at one of their favorite restaurants. And if anyone has somehow missed the new life that has revitalized Montgomery, Hitchcock emphasizes it after David gets off the phone, and he rewrites from Miss to "MisTress Krausheimer."

What Montgomery has not planned on is that because his bearer of *unmarried* tidings happened to have been a former friend of Lombard by way of a sister, Halton decides to look her up, too. After all, he has come a long way, and since he is in New York anyway.... This allows the introduction of another Hitchcock given—the controlling mother. Lombard's matriarchal bully, Esther Dale, who placed the same rein on Ralph Bellamy in Leo McCarey's screwball classic *The Awful Truth* (1937), is there when the surprise visitor arrives with the territorial bungle. Mrs. Krausheimer immediately acts as if David has hatched up this geographical mistake. And one immediately sees from whom Lombard's Ann inherited what writer William H. Gass might have described as her extra "dab of the dizzies."[26]

Indeed, while this old neighbor turned marriage revoker is on screen, one learns that as a little girl Lombard's Ann once chased an alleged adversary a half mile with a baseball bat. It seems that a homicidal cloud has always shadowed her. Naturally, there is neither mention nor sight of Ann's father. One might even ponder Mrs. Krausheimer's views on straight-edged razors. Plus, given the nature of the Krausheimer women, even if Ann's absent father had supposedly died of natural causes, one is reminded of Groucho Marx's *Duck Soup* (1933) line, "He might just be using that as an excuse." However, to Lombard's credit, despite normally having a sheer grasp of confusion, she assumes Montgomery will do the right thing—thinking he is taking her to an old dating location so that he can propose again.

Naturally, that is not Montgomery's plan at all, which ultimately results in Lombard kicking him out of their apartment at the end of the evening. This represents Hitchcock's further unveiling of the love lie (breaking the key codified rule) at the heart of American farce/screwball comedy. In a *Hollywood Reporter* review of *Night Train to Munich* (1941), a Carol

Reed-directed film reminiscent of *The Lady Vanishes*, a fleeting aside loosely links Hitchcock and Preston Sturges—the brilliant American screwball comedy director with European ties who made any question of lasting love in the genre inconceivable during the war years.[27] For example, what Hitchcock plays with casually (Miss to MisTress) during *Smith*, Sturges has fun bluntly stating via one of his regular stock players (Al Bridge as a lawyer) in 1944's *The Miracle of Morgan's Creek*:

> The responsibility for recording a marriage has always been up to the woman. If it wasn't for her, marriage would have disappeared long since. No man is going to jeopardize his present or poison his future with a lot of little brats hollering around the house unless he's forced to. It's up to the woman to knock him down, hogtie him, and drag him in front of two witnesses, immediately if not sooner. Anytime after that is too late.

Also, keep in mind that in Preston Sturges' last rule-bending dark screwball comedy, *Unfaithfully Yours* (1948), Rex Harrison plays a famous symphony conductor who fantasizes about murdering a cheating wife, with a throat slashing reminiscent of Ann's razor.

Regardless, while screwball comedy has always spoofed the love story, Hitchcock goes further on the subject to a reaffirmation level only rivaled by the much later *Arthur* (1981). For instance, when David and Ann go to their old restaurant, "Mama Lucy's," it is now a dump, with its namesake having returned to the "old country," and presumably her disgruntled husband running the place under her name.

Furthermore, at home, just prior to David's surprise boot from Ann, he is happily whistling along preparing for his tryst with MisTress Krausheimer when the sliding bedroom doors protect him from a Lombard-thrown crystal water container. It is as if Hitchcock is affectionately spoofing two of his filmmaking influences, Fritz Lang's greatest creation (the two-faced whistling Lorre of *M*, 1931), and the "Lubitsch touch" of telegraphing Lombard's gathering storm, before she turns baseball pitcher. Remember, parody frequently has a scattergun effect, holding "nothing sacred" in its broad dissemination of comic targets.

Hitchcock further mocks love in myriad ways. The second night Montgomery is forced to sleep over at his men's club, the night attendant observes to himself, "when they come back a second night things are bad." Montgomery then develops a friendship with another of the club's homeless husbands, the underrated comedian Jack Carson. This results in the world's worst double date, especially after the arrival of Lombard with an escort. Once again, however, it allows Hitchcock to sow a variation on the anything goes nature of parody. For instance, Hitchcock, the silent filmmaker at heart, peppers the film with pantomime, with the best extended sequence belonging to Montgomery. His David is tightly wedged between two women at the restaurant.

One is his less than attractive date, the other is a Hitchcock blonde. In order to make Lombard jealous, he pretends to mouth words in a silent conversation with the unaware Lombard look-alike.

Naturally, Montgomery's enchanting idea fails when this unenlightened woman becomes enlightened. Yet again, Hitchcock seems to be reaching back into his early silent film apprenticeship. Now, however, instead of burlesquing basic silent comedy models, he is taking on the "talkies" more ambitiously. That is, in a *Theatre Arts* article from the same year *Smith* appeared, pioneering American film historian Lewis Jacobs notes a rule upon which Hitchcock insisted:

> ... it is silent training which counts. Naval men have a theory that the finest navigators nowadays are the men who learned their craft in out-of-date sailing ships. I maintain that the young men who strike out into the game should first go through a course of silent film technique.[28]

Consistent with this comment, Hitchcock even tops Montgomery's fetching pretend conversation with the unaware nightclub beauty. Desperate to get out of this awkward situation, David decides his exit excuse will be a random bloody nose. Thus, he hits himself in his schnozzola. But it has all the power of the baby-like comedy star Harry Langdon. Nothing.

Moving up a notch in punching power, à la Hitchcock's favorite Chaplin, he manages a respectable jab. Still nothing. Then he has a rougher Buster Keaton–style epiphany—he wraps his cloth napkin around a salt shaker and really slugs himself. Bingo. Unfortunately, however, this only creates a more awkward situation when his blind date, who looks like she might have been able to go a few rounds with Jack Dempsey, jumps to his assistance. Sure enough, if the woman had not been a boxer, she could have doubled as a boxer's "cut man"—the individual in each fighter's corner who can always stop the bleeding in order that a fight can continue.

Consistent with a darker screwball comedy, her surefire remedy, ironically enough, is to quickly produce a knife and hold it under Montgomery's nose. It immediately stops the bleeding, and almost assuredly guarantees, if there had been any doubts, that she does not have a midtown address. Fittingly, for the straight edge razor-shaving Lombard, who has witnessed the scene, Miss Krausheimer comments, "I don't care who holds a knife to him, though I'd certainly like the chance myself." One assumes she would go for his jugular, though if one merely wanted to put an ex-husband out of romantic commission, slicing off his proboscis would certainly wreak havoc with his dance card.

Of course, Hitchcock's ongoing suggestion that love fades, whether the picture be a comic thriller, or a quasi-screwball comedy turned dark, is not without verbal thrusts, too:

6. Mr. and Mrs. Smith *(1941)*

MONTGOMERY: What's wrong with me [romantically]?"
LOMBARD: I don't want the discussion to run into hours.

With this new threat of violence, Hitchcock cannot help pinballing back to parody, with himself now a target. The director is unable to resist kidding his own screen reputation by briefly turning Montgomery's David into an amateur sleuth, with a well-paid taxi driver sidekick. However, even Montgomery's hard work playing a novice shamus does not prepare him for a final blow at the ephemeral nature of love, with a sideorder of betrayal.

Montgomery's law partner, college buddy, and fellow football player at Alabama (Gene Raymond) turns out to have designs on Lombard. And she seems to reciprocate his favor. The viewer, however, is well aware of this before Montgomery. After the nightclub fiasco, Raymond's character (Jeff Custer, not the most promising name), takes Lombard to the New York World's Fair (1939–1940), the biggest international event since World War I. Planned and promoted for several years, with its theme being the future, it was also meant to be both an economic and entertainment counterweight to the Depression, as well as marking the 150th anniversary of George Washington's first inaugural speech, which had taken place in New York. Paradoxically, though hardly surprisingly, despite all the educational developments (including the huge promotion of early television), the most popular area was the large amusement park. And *the* ride was the giant "parachute jump."

Naturally, Hitchcock spoofs his signature tendency to regularly showcase famous locations by having Lombard and Raymond not only visit the fair but also go up in the "Parachute Jump." Not surprisingly, the director treats his viewers to several dizzily high shots as the excursion takes the couple to a seemingly unrealistic altitude. Consequently, here was more Hitchcock parody of himself on two levels. First while *Smith* was not a thriller, if one can get beyond the image of Lombard and a straight edged razor, this is a *scary* height. One rightly assumes there will be no typical Hitchcock high above the ground danger, such as the dome of the British Royal Museum in *Blackmail* (1929, see Chapter 1), or the later Mount Rushmore scenes of *North by Northwest* (1959).

However, Hitchcock overhead shots are still never a good omen for those involved. So how could the director play with part of his formula? Simple solution—the ride malfunctions and grinds to a halt, with the couple stuck in the clouds. It is a funny though modest twist on a Hitchcock auteur trait. Yet, it no doubt drew in more viewers, because who has not suffered through some such thing? Plus, it allowed the director to dovetail into comedy's rule of threes. That is, he ups the comedy anty by having a storm come up and soak them—more amusing, as well as cosmic revenge on Lombard for getting involved with Montgomery's partner! Moreover, still in silent comedy mode, Hitchcock has again aped Sennett's surefire conclusion to any comic sequence or short subject—get the principals wringing wet.

Third, by the time Lombard's All-American replacement gets them home, he is just a few sneezes short of "pneumonia," also a period euphemism for Hollywood, defined as "a cold with a press agent." Regardless, this was not only Hitchcock's topper trifecta, it also was the catalyst for another soon-to-be basic element in the director's oeuvre. Made during Hitchcock's extremely heavy drinking period, the film includes a version of his expression "It isn't alcohol, it's like medicine." Lombard has the teetotaler Custer take a glass of brandy to "kill the germs," telling him "This isn't alcohol—it's medicine." After this picture, a variation of that line would be included in numerous Hitchcock films to come, including *Vertigo*.

Lombard now begins to see some colorless cracks in Custer's persona, from him claiming to have been greatly influenced by a temperance meeting as a young man, to extolling the virtues of vegetables. She does compliment him for not making a pass at her after some more "medicine." It would not have been possible anyway—his pantomime of a drunken stiff is priceless. Regardless, her expression when she realizes he is essentially a prohibitionist captures the essence of one of Dean Martin's later signature jokes, "I feel sorry for people who don't drink. Because when they get up in the morning, that's as good as they're going to feel all day."

Keep in mind, screwball comedy is the most pickled of genres. Examples include its all-important birthing year of 1934 and *The Thin Man*'s well-oiled Nick and Nora Charles (the sophisticated comedy-mystery duo which inspired *five* sequels), to such later energized pictures as *Arthur*, with Dudley Moore's droll drunk title character poignantly observing, "Everyone who drinks is not a poet, some of us drink because we're not poets." Indeed, when I interviewed pivotal 1930s producer Pandro S. Berman, a close friend of screwball comedy auteur Gregory LaCava, I was told that LaCava's Lombard starring in *My Man Godfrey* was not only lubricated on screen, but the set itself was essentially an ongoing cocktail party.[29]

Regardless, other Hitchcock autobiographical touches occur late in the film when Lombard and Raymond get away to New York's Lake Placid skiing resort. This is another link to Hitchcock's British farcical thrillers, which often spent time in settings not unlike Lake Placid, inspired by Switzerland's St. Moritz—where the Hitchcocks honeymooned in 1926. Naturally, these were times in which to sometimes patch-up rifts in their relationship. Consequently, Montgomery is able to win back Lombard at Lake Placid, by booking a cabin near the one in which Lombard and Raymond are visiting his parents.

Ironically, the Hitchcocks were going through a less congenial period in their marriage at that time, versus their last years in Britain.[30] Several factors were involved, including wife Alma not feeling as totally involved with some of her husband's early American projects, as well as his excessive drinking during this period. And sadly, St. Moritz had been, and would continue to be, cut off from them during Great Britain's World War II years, 1939–1945. Consequently, the eventual reconciliation of Lombard and Montgomery at the close seems almost like a personal gift/wish from Hitchcock to Alma.

That being said, there remained some entertaining ambiguities about the ending. Though there was not going to be any Lombard-Raymond future relationship, she was not quite ready to take back Montgomery. Alone with her ex in his cabin, after Raymond and his parents had left, she decided to put on her skis and go back to the main lodge. (Alma skied; Hitchcock did not.) Though Lombard had carried the brunt of the slapstick until then, Montgomery stops her by simply pushing Ann over, with her feet and skis comically up in the air. He also pretends to act like he is finally ready to stop trying to get her back. Lombard is also ready to capitulate but is too proud to say anything. However, Montgomery is soon standing over an unseen Lombard, and her hands slowly reach up to him. Presumably, she will be pulling him down for an out of sight kiss—a bit of the "Lubitsch touch." However, since one does not see the kiss, and Lombard's hands are drawing his neck down, can one completely rule out that Ann's bipolar character is not about to strangle him? After all, for Hitchcock strangling is right up there with straight edge razors. (As an addendum to the Lubitsch reference, the following year, 1942, this director took both the genre and Lombard to a much darker place with his Nazi strewn *To Be or Not to Be*, the actress' last picture).

Be that as it may, since the final *Smith* image is of Lombard's still-in-the-air skis crossing, it must be a truce. However, what kind might that be, given the director's nickname—"just Hitch, no cock"? In Britain, an "x" means a kiss, while in America it represents more of a sign of affection. But to take a more somber metaphorical meaning from this "criss cross," it inadvertently foreshadows Hitchcock's noirish dark comedies to come, be it *Shadow of a Doubt* or Lombard's "first cousin" Bruno and *Strangers on a Train*. After all, *Smith* has been suggested as a bridge from Hitchcock's somewhat lighter British films. There is even a classic film noir with that name, *Criss Cross* (1949).

Nonetheless, I am content to simply call *Smith* a darker than normal screwball comedy, which loosely plays with the genre template, and has ties to Hitchcock's British farcical thrillers, with an added visual shtick, and some autobiographical touches. Moreover, screwball comedy stories often conclude in the country and/or mountains including two mega-hit productions from the underrated and *visual* screwball comedy accented Leo McCarey, *The Awful Truth* (1937) and *My Favorite Wife* (1940).[31] Both starred Irene Dunne and Cary Grant, the latter of which both Hitchcock and Lombard had attempted to sign as their *Smith* leading man.

Coming back to the notion that *Smith* was some sort of slumming anomaly in the Hitchcock canon, hopefully the preceding pages have demonstrated that a revisionist "reading" suggests much more. Besides being a decisive bridge in his oeuvre, and much more—it was a critical and major commercial success for RKO. For any period critics who quibbled, the previously cited *New York World-Telegram*'s "a plague on them" comment said it best, after giving *Smith* impressive comedy kudos. This also couples nicely with the *New York Daily News*' praise of its pantomime:

> Hitchcock's knowing directorial hand has made it into an interesting screen exhibit. He has reverted to the technique of silent films, as most of the comedy is engendered by the facial expressions of his players ... [Lombard, Montgomey, and Raymond] prove themselves adept at pantomime.[32]

The *New York Herald Tribune*, after saying, "chalk up another triumph for one of the screen's top craftsmen," went on to second the *Daily News*' praise of his silent comedy touch:

> As in the past, the great director has avoided using dialogue when pictorial pantomime would suffice. Thus, the sequences bridging the temporary separation of the Smiths are narrated frequently in pure imagery. It makes for a refreshing and even exciting treatment of farcical material.[33]

New York Post critic Irene Thirer's review, however, was simply one continuous hosanna:

> ... an American farce, gay and witty and sophisticated: he's (Robert Montgomery) an attorney, she's (Carole Lombard) a spitfire.... Reconciled after a chair throwing quarrel (it happens often) ... she asks him sweetly: "Darling, tell me the truth. If you were single again, would you marry me?" To which he honestly (ducking) replies: "No" ... It's a smart little picture."[34]

Quotes from two final period *Smith* reviews underscore how natural—almost to be expected—the movie is to Hitchcock's filmography. First, the *New York Sun*, which will go on to call it an "expert farce," opens by stating:

> Alfred Hitchcock, whose mixture of comedy and suspense have been the delight of the movie-going world since first his pictures began to drift over here from England, now has made a picture that is all comedy ... [*Smith* is] a domestic comedy, directed knowingly by Mr. Hitchcock.[35]

And the *New York Times*, describing Hitchcock's work on the screwball comedy as having a "Machiavellian cunning," suggests how easily he could have veered this comedy into mystery:

> What distinguishes Mr. Hitchcock's magic mountain is the angle at which he has set his camera, the means by which he has underscored the ludicrousness of a situation [the director loved tossing logic out the window] ... when Mr. and Mrs. Smith try to recapture an ardent courtship in a half-forgotten spaghetti tavern, the director sets a most sinister cat on their table to stare at the soup....[36]

6. Mr. and Mrs. Smith *(1941)*

One cannot close this chapter on such a multifaceted film without noting a period significance lost on modern viewers. From the coverage of *Smith's* production, starting with day one, this picture arguably helped America fully embrace a great director who was thus far a difficult character to get a handle on. There was his gargantuan consumption of food, the odd pleasure he claimed to get from breaking crockery, his seeming indifference to actors, and so on. In contrast, Lombard was adored by a public that was especially happy to see her returning to screwball comedy. (Indeed, when she did not receive an Oscar for *My Man Godfrey* no less an eccentric talent than W.C. Fields felt called upon to make his displeasure known. The title of a *Washington Post* article said it all—"Noted Comic Is Slightly Irked by Film Awards."[37])

And no single person better helped Hitchcock be fully embraced by the general American public than Lombard. This is unquestionably best demonstrated by her direction of his *Smith* cameo. It demonstrated he could take a joke at his own expense—directed at his signature image—by a most comically demanding Lombard. Hitchcock was famous, or infamous, for the statement, "Actors should be treated as cattle." So, when the director appeared for the first day of shooting, he found a small corral holding three calves with accompanying name tags for each of the stars. When it came time to shoot Hitchcock's cameo, the actress took over. She relished the opportunity for comedy payback, or as a contemporary article proclaimed, "Carole Lombard Gets Revenge by Directing Alfred Hitchcock."[38]

The scene had the director being mistaken for a panhandler and Montgomery giving him a dime. Lombard was relentless in her direction of Hitchcock: "Try again. Now Alfie, when he gives you that dime, I want you in a pensive mood, Alfie. [Hitchcock tries to follow Lombard's direction.] I don't like it. Stop your mumbling. [He protests.] I'd like it a little clearer. This is for an American audience."[39] The situation would have played even funnier for period readers, since the dialogue for early 1930s British imports was often criticized for being hard to understand.

Hitchcock was being assimilated. However, it was now time for darker things.

7

Shadow of a Doubt (1943)
Beginning of Hitchcock's Nietzschean Dark Comedy Trilogy

> This was my father's favorite movie because he loved the thought of bringing menace into a small town—Pat Hitchcock[1]

If every film is an unwitting documentary to the time in which it was made, it is also a letter written to the future. Nothing chronicles this more effectively than *Shadow of a Doubt*. Indeed, it even starts to anticipate film noir. However, while the story begins in a noirish New Jersey boardinghouse, it ends up in a variation of Thornton Wilder's Grover's Corner—the universal American small town which was the setting for the author's 1938 Pulitzer Prize winning play, *Our Town*. (Wilder co-scripted *Doubt*, and Hitchcock greatly admired both his modesty and the fact that the writer was arguably the first great American artist to accept him on equal terms, once the director moved to this country.) That being said, *Doubt* more than anticipates the inhumanity of man during World War II (when the film was made), and the Theatre of Absurd world to follow.

While this text's ongoing motto has been Hitchcock's view that most of his films were dark comedies, and that Darwin was decidedly wrong about humankind having evolved, *Doubt* is his ultimate scary testimonial to that world view. The director's slaughterhouse justification was randomly reported earlier in the text. However, when placed in its proper *Doubt* context, its chilling content is exponentially more disturbing. Before fleshing out the film's full storyline, it is enough at this point to simply state that a visiting beloved Uncle Charlie (an engaging Joseph Cotten) rather indiscriminately observes, in part, at a family dinner:

> ... silly [wealthy widowed] wives. What do the wives do, these useless women? You see them in the hotels, the best hotels, the best hotels by the thousands. Drinking

their money, eating their money ... smelling of money. Proud of their jewelry but nothing else. Horrible, faded fat greedy women....

What has started as a monologue briefly becomes a distressing dialogue with his once beloved namesake niece, Young Charlie (Teresa Wright):

WRIGHT: But they're alive. They're human beings!
COTTEN: [In a brutal close-up response] Are they?

As filmmaker/historian Peter Bogdanovich later observes in the documentary *Beyond Doubt: The Making of Hitchcock's Favorite Film*: "Hitchcock definitely gives Cotten his position. He lets the character say what he [the director] means ... 'This is how I feel.'"[2] Be that as it may, this is hardly a 1943 press kit revelation, or Hitchcock's American career would have taken a decidedly different direction. However, the disclosure grants *Doubt* the rare distinction of arguably having a greater disturbance quotient today than when it was released.

Regardless, the film briefly begins with a dream-like reverie of couples dancing in ballroom attire to the title waltz in Franz Lehár's 1905 *Merry Widow* operetta. Lehár's comic tale is about a rich widow and control of her money. This trance of an image will frequently reoccur throughout the movie and is like *Doubt's* yet to be defined coded message. The movie then cuts to some seamy East Coast contemporary (1940s) imagery before arriving in Uncle Charlie's room in the aforementioned rooming house. Cotten's dapper character is dressed and lying on his bed bored, smoking a cigar and presumably thinking about that ephemeral waltz imagery—its unnoted lyrics suggest that true love only exists in one's dreams.

There are dirty wads of money on the floor and the bed's end table. The presumed owner of the dwelling, an older, sympathetic woman, next makes an appearance. She tells Cotten about two men who have been asking about him. But per his directions, the matron has revealed nothing, and then gently chides him about leaving out all his money. Consistent with a theme which seems to be developing, she warns him people are not to be trusted ... though she makes an exception with herself. Before exiting, she maintains a motherly manner (though her maternal instincts seem assisted by all that cash), by encouraging Cotten to continue resting and promises she will go on being a gatekeeper, with regard to those men.

After her exit, Cotten suddenly and uncharacteristically throws his shot glass against the wall. The unwanted visitors are waiting at the corner outside. Still in his room, Uncle Charlie confidently says out loud, "You're bluffing. You have nothing on me." And unlike *The 39 Steps*' (1935) Richard Donat, who is also being stalked by two men down at the corner, Cotten brazenly leaves the boardinghouse and walks right by the men—whereas Donat must devise a ruse. Immediately, one has dark comedy *absurdity*; the "wrong man" must slip away, the guilty one cannot be touched.

Cotten has decided to visit his beloved sister Emma Newton (Patricia Collinge) and her family in the innocent average city of sunny Santa Rosa, California. Uncle Charlie is also particularly close to his namesake niece, Teresa Wright, who reciprocates these feelings. Cotten and his niece are another example of Hitchcock's use of the doppelganger phenomenon—the evil adult Charlie, and the young innocent Charlie. An immediate example occurs after he loses the detectives and telegrams his family he is coming for a visit; the viewer first sees a dressed Young Charlie lying in her bedroom in Cotten's previous pose. Paradoxically, she too is bored and wants her dull existence transformed. That much and more is on its way; be careful what you wish for. Moreover, consistent with the twin factor, she decides to send a telegram to her uncle. Thus, she is overjoyed upon reaching the cable office, because Cotten's telegram announcing his visit has already arrived.

Before moving this *Doubt* table of contents along, Hitchcock's tale of "bringing menace into a small town" merits comparison to two other significant works of American literature. The first, Wilder's *Our Town*, has already been mentioned. The playwright's story of another universal sleepy American town, Grover's Corners, is usually given just that sort of stereotypical brief reference in Hitchcock criticism, à la "How fitting that a mainstream American author should assist the director in creating this 'Aw shucks' location for a menace coming to town."

However, as this text has observed ad nauseam, such materials do not seem to be reviewed by Hitchcock authors. Wilder's play is three acts of nice people, whose message is essentially "savor every moment." So far so good for Hitchcock's *Doubt*—an innocent destination. However, one soon hits a speed bump; Grover's Corners' dark comedy philosophy is without any need for the devilish Cotten. That is, *Our Town*'s Act One is about daily life in 1901; Act Two is love and marriage in 1904, with central figures George and Emily marrying, and Act Three moves to 1913, with Emily having died in childbirth. One is reminded of Norm Macdonald's *Hitler's Dog* comedy special which the *New York Times* called 2017's best comedy special.[3] That is, to paraphrase Macdonald's riff about suddenly coming out of a "cotton candy world," one might consider it is "time to go down to the rope store, which is conveniently located by the rickety stool store."

It gets better/worse, as Emily mingles with other dead acquaintances, like you do, after the funeral. Emily discovers she can go back but in a dual capacity—as naïve Emily and as her observing spirit, who has passed. The dead advise against it—death's purpose is to forget. However, Emily decides to return just for her 12th birthday. Yet she is unable to stay long before she requests a return to death:

> I can't. I can't go on. It [life] goes so fast. We don't have time to look at one another....
> I didn't realize. So all that was going on and we never noticed. Take me back—up the

7. Shadow of a Doubt (1943)

hill—to my grave.... I should have listened to you [the dead]. That's all human beings are! Just blind people.[4]

Another member of Emily's new group puts it even more bitingly, rather in an Uncle Charlie perspective:

> Yes, now you know. Now you know! That's what it was to be alive. To move about in a cloud of ignorance; to go up and down trampling on the feelings of those ... of those about you. To spend and waste time as though you had a million years. To be always at the mercy of one self-centered passion, or another. Now you know—that's the happy existence you wanted to go back to. Ignorance and blindness.[5]

As *New York Times* critic Mel Gussow later wrote, "Though certainly less mordant there is a kind of Becket-like aspect in the author's [Wilder] intention. In *Our Town*, as in *Waiting for Godot*, one is born astride the grave."[6] Dark comedy does not get any more existentially basic than that—killing time until it kills you. This film is where Hitchcock *really* moves the needle to dark comedy.

Consequently, while a contemporary *Doubt* audience might bring the added macabre Hitchcock insight to a screening, a literate period audience quite possibly saw the human black humor irony of bored Young Charlie as a potentially soon-to-be Wilder's dead Emily—yet another blind person in a world of deaf people. Uncle Charlie, where is thy sting? Why, one could christen him a handsome young Dr. Kevorkian in a Panama suit. It also evokes today's revisionist take on *It's a Wonderful Life* (1946)—"...the American dream was so close to the nightmare ... uplifting fellowship, yet it was a film noir full of regret, self-pity, and the temptation of suicide."[7] Interestingly, both Capra's film and Wilder's play feature a pivotal "George" character who ultimately abandons his college goal for love and the questionable *Truman Show* (1998)-like sealed bubble permanency of a small town.

Moreover, this Grover's Corners link is not just some academic proposing connecting certain dots. David Freeman's *The Last Days of Hitchcock* chronicles the lengthy time the writer was with the director crafting the unproduced screenplay, "The Short Night." As with most Hitchcock collaborators, Freeman spent lengthy periods listening to the raconteur's nonstop eclectic monologues about almost everything but the subject at hand. During one of these sessions, however, Hitchcock said, "...the [*Doubt*] script was just an extension of 'Our Town.'"[8] So there is the direct link.

Wilder notwithstanding, however, one might credit *outsider* Hitchcock for cinematically skewering the clueless mindset of small town America. However, there is another literary classic which merits coupling with *Doubt*—Mark Twain's homegrown darkly comic iconoclastic novella *The Man That Corrupted Hadleyburg* (1899). It too features another basically unknown wanderer "bringing menace" into a self-righteous burg. (Indeed, one could also couple *Hadleyburg* with Twain's later unfinished 1916 novella *The Mysterious Stranger*, in which Satan's nephew appears in the nice medieval Austrian village of Eseldorf—German for "Assville.")

Since "Assville" rather simplistically gets at the cinder-black comedy of Twain's perspective, one might better focus on a brief comparison with *Doubt* and *Hadleyburg*. Hitchcock's Cotten is essentially bringing the dark side to Santa Rosa simply by visiting. In contrast, Twain's Hadleyburg's dark comedy figure has a specific revenge in mind for a smugly self-righteous town that has somehow slighted him in the past. Thus, one does not enter Santa Rosa with the same distaste as for Hadleyburg. Still, the text will eventually show several basic parallels. Ironically, moreover, one might end up liking Hadleyburg more, since Santa Rosa remains in its black comedy obtuseness, without an ounce of existential awareness. (This is another Hitchcock dark comedy in-joke.)

Interestingly, the sum of $40,000 plays an important part in both stories. (This is also the amount of money Janet Leigh steals in *Psycho*—coincidence?) In Twain's Hadleyburg, the amount is a trap—a gift for a claimed kindness given to a poor stranger. The catch is only to have the winner repeat the advice s/he gave the plotter. The trickster has made the scam possible by sending the sage counsel in letter form to several prominent citizens of this allegedly most honest town ... to tempt them into hypocrisy. Naturally, it works, playing up one of dark comedy's basics that people are not to be trusted. The town, however, does learn a lesson; its motto drops a pivotal word, "Lead us into temptation." Otherwise, how else can one claim honesty without enticement?

In *Doubt*, it might be inviting to call the money Hitchcock's proverbial MacGuffin. Yet, the constant presence of Cotten's cash, a comic bank deposit scene (to be addressed shortly), Uncle Charlie's philanthropy, and the flowery closing comments spoken over his elaborate funeral procession all speak towards money making anything okay. Bank notes are the foundation of the establishment—the ongoing target of dark comedy. Be that as it may, there is another interesting parallel between the Twain and Hitchcock works. Without suggesting that this is anything more than a coincidence, the additional analogous point is that the director had felt so slighted by American intellectuals that Wilder's work on *Doubt* had meant enough to him that the opening credits even include a conspicuous acknowledgment to the playwright. Thus, it is difficult not to think of prankster Hitchcock when reading, in part, the letter Twain's mysterious figure has included with the $40,000, especially since the director is also going to find another American town wanting:

> I am a foreigner, and am presently going back to my country, to remain permanently. I am grateful to America ... to one of her citizens—a citizen of Hadleyburg— I am especially grateful to a great kindness done me a year or two ago....[9]

Regardless, attempting to stay within the chalk marks, Hitchcock accents Cotten as the devil coming home to Santa Rosa by having the arriving train belching darker than normal smoke. In true black humor fashion, however, what the audience knows to be a negative situation visually—the Evil One arrives—is juxtaposed with what the soundtrack suggests, upbeat music. Dark comedy is unique along these lines, like Malcolm McDowell warbling "Singin' in the Rain" while beating people to death in *Clockwork Orange* (1971). Regardless, producer Stanley Kramer would later use the darker smoke ploy when his Western train brought another evil figure into *High Noon*'s (1952) soon to be compromised town—a classic McCarthyism allegory about the nefarious times soon to follow *Doubt*. By then, *High Noon*'s blacklisted screenwriter, Carl Foreman, had consciously written this political parable about another flawed and naïve American small town. Twain also surfaces again, too, with Foreman's burg being called *Hadley*ville.

Doubt and its specific uses of humor essentially begin with Cotten's arrival at the home of his beloved sister's family. Naturally, Young Charlie has insisted that Cotten take her room, while she doubles up with her younger

"Uncle Charlie" (Joseph Cotten), or is that the devil come to Santa Rosa? He is flanked by Charles Bates and Edna May Wonacott as nephew and niece; Teresa Wright as Young Charlie is at left. Clarence Muse as a porter stands at right.

sister, Ann (Edna May Wonacott). Ironically, while this girl is reading *Ivanhoe*, Walter Scott's novel of chivalrous knights during the Middle Ages, she is a pint-sized realist who is never impressed with Uncle Charlie.

Moreover, like the Preston Sturges screen sisters in another tale of a less than ideal American small town in *The Miracle of Morgan's Creek* (1944), the younger girl acts the part of a cynical personality comedian. For example, when Uncle Charlie begins to produce gifts, Young Charlie claims to not want anything. With vaudeville timing, Ann immediately responds in the fifth columnist aside tradition of W.C. Fields, "She doesn't mean it. If you ask me, I think she's putting on, like girls in books. The ones that say they don't want anything always get more in the end."

However, the real personality comedians of *Doubt* are yet another Hitchcock comedy team of sorts—the girls' father Joseph Newton (Henry Travers) and the family friend Herbie Hawkins (Hume Cronyn). Indeed, Cronyn's bachelor character is a joke unto himself, only appearing at meal time. In fact, Hitchcock seems to be parodying himself. Besides Herbie's interest in food, he still lives with his mother and is obsessed with crime stories—especially the perfect murder, another Hitchcock fixation.

One might draw a comparison with Hitchcock's use of Basil Radford and Naunton Wayne in *The Lady Vanishes* (1938). A later 1941 *Theatre Arts* article said of the two that they "compositely personify the [British] caricature John Bull—golf and cricket addicts, heavy-witted [fellows]...."[10] Its author, pioneering American film historian Lewis Jacobs, might have likened Travers and Cronyn to a then popular personality comedy type in American pictures—the amateur murder infatuated character. For example, Red Skelton's breakout film was 1941's *Whistling in the Dark*, in which he played a radio murder mystery expert who is kidnapped by real killers to create the perfect assassinations.[11] It was so popular there would be two sequels.

This was the height of pulp fiction mayhem stories. Indeed, the *Doubt* viewer first sees Herbie with his arms full of magazines with "Crime," "Murder," and so forth showing on their covers. When Young Charlie mildly complains about such literature, another family member observes with dark comedy absurdity that crime puzzles are actually good for you. Indeed, much of Uncle Charlie's arrival time is taken up by one of what will be innumerable perfect murder discussions between Joe and Herbie. This extended foray into homicide land first occurs when the duo go out on the porch following supper. The father's best friend is beside himself with admiration for fictional detective Hercule Poirot—"That little Frenchman beats them all ... including Sherlock Holmes." What soon follows is an extended conversation which amounts to another Hitchcock example of personality comedy team shtick doubling as dark comedy—since an actual murderer is now living with these amateur detectives:

7. Shadow of a Doubt (1943) 141

JOE: Best way to commit murder—
HERBIE: I know. I know. Hit them on the head with a blunt instrument.
JOE: Well, it's true, isn't it? Do you think if I wanted to murder you tomorrow, do you think I'd waste my time on hypodermic.... Listen, I'd find out if you were alone. [And] Walk in, [and] hit you on the head with a piece of lead pipe, or a leaded cane.
HERBIE: Where's your planning? Where's your clues?
JOE: I don't want any clues. I want to murder you. What do I want with clues?
HERBIE: Well if you don't have any clues, where's your book?
JOE: I'm not talking about writing books. I'm talking about killing you.
HERBIE: If I'm going to kill you I wouldn't do a dumb thing about hitting you on the head. First of all, I don't like the fingerprint angle. Of course, I could always wear gloves. [I'd] Press your hands against the pipe when you were dead and make you look like a suicide.... Except it doesn't seem hardly likely you'd beat yourself to death with a club. I'd murder you so it didn't look like murder.

The beauty of Hitchcock creating yet another comic team which works with perfect paradoxical plot purposes is again grounded in personality comedian basics. Joe and Herbie, with their little boy names, are childlike figures both obsessed with their play and oblivious to the world around them. Moreover, their ties to dark comedy are hardly limited to the incongruity of murder, or that a killer now lives with them. That is, another key to black humor is the constant presence of death, and the duo are totally impervious to two later rather mundane murder attempts by Cotten on Wright's Young Charlie. For example, Cotten partially saws a backyard stairwell step, hoping his niece will fall to her death. Later he rather clumsily attempts the old asphyxiation in the garage trick, based upon an easily stuck door.

If one were writing a text on killing, there would be very few bookmarks stuck in chapters on sawed steps and asphyxiation, unless it was a survey class. But herein lies the pivotal personality comedian reason—Herbie and Joe are stun gun stupid, as seen in their idea of staging a murder where the victim beats himself to death. Most screen clowns are just that way, be it God-given (which is the kind of god dark comedy would have, if s/he had not already become an atheist), or self-induced idiocy, like potheads Cheech & Chong. Moreover, Hitchcock's pièce de résistance here, and he could not have populated his films with so many comic teams (whether Laurel & Hardy types or screwball couples) without putting just as much thought into it as anything horrid, was casting Henry Travers as Joe the father.

Travers was an actor Hitchcock knew from the London stage and 1930s films—invariably playing amiable senior citizens. The kind of person for whom the term *milquetoast* was invented. Consequently, having such statements coming from him add an incongruously funny factor. Moreover, he is even made the more practical philosopher of murder—"I'd find out if you were alone. Walk in, [and] hit you on the head with a piece of lead pipe" is the topper, especially for period audiences. However, the modern viewer will get a darkly comic bonus; killer Joe here is the same actor who plays "Clarence, the second class angel" in Frank Capra's *It's a Wonderful Life* (1946).

In this comic thriller *Doubt* finally gets back to Uncle Charlie, hidden behind an open newspaper at a time when the oversized tabloids were rightfully called a "broadsheet." In these chauvinistic days the newspaper was seemingly also the domain of men. In fact, in the tony households this sacred chronicle was also often ironed by a wife or servant—news seemed to read better if the facts were nice and crisp.

Cotten's comfortable escape into reading is disturbed, however, when it becomes apparent he has found an upsetting article—possibly something that implicates him in his Bluebeard "career." He immediately sets out to eliminate the piece in yet another example of Hitchcock's disregard for logic. Cotten condescendingly calls Ann over to demonstrate how by a little tearing here and there, a portion of the newspaper can be reduced to a paper house—which also eliminates some unwanted news.

Keep in mind this subterfuge is a bit of "magic" befitting a preschooler, not a cynical 10-year-old going on 20. Plus, he has already insulted her, which she has made no attempt to hide, when upon arrival he gifted her with a tyke's small stuffed animal. With Joe being a simple bank teller, this is hardly a household in which a newspaper merits an ironing. However, it is swiftly apparent that this document is still strictly Dad's domain. Consequently, both daughters express concern over what Uncle Charlie has done, with Young Charlie attempting to rectify things by neatly folding up the newspaper in the hopes that her dad will not notice the missing section.

Things still might have blown over, but Cotten does not destroy the article, and after he has gone up to his room, Wright's character brings him some water. Their feelings towards each other almost feel incestuous, especially after he has privately given her an expensive ring upon his arrival. She speaks again lovingly of their telepathic (twin-like) bond, and how she knows the torn piece of paper involves him. The catalyst for the observation is that she has spied the article in his coat pocket and taken it out—which results in his roughly grabbing it back.

From this point on, her doubts about Uncle Charlie will slowly grow, until she plays detective herself—finding the article at the library. Titled "Where Is the Merry Widower?," it states there is a "Nation-wide search under way for the strangulation of Three Rich Women." The press has named him the "Merry-Widow Murderer," which coincides with the film's periodic use of the dreamlike couples dancing to Franz Lehárs "Merry Widow" waltz, from the operetta of the same name. The newspaper states the latest victim was "Mrs. Bruce Mathewson, former musical comedy star known at the beginning of the century as the 'beautiful Thelma Schenley.'" The time period parallels the composition of the "Merry Widow." There is also the added black humor touch of choosing to kill a comedienne. Finally, one also comes back to the incestuous theme, because the ages of his victims approximate that of his sister with whom he is also unusually close.

Just as Young Charlie has been given a most valuable emerald ring, her mother Emma (also the name of Hitchcock's mother) has received an expensive fur piece from Cotten's character. Regardless, the unnatural relationships, particularly between the two Charlies, have been sometimes noted by Hitchcock authors. However, they do not seem to have done their full dark comedy research. The emerald is the stone of the goddess Venus—which in Latin means love and sexual desire. (How is that for upping Uncle Charlie's creepy meter?) Moreover, the strict Catholic school the fearful young Hitchcock attended specialized in teaching Latin, and the evils of sex.

And remember love does not exist in dark comedy. It is replaced by lust and/or unnatural sexuality. And that is precisely how Cotten looks at the bedroom pictures of his niece. How appropriate for Hitchcock, whose social and sexual mores had been stuck in adolescent amber by the exacting priests and a martinet mother, with whom he lived and to whom he answered well into his twenties. A further dark comedy irony attached to the emerald ring is that the stone also has a *double* paradoxically comic meaning—hope. Thus, the ring scene, more than the "newspaper house," represents hope going down all the toilets and water closet visuals and references which often appealed to Hitchcock's little boy sense of humor, as well as his fondness for ribald jokes. And naturally, the emerald played into Hitchcock's fixation on duality, too.

So why does the ring development play out so badly for Uncle Charlie? Cotten has neglected to notice that the piece of jewelry has an engraved inscription "From T.S. [Thelma Schenley] to B.M. [Bruce Matthewson]." Because of the seriousness of the situation, given Hitchcock's "adult" weakness for bathroom humor and abominable pranks involving laxatives, it is not out of the realm of possibility that Hitchcock had yet again created a crude personal joke of "T.S." as "Total Shit" to "B.M." "bowel movement"—slang dictionary abbreviations not out of keeping with his often naughty little boy comments from the Truffaut interview. The letters would fall under what *New Yorker* critic Anthony Lane has also referred to as Hitchcock's sometimes "clammy-comic touch."[12] One might not note such a "reading" at a first screening, but it is more apparent at a second viewing. And remember, Hitchcock's dark comedy core lines were especially written for *his* enjoyment, well before the video/DVD/Blu-ray era of numerous screenings. Indeed, as noted earlier, the director frequently included dialogue that could only be funny after a second examination, such as *Psycho*'s Norman Bates (Anthony Perkins) observing, "Mother—what's the phrase?—isn't quite herself today." This black humor only later registers when a viewer discovers Mother is mummified—at which time s/he might have even forgotten Perkins' comment.

The lettering joke is merely hypothetical but compatible with Hitchcock's toilet variety of dark humor. Moreover, it is also consistent with his and Uncle Charlie's view of marriage, which the ring suggests. That is, this "institution" to them is "total shit," no more important than a "bowel movement." Keep in mind, in black humor any establishment institution is there to be trashed. That is why Uncle Charlie embarrasses Joe at the bank, with his cracks about embezzlement and doctoring the books when Cotten comes to deposit $40,000. Banks are part of the establishment and not to be trusted, as Uncle Charlie suggests by saying who knows what goes on behind closed bank doors. Hitchcock underlines this by soon repeating the same line with a different intonation. That is, Cotten sarcastically says he is "not interested in money," while the bank president has a near apoplectic moment, "Not interested in money?" One could also broaden the foulness metaphor (total shit) with yet another black humor given (absurdity). Joseph Heller expresses it best in his later novel *Catch-22*—how is it that one moment thinking "Man was matter.... Bury him and he'll rot like other kinds of garbage. The spirit gone, man is garbage."[13]

As long as one is warbling about with provocative dark *Shadow* tidbits, naming an urbane *Bluebeard* "Uncle Charlie" is a brilliant black humor stroke—how can an individual with such an innocuous name be a murderer? One might liken the irony to courtly killer and water controlling John Huston's name in 1974's dark comedy revisionist noir classic *Chinatown*—Noah Cross.[14] Names in the arts are seldom casually given; for instance, *Doubt*'s money-hungry banker is named Mr. Green (an uncredited Edwin Stanley, who was actually president of that Santa Rosa bank). Regardless, one gets the same feeling when considering Charlie Chaplin's *Monsieur Verdoux* (1947), about another Bluebeard marrying and murdering rich older women, played by an iconic actor internationally known as "Charlie." Indeed, some might even think Chaplin was inspired by Hitchcock's work, especially with Cotten sometimes even carrying a cane. However, the gestation period for a Chaplin film was a matter of years. Thus, news that the comedian was going to play such a character had already appeared in a 1941 front page *Hollywood Reporter* article.[15] Of course, the critical success of *Doubt*, to be addressed shortly, might have encouraged the mercurial comedian to stay on course.

As an addendum to the phrase "Uncle Charlie," while Hitchcock was not much of a sports fan, the Pacific Coast League in baseball was then very popular, especially with no Major League clubs west of the Mississippi River. Most studios had their own teams, with frequent professional-amateur games between the stars and the local Los Angeles Angels team. One could compare it to the pro-am golf tournaments which became so popular years later. At a time when baseball *was* the national game, some European filmmakers embraced the sport to help fit in, as immigrants all over the country were doing. Indeed, Austrian-born Billy Wilder, soon to be a multiple Oscar winner, claimed to have learned English by listening to baseball games on the radio! And, whether Hitchcock was aware of it or not, the then popular slang phrase for a curve ball was an "Uncle Charlie." This pitch also has a dual character, seeming about to hit/harm the batter before suddenly dropping down near the plate.

Regardless, between Cotten's newspaper house mistake and missing the ring engraving, one might suggest the murderer was becoming sloppy at his "job." Yet, a random dark comedy comment he later makes, "The whole world's a joke to me," explains a lot about him and Hitchcock. (Fittingly, Hitchcock contemporary Charlie Chaplin, also a fellow student of dark comedy, also frequently made a similar comment, "In the end, everything is a gag." Consequently, in theatre of the absurd black humor, what is the point, or fun, of trying to be logical in this cling-to-the-wreckage modern world? Hitchcock had repeatedly claimed he made dark comedies and related more to his colorful villains (which is especially true versus the stiff detectives who eventually trace Cotten to Santa Rosa). Thus, it is consistent that Hitchcock's production should have slapdash qualities, too. Indeed, Hitchcock forever put down logic in storytelling, and like Chaplin, he believed if the audience caught an error, he had lost them anyway. Eventually, Chaplin also embraced Hitchcock's German Expressionistic fatalism, which always saw life as simply a joke. Yet, one of Hitchcock's mantras was "It's only a movie," words inimical to Chaplin. In fact, for much of the comedian's life, despite his disappointment with the reception of *A Woman of Paris* (1923), he felt his audience could grow with him.[16]

Consequently, one can take Cotten's lackadaisical attitude about the engravings several steps further. For instance, Uncle Charlie justifies killing rich widows because they burn through their late husbands' earnings. Yet, the victim whose ring he has given Young Charlie had been a famous *working* actress (Thelma Schenley), presumably the breadwinner in her relationship with husband Bruce Matthewson. And this seems borne out by the engraving "T.S. to B.M."—it is the woman who has given the man the ring! Yet, the emerald ring Uncle Charlie gives his niece is clearly a delicate lady's ring. It is merely a compounding of Hitchcock's belief in the easy manipulation of his audience.

Moreover, while *Doubt* has always been portrayed as "the devil comes to perfect small town USA," as previously noted, even Hitchcock admitted late in his life that Santa Rosa was at least partly the darker world of Grover's Corners. Though Hitchcock never does a David Lynch *Blue Velvet* (1986), and completely pull back the curtain on Santa Rosa's dry rot, there are inklings. For example, late in the movie when Young Charlie really knows what her uncle is all about, she angrily leaves the dinner table and rushes from the house when Joe and Herbie start one of their time-warp vaudevillian sketches on murder. Uncle Charlie immediately follows her and drags her into a bar that looks like something out of Pottersville in *It's a Wonderful Life* (1946).

The dive is right off the cotton candy main street, seemingly seconds from the house. And the exterior shot angle of a neon sign only reveals the term "cock." Moreover, the waitress is a tormented high school friend of Young Charlie, only she acts like a somnambulist slumming from *The Cabinet of Dr. Caligari* (1920). Yet, the girl somehow does not seem unique to the town; Hitchcock has just not visited her neighborhood. Indeed, in William Rothman's excellent *Hitchcock: The Murderous Gaze*, which devotes a chapter to *Shadow*, he describes Cotten as periodically acting "like a somnambulist, too."[17] And in Uncle Charlie's bar conversation with his niece, he calls her a sleepwalker. One gets the sense if you open the wrong door it is "Hello German Expressionism," or a comically twisted episode of *The Twilight Zone* (cue Rod Serling's voice). Moreover, after seeing the noirish, blighted East Coast from which Uncle Charlie has arrived, anything good about Santa Rosa does not seem real. It is like one has gone through a portal to a fairy tale like *Brigadoon*, the Scottish tale of a village that appears for only one day every hundred years. (Moreover, the movie never conveys we are in the midst of World War II.)

Returning to the somnambulist waitress, and the suggestion of a darker Santa Rosa, when she sees Young Charlie's ring it somewhat awakens her, and she says, fittingly for this dark comedy setting, "I'd just die for a ring like that"—talk about the appropriate customer! The waitress then shares her instinctual awareness of gems, as if she has come to her present plight because of them. One might even imagine a noirish victimization, like *Blue Velvet*'s Isabella Rossellini's need for help/protection and/or sexual gratification in another American small town. Though Cotten might have come to Santa Rosa as the devil, it is not as if he is without strategically placed wicked way stations.

Moreover, Wright is moved to threaten to kill her formerly beloved Uncle Charlie. Playing upon the twin philosophy, she has now embraced his dark side. One might argue, however, this is a desperate situation, involving a killer. Yet, the potential for homegrown violence in corny small town America has always been a source of macabre humor. For example, one of *Doubt*'s screenwriters, besides Wilder, was Sally Benson, who wrote the story upon which *Meet Me in St. Louis* (1944, the classic American musical with the small town ambience) was based. However, even this film sometimes has a disturbing dark subtext to it. As early as 1976, British film scholar Geoffrey Nowell-

Smith stated in a lecture this was best exemplified by the scene following Judy Garland's attempt to comfort her upset little screen sister Margaret O'Brien.[18] It was Christmas time back in that era in which the "Merry Widow" was written. The banking father of the family is moving them to New York sometime after the holidays.

Garland's attempt to ease O'Brien's hurt, despite a poignant rendition of "Have Yourself a Merry Little Christmas," fails. The two are overlooking the family's courtyard, which contains several snowmen. The still unsettled little O'Brien runs into the yard with a shovel and begins to hack away at the snowmen. As she chops, her crying refrain is that if they cannot go to New York with the family, no one else can have them. Nowell-Smith's point was that if this musical melodrama was remade today, it would probably be a new age horror film, with the youngster hacking away at father.... Then, with a mischievous smile, Nowell-Smith also suggested it might have happened in a 1940s noir world, too.

With Hitchcock's dark comedy, whether it was a ring engraved with "B.M." initials or Joe and Herbie forever talking murder while a strangler slept in a daughter's bedroom, the director seems more inclined than ever to showcase how easy it is to fool screen characters, and by extension, the audiences watching them. The dark comedy theme of man as beast is a perfect fit for Uncle Charlie. And like Young Charlie, many people are bored and want the excitement a "mysterious stranger" can bring, even though here he is a roving (or is that "raving"?) relative. Consequently, the not overly intelligent creatures in Hitchcock's world (inside and outside his films), are all the more easily deceived.

In this case, only Young Charlie really figures it out, linking the double factor between them all the more. Indeed, at the end of the film, when Cotten attempts to dispatch her yet again, she inadvertently kills him. Granted, it is part self-defense and part accident, when he attempts to push her from the train, and in the struggle it is Uncle Charlie who is shoved under the wheels of an oncoming locomotive.

Enough, however, for the moment on Cotten and Wright. *Doubt* belongs as much to his personality comedian duo, another doubling with Travers' Joe and Cronyn's Herbie. They steal the picture as they wonder in and out as the dumbest of amateur sleuths. While their other murder seminar dialogues are not as drawn out as the earlier example, the routines keep coming. For example, Herbie gives Joe some coffee with a touch of soda and the comic dialogue eventually ends as follows:

> JOE: Well, you don't say. I never tasted a thing. Of course, I might not notice the soda [as a rule].
> HERBIE: [You'd] Notice the soda more than you'd notice the poison. Heh, for all you knew, you might just as well have been dead.

In this American film, Joe and Herbie seem more feeble-minded than the comedy teams with which Hitchcock so often populated his British pictures. For example, the cricket obsessed duo of *The Lady Vanishes*, Caldicott (Naunton Wayne) and Charters (Basil Radford), are a regular pair of slumming professors compared to Joe and Herbie. By the end of *The Lady Vanishes*, Caldicott and Charters have come to realize that their observations about the do or die nature of their beloved sport actually better apply to the approach of World War II. Moreover, and most impressively, the pair actually play a large part in making it possible for the film's title character, Dame May Whitty's spy Miss Froy, to escape. Plus, who knew Caldicott and Charters would also be crack shots when the time came? In contrast, Joe and Herbie *never* realize the truth, let alone protect Young Charlie from her murdering uncle. Joe and Herbie remain stupid squared throughout. Plus, even when Caldicott and Charters struggle, they do it on their own playtime. Joe is a henpecked husband (more Hitchcock trashing of marriage), and mama's boy Herbie comes up with all his perfect murders while living with mother. He is Norman Bates in the making. One could argue that while future American Hitchcock comedy twosomes seem smarter, the director was having more personal in-joke fun with *Shadow*. After all, so much was made of the setting being an *average American* town.

The dark comedy brilliance of *Doubt* is directly connected to all the hullabaloo then and now, about how the film was finally Hitchcock's first American movie—about the perfect wholesome town. Granted, his previous American films, like *Rebecca*, *Foreign Correspondence* (both 1940), *Suspicion* (1941) and *Saboteur* (1942), had British settings and/or were propaganda pictures for the war effort. Of course, that ignores how historians disregarded Hitchcock's derailing of All-American screwball comedy in *Mr. and Mrs. Smith* (1941).

Still, *Doubt* was about shooting on location, in part, in Sweet Santa Rosa, and supposedly getting all warm and fuzzy about Americana. But as the previous pages have demonstrated, with Santa Rosa's parallels to other American literary towns with frayed edges and festering foundations, Hitchcock still applied his down-on-humanity bag of tricks to this setting. Moreover, it was a real sucker punch. As already implied, in this particular film he managed to dumb down his normal take on humanity *even more* as applied to America. To paraphrase a Woody Allen line from *Play It Again, Sam* (1972), when he is encouraged to say something he cannot believe another party will believe— "They bought it." Hitchcock has arguably created another inside dark humor joke just for himself.

This only enhances it as his greatest film. No wonder it was his own personal favorite. Plus, the people of the earlier Twain and Wilder towns eventually, one in life and the other in death, at least learned Hitchcock's

7. Shadow of a Doubt (1943)

ongoing dark comedy message—"it's all a joke"—about life. Instead, Santa Rosa is an upscale DogPatch, USA, à la Al Capp's hugely popular period newspaper comic strip—*Li'l Abner*, about a hillbilly community without a clue.

Of course, maybe I am being too hard on good old gullible America. Winston Churchill once said, "The best argument against democracy is a five-minute conversation with the average voter." Ironically, this perspective was given a left-handed endorsement in a 2002 BBC survey on Great Britain's hundred greatest individuals in their long storied history. Churchill was chosen number one. However, in a photo finish, he was nearly beaten out by the third choice. Who would that have been—Shakespeare, Dickens, Darwin, Isaac Newton ... maybe even Chaplin or Hitchcock? Nope. The answer is Princess Diana. Let that soak in a moment, if you are still conscious. One might liken it to a Robin Williams concert ad-lib at a very upscale smoking audience of decades ago, "Ah, more smoke. I want to die."

Ironically, one could dust off *Blackmail*'s (1929) painting of the accusingly pointing jester and apply it here, too. Except in that first British sound film, eventually the clown's satire is understood in a broader context. But in *Doubt* Hitchcock hoodwinks everyone. Of course, Young Charlie and a detective with whom she eventually teams have a kindergarten-level, mind-numbing exchange near the close.

> YOUNG CHARLIE: He [her uncle] hated the whole world. You know, he said that people like us had no idea what the world was really like.
> DETECTIVE: It's not quite as bad as all that. Sometimes it needs a lot of watching. It seems to go crazy every now and then, like your Uncle Charlie.

The *New York Times* was a rare period publication to call the film on it: "the bathos is enough to knock you down."[19]

Hitchcock then underlines the asinine ludicrousness of these words by using dark comedy to take down another establishment institution—the church. In closing, the director increases the soundtrack volume of an unseen minister praising Cotten. It is heard over the long shot of Uncle Charlie's funeral procession. Cotten's philanthropic community action cover has sainted him to Santa Rosa. Consequently, the religious leader closes with a final dose of the genre's use of absurdity. One hears Uncle Charlie inspiring a statement about the "beauty of the souls" like his, and how "the sweetness of their characters lives on with us forever."

Before circling the wagons around some of *Doubt*'s period reviews, which document how Hitchcock's typical dark comedy tricks deserve added kudos ratcheting up the skewering of small town America, a few additional genre examples merit including. First, as noted earlier in the text, Patricia Collinge's often moving mother Emma is one of the last positive Hitchcock matriarchs—with his own mother dying during the production. (In Pat Hitchcock O'Connell's biography of her mother Alma, she said her father's own mother only shared the same name.[20]) Regardless, despite Collinge's poignant love for her brother Charlie, her description of his childhood accident, though innocently shared, has a macabre, almost laugh-out-loud nature to it. One actually almost feels sympathetic for Uncle Charlie. She describes at length how he suffered a skull fracture in a biking accident as a boy—the same day he had his picture taken for school. It resulted in a long recovery, with the formerly bookish Charlie now needing

> to get into mischief to blow off steam. He didn't do too much reading after that, let me tell you ... when the pictures came home, how mama cried ... she wondered if he'd ever be the same.

Gosh, do you think Emma and Charlie's mom was onto something? Plus, Emma tells her long tale in front of the whole family, including future Uncle "Killer" Charlie.

Second, a dark comedy MO is providing body blows to establishment institutions, such as the aforementioned example of religion—which Hitchcock mocks at *Doubt*'s close. However, the movie is peppered with such digs both direct and subtle. An example of the former would best be served by a Sunday service Uncle Charlie skipped. When the family comes home he asks his niece, "How was church, Charlie? Count the house? Turn anybody away?"

Cotten treats the institution like an entertainment business, mixed with the crutch of hope. Yet, he does spread money around for cover. Thus, please do not kill the genre messenger. But *Doubt* consistently showcases religion as the perfect scam franchise. However, if major donations have been made, à la Uncle Charlie, one might get a flashy exit. Plus, one does have their personal IOU for eternal life ... without even the need to offer up testimonials from satisfied customers. *Doubt*'s unnamed minister, like Banker Green, should have been christened Green, too.

A more muted assault comes from Uncle Charlie using Saint Paul's name in a toast. There is a personal in-joke in this saint's name. It is not just Hitchcock possibly kidding the fact that he himself was a budding alcoholic. The director was not religious but ironically, many such people, such as dark comedy atheists Mark Twain and Kurt Vonnegut, also seem to be well-versed in the "good book." And I believe "Hitch" goes further than the response a surprised visitor received from the dying W.C. Fields, when he caught the nihilist reading a Bible, "I'm looking for loopholes." How did Hitchcock go Fields one better? What follows is a paraphrasing of a line from John Russell Taylor's family authorized biography of the director, *Hitch: The Life and Times of Alfred Hitchcock* (1978). Upon seeing a boy talking with a priest, the director leaned out of a moving car and yelled, "Run, little boy, run for your life!" Hyperbole or not, it rings as true for his films as the hyperbolic tale of a young Hitchcock being briefly jailed as punishment by his father.

7. Shadow of a Doubt (1943)   151

So what about Saint Paul? As the preceding pages have documented, Hitchcock's art was invariably down on marriages. This was also pivotal to Saint Paul—the Bible's main cheerleader on the subject. However, Paul is also pertinent here for another reason. In Romans 7:15–17, this righteous figure might have offered more insight about Uncle Charlie detesting religion and dark comedy's unmasking the absurdity of church solace: "I don't understand myself at all.... I know perfectly well what I am doing is wrong.... But I can't help myself."[21] That is the best a headliner saint has got? Why even Norm Macdonald's advice about the rope and rickety stool stores makes more sense than that.

Third, while the chapter has done much to demonstrate that the idealized Santa Rosa was not so different from Twain's Hadleyburg, or Wilder's Grover's Corners, space has not allowed itself all the chances to demonstrate that Hitchcock's town had the same superstitions of not wanting to be tempted. For example, when Joe shows Uncle Charlie to Young Charlie's room, while his niece doubles up with her sister, he makes a gesture to toss his hat on the bed. Yet, Joe's response initially keeps him from doing it. It was once believed a hat on a bed meant death would soon follow. Joe observes, I just "don't believe in inviting trouble." However, Hitchcock gives it a dark comedy twist by having it happen—since Uncle Charlie tosses his fedora on the bed as soon as Joe leaves, and will die before you know it. Such gestures represent more of Hitchcock's black humor foreshadowing, which, of course, only he can fully enjoy at the initial screenings.

Fourth, the text has posited that Hitchcock was not really out to create that idealized American small town. Indeed, just his admiration for Wilder's Grover's Corners blows that out of the water. Still, it is a nice little story which has been propagated through the years and then topped off with—*Hitchcock even went on location to find such a place*. Yet, even a modicum of period research compromises that perspective.

Ironically, one of America's most down home publications, the pictorial *LIFE* magazine, somehow manages to punch the hole in that perspective, while still celebrating Hitchcock's alleged goal. The director who normally hated to go on location was essentially forced to do so—which is all captured in the title to *LIFE*'s coverage of *Doubt*—"$5,000 PRODUCTION: Hitchcock Makes Thriller under WPB [War Production Board] Order On New Sets."[22] *Doubt* "was one of the first movies to be produced under the Government restrictions placing a $5,000 ceiling on new materials used for sets...."[23] While there were many benefits from going on location, such as discovering the scene stealing screen sister of Wright (10-year-old Edna May Wonacott), Hitchcock was *forced* to use Santa Rosa over cost restrictions.

There are additional qualifiers which go against the grain of Hitchcock's goal of making a rah-rah, average small town American picture, but they add more to Hitchcock's insider dark comedy. How did period reviewers rate *Doubt*? The critiques were mixed to good, though *Doubt*'s closing stumble reduced its dark comedy for a few critics to more of a bruise. A small minority of reviewers, such as the *New York Post*'s Archer Winsten, did agree with the *New York Times*' suggestion that the ending was rather simplistic blathering, after much of the picture had anticipated some Theatre of the Absurd situations.[24] After all, if Uncle Charlie had not attempted to kill her, and then died in the attempt, Young Charlie had made an accord with him—a pact with the devil—to keep his secret if he would just leave town. But the public generally bought it.

However, it was obvious Cotten's killing ways would continue. Indeed, one of his sister's wealthy widowed friends, Mrs. Potter, was *dying* to get better acquainted with him. She had even booked passage on Uncle Charlie's exiting train to San Francisco. She would be an easy mark—one less "animal" to ruin his idealized "Merry Widow" dancing apparition of the past. Regardless, would not Wright's pact have made her character an accomplice to murder(s)? She was flirting with becoming a true twin of her uncle. Moreover, as endearing as Young Charlie often is, her early lazy teenage boredom reminds one of writer Lillian Hellman's description of actress Norma Shearer—"a face unclouded by thought." Still, she could not be a "twin" to her uncle without figuring it out.

At the close, when Young Charlie decides to share everything with the cipher of a detective she *might* become romantically involved with, it could be *Blackmail* all over again. If their tryst did not work out, he could always hold it over her, just as the *Blackmail* detective lover could hold the real story of the artist's death over that heroine. Until an *Eternal Sunshine of the Spotless Mind* (2004) scenario can truly create a brain wash, or even a spin cycle to reverse it, these heroines are screwed. Ultimately, *Doubt* works for the same reason much of Hitchcock works, "The profound unease we feel in identifying with an evil character in a movie is the recognition that we may be capable of such evil."[25] Absorbingly, Kate Cameron's *New York Daily News* critique of *Doubt* anticipates this observation, without quite being able to articulate it in a black humor manner.[26] However, while the house of Hitchcock was honing the genre, the world was going to catch up with his belief that all his films were essentially dark comedies.

8

Rope (1948)
Film Two of Hitchcock's Nietzschean Dark Comedy Trilogy

> High from the opening shot in which a young man gives a last gurgling gasp as he's being garroted with a piece of rope, Hitchcock rivets audience attention ... it is an uncomfortably arresting psychological study—*New York Journal-American* (August 27, 1948)[1]

Despite there being three Hitchcock films between *Shadow of a Doubt* (1943, see the last chapter), and *Rope*—*Lifeboat* (1944), *Spellbound* (1945), and *Notorious* (1946)—*Rope* plays like a sequel to *Shadow*. Though weakly denied at the time, the picture is a variation upon the 1924 Leopold and Loeb murder case.[2] This particular homicide is arguably Hollywood's favorite "crime of the century," with regard to inspiring deviations upon the same theme in other pictures.[3] Hitchcock's take on the murder remains the most riveting.

This case, which has so creatively resonated with filmmakers throughout the years, involved Nathan Leopold (1904–1971) and Richard Loeb's (1905–1936) self described "thrill" killing of 14-year-old Robert "Bobby" Franks on May 21, 1924. Leopold and Loeb were child prodigy lovers from wealthy Chicago families. At the time of the murder, the duo were still teenagers themselves ... yet both had already graduated from the University of Michigan, and Leopold was, ironically, a University of Chicago law student.

Fittingly, given their off-the-charts intelligence, Leopold and Loeb believed themselves Nietzschean Ubermensch/supermen, after the teachings of German philosopher Friedrich Nietzsche (1844–1900). That is, Nietzsche wrote that superior people were neither governed by mankind's normal laws, nor subject to guilt over anything they might do. Killing the boy was a chilling application of this theoretician's signature belief. (*Shadow*'s Bluebeard "Uncle

Charlie" would have been right at home with the "boys.") Fittingly, Nietzsche and Hitler are also referenced in *Rope*.

The murderers and their victim all lived in the aristocratic Kenwood district on Chicago's South Side. Indeed, Franks was a neighbor and second cousin of Loeb, so it was easy to offer the unsuspecting young teen a ride home on that May Wednesday afternoon. While the two young men (both just short of twenty) had planned the crime for months, the child was randomly selected. After Leopold and Loeb lured Franks into their rented car, they stuffed a sock into his mouth and the youngster was dispatched by several chisel blows to the head. It has never been conclusively proven which of the two men sat in the car's backseat and administered the fatal attack. Each of them later blamed the other for the actual murder.

After the killing, they stripped Frank of his clothes and poured acid on his remains to make identification more difficult. After hiding the body in a nature preserve, they sent a ransom note to Franks' family. This action was a pure diversionary tactic, since the duo had no money needs and ransom was never the purpose of their Nietzsche experiment. However, the body was discovered before a $10,000 ransom was paid. Moreover, their "perfect crime" soon unraveled. Leopold left his eyeglasses near the body, and an unusual frame hinge mechanism allowed the police to trace them directly to the law student. The two killers were soon arrested.

Hitchcock's version of the Leopold and Loeb murder is transformed to a 1940s fashionable New York penthouse with a sweeping view of Manhattan's skyline and another pair of lovers—Phillip Morgan (Farley Granger) and Brandon Shaw (John Dall). The film opens just as they strangle to death old friend David Kentley (Dick Hogan). Here the couple are in their mid-twenties and more sophisticated, except for their movie opening parlor trick. The victim is then placed in an Italian antique coffin-like wooden chest, just before there is to be a party.

However, before addressing Hitchcock's use of dark humor and a farce-like atmosphere, several curiosities about the production need to be addressed. First, *Rope* is an unusual non-commercial pick as Hitchcock's first venture as a producer. The director was blowing smoke when he later told François Truffaut, in the latter's groundbreaking book-length Hitchcock interview, that the movie made money and "had good notices."[4] *Rope* laid an egg at the box office. Indeed, it was occasionally banned in smaller towns, and some foreign distributers even requested replacements. Period reviews were mixed at best. Making it Hitchcock's first Technicolor film made even less sense; while the canned theatre set was ironically lush and inviting in its rich hues, this further drove up costs.

Second, despite the controversial subject matter, Hitchcock and some of the critics were more interested in what might be called the director's sec-

8. Rope (1948)

As one begins *Rope*'s examination, (1948), this still provides a rare showcasing of its principal players, from right to left: Hitchcock, Jimmy Stewart, Joan Chandler, Cedric Hardwicke, Constance Collier, John Dall, Douglas Dick, Edith Evanson, and Farley Granger.

ond major film experiment. That is, in *Lifeboat* he challenged himself to see if he could make a picture in the most confined space possible. In *Rope* the test was to both make the movie in real time and to piece it together as if it were one continuous shot. Thus, it was filmed in uninterrupted takes of ten minutes (the amount of raw stock a period movie camera magazine could hold), with the breaks being covered by someone or something suddenly coming in front of the camera to suggest it was one long take. Moreover, this meant actors had to navigate through a two-and-a-half-room set as walls, furniture, and film equipment were continually moving out of their way and screen visibility.

Plus, if any mistake was made, from a forgotten line to dancing into an object that should not have been there—the *whole* ten-minute take had to be redone. Naturally, this greatly added to the tension, à la Peter O'Toole's character shouting in *My Favorite Year* (1982), "I'm not an actor, I'm a movie star!" (Normally, simple movie retakes are easy.) Ironically, the added stress, however, did favor actors Granger and Dall. Despite their characters' belief in being superior, the killing put a strain on the duo, particularly Granger's Phillip, who committed the rope strangulation, while Dall's Brandon held the victim. Consequently, any increased worry contributed by Hitchcock's production experiment would undoubtedly have strengthened their "acting."

Third, in a homophobic era, when even the American Medical Association considered homosexuality abnormal, there is little attempt to disguise the fact that Phillip and Brandon, if not glaringly gay, are obviously a couple. This might also have contributed to low attendance. Of course, one could justify this by saying *Rope* was merely being factual to the Leopold and Loeb case. Moreover, Hitchcock might also have been attracted to tweaking a real "thrill" murder to better disguise and/or justify his own misanthropic nature. As a footnote to the casting, as noted earlier, Hitchcock frequently selected closeted gay actors, since he felt they had to "act" 24/7. Both Granger and Dall were gay in real life.

Though Hitchcock was *hardly* an Italian Neo-realist, one must also note that *Rope* also appeared in the midst of a film movement defined by long takes and playing with real time. Plus, shortly after the horrors of World War II, more people, to a degree, had embraced the director's misanthropic nature. Thus, cinema was ready for provocative new subjects done in provocative new ways, even transplanted to Hitchcock's Hollywood.

While *Rope*'s tone could have made it a perfect follow-up to *Shadow*, the director did a 180-degree flip from his 1930s British films with regard to how he presented dark comedy and farce. This is best exemplified by comparing *Rope* to *Secret Agent* (1936, see Chapter Four). The topsy-turvydom begins with the beginnings. Both films essentially start in la-de-da high society settings with wealthy couples. However, the storylines are then twisted mirror opposites.

Secret Agent quickly provides viewers with screwball comedy-like banter between a flirting heterosexual couple. The audience's expectations are vague, yet one is led to believe a deserving unknown enemy will be killed by the picture's close. In contrast, *Rope* immediately begins with the killing of a known undeserving *friend*, whose death parallels the senseless Theatre of the Absurd killing in Albert Camus' novel *The Stranger* (1946). Moreover, instead of *Agent*'s spy backdrop, once the *Rope* victim is comfortably tucked away in the casket-like box, a skewed farce/party will begin, also with witty banter. Plus, there is a sexual ambience to each scene—except in *Rope* it is driven, at least for Brandon, by the almost orgasmic thrill of taking a life. However, while a "husband" will soon surprisingly appear in *Secret Agent*, à la the helter skelter traditional world of farce, *Rope*'s corpse will quietly rest, as *expected* guests begin to arrive. Of course, the audience wonders *if* a surprise will occur, as in a possible sudden opening of the box. The tension is even satirized by Brandon's dark comedy quip to Phillip about dead David having a Lazarus moment.

The party preparation of killing the first guest is pure black humor, with David first getting a drink, so even his evening is not totally ruined. Regardless, given Hitchcock's perspective on humanity, one can assume he would have loved the signature scene in Clint Eastwood's later *Unforgiven* (1992). A failure of a wannabe gun for hire, the Schofield Kid (Jaimz Woolvett), who has bragged about his shootings, gets sick after what turns out to be his first killing. Ultimately, to justify it to Eastwood's veteran killer, he says the victim "had it coming." The battle-scarred, unvarnished Eastwood straightforwardly responds, "Kid, we all have it coming." However, it seems "Uncle Charlie" Hitchcock would have felt no pain about dispatching *Rope*'s David. Indeed, from Hitchcock's extreme Catholic upbringing, can there be any doubt that we all have coming?

Now for the remainder of the *Rope* party there will be frequent dark comedy repartee, some of it droll, while other examples will fall to Hitchcock's propensity for black humor from an adolescent perspective. However, before one gets to cataloging them in all their gray to black hues, Hitchcock still provides a wealth of wit which would not be out of place in a standard farce. One might even compare it to a *39 Steps* review line from celebrated Latin American author Jorge Luis Borges, "He [Hitchcock] has invented episodes, inserted wit and mischief where the original contained only … [seriousness]."[5] And why not—*Rope* does take place at a polished party gathering of several well-heeled New Yorkers. Moreover, like his beloved Buster Keaton, Hitchcock will occasionally find time for parody, with nothing having to do regarding that fellow in the box.

Consequently, before getting into the sticky wicket of dark comedy, Hitchcock has a comically well-scripted soirée/farce which could be broken into three general comedy categories. First, one must start with the key guest, besides David in the box—publisher Rupert Cadell (Jimmy Stewart), who almost doubles as a biting personality comedian. He was the former housemaster to Brandon and Phillip, as well as their Nietzsche guru. He is a wannabe Oscar Wilde on acid. Rupert is late to the party, and Brandon provides the perfect sarcastic profile to another guest, "Rupert's extremely radical. Do you know he selects his books on the assumption that people can not only read but actually can think?"

When Stewart's Rupert arrives, he does not disappoint, and is miles away from his pre-war Frank Capra innocent. Shortly after his entrance, he is introduced to another guest, the victim's snobbish fiancée, Janet Walker (Joan Chandler), who is about to become part of the most twisted of farcical scenarios. When she makes small talk with Rupert, the publisher shares that Brandon had previously spoken of her. Curious, and with a touch of arrogance, she asks if Brandon had done her justice. As quick as Groucho in *Duck Soup* (1933), Rupert replies, "Do you deserve justice?"

Brandon and Phillip's practical housekeeper Mrs. Wilson (Edith Evanson) is an older, endearingly favorite aunt type, who has always had something of a crush on Rupert. Thus, she has gone out of her way to get Stewart's favorite pâté. When she tells him about it, he casually observes he does not like that pâté anymore. However, unlike as with Janet, he does not let the wallop linger. He is not so thoughtful with Brandon, who stumbles over his words upon greeting his Nietzschean hero. Rupert matter of factly digs, "You always did stutter when you were excited." Curmudgeon is his style.

However, Rupert's interactions with Janet and yet another guest, the victim's aunt, Mrs. Atwater (Constance Collier), are an extended slide into part two—movie parody. This both allows Hitchcock to spoof films, which he had done as far back as *Blackmail* (1929), and is also the category into which his cameos would fit. Regardless, Janet has a thing about James Mason but ultimately prefers Cary Grant. Those actors seem to remind both women they have just seen an excellent film starring Ingrid Bergman, with a title like *Something*. They then vacuously ramble on about this "something" movie.

Before moving on to Rupert's coup de grâce of this whole cinema routine, Hitchcock has scored parody points on four levels. First, the picture the women are struggling to remember is the director's own *Notorious* (1943), which starred the three aforementioned actors. Second, being an extraordinary picture—heralded both then and now—it implies even a film classic is unimportant, with neither viewing character recalling its name. Third, despite the detail he put into his pictures, it again echoes one of Hitchcock's signature self-deprecating expressions, "It's only a movie." Fourth, it also allows the director to indirectly apply his misogynistic/misanthropic views under cover of a nearly incoherent movie conversation. (Moreover, Mrs. Atwater could not have been more of a definitive target for the director's alter ego from *Shadow*, Uncle Charlie.)

Consequently, how does Stewart's Rupert further spoofingly derail both the movies and the women? He is as patient as a captain turning a super tanker. Yet, once this chitchat to nowhere ends, he earnestly seems to restart it with his own cinema experience: "I once went to the movies and saw Mary Pickford." However, when asked what the film was he quickly displays his scorn for them by burlesquing their "something" mantra when attempting to recall the Pickford moniker. Consequently, he has sideswiped both the women and the topic at hand, the movies, in another four-part way. First, Pickford had not starred in a movie since 1933; how important could moving pictures be if he had not attended one in 15 years? Second, even though it had been that long, Pickford, with Charlie Chaplin and Douglas Fairbanks, Sr., were silent cinema legends. Moreover, her then marriage to Fairbanks had made them what is still considered Hollywood's First Couple. Consequently, this suggests he had never seen the movie but felt he could better trash the industry by flattening pioneering stars. Third, it also allowed Hitchcock to use more self-deprecating parody, because he revered the pre-talkies, and still essentially saw himself at his best as a silent director. Fourth, the mere fact the women were so far out of their element they did not even seem to inhabit the words they spoke further flayed films. One half expected to see subtitles of their thoughts confessing just that, as Woody Allen later did in *Annie Hall* (1977).

As a footnote to Hitchcock's films usually spoofing the movies and/or himself, one would think his most compressed examples would be the cameos, lasting only seconds. Yet his definitive squeeze play example transpires in *Shadow of a Doubt*, when Teresa Wright's little sister is saying her prayers. The serious bespectacled preteen's "God bless" requests are all to be assumed, except one. She mentions Mama, Papa, the president (this is during World War II), and Captain Midnight (a popular period action adventure radio star). But she also names Veronica Lake, the film star known by her peekaboo hairstyle. Though Lake's career was short, she was arguably one of cinema's most provocative sexy leading ladies. To paraphrase Woody Allen, "She could make men's teeth sweat."

This is the last person the girl would have added. She did not even include her sister, whom the child no doubt saw as Lake-like, using her beauty and misdirection dialogue to get what she wanted. However, it gets better, Lake is *the* Hitchcock type, the beautiful cool-to-men blonde. Indeed, Lake is even best known for the genre famous for this type—film noir, to which *Doubt* is a precursor. Consequently, Hitchcock has dropped in the briefest bit of self-parody, too.

Regardless, *Rope*'s four-part movie rebuffing by the seemingly witless two women arguably motivated Brandon's best non murder-related crack. Shortly after the two women stopped their Gracie Allen squared routine, Mrs. Atwater observed, "Do you know when I was a girl I used to read quite a bit." Dall's Brandon, like his mocking former mentor, sneered, "We all do strange things in our childhood." Again, the seemingly widowed wealthy older Mrs. Atwater is like a template for all those women "Uncle Charlie" was so anxious to dispatch.

Be that as it may, *Rope*'s third common Hitchcock bit of comic shtick which is not necessarily tied to black humor surfaces here with the frequent controlling mother. Indeed, in this case, the mother in question was to have been a guest, but proves to be a bothersome presence just the same. The alleged catalyst for the gathering was tied to David's father visiting Brandon and Phillip's penthouse to examine some first edition books with which Dall's character was willing to part. It also coincided with Brandon and Phillip preparing to leave New York for a country getaway, which would also allow Granger to practice for a forthcoming piano concert tour.

Granted, the underpinnings of the party were really a dark comedy celebration of murder, which would be topped off by having David's parents arrive shortly after the deed. Yet, the dig at controlling mothers mixed nicely with another Hitchcock theme—relationships just do not work in his world—as was the case in the Hitchcock-favored Keaton silents. This is apparent when David's father, Mr. Kentley (Sir Cedric Hardwicke) arrives. Escorting his sister, Mrs. Atwater, he is obviously an antiheroic husband also controlled by his wife. Even Hitchcock's last sane sweet cinema mother, *Shadow*'s Emma Newton (Patricia Collinge), always keeps her meek and mild bank clerk husband, Henry Travers, in comic line.

With Mr. Kentley's opening lines, one has a full picture of the henpecked world through which he has long suffered. One is immediately reminded of the period female-dominated comic antiheroic males of James Thurber, especially the Mr. and Mrs. Monroe stories, or the more famous "Secret Life of Walter Mitty."[6] The title of the first Thurber anthology including "Mitty" seems to say it all, *My World—And Welcome to It*.[7]

Rope's Mr. Kentley shares that "Mother, as usual" is sick. This time it is a cold, and he hopes that David arrives soon, because she wants him to call her. Since Janet is engaged to David, she gently reminds her never-to-be father-in-law that her fiancé is their only child. Mr. Kentley promptly responds, "He's my only child, too, but I'm willing to let him grow up, too." Her repeated calls throughout the party, both to the penthouse and other locations, eventually become more justified. However, while this type of behavior usually reminds viewers of some controlling person, and a comic shrew, soon one guiltily flirts with an Uncle Charlie moment.

This also reminds one of Hitchcock's real life relationship with his own mother, and how mothers were portrayed in his subsequent movies. Though there is a father here and in the earlier *Doubt*, the male parent of his dominant characters is often missing, just as young Hitchcock's father died ... or as the old punch line goes, "maybe he was just using that as an excuse." However, there is still something absorbing about these three Hitchcock norms which manage to surface at this farcical party from hell.

First, even Stewart's generally misanthropic, late-to-the-party, twisted comedian/amateur sleuth can still manage to deliver seemingly innocuous, lightly amusing lines in awkward situations. For example, "I'm in an embarrassing situation. I seem to be the only one having a good time." Yet, this chapter will soon be itemizing first Dall's and then Stewart's much more common nihilistically dark comedy digs, to the point of even encouraging other guests to join in.

Second, with regard to parody, *Sight and Sound*'s later application of reaffirmation parody to the dark comedy horror film *Scream* (1996)—going "beyond parody into post-modernism"—applies here, too.[8] Put less obtusely,

8. Rope (1948)

Rope comically toys with explaining contemporary terror by blurring the differences between art and reality. Thus, Hitchcock's black humor murder story is self-referential parody. That is, while there is a dead body in *Rope*'s coffin-like box on which people are eating, several guests are also discussing another thriller, *Notorious*, by the same director.

Third, while Hitchcock's seemingly autobiographical mother complex can be played for safe comedy in which women control antiheroic males, be they mothers or wives—the worm can turn. After all, even a Thurber husband eventually gets a miserable mate committed to a mental institution in "The Unicorn in the Garden," and Hitchcock's whole filmography leads directly to what Norman Bates does to Mommy in *Psycho* (1960).[9] Few would ever do so, but by merely making one ponder the idea, Hitchcock has implicated viewers. And this chapter is just now coming to *Rope*'s real blitz of black comedy.

Period critics were iffy on how audiences would respond. For instance, the *New York Times* observed, "...the emphasis on the macabre in this story is frightfully intense," while *Variety* added, "[The] Theme of a thrill murder, done for no reason but to satisfy a sadistical urge and intellectual vanity, is in questionable taste."[10] This precisely captured the spirit of 1948 audiences, who stayed away just as they did with another artfully done dark comedy from the same year—Preston Sturges' *Unfaithfully Yours*. Yet how much the world has changed in the interim. My college students treat both *Rope* and its dialogue like comic business as usual. Indeed, even forty-plus years ago Woody Allen's *Annie Hall* character attributes this crack to Leopold and Loeb: "I think there's too much burden placed on the orgasm, you know, to make up for empty areas in life."

This film, more than any other in the text, embraces the fundamental elements of dark comedy. What could be more *absurd* than killing someone like a lab experiment in a philosophy course? Then, why not increase the absurdity by throwing a party and essentially using the coffin-like box as a serving table? However, why stop there? Invite his parents and fiancée to the party, as well as her former lover, Kenneth Lawrence (Douglas Dick). And why not then have Dall, overconfident in his superiority, play an unbeatable matchmaker in getting Kenneth and Chandler's Janet back together again. One merely has to kill the competition—done!

Normally a screwball farce, such as Lee McCarey's *The Awful Truth* (1937), has a *living* lover or two secretly just-out-of sight (in this case, first Cary Grant, and then Alexander D'Arcy), while the leading lady (Irene Dunne) is entertaining her current beau (Ralph Bellamy). Dall has so simplified the process in his *man as beast* process that his mischievous (I mean murderous) "Puck" can keep everyone in the same twisted space, with nary a nasty quarrel, and time for drinks all around, except for dead David. Though as in any good dark comedy, death is omnipresent.

Hitchcock also overturns his normal set of rules in orchestrating his "all my films are dark comedies" precept in three key ways. First, there is no waiting around for death to happen, like poor sexy spy Annabella Smith (Lucie Mannheim) in *The 39 Steps* (1935). Nope, David is toast before a viewer can even get at that popcorn. This is perplexing if one is following the old Hitchcock playbook.

Second, what about this director's normal inside joke policy that an audience member can only savor the black humor crack *after* a second screening, like Robert Donat telling the aforementioned hapless Lucie Mannheim's double agent, "It's your funeral," *before* she stumbles into his bedroom with a knife in her back the next morning. Nope. In Hitchcock's *Rope* there is no director's private form of the predestined black humor observation about any of his marionette-like characters. Thus, the black humor hits one more quickly. This is the genre's modern updating of the ancient comedy theory of surprise—instant provocative Pop! David died in a millisecond compared to Hitchcock's *Torn Curtain* (1966) *forever* killing of the enemy East German security guard via stabbing, battering with a shovel, and eventually gassing in an oven—doubling the dark comedy quotient for a villain from Nazi country.

Third, Hitchcock usually has an idiotic personality-comedy duo wandering around the film without a clue, like *Doubt*'s Henry Travers and Hume Cronyn. There is a murderer in-house, and not only are the dumb duo oblivious, their obsession with a perfect murder (also Hitchcock's) is studied but never acted upon—again like the director playing pretend movie murder. In contrast, Dall and reluctant Farley Granger *act* on this goal. And as conscious killers, *this* dark comedy "team" are neither supporting characters nor just kidding around. Moreover, unlike Travers and Cronyn receiving joy from just playing with the macabre, at least Dall is feeling "tremendously exhilarated."

Moreover, while this book has periodically noted that dark comedy's holy grail is the "perfect murder," less time has been granted the premise of killing as a form of art, another Hitchcock interest. Yet, Brandon literally observes, "I'd wished for more artistic talent. Well, murder can be art, too." Nodding towards the boxed David, like a museum piece about to be shipped, he further states, "[By combining it with a party, we're] making our work of art a masterpiece." Consequently, Brandon even provides a further insight into the perfect murder, with links to Hitchcock. Dall's lover/co-killer, concert pianist Phillip, is already an artist about to perform in New York's famous Town Hall setting. The killing of David, for Dall, makes him an artist ... of death. Moreover, while Hitchcock often said his films "were only movies," his meticulous crafting of these deadly moving picture tabloids of death—especially one based on a real "crime of the century"—makes Hitchcock sort of a first cousin to Brandon's character. Moreover, while the great often improvisational director Nicholas Ray, whose work often dealt with death, too, was fond of saying of his work, "I'm a stranger here myself," Hitchcock was no stranger to this world.

Ultimately, *Rope*'s flip-flop on Hitchcock's norms also makes it an artist spoofing himself, as if to say, "Maybe I need to flaunt this dark side more, for fear my lemming audience, as a misanthropic former marketing person, will miss what I am accomplishing here." Again, Brandon comes to mind; Dall's character is so proud of finding his artistic persona that he cannot help but flaunt it via comments he makes to the guests.

Not to become too psychoanalytical, while Dall discovers delight in murder (to the point of saving David's wine glass as an artifact for a place like Madame Tussaud's special "Chamber of Horror" section, (a favorite with Hitchcock), Brandon's straight man in crime, Phillip, is about to lose it. His reaction to what they have done could be said to represent Hitchcock's inner little Catholic boy full of guilt. This tension even complements another ongoing Hitchcock point of dark comedy—couples are never meant to be happy for long.

However, in this case, the little things all twosomes periodically argue about take on a wonderfully deformed bit of dark comedy parody. For instance, Philip asks, "You don't think the party's a mistake do you ... [after a murder]?" Then, there is Phillip's questioning of Brandon's sudden impulse to move the party food from one place to another—but the "other" is the top of David's quasi-coffin ... which then squeezes out more black humor with Brandon's vexed response, "[You] Don't want to leave our guest of honor alone during supper."

Phillip is upset that one particular guest is invited, a common enough difference between couples. But not over a party list based upon murder! Phillip is afraid that Stewart's Rupert, whose recycling of Nietzsche to the men when they were boys was the catalyst for the murder, will figure out what has occurred. However, for Brandon, it is a further validation of his newfound artistry. Only their mentor in the macabre would have fully appreciated what they had done. In fact, at one point Dall's character had flirted with inviting Rupert to taking part in David's exit.

Regardless, even this early in the movie it is already clear that Dall is the dominant member of the couple; such a dynamic is also typical in comedy teams. Yet, again this petty bickering, often funny in and of itself, is standard farce—which immediately zips to dark comedy, as predicated by dead David essentially functioning as the serving table. Moreover, many couples and/or comedy teams have one member who is easily rattled by everything, such as Stan Laurel's patented crying shtick.[11] Consequently, when Phillip suddenly sees a short portion of the rope used to strangle David protruding from the

The rope held by Jimmy Stewart, which so rattles Farley Granger (far right), with John Dall.

box, he freaks. In response, a mildly disgruntled Brandon tells his partner there is nothing more common in a home than a bit of rope—which he casually places in what at that time was commonly called the kitchen "junk drawer."

While the chapter will shortly return to other instances of discord turned to dark comedy, or ongoing Bob Hope–like lines in Ingmar Bergman-land, Granger's Phillip also occasionally plays the comedy team setup man with a bit of his own relatively rare black humor. For instance, Phillip says before the party, "[It was] out of character for him [David] to die this way." Well duh, that feels like a yes. Moreover, it seems to be a fair assessment for *any-one*—to be strangled to death by "friends" and stuffed in a box just before a party.

Brandon's response on this occasion is not funny but it is more valuable with regard to underlying a basic dark comedy component which separates it from most other genres. That is, he says, "[Yes] Good Americans usually die young on the battlefield." To decode this is to say, "In dark comedy death is random, without any point. And once an individual is gone it is like s/he never existed. In most other genres, death has a positive purpose."

8. Rope (1948)

To illustrate, in Frank Capra's seminal populist film, *It's a Wonderful Life* (1946), George Bailey (Jimmy Stewart) loses his father early in the film, yet the ideals and love represented by this parent's savings and loan company, versus the evil banker Mr. Potter (Lionel Barrymore), live on as Stewart's character continues to follow in his father's humanistic footsteps. Moreover, that same year, a pivotal John Ford Western, *My Darling Clementine* (1946), which showcases a version of the genre's iconic gunfight at the O.K. Corral, makes the same point about death. Early in the story Wyatt Earp's (Henry Fonda) youngest brother is murdered by the Earps' nemesis family, the Clantons. (Historically, he was killed later.) After the burial of the boy, Wyatt and his remaining brothers, who had just been driving their cattle to market, stay on in Tombstone as the law—in order to avenge their brother and bring peace to the most disorderly of towns. Fonda regularly visits his brother's grave site and tells his loved one that his death will not have been in vain. Consequently, in both films the spirit of a lost individual lives on, as well as rescuing two towns, otherwise, Tombstone would soon live up to its name, while the Bailey Savings and Loan saved Capra's Bedford Falls from becoming the horrendous Potterville.

Be that as it may, it is past time to note the numerous dark comedy quips that often come at a rapid pace. For instance, a whimsical Dall attempts to comfort an upset Granger before the quests begin to arrive, with the jocular comment, "Of course, he [David] was a Harvard graduate, which might make it justifiable homicide." Later, after the deed, the twosome decide to have a special drink. When Phillip asks who or what they should toast to, Brandon says at warp speed, "To David, of course!"

Along drinking lines, when first guest Kenneth realizes they are having champagne, he surprisingly asks, "It isn't someone's birthday?" And Dall, with an amusingly quizzical look on his face that slowly turns to brilliant bemusement, replies, "No, almost the opposite." Indeed, almost all roads lead to black humor, with Hitchcock sometimes incorporating them into core components of his oeuvre. For instance, the text has chronicled how Hitchcock often ties objects of art to his narrative. Thus, in *Rope* Janet asks Brandon about a new painting in the penthouse. With a straight face he replies it is by "...a new American primitive."

Hitchcock also uses Phillip's legitimate talent as a pianist for ironic black humor. One's gift here is his hands, and it is Phillip that does the actual strangling. One might even think Hitchcock is spoofing his friend Peter Lorre's *Mad Love* (1935), in which the actor's mad surgeon character grafts the hands of a murderer upon a pianist involved in an accident ... with the expected results. However, Hitchcock also telegraphs the connection in a series of broad dark comedy observations. For example, when Janet hears about Phillip's upcoming concert she tells him, "I bet you're going to play a foul trick on all of us and become horribly famous."

However, more pointedly, Mrs. Atwater allegedly has a gift for predicting the future via the horoscope. And at least with Phillip, her skills are spot-on. She tells him, "These hands will bring you great fame." Plus, given Hitchcock's wordsmithing obsession on scripts, one cannot help but think he also enjoyed playing upon the pun that this prophesy involving murder was a result of a *horo*scope.

These unintentional dark comedy hits by party guests also provide the perfect segue for when the visitors transition into a reaffirmation parody sequence, in which they consciously and self-referentially make merry with comic killing comments in a movie murder story. Brandon is the catalyst, with a sardonic comment about how the flick of a knife could get one a better table in a classy restaurant. Kenneth then chimes in with how he recently could have knifed a hotel employee. With that comment, Rupert fittingly becomes the moderator and chief contributor to what essentially will become a dark parlor game in a farcical setting.

Playing off of Kenneth's comment, Rupert disagrees, "Knives may not be used on hotel employees, please. They are in the death by slow torture category, along with bird lovers, small children, and tap dancers." (These are all characters of whom Hitchcock was not fond). Rupert then continues down the Hitchcock homicide highway while punning the title of Gilbert Seldes' still enormously influential book *The Seven Lively Arts* (1924, which advocated pop culture as art). Rupert's play on words declared murder should be considered an art, though "not maybe one of the seven lively" ones.

Rupert's raconteur manner makes dark comedy an infectious panacea for whatever ails you—"Think of the problems it would solve: unemployment, poverty, standing in line for theatre tickets…." Again, such verbal jabs are in the period tradition of America's transition to a more antiheroic humor during the early blossoming of Hitchcock's career—with both the director and the movement capable of going abruptly into a mischievous dark mode. Consider Thurber's aforementioned "The Unicorn in the Garden," or Robert Benchley's even more Rupert-like comment on what to do to a disruptive audience member in "Matinées—Wednesdays and Saturday": "I once heard a woman laugh at the most tragic moment in all drama, the off-stage shot in 'The Wild Goose,' and I afterward had her killed, so there will be no more of that out of *her*."[12] And to underline the dark comedy base he shared with Hitchcock, Benchley's essay collections always sealed the genre's absurdist component with their titles. Thus, "Matinées" was anthologized in *No Poems, or Around the World Backwards and Sideways*.[13]

Regardless, Rupert's contagious tutorial on this less "lively art" soon had the guests joining in a litany of ways to popularize this pastime, such as "Cut a Throat Week," or "Strangulation Day." Ironically, the one guest bothered by the game is David's father, who questions the seriousness of Rupert's com-

Hitchcock's sophisticated dark comedy world was greatly impacted by *New Yorker* writers such as Robert Benchley (shown) and cartoonists like Charles Addams.

ments. And Brandon quickly answers for his old mentor, "Of course he is." Mr. Kentley interjects that this means an embracing of Nietzsche, to which Rupert quickly acquiesces. Naturally, so soon after the 1945 end of World War II, Kentley sharply replies, "So did Hitler." Clearly, he is correct, and with another spot of dark comedy absurdity, Leopold and Loeb were actually more topical in the 1940s than in the 1920s.

Before addressing the perverse farcical situation Brandon has cooked up, which contributes to his downfall, one must examine a seemingly throwaway literary reference which allows Hitchcock one of his more traditional inside dark comedy jokes—a phenomenon not as prevalent in *Rope*. In party conversation, it comes out that of all the tales Rupert had imparted to his young charges, "The Mistletoe Bough" was by far Brandon's favorite—keeping mentor and pupil up to all hours in the pleasure of its repeated telling.

"The Mistletoe Bough" was actually a poem converted to song in 1830s England. It soon became a long running rage during the Victorian and Edwardian era, which would have carried its great popularity into Hitchcock's childhood. The English folktale–inspired song produced several literary variations, with the short story Rupert would have no doubt been telling Brandon being Susan E. Wallace's "Ginevra or The Old Oak Chest! A Christmas Story" (1887). So what was the tale? An encapsulation is best left to some lyrics from the now public domain song, about how a new bride's boredom at her party motivated her to propose a game of hide-and-seek. Indeed, its dark comedy Christmas song adoration, all the more absurd for its holiday time fashion, might begin with it sometimes punningly referred to as "bride-and-seek":

> They sought her that night, they sought her next day,
> They sought her in vain when a week passed away.
> In the highest, the lowest, the loneliest spot
> Young [husband] Lovel sought wildly, but found her not.
>
> The years passed by and their grief at last
> Was told as a sorrowful tale long past.
> When Lovel appeared, all the children cried,
> "See the old man weep for his fairy bride."
>
> Oh, the mistletoe bough
>
> At length, an old chest that had long laid hid
> Was found in the castle; they raised the lid.
> A skeleton form lay moldering there
> In the bridal wreath of that lady fair.
>
> How sad the day when in sportive jest
> She hid from her lord in the old oak chest,
> It closed with a spring and a dreadful doom,
> And the bride lay clasped in a living tomb.
>
> Oh, the mistletoe bough

The story provides so much more context to the throwaway *Rope* reference. While briefly sketched, ironically by David's father, as something horrific, it originated from a long celebrated *darkly comic song* in Hitchcock's youth, and continues today. Who knew? It helps explain or suggest why David was placed in a chest-like box. It underscores the random tenuous nature of life, even a party—both in the song and *Rope*. The lyrics, "in sportive jest she hid from her lord [husband]…" proposes Hitchcock's misogynist nature. The fact that "Oh, the mistletoe bough" is an ongoing refrain encourages punishment for young love/lust, that "mistletoe" is drawn from a pagan fertility ritual, and schoolboy Hitchcock had been so impacted with Catholic guilt related to sexuality.

The potential defining *Rope*/dark comedy connections seem endless. For instance, the genre associates sexuality with death as a loss of control. And while not a bride, David was about to be married, and his fiancée was a guest at the party. Plus, throughout the movie everyone constantly wonders what has become of David, the same question asked about the bride. During *Rope*, ongoing phone calls are made and received, with theories incessantly put forward. Moreover, between the fact that Janet had once dated both Brandon and Kenneth and is now engaged to dead David, the scenario again envelopes Hitchcock's bugaboo about the transitory and ultimately unhappy nature of relationships.

Indeed, this interpretation is given added credence when one considers another short story whose catalyst was "The Mistletoe Bough" song—American/British author Henry James' "The Romance of Certain Old Clothes." This work merits special consideration for several reasons, starting with James being the most august author to bring his talents to the tale. Second, though initially published in 1868 America, its 1885 British debut occurred just the decade before Hitchcock's birth, and is easily the most available of any reworking of the story. Third, besides being the most significant writer to address the folk tale, James' British profile took on added significance when he became an English citizen during Hitchcock's teen years. Fourth, starting as a child, Hitchcock had amassed a huge library collection of Gothic and macabre tomes. Thus, it would seem unlikely that he would have been unaware of James' version, especially since the original tale is noted in *Rope*.

Regardless, James' tweaking of "The Mistletoe Bough" joins the story to another Hitchcock and dark comedy basic—another relationship gone sour. Two sisters, Perdita and Rosalind, desire to marry the same most eligible of bachelors. Sweet Perdita succeeds, only to die shortly after giving birth to a daughter. However, before the young mother passes, she elicits a promise from her husband that all her beautiful and valuable clothing and jewelry will be carefully wrapped and placed in a double-lock chest in the attic. The items are to be sequestered for their daughter until she is grown. And so it is done.

With Perdita's death, however, her grieving husband must get away from what has transpired. So, when a business opportunity in England arises, he leaves his daughter in the loving care of his mother-in-law, in whose home Rosalind still abides. Given that this all transpires well before the Revolutionary War, his journey to and from Britain is lengthy, as are his business dealings. Over a year passes, and now he longs for his daughter. However, Rosalind, still angry at not being chosen, has so ingratiated herself with the daughter that this propels a marriage to the father.

The departed Perdita has anticipated this happening, knowing that the romantic rivalry she and her sister had had was vastly different. She had loved the young man, while her sister was more interested in his ability to provide her with fine things. Still, all would have no doubt transpired as planned, because while Rosalind did not love her new husband, she controlled him via her sexuality—what James veils as the woman's "devilish" nature. However, her former brother-in-law turned husband has business setbacks, and suddenly there is no longer money for lovely regalia.

Rosalind now desires the riches in the trunk. Lloyd, the husband, will have nothing of it. However, his wife keeps at it. And if the truth be told, he had always secretly "coveted" the "devilish fine woman" which Rosalind represented.[14] Finally, worn down by her arguments, and denied of the lust which seems to have driven the marriage, he gives in. Ultimately, Lloyd produces the trunk key. Yet, Rosalind does not want to overplay her hand. Thus, she does not initially take it.

However, over the course of the day Rosalind seems to have disappeared. As in *Rope*, hours pass without the missing person turning up. Since Lloyd had thrown down the key with great shame, and had not seen her retrieve it, he only goes to the attic as an afterthought. However, now a premonition tells him to go alone. What he finds is an open chest and his wife having fallen backward from a kneeling position.

> ...one hand supporting her on the floor and the other pressed to her heart. On her limbs was the stiffness of death, and on her face, in the fading light of the sun, the terror of something more than death. Her lips were parted in entreaty, in dismay, in agony; and on her blanched brow and cheeks there glowed the marks of ten hideous wounds from two vengeful ghostly hands.[15]

Besides reinforcing Hitchcock questioning a "they lived happily ever after" scenario as well as bolstering his Catholic guilt over the penalty for lust, James' story is also a natural segue to Brandon's twisted farcical actress in *Rope*. Dall's character keeps hinting to Janet and Kenneth that maybe their former relationship could have a second act without, of course, telling them about dead David. Nothing kills farce quicker than, well, killing off the competition. Yet, Janet's character seems a bit like the "devilish" Rosalind, since she seems to have dated half of the party's male population. Moreover, Brandon suggests she seems more interested in David than Kenneth, because her late fiancé's family is better off.

Moreover, if one adds James' rendition to Susan Wallace's short story, "Geneva, or the Old Chest," and the additional linked poems accompanying the H.W. Hageman Publishing Company's 1894 novella-length compilation, some potentially connected-to-Hitchcock/dark comedy components surface.[16] The victim is a spoiled naïve beautiful blonde who turns down many suitors, including a prince in one telling. Thus, many Hitchcock historians, including François Truffaut, have suggested the director's cinematic misogynist nature probably stems from a shy, chubby childhood in which he either knew or feared romantic adolescent rejection, especially from those seemingly unattainable gorgeous girls. However, it gets better, with regard to Hitchcock and dark comedy. In the many variations of the victim's story, her babied and foolish inclinations—randomly hiding in a chest because she is certain people will want to come find her—come from wealth and in one case, quasi-royalty. She comes off sounding like an empty-headed farcical screwball heroine.

Moreover, recall Hitchcock's hatred of the class system, as well as dark comedy's desire to destroy all establishment institutions. Plus, much of the humor in screwball comedy/farce comes from the fact that the blue collar help really run the system, including being aware of spring locks. Thus, it is easy to see how a privileged dead girl in a box might provide a dark comedy giggle for the working class. Indeed, even today, a quick look on the internet chronicles laughing contemporary pub patrons from the British Isles (especially in the anti-monarchy Republic of Ireland) still singing "The Mistletoe Bough." Consequently, Hitchcock's patented inside black humor joke would not have played that way in his home country.

In addition, Christmas has another dark comedy connection. The genre is out to shock, and during this holiday, with much of the public briefly letting down their possibly otherwise cynical nature—black humor can get its maximum buck. Ironically, this is further maximized, because with patrons now possibly even more receptive to something sentimental during this brief window—BAM, they are hit with dark comedy. Indeed, through the years many signature dark comedies have been released at Christmas, such as the pioneering example of the genre, *Harold and Maude* (1971). So, it is most appropriate that *Rope* references "The Mistletoe Bough."

Actually, a bigger *Rope* surprise, sans the opening, is possibly Stewart's Rupert getting a little too self-righteous at the close, when he has pieced together all the clues and is lecturing his mentored murderers. Mainly one can chalk it up to a censorship era dictating the ending, such as occurred most famously with Hitchcock's *Suspicion* (1941), in which all clues seem to indicate that Cary Grant has murdered screen wife Joan Fontaine. Even period censoring would have had a hand in the "comfort the masses" lame finale to *Doubt*.

Rupert's sanctimonious preaching only mildly dampens Hitchcock's dead-on dark comedy. It is an exercise in the establishment winning, never a popular posture in this genre. However, one might reframe its rather arch commentary as a reversal of the dark comedy which ends unbelievably happily, such as *Catch-22* (1970) or *Brazil* (1985)—none are to be accepted as credible. Hitchcock always has a strong sense of space; thus, most of the New York sophisticates at the party recognize what Rupert's drolly dark humor makes him—a provocative raconteur. Why he could be the painting of 1929's *Blackmail* jester come to life. However, labeling him merely a tongue-in-cheek comedian of black humor does not exactly mesh with his serious admission of being a disciple of Nietzsche—now that is black comedy.

Regardless, what of the critics? The reviews were mixed at best but there were plenty of puns. For example, the *New York World-Telegram* critique was titled "Hitchcock's 'Rope' Hangs Up Bravos."[17] In contrast, one might recycle an old Western line to describe the *New York Times*' review—critic Bosley Crowther "took the long way around the barn" for his gentle pan:

> The fondness of Alfred Hitchcock for cinematic tours de force is admirable.... But it also ... leads him to stick out his neck and place it ... in positions of evident peril. It is in such a delicate position ... as the consequence of having stretched it in his new film, an item called *Rope*.[18]

Variety was not without praise but its opening was enough to no doubt discourage patronage: "'Rope' undoubtedly will be ballyhooed as a super-horror film. It is and in so being may defeat itself. It's a cold-blooded account of wanton murder."[19]

Neither review even mentions humor, let alone dark comedy, despite elements of that genre, personality comedians from hell, reaffirmation parody, traditional parody—all wrapped up in a farcical screwball comedy-like cocktail party. The *New York Sun* buries any praises of humor well into its description of the Dall-Granger team, "Brandon, the bright-eyed amusing Brandon, and the quietly neurotic Phillip are certainly insane."[20] *Sun* critic Eileen Creelman seemed to be one of the more articulate period reviewers but one can sense she has little sense of the compound genre Hitchcock has mixed, nor a ready vocabulary with which to explain it:

> "Rope," [the] latest Alfred Hitchcock study of the macabre, goes about as far in that direction as even Hitchcock dares and maybe even a little further.... It is a tour de force.... All that admitted, one may still wonder if it were worth doing.[21]

Howard Barnes' *New York Herald Tribune* review of *Rope* has a promising moment, only to fumble the film's dark comedy concept: "...a brutal and willful murder is examined in drawing room comedy terms. Immaculate staging has made the mixture of small talk and violence properly horrifying."[22] However, Barnes then finds *Rope* safety in the way many other period critics often did; he turned to Hitchcock's interest in experimenting. The critic brought in a modest comparison of *Lifeboat*'s study in limited space, versus *Rope*'s suggestion of a single take in real time.

In the jargon of baseball, dark comedy film did not regularly start to "hit a home run" with mainstream audiences until the 1960s and 1970s.[23] Even then, since the shock value had to be an increasingly traumatizing mix of comedy and the unsettling, it was always a more iffy proposition as it morphed (as all genres do) into something else. Moreover, *Rope* was still too close to what history has defined as "the good war" (World War II) to readily embrace Nietzsche publishers, or the black smoke from a small crematorium which opens Chaplin's Bluebeard *Monsieur Verdoux*.

While *Rope* was embraced as a trailblazing dark comedy decades ago, it is stunning how a mid-century provocative picture can transition into a ho-hum genre template years later. Consequently, a fitting close to this chapter is a random review snippet by the forever insightful *New Yorker* critic Anthony Lane from 1995: "[The film] is a new twist on that old Hitchcock teaser: How do you get rid of a body without losing your mind? Like *Rope* and *The Trouble with Harry* [1955], it seems more of an exercise in logic than a chiller ... it fights to keep a straight face...."[24]

9

Strangers on a Train (1951)
Completion of Nietzschean Dark Comedy Trilogy

"Any kind of person can murder. Purely circumstances and not a thing to do with temperament! People get so far—and it takes just the least little thing to push them over the brink. Anybody. Even your grandmother. I know!.... [And] A lot of little people ... don't matter."[1]—Bruno's character in Patricia Highsmith's novel *Strangers on a Train* (1950), from which the film was adapted

Coupled with *Shadow of a Doubt* (1943) and *Rope* (1948), one might call *Strangers on a Train* the completion of Hitchcock's "Nietzsche Trilogy." Two nondescript pictures, bordering on duds, had followed *Rope—Under Capricorn* (1949) and *Stage Fright* (1950). However, the esteemed auteur came roaring back with *Strangers*. Indeed, it would also be the catalyst for Hitchcock's most sustained period of extraordinary creativity since the British span between 1934 and 1938, which included the underrated original *The Man Who Knew Too Much* (1934, see Chapter 2), *The 39 Steps* (1935, see Chapter 3), *The Secret Agent* (1936, see Chapter 4), and *The Lady Vanishes* (1938, see Chapter 5).

Engagingly, however, there seems to be a straight Nietzsche line from *Strangers* to the earlier *Shadow* and especially to *Rope*. Indeed, there are actual scenes from the latter picture which play as if only tweaked for *Strangers*. Moreover, there are times when it seems like Hitchcock and Highsmith's dark philosophical thoughts mesh. (Do *not* be persuaded by Donald Spoto's puzzling attempt to radically distance the film from the novel.[2]) Nonetheless, if the *Strangers* scenario seems familiar for non–Hitchcock aficionados, Billy Crystal and director/co-star Danny DeVito did a very popular *Strangers* spoof years later—*Throw Momma from the Train* (1987). Their only flaw is that *Strangers* is already so immersed in dark comedy that *Momma* is, at times, uneven in Crystal and DeVito's attempts to make their film the broadest of black humor burlesques.

The *Momma/Strangers* comparison might just seem like a bonus addendum, yet it ties into another real challenge for spoofing dark comedy—pushing the macabre envelope ever further. For example, what follows are two review excerpts which did *not* appear in the preceding *Rope* chapter. One is drawn from a period (1948) *Los Angeles Daily News* critique; the second is a *New York Times* 1984 reassessment. The first warns that "Hitchcock's suave direction and a competent cast make 'Rope' a rather disturbing dissertation— in strictly melodramatic terms."[3] As previously noted, other 1948 reviews found at least some of *Rope*'s humor, but there were usually qualifiers not unlike the *Los Angeles Daily News* evaluation. However, contrast this with Vincent Canby's *New York Times* revisionist (1984) reporting on *Rope*:

> When I saw the film last week at the Cinema Studio the audience collapsed with laughter at Philip's tentative suggestion that the party might be a mistake.... There are lots of laughs in "Rope."...[4]

More and more one must acknowledge that the public has caught up with Hitchcock.

Consequently, if *Rope* now plays more like a broad dark comedy farce— with a savoir faire stiff in the serving chest/coffin doubling as a party serving table—*Doubt* still often plays black humor more seriously. This is most fitting, since multiple sources (see Chapter 7) chronicle Uncle Charlie's (Joseph Cotten) Bluebeard as channeling Hitchcock's real views. Naturally, this brings to mind Charlie's dinner monologue about old "horrible, faded, greedy women...." However, upon further supposition, does not Hitchcock reveal more of his dark side when Cotten's character dresses down his namesake niece (Teresa Wright)?:

> What do you know, really? You go through your ordinary little day and at night you sleep your untroubled ordinary little sleep filled with peaceful stupid dreams. And I brought you nightmares.

While there are no reports of Hitchcock killing rich old ladies, the aforementioned ugly scolding of Young Charlie might very well be the director talking directly to his audience. Here is Hitchcock himself embracing the first and most central of dark comedy's three core themes—"man as beast." Without that component, the other two, "the absurdity of life" and "the omnipresence of death," fade considerably.

The beauty of *Strangers* being third in this Hitchcock Nietzsche trilogy of dark comedy is that Hitchcock has improved upon the first two pictures' execution of the genre. For instance, while Cotten's often charming nature is what makes him such a winning villain, his ultimate motive for killing these benign elderly ladies exposes a dark side to which most viewers hopefully cannot relate.

Another variation of this dark comedy perspective which one cannot quite also embrace as a potential act of a viewer's alter ego exists with *Rope*. For example, when Los Angeles theatre director Jack Shouce staged the film as a 2001 play he stated:

> The most important reason for bringing *Rope* to the stage is the enduring significance of the subject matter. I'd always been fascinated by the Leopold and Loeb case.... They were wealthy, handsome intellectuals who killed another boy simply as an experiment ... a black comedy [with] philosophical depth.[5]

Now follow that "experiment" up with a sophisticated penthouse party, with farcical lines like, "Everybody talks about committing the perfect crime, but nobody does anything about it," and presto—dark comedy. However, one's laughter hardly makes one want to perform his own random experiment.

However, when *Strangers* has Robert Walker's Bruno propose a crisscross exchange of random (fail-safe) murders to Farley Granger's tennis-playing Guy, a hated father for an estranged wife, there is a distinct difference. First, Bruno is arguably cinema's most entertainingly sympathetic psychopath, which will be expanded upon shortly. However, his likability factor runs diabolical circles around the other two films' dark comedy rogues.

Second, and of greater importance, Hitchcock seems to have taken an invaluable lesson from Frank Capra's adaptation of the Broadway play *Arsenic and Old Lace* (1944), Charlie Chaplin's *Monsieur Verdoux* (1947), and Robert Hamer's Ealing Studio's (Great Britain) *Kind Hearts and Coronets* (1949). In each case, besides featuring likable killers, the victims are expendable. Capra's picture has two pleasantly unhinged elderly sisters, Abby (Josephine Hull) and Martha (Jean Adair) Brewster, who perform their own form of euthanasia. With a touch of elderberry wine and some less healthy ingredients, the two periodically dispose of lonely old bachelors, who are then benevolently buried in their basement by the sisters' equally batty nephew Teddy (John Alexander), who believes he is Theodore Roosevelt. Teddy also enjoys running up the stairwell yelling "Charge!," à la Roosevelt's charge up San Juan Hill. One might actually say the Brewsters are performing a public service as yet another far-sighted program under then President Franklin Delano Roosevelt.

With Chaplin's title character of Verdoux, who also marries and murders wealthy older widows, he reminds one of Chaplin's beloved alter ego, the Tramp. Seminal film theorist Andre Bazin has even written a notable essay on the subject, "The Myth of Monsieur Verdoux," stating, "Charlie is always there as if superimposed on Verdoux, because Verdoux is Charlie."[6] Consequently, the friendly factor is even a more substantial given than the viewer's fondness for Abby and Martha. Also like the pixilated older sisters, Verdoux is always engaging. In contrast, Cotten is not always nice "Uncle Charlie," and *Rope*'s duo actually perform their killing on screen.

9. Strangers on a Train *(1951)*

This is neither the case with the Brewster women nor Verdoux. Plus, the sisters are seemingly acting out of kindness. Chaplin's Bluebeard presents decidedly disagreeable victims. Indeed, the one he fails to kill, Martha Raye, is *so* comically irritating that audiences root for her demise. (In later years, while visiting France, Raye was affectionately hailed as "Mme. Verdoux." *Kind Hearts* was arguably inspired by Chaplin, since Ealing Studio management were serious fans of Chaplin's post–Tramp work, presenting an equally winning reason for a series of off-camera killings.[7] Central character Dennis Price's titled mother marries a commoner and she is cast off from her disagreeable regal family. Upon her death, Price decides to vengefully work his way back to prominence by knocking off "royal" relatives who stand in the way of his becoming a duke. Price's termination of various kin is further softened by all his victims being played by Alex Guinness. And as in any good dark comedy, his eventual conviction for murder embraces *absurdity*—since the victim is someone he did *not* kill.

While naturally no wholesome viewer would ever kill anyone, *Arsenic*, *Verdoux* and *Kind Hearts* still have most audiences rooting for the potential prison team. A similar *Strangers* scenario is at work via Walker's tour de force psychopathic performance as Bruno. He meets Granger's famous athlete Guy on the train, after viewers follow a comic crisscross path of their shoewear in boarding. Bruno's shoes are expensive but gaudy two-tone gunboats, while Guy wears a nondescript pair, as lackluster as he is—despite being the star tennis player.

Both end up in the club car, their feet accidentally touch, and Bruno starts a conversation. His outfit is as outlandish as his shoes, especially his garish monogrammed tie. He seems to be an overgrown kid, which is immediately confirmed when he explains he has to wear the tie because of his mother. Highsmith's novel accents the adolescent slant further by how she has Guy describe Bruno, fittingly topped off by a distracting pimple:

> The long rust-brown body was sprawled vulnerable now, the head thrown back so that the big pimple [on his forehead] ... might have been the topmost point.... It was an interesting face, though Guy did not know why. It looked neither young nor old, neither intelligent nor entirely stupid.... The skin was smooth as a girl's, even waxenly clear, as if all its impurities had been drained to feed the pimple's outburst.[8]

Hitchcock, sans the pimple, projects that same sort of child/man Bruno image, which is further reinforced when he and Guy retreat to his cabin for lunch. That is, Bruno's compartment looks like a stereotypical teenager's messy bedroom—an explosion at a clothing store. Walker's Bruno also has that friendly factor one might associate with Chaplin's Tramp. That is, his youthful appearance was still associated with the innocent boy-next-door persona which had so contributed to such hit films as *See Here, Private Hargrove* (1944, as a sad sack soldier opposite Donna Reed) and the poignant wartime romance *The Clock* (1945, paired with Judy Garland). Even the sardonically biting wordsmith of a critic David Thomson was later poetically moved to write:

> Walker had the kind of heartbreaking smile that tells an audience he is doomed. He was so thin, so earnest, so likable ... as Jennifer Jones' [his then estranged wife] boyfriend in *Since You Went Away* (1944) ... You wanted to reach out and warn Walker, or put an umbrella over his head.[9]

For this reason, Walker had been Hitchcock's first choice for Bruno. However, the director's reasoning had an additional darker motivation—the "ends justify the means" perspective which so fit his dark personality. That is, Walker's post–World War II personal life had been one of turmoil following his divorce. The open secret of how producer David *Gone with the Wind* Selznick first played Svengali and then husband to Jones devastated Walker. Though continuing to act, he developed an extreme drinking problem and had two short marriages (the second, to John Ford's daughter Barbara, lasting all of six weeks) and a series of nervous breakdowns—which eventually resulted in an extended stay at Houston's Menninger Clinic.

Robert Walker (right) as Bruno charming Farley Granger as Guy early in *Strangers on a Train* (1951).

9. Strangers on a Train (1951)

So why the reference to Hitchcock's dark side? *Strangers* was Walker's first role after leaving Menninger. When the director invited Granger to his home to tell him the film's story, something he did with many of the actors he cast, Hitchcock mentioned he would be playing opposite Walker. Granger responded:

> "Oh, I think that's terrific. He's just a wonderful, wonderful actor." Hitch said, "Yes. Wouldn't it be interesting if something happened during the movie?" I said, "Hitch, that's *terrible* to say that," and he laughed. I *think* he meant a scandal.[10]

Whatever Hitchcock meant, he was casting Walker as a most entertainingly unstable individual in a story that revolved around Guy's unfaithful wife. The result was the actor's greatest performance, though a later mistaken dose of medication to a ragingly drunk Walker would kill him within a year. According to Granger, however, who became quite close to Walker during the shoot, there was only one minor Walker drinking snag at the beginning of the production, and his co-star was able to cover for him. Consequently, the dark comedy *Strangers* had some personal dark comedy—the character playing the potential victim helped his cinema adversary—and Hitchcock did *not* get his wish.

Regardless, while Hitchcock followed the leads of the earlier dark comedy trio by creating a more sympathetic villain in Bruno, he actually does Capra, Chaplin, and Hamer one better in the casualty department. While one feels nothing for their victims, Bruno's elimination of Guy's estranged cheating wife, Laura Elliott's Miriam, is like a good deed. Yes, that sounds like a major slide from one moral guardrail to another. However, there are many extenuating circumstances. Bruno's immediate puppy dog-like support for the athlete catches Guy at a particularly weak moment. He is attempting to facilitate a divorce from the promiscuous Miriam in order to marry Senator Morton's (Leo G. Carroll) daughter Anne (Ruth Roman). And as a popular tennis champion, he is thinking of a political career.

Moreover, Hitchcock never created a better dark side alter ego than Bruno is to Guy. While Walker does his amusing tightrope walk between loose cannon kid brother type and charming host—telling the tennis player the only type of doubles he plays involve alcohol—he is fueling Guy's dark side. Consequently, when Granger's character soon meets with Miriam, her hustling harlot behavior has him turning ugly. Plus, she is peerless in stoking his anger. After a year of hounding him for a divorce, Miriam now feels that she can further "milk" their "marriage," given Guy's rising star. Plus, she is now pregnant with someone else's baby, and threatens a scandal if he attempts to walk.

Naturally, there is an ugly public argument at Miriam's place of work, culminating in Guy grabbing her and making the threat, "I'm warning you!"

At this point her boss intercedes, telling Guy, "This isn't a place for a family quarrel." Guy immediately calls Anne and relates Miriam's slutty opportunism. What follows is a segment of that conversation:

> ANNE: You sound so savage, Guy.
> GUY: Sure, I sound savage! I feel savage! I'd like to break her neck! I'd like to break her foul little useless neck! [calling from the local train station, shouting over the noise from a passing locomotive] I said I could strangle her!

The shot then dissolves into Bruno's hands as his mad as a March hare mother (Marion Lorne) files his nails. Besides a sublime encapsulation of why Hitchcock liked to refer to the film as *Stranglers on a Train*, the transition executes another dark comedy basic—life's tendency to absurdly juxtapose the most antithetical of events. Fittingly, for a film so wrapped in twos (Hitchcock's cameo even has him carrying a double bass), the black humor juxtapositioning works on two levels.

First, one is moving from violent rage to the most tranquil of events—Mommy is doing her boy's nails, further reinforcing Bruno as the humorous child. Second, the scene is then couched in verbal absurdity. What about Bruno's pitch for a crisscross murder plan on the train, one might ask. Odd, yes, but Guy and Bruno had been downing doubles on the train, and pouring down liquid fun often guarantees a seemingly smooth takeoff on the most outrageous of subjects, especially when briefly talking to a traveling stranger. Indeed, that was how Guy had interpreted the encounter.

Now, the dissolve to Bruno's mom working on his nails reveals a sober take on just how far both of them are parked in left field. In fact, one should preface it with Yogi Berra's philosophy of life, "If the world were perfect, it wouldn't be." In any case, Bruno's mom ever so casually observes, "I hope you've forgotten that silly little plan of yours about blowing up the White House." Is this a prequel to Norman Bates and his mommy?

Bruno's mother next certifies their crazy town existence, in their big old house à la *Psycho* (1960), when she adds, "You're a naughty boy but you can always make me laugh." As the absurd scene continues, it appears that mom can have that effect on Bruno, too. And this involves Hitchcock's tendency to frequently use paintings in black humor, such as the multiple readings applied to *Blackmail*'s (1929) painted jester, each time it resurfaced.

Wishing that Bruno would take up drawing, she says, "Don't lose control. Come see my painting." Said work then produces the most prolonged demented laugh from her son—which rather seals the deal on his mental condition. However, this really kindles the viewer's curiosity. One had hoped that maybe mom was some sort of idiot savant with a special gift that could calm the "man as beast" tendencies of junior. Instead, the painting more closely resembles the comic horror show ending of 1945's *Picture of Dorian*

Gray—the previously closeted painting of the effects of ongoing debauchery in this haunting Oscar Wilde adaptation. (It can now be seen at the Art Institute of Chicago.)

Before getting back to how Miriam's death frequently produces verbal comments of "Yes!" from my college classes, not to mention how effectively Hitchcock showcases the event in a dark comedy manner, one must briefly address the various comic ways the *Strangers* painting is a given in his oeuvre, beyond the black humor. First, the director was all about inside jokes and self-parody. After *Doubt*, he enjoyed trashing motherhood. This painting has matriarchs taking another one on the chin.

Second, however, the director personally collected modern art. And this *Strangers* painting, if the phrase was used loosely, would fall under that umbrella. Thus, one could argue the director was spoofing himself and/or a general public which enjoyed mocking the phenomenon. Modern art collector Steve Martin does a more drawn out variation on this theme as he roller skates through a gallery in *L.A. Story* (1991, which he wrote). Ironically, or maybe fittingly, both filmmakers had/have a fascination with the lonely paintings of Edward Hopper. Third, a subtext to all Hitchcock films is the question of examining murder as an art form. Bruno's mother, when suggesting he take up painting, is not aware that her son is just discovering his own macabre art form. Finally, dark comedy always attacks the establishment. And since his mom was attempting to paint St. Francis, Hitchcock can get yet another dig in at the Catholic Church.

Be that as it may, when responding to the murder of Miriam as something audiences lost little sleep over, one must return to the time shortly before it occurs. Appropriately for the child-like Bruno, the setting is in an amusement park, to which she has gone with two young men. Relatively early, she is aware that Bruno is following them, or more specifically, that he is interested in her. She broadly "reads" this attention along sexual lines, especially since the two young men are not much more than boys. In contrast, while Bruno has been psychologically described as child-like, he is a handsome, slightly older figure, who looks worldly in a tailored and much more subdued wardrobe; loud clothing, such as flashy two-tone shoes and gaudy ties, are never recommended when murder is your game. It is in all the handbooks.

Moreover, Hitchcock portrays Miriam in a manner which suggests she rents by the hour. And period reviews were not exactly shy about proposing the same thing. For example, the *New York Post*'s dark comedy take on Laura Elliott's (later known as Kasey Rogers) performance states she plays "the wife no husband would want to keep very long."[11] Indeed, *Variety* is much more succinct about the character—"his tramp wife."[12]

Of course, with black humor relish Hitchcock has put some pump priming dialogue in the script. When Ruth Roman's senator father hears of the murders, he starts to observe, "[The] Poor unfortunate girl." But he is cut off by Hitchcock's own daughter Patricia (playing Roman's sister Barbara) with the crack—"She was a tramp!" It is as if young Hitchcock was channeling her father's own dark comedy world view, especially with the dialogue then morphing into a variation of a verbal exchange reminiscent of the director's favorite movie *Doubt*, which showcased his dark comedy philosophy so directly:

> SENATOR MORTON: She was a human being.... She had the right to life and the pursuit of happiness."
> BARBARA MORTON: From what I hear she pursued it in all directions! [She does not quite ask the Uncle Charlie question about whether a person in question is human or not. But she continues in that direction, telling her sister:] Now you [Anne and Guy] can be married. Think of it, you're free!
> SENATOR MORTON: One doesn't always have to say what one thinks.
> BARBARA MORTON: Father, I'm not a politician [score another dark comedy dig at the establishment. At this point she briefly leaves the setting, only to quickly stick her head back into the room and say:] I still think it would be wonderful to have a man love you so much he'd kill for you.

Again, besides Barbara having an entertainingly dark comedy glee to her dialogue, the fact that Hitchcock has his own daughter parroting a variation on his and Uncle Charlie's misanthropic views (from the director and his wife's own favorite film, for which she shares screenplay credit) is further fuel for *Strangers/Stranglers* being the topper to a Nietzschean trilogy. This philosophy was not exactly 1940s press kit fare, or Hitchcock's career might have been considerably shorter. Yet, it is certainly further evidence of the artist's position.

Regardless, at this point the traditional Hitchcock study then implicates the viewer in the nefarious act by relating to the villain, as Robin Wood has so concisely stated: "Bruno forms a link in a chain of fascinating insidiously attractive Hitchcock villains who constantly 'take over' ... as the center of [our] sympathy ..."[13] Few would really question the point, especially since the weight of Hitchcock scholarship has so calcified the position. However, one might state that some cracks have formed in this Hitchcock edifice as it relates to shared guilt with some of these Hitchcock villains, beginning as early as the director's British work with Peter Lorre.

Indeed, as just noted, even period *Strangers* reviews were shedding few tears over Miriam. About as warm as their description became was the *New York Daily News*' critic Kate Cameron calling her "heartless."[14] One is not suggesting society should embrace Cotten's chilling implications about justifiable homicide ... but the postmodern world of dark comedy has already, in many cases, parked in that garage. Now at this point, someone should jump up and cry "stay, illusion," à la Hamlet's cry to the ghost in the play's Act I, Scene I. And as the author, I will volunteer as the Disney character who metaphorically shouts that plea for the inherent innocence of humanity. However, in *Strangers* Hitchcock has certainly made the question relevant. The aforementioned David Thomson has best described the situation Bruno has put the audience in, with regard to killing Miriam:

> [Bruno is a] landmark among villains—a man of piercing ideas ... [who] manages to be very disturbing and yet never loses our sympathy ... the inactive man who dominates the athletic Granger ... including that beautiful moment when he leans back, sighs, and tells how he "puts himself to sleep scheming up [murder] plans." Bruno is one of Hitchcock's greatest creations...[15]

Regardless, the setting of the *Strangers* murder, and how it plays out, ooze dark comedy. First, the genre is all about sexuality, and Hitchcock never formatted a killing with more sexual suggestion. However, before dissecting the scene along those lines, why is sex so central to dark comedy? Simply put, it plays towards the "man as beast" dark side of the genre. First is the perversity factor. For example, in *Harold and Maude* (1971), the establishment priest counsels against teenager Harold's relationship with the seventy-nine-year-old Maude in such a passionate, drawn-out manner that he reveals his own pedophilic feelings. Speaking slowly, at eventually a stuttering pace, the priest observes, "I would be remiss in my duty, if I did not tell you, that the idea of [pause] intercourse—your firm young [pause] body [pause] co-mingling with [pause] withered flesh [pause], sagging breasts [pause], flabby b-b-buttocks [pause] makes me want [pause] to vomit." Why, given the pedophile revelations about the Catholic Church in the decades since *Harold and Maude*'s release, the film seems even more timely today.

Sex also represents an absence of self-control, consistent with man's plight in black comedy. This breakdown is comically presented in the bug-eyed panting of Yossarian and his *Catch-22* (1970) company after they meet the sexy companion of Orson Welles' General Dreedle—completely ignoring their bombing mission briefing. One is also reminded of Slim Pickens' Major King Kong happily astride a falling phallic-shaped atomic bomb called Lolita, whooping his way to world oblivion in *Dr. Strangelove: Or, How I Learned to Stop Worrying and Love the Bomb* (1964).[16] As Luis Buñuel, a most acclaimed foreign director of dark comedy, observed, "In a rigidly hierarchical society, sex—which respects no barriers and obeys no laws—can at any moment become an agent of chaos."[17]

Besides black humor's use of sex to get at that "man as beast" theme, incest moves the subject further into the Hitchcock wheelhouse. Indeed, critic Anthony Lane could have been speaking of that very subject when he wrote, "[This] humor is so black that it might have been pumped out of the ground."[18] And since Bruno's position with his mother is fast tracking toward that very subject with Norman and his mommy in *Psycho*, this merits noting.

Walker's (asleep) strangulation demonstration has aped Kafka's sensation of a violent sexual ejaculation at Senator Morton's (Leo G. Carroll, right) party, with Farley Granger.

Yet, just after *Rope* generated broad dark comedy laughter from another generation, it took an even shorter time in the post–*Psycho* world for a film like *Where's Poppa?* (1970), the absurdist cult classic, to comically play the incest card with such blasé ease. Black humor's latest shock never lingers long. In *Where's Poppa?* George Segal plays a repressed lawyer saddled with a live-in, senile mother played by Ruth Gordon. Segal's character is attempting to honor a family promise to keep her from a nursing home. However, her presence has curtailed any possible sex life for him. He is already so desperate that early in the film he dons a gorilla costume and attempts to scare her to death. At film's end, with one more girlfriend lost because of mother, he falls in bed beside her. The implication is that he will be replacing the long-time-dead "Poppa."

Moving dark comedy's use of sexuality further into Hitchcock territory, the genre frequently makes direct links between sex and death—the ultimate lack of control. Indeed, biographer Deborah Crawford's *Franz Kafka: Man Out of Step* chronicles that the suicide of George in her subject's "The Judgment" was linked in Kafka's mind to the sensation of violent sexual ejaculation. Fittingly, in the dark comedy film *Heathers* (1989) the sexual cliché, "Is this as good for you as it is for me?" actually refers to murder ... several of them.

A "violent sexual ejaculation" is also precisely what one thinks of as Bruno demonstrates strangulation on a guest's neck at Senator Morton's cocktail party in *Strangers*. In fact, Bruno becomes so transfixed by the action as he looks across the room at Miriam's double (Barbara), he actually passes out. The scene might have been inspired by a similar sequence from the previous year's *In a Lonely Place* (1950), a film also with a plot of confused identity, murder, and twisted sexuality. In this Nicholas Ray noir, Humphrey Bogart's character nearly chokes a woman to death with another "innocent" demonstration. He has a friend's wife place her neck in the seemingly affectionate crux of his elbow and he begins to squeeze. However, the same Bruno-like orgasmic look comes over him and the woman is nearly choked to death.

Of course, sex and death bring one back full circle to this proposed Hitchcock Nietzschean trilogy of *Shadow*, *Rope*, and *Strangers*. In the first film, Cotten marries and murders, while *Rope* opens with a strangulation that elicits from at least one of the murderers (John Dall) that same loss-of-control orgasm demonstrated by Bruno and Bogie.

Interestingly, in just noting the trilogy, Walker's character at the party, prior to the choking incident, would seem to be aping *Rope*'s Jimmy Stewart's charmingly cynical manner of drawing people into plausible dark comedy possibilities:

BRUNO: Oh, come now. Everyone is interested in that [murder]. Everybody has somebody they want to put out of the way. Oh now surely madam, you're not going to tell me there hasn't been a time when you didn't want to dispose of someone. Your husband, for instance.
MATRON: [giggling] By heavens no.
BRUNO: Are you sure? Are you sure there wasn't a tiny moment when you were made very angry, and what did you say?
MATRON: [more giggling.]
BRUNO: There you are. There you are. Now, you're going to do the murder [matron and friend are entranced]. How are you going to do it? That's the fascinating part. I didn't get your name?
MATRON: Mrs. Cunningham.
BRUNO: Mrs. Cunningham, how are you going to do it?
MATRON: Well, I suppose I'm going to have to get a gun from somewhere.
BRUNO: [Disappointed] No, Mrs. Cunningham. Bang, bang, bang all over the place. Blood everywhere.
MATRON'S FRIEND: How about a little poison?
BRUNO: Ah, that's better ... [he struggles for her name].
MATRON'S FRIEND: Mrs. Henderson.
BRUNO: Oh, that's better, Mrs. Henderson. But see, Mrs. Cunningham is in a dreadful hurry. Poison could take anywhere from 10–12 weeks if Mr. Cunningham is to die of "natural causes."
HENDERSON: You know, I read of a case. I think it would be a wonderful idea. I can take him out in the car and when we get to the very lonely spot [I] knock him

on the head with a hammer, pour gasoline over him and the car and set the whole thing ablaze. [She is pleased with herself and begins to laugh.]
BRUNO: And [you'd] have to walk all the way home. Oh no, no, no, no. I have the best way. [He holds out his hands.] Simple and silent and quick. The silent part being the most important. Let me show you what I mean. You don't mind if I borrow your neck for a moment?
HENDERSON: If it's not for long.
BRUNO: Now, when I nod my head just try to cry out, and I bet you can't do it. All right, now wait for the nod of my head [as he places his hands around her neck. But as he begins his demonstration he sees Barbara....]

Regardless, it is past time to scrutinize Hitchcock's darkly comic sexualization of Miriam's murder. It also doubles as an inspired parody of a murder story—because instead of back alleys and noir darkness, Hitchcock's twisted comic homicide takes place at an amusement park. Regardless, licentious Miriam leaves on her date with two young men all over her. Soon spotting a trailing Bruno, she looks like she could do a cinematic replication of Clara Bow and take on the whole UCLA football team. For film fans, it reminds one of Sam Fuller's striking use of the word "Nymphos!" from 1963's *Shock Corridor*.

Hitchcock utilizes about every sexual suggestion possible in the brief time left for party girl Miriam. These range from the phallic support poles on the bus ride to the park, to Miriam's tongue doing double time on an ice *cream* cone at the park. Again, Miriam seems to conjure up a provocative movie line. If it is not "Nympho!" her tongue craftsmanship reminds one of Willie Nelson's *Electric Horseman* (1979) observations, "I'm gonna ... find me one of them keno girls [sexy gambling casino assistants] that can suck the chrome off a trailer hitch and just kind of kick back."

Hitchcock also manages to keep the murder mood light by scenes such as a stalking Bruno going past a little cowboy-attired youngster who "shoots" the man/child twice with his toy pistol. Ironically, it is like Bruno meeting an apprentice assassin. (Ah, how early America implants violence, to which Hitchcock was attuned, since it made his form of entertainment so much more marketable.) Be that as it may, Bruno's response to the bratty kid is just another reason why he walks away with the movie, and Miriam is minimized—he uses his cigarette to pop the child's balloon. He does it with such entertaining aplomb, one cannot help but think of the child-hating W.C. Fields. Moreover, almost every major American comic had done a variation of that joke.

Soon Miriam's slender wannabe stud companions want to sexually impress her with their strength. Hitchcock then introduces a bit especially prevalent in the cartoon world that sometimes passes for the director's adolescent take on relationships. Both of her dates attempt to display their skills (such as they are) by playing the carnival game in which one strikes a lever with a hammer-like mallet which catapults a marker up a pole and maybe a bell is made to ring—another veiled "you scored" sexual metaphor.

Neither individual succeeds, and Miriam is disappointed for two reasons—they do not have what it takes, and she has lost track of Bruno in the crowd. However, he surprises her by suddenly turning up at the same game of strength. He looks at his hands and then at her—more dark comedy sexuality is suggested. Both of them have different plans for those hands. Naturally his mallet swing has Babe Ruth power. In fact, he has hit it so hard that someone yells, "He's broken the thing!" Wow. Dare we say he has reached Kafkaesque ejaculation power of death. Bruno then gives Miriam his most flirtatious look and her hooker mentality is hooked.

Next stop is the merry-go-round. And Hitchcock has just hit the triple crown of sexual connections leading to death. His inspired elements of dark comedy combine with parody to spoof America's then favorite genre. During the 1940s and 1950s roughly one of every four American films was a Western. The motion picture industry even had two annual Top Ten Box Office stars lists, one generic and the other for its horse opera heroes. Plus, there was so much sagebrush crossover the year *Strangers* came out that John Wayne *topped* the all-purpose list and was closely followed by Randolph Scott and Gary Cooper.[19]

Moreover, Westerns were all over the small screen, too, with the TV's first cowboy star, Hopalong Cassidy (William Boyd), having a series initially created by recutting many of his B-Westerns from the 1930s and 1940s. Bruno's undersized cowboy antagonist even seemed to be wearing a variation on "Hoppy's" garb—a brilliant move by Hitchcock to turn what seemed like a one-joke throwaway into a set-up for the Western spoofing to come. There were so many horse operas on the small screen that Bob Hope was given to saying that he had to blow the hay off his set before he could even turn it on.

Thus, as this goofy dark comedy murder segment moves to a merry-go-round, what better place could one pepper with sexual suggestions? Bruno mounts a horse right behind Miriam on her pony. The ride starts and so do the sultry propositions as the mounts go up and down. One expects to hear period cowboy star Gene Autry's signature song "Back in the Saddle Again" on the soundtrack. For Miriam it's a small town tramp thinking she has reeled in a more worldly catch, and for Bruno it is completing his task of making her the easiest of victims. Plus, Hitchcock's merry-go-round is the perfect metaphor for another dark comedy theme—the absurdity of life—a ride that takes you nowhere. One wonders if he was thinking of favored comedian Buster Keaton's treadmill sequence in *Day Dream* (1923).

Regardless, Miriam's next ride will be her last. She wants to go by boat to the "Magic Isle," a small island so full of amorous horizontal couples it might better be called "Lust Isle." And thus, one has yet another sexual veil, or is that a blanket, connected to the murder. The isle's only feature is ironically titled, given its unchaste setting, "The Tunnel of *Love*" (italics mine). Miriam has fittingly saved it for last. This is dark comedy to the max—a married woman pregnant by someone else, now out with still two other men, hoping to soon have sex with a stranger she fancies. Her screen name might better have been Sadie Thompson, early film's most famous trollop.

Miriam and company enter a boat and Bruno then follows in another paddler. They soon disappear and one hears screams. Has he somehow managed to kill her? How would that be possible? No, the sex-death link is demonstrated between orgasmic cries and those of being murdered. Again, a more contemporary film fan might be reminded of the porno theatre close of the dark comedy *An American Werewolf in London* (1981), when the moans heard outside the theatre, like those cries outside "The Tunnel of Love," cannot be distinguished as sounds of ecstasy or extinction.

However, both boats come out the other side with everyone intact, save for Bruno having finished his popcorn—it's always rather a dark comedy touch when murder and meals can be mixed. For instance, James Cagney's *White Heat* (1949) noirish gangster kills a stoolie locked in a car trunk as the gangster chews on a drumstick. (Everyone needs their strength. Indeed, since a funny fatal food-related focus drives such a character, maybe he could be named "Sal Manella.") Regardless, Miriam runs ahead of her two dates, trying to lose them in order to find Bruno for her special talent—what one might call her *art* in a Hitchcock film.

She turns and Bruno is suddenly sexually close. He asks her name; one must be sure about these things. From her perspective, it is almost an act of a gentleman—since her goal had been to be with a total stranger. Once she says "Miriam," Bruno performs his art. The audience views the action as if it is a performance once removed—reflected in the lens of her fallen glasses. This makes it seem more timely today—because it is a secondhand experience. It could be one of today's violent video games, moved a step from reality. Maybe this further softens one's view of Bruno's truly likable villain.

Along these lines, if Miriam's whorish character also contributed to the ease with which one makes allowances for Bruno's bewitching figure, Granger's bland Guy, despite his status as a famous world-class tennis star, further thrusts one toward Walker's Bruno. Before further exploring Granger's lackluster *Strangers* character, one really has to retreat to his figure in *Rope* (see previous chapter). He is clearly the weaker individual in the reworking of the Leopold and Loeb murder case, too.

As with *Strangers*, there is an additional parallel connection to the weakness of his *Rope* figure. That is, though his male companion (John Dall) in the latter picture also dominates him, Granger's public persona in that film is also greater—he is an accomplished professional pianist about to give a high profile concert date. One expects top-notch talent, be it on a tennis court or in a concert, not to be so easily controlled by a demented character—even one so winningly played as Walker's Bruno.

Of course, in fairness to Guy, such calculations are being made in the realm of drama. And this text is looking through the other (comic) end of the telescope. Cinema clowns are often thought to be pleasantly loony—more allowances for Bruno. Remember for *Secret Agent* the Bruno-like Peter Lorre was routinely compared to Harpo Marx by period critics. And what does Bruno do right after exterminating Miriam? He kindly helps a blind man cross the street in front of the park. (That shows a nice spirit.) More importantly, it is reminiscent of W.C. Fields attempting to help another blind man (the local hotel detective—further absurdity) cross the street in *It's a Gift* (1934). Fields' act of assistance also seems comically ludicrous, since the blind old curmudgeon has nearly destroyed his general store (including a large display of light bulbs) by wildly swinging his cane about as he walked. Many period critics found this classic dark comedy sequence in poor taste.

Moreover, Bruno's character appears in a unique time in American film comedy history, when one can start to draw a direct line from the Eddie Bracken characters of his mid–1940s Sturges films, to Danny Kaye, to Jerry Lewis, and right on to the crazy young Jim Carrey. As biographer James Ursini has observed of Bracken, "He is a complete failure—physically handicapped with high blood pressure [and] rather confused mentally...."[20] Indeed, Walker's early sad sack "Private Hargrove" roles were essentially aligned with Bracken's work both in time and tone. Walker's Bruno was just taking this character to the darkly comic crazy town next level.

Compellingly, another unique transition was happening around the production of *Strangers*. In the early 1950s the young *Cahiers du Cinéma* critics who would launch the French New Wave film movement at the end of the decade, especially François Truffaut and Jean-Luc Godard, gave the world a new postwar litmus test for screen viewing. An earlier "golden era" norm was tied to plot, heroes with consistent positive personae with which to identify, and happy endings. These critics rejected such standards. They wanted slice of life stories, provocative interesting characters but not ones the viewers would necessarily want to be, and realistic endings which would be ambiguous and/or even troubling. Hitchcock was their man. As previously noted, Truffaut's book-length interview transitioned the director from being perceived as *merely* a popular commercial director to an artist worth serious study.

However, there remains a partial disconnect here. Hitchcock often fulfilled these new values, yet critics, including *Cahiers* reviewers, sometimes held on to old school values. And it is most glaring in *Strangers*. For example, let us flash forward in the picture. Since Guy has not lived up to the proposed criss-cross murders (by killing Bruno's father), Walker's character is heading back to the amusement park to plant Guy's lighter, which he has carelessly forgotten the first time the two met.

Guy must get to the amusement park first. However, since he has already become suspect number one, he cannot deviate from his normal schedule—playing an important match. Both men run into snags. Guy changes his conventional methodical tennis style (like his normal persona) into a more aggressive attack mode—again Bruno has provoked the darker side—in order to win as quickly as possible. However, it does not work. Guy wins but it is a more drawn-out affair. Bruno makes a potentially much more grave error—he accidentally drops the lighter through the iron sewer grating near the curb of the sidewalk on which he is walking.

If the lighter goes down the drain he will not be able to frame Guy; yet it is seemingly just out of reach, close to disappearing down the drain. Audiences find themselves rooting for Bruno to squeeze his hand through the grating, despite what that means—guilt for relating to the assigned bad guy. Please! In this post-modern darkly comic cynical world, we as an audience have caught up with Hitchcock. Guilt—Pshaw! Bruno is no reason to page Dr. Freud.

Returning to Guy—he is not fun. Besides being colorless, there is no chemistry between his character and the senator's daughter. As Bruno implied early on, she appears to be merely a stepping stone to Guy's desire for a career in politics. Moreover, despite another happy ending, when Guy and Anne are on yet another train and a minister asks if he is not that famous tennis player and they bolt—avoiding the risk of another Bruno—it is too sweet to be believed. Yet another dark comedy takedown of an over-the-top happy ending.

For instance, how can Ruth Roman's Anne forget what has just occurred? Soon after Guy had exposed his dark side to her, she had asked him, "How did you get him [Bruno] to do it?" And even when it is proven that Guy is innocent, she has seen that he was capable of killing Miriam. The reality of such a situation takes one back to *In a Lonely Place*. Bogart is innocent of a murder rap. But his lover (Gloria Grahame) cannot marry him—how can she be sure such rage will never be turned on her?

As a study of Hitchcock and humor, this is the pivotal turning point—the completion of a Nietzschean trilogy which nails all the dark comedy, driven by Bruno's wonderfully twisted clown of character. These range from interactions with Guy and his mother, to the farcical cocktail party that eventually goes south. Also, Hitchcock spoofs the odd Western merry-go-round murder setting not once but twice. The finale has a down-and-out parody of a horse opera fight on a now out-of-control ride. (Another of Hitchcock's incompetent cops has managed to shoot the merry-go-round operator and caused the ride to go faster and faster.)

9. Strangers on a Train *(1951)*

Yet, everything is subtextually comic about this sequence. As in a cartoon Western, Guy and Bruno fight under the hooves of the ride's pretend horses. A mother on the merry-go-round stands by her saddled son—hysterical that something will happen to him. But when Hitchcock cuts to the kid he is having the time of his life. The little cowboy even attempts to help Guy by hitting Bruno, and when the child is knocked off his pony—Hitchcock gives the audience the stereotypical Western expectation. Guy somehow manages to stop fighting and make sure the kid is safe, before returning to his fisticuffs with Bruno.

Naturally, this out-of-control ride must be stopped. Period viewers were quite possibly thinking of the signature line from my favorite 1940s Warner Brothers cartoon cowboy, Yosemite Sam, "When I say whoa, I mean WHOA!" Unfortunately, since Sam was not available for the movie, Hitchcock does the necessity for a "WHOA!" with a *double* comic solution. First, and consistent with the Western theme, an old toothless guy risks crawling under the ride to stop it. The fellow is very reminiscent of the era's perennial Western sidekick George "Gabby" Hayes, who played in dozens of B-pictures with Hopalong Cassidy and Roy Rogers, not to mention A-turns with Randolph Scott and John Wayne.

The second part of the gag allows Hitchcock another dig at the establishment police authorities he so enjoyed satirizing. Consequently, while a trigger-happy cop had started the problem, our substitute Gabby Hayes now allows the director to suggest that law officers are cowards. As Gabby starts his brave act, the cops tell him to stop and the following exchange occurs:

OLD GUY: Want to do it yourself?
POLICEMAN: No, I guess he can make it all right.

The Gabby–like character succeeds. But the speeding merry-go-round comes off its base for a chaotic stop. However, like most Westerns from this era, only the nominal bad guy, Bruno, dies, and Guy is both a hero and proven innocent. And as a random addendum to Hitchcock's spoof of period Westerns, Granger's character name, Guy, was already established in the novel. However, as a stroke of luck, one of the most popular TV cowboys at the time *Strangers* appeared was *Guy* Madison, who played *Wild Bill Hickok* on the small screen.

Regardless, the following chapter on *Rear Window* (1954) continues this revisionist examination of Hitchcock's black humor, and other forms of comedy—highlighted by a provocative take on Jimmy Stewart's role. However, *Strangers* marks a major turning point towards the public having caught up with Hitchcock.

10

Rear Window (1954)

> "We've become a race of Peeping Toms. What people ought to do is get outside their own house and look inside for a change!"—Nurse Stella (Thelma Ritter) to convalescing action photographer L.B. Jefferies (Jimmy Stewart) as *Rear Window* begins

As noted earlier, Hitchcock has always been a front man for dark comedy, but in this film, he pulls back the tent flap to reveal that his sense of humor has an even broader comedy palette. Between *Strangers on a Train* (1951) and *Rear Window* Hitchcock had done two lesser pictures, *I Confess* (1953) and *Dial M for Murder* (1954). Interestingly, given this text's focus on comedy, the director felt the pivotal problem with *I Confess* was its total lack of humor.[1] Regardless, with *Rear Window* Hitchcock was back on artistic high ground. Indeed, the director would later state:

> I always say *Shadow of a Doubt* was my personal favorite but I am very proud of *Rear Window*. It's a movie about a Peeping Tom, to be blunt. I think it's human nature. People love to peek, or they would if they weren't afraid of getting caught.... In *Rear Window* I wanted to show the claustrophobia of Stewart's situation and the extent of his boredom....[2]

The observation is both superficially true and overly kind. Stewart is an American iconic Everyman. However, his broken-legged character's use of binoculars and then a telephoto lens to spy on his Greenwich Village neighbors across a courtyard—which is surrounded by four apartments—is comically creepy. In contrast, Ritter's wisecracking nurse starts out more like an American crackerbarrel humorist, spouting truisms which are even more timely today—such as the chapter opening suggestion that people need to be more introspective. Intriguingly, the *New York Post*'s review of *Rear Window* opined, "perhaps it has taken Hitchcock all these years to find an American humor that is ... equivalent in entertainment ... [to his] British brand...."[3]

While the movie was a great critical and commercial success, period

10. Rear Window (1954)

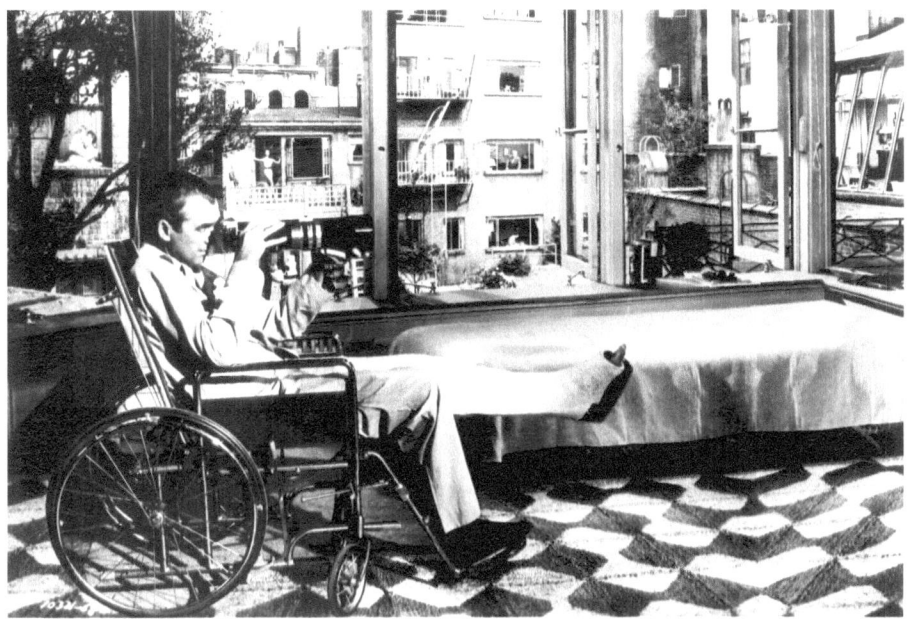

"Peeping Tom" Jimmy Stewart with his signature "erection" cast.

critics sided with Ritter's lecture to Stewart about Peeping Toms being unsavory. For example, the *New York Daily News* reviewer Kate Cameron said, "[He is a] snooping photographer who takes a mean advantage of his neighbors."[4] One can balance this by saying this is the beloved Stewart in off-beat Greenwich Village, and he does *seem* to discover a murder.... However, the manner of detection is still capable of producing sympathy for the killer (Raymond Burr's Lars Thorwald).

For instance, *New York Herald-Tribune* critic Otis L. Guernsey, Jr., wrote, "[There was] even a sharp pang of pity for the murderer."[5] And almost in a nod towards reviewers' treatment of the "trampish" murdered Miriam of *Strangers*, *Variety* described *Rear Window*'s victim (Irene Winston) as a "shrewish wife."[6] Add all this irony to a great deal of comic dialogue, and one would be entitled to do a variation on Rod Serling's sardonic mantra, "You are now entering the dark comedy zone."

Of course, Stewart is going to be seen in a more twisted manner here. He is essentially playing the part of dark comedy Hitchcock in a director's chair–like stationary position, and largely showing the audience only what this Hitch/Jeff doppelganger wants us to see. One is further nudged in that direction by Stewart's character constantly holding a camera lens. Even more than their joint director-like makeover of *Vertigo*'s (1958) Kim Novak, one is seeing an actor channel an auteur.

Moreover, *Rear Window*'s large cast of peripheral characters are presented as if one were panning a series of movie screens, all encased in a black humor series of boxes. Plus, this is a hot New York summer, with the film opening on a sweating Stewart and a temperature gauge well over 90 degrees; this is not a movie which would have been done 10–15 years later, when air conditioning was more common. Billy Wilder also used the same situation to comic effect soon after in *The Seven Year Itch* (1955). Consequently, window shades were open 24/7. And many Americans, especially someone like action photographer Jeff, did not yet have a television set. The absence of this "vaudeville in a box" distraction was yet another invitation for comic voyeurism. In addition, Stewart's persona was then being given a noirish makeover from his Westerns with director Anthony Mann. So the sight of him out of the saddle with a leg comically propped up in a cast would also have increased the humor for period viewers. Hitchcock further goosed the situation by having the following lines written on the cast: "Here lie the broken bones of L.B. Jefferies." There is so much comedy peppered throughout the film that the *Christian Science Monitor* critic complained, "As thriller entertainment, *Rear Window* is sufficiently above average to make one wish … [Hitchcock] had buried some of his [train] smoking car humor in Thorwald's flower bed."[7]

Moreover, there are other physical and/or visual components to Stewart's *Rear Window* persona that often mesh nicely with the Ritter personality nature soon to be examined. For example, for anyone who has ever had a cast, there is an instant comic connection to his attempts to use a back scratcher device to get at an itch under the plaster of paris. This also applies to that equally itchy exposed big toe that his stiff cast makes extra hard to reach. And speaking of stiff, for a manful chest-thumping type who somehow can be seemingly oblivious to the lovely Grace Kelly, his propped up leg-in-a cast ironically looks like a permanent erection. This is even more comically provocative when he gets out his long telephoto camera lens for his growing Peeping Tom interest in his neighbors.

However, there were all those tempting portals to other worlds (like the movies) for him to spend his time metaphorically channel-surfing from one human comedy story to another. Moreover, though the picture used lots of natural sounds, without a regular score (which was unusual for the time) many reviewers described these across the courtyard scenes, "like stories in pantomime," almost as an homage to Hitchcock's beloved silent cinema.[8]

While there were many quasi-genres at work here, at first personality comedy seems the most prevalent. These included a couple who periodically lowered their small dog in a basket from a second story apartment whenever nature called, another twosome who always seemed to be in some slapstick routine involving wrestling their mattress on and off the fire escape for nighttime sleeping, and the neighbor the *New York Telegram* described as "a fat old sculptress [who] waddles out to sun herself."[9]

10. Rear Window (1954)

In fact, the last two routines have back stories which replicate common Hitchcock humor habits one associates in his oeuvre with personality comedy. For example, he often used his large round shape for comic cameos, which was especially popular in silent comedy, from the pioneering odd shaped duo of round John Bunny and Olive Oyl-thin Flora Finch, to Laurel & Hardy. That seemed to be the purpose of the heavy uncredited artist (Jonni Paris). Yet, her work involves Hitchcock's frequent use of art for sardonic purposes. Throughout the picture, though caught in mere film snippets, she is struggling with a sculpture piece which resembles a chubby shirt form store mannequin. At the film's close she finally happily completes her statue, calling it *Hunger*—a comic reflection on her round physique and a director who consumed massive amounts of food.

Speaking of a torso is a natural transition for added comic background on the mattress couple. This information was later provided in a documentary interview by another of Jeff's menagerie of misfit neighbors—the lovely Georgine Darcy, whose shapely dancer Jeff has named Miss Torso. In the film *Rear Window Ethics: An Original Documentary*, Darcy shared how Hitchcock orchestrated improvisational bits for further humor. The fire escape couple were funny as a given—what is now often called "Theatre of the Real." Who has not grappled with moving a mattress?

Thus, one day on the set Hitchcock invited Darcy to watch how he could have some fun manipulating this couple (Frank Cady and Sara Berner), and make their mattress routine more comically realistic.[10] A planned "studio shower" was occurring to hurry their attempts to get the mattress back through their bedroom window. Hitchcock had had the two actors equipped with ear plugs in which he could separately direct their movements. However, Hitchcock was giving them conflicting commands, which essentially had them pulling in separate directions. The comic bonus was how their unplanned opposing tugs had sent the twosome and the mattress entertainingly falling back through the window.

Miss Torso's window frame represented another form of comedy—burlesque. Today that term is simply synonymous with strippers. Yet any faithful thesaurus will start its "burlesque" entry list of closely related words with the term "parody." So where is the disconnect? While "burlesque houses" might have eventually succumbed to being "strip joints," there was a time, such as the early 1930s, when to comedians like Red Skelton "burlesque" meant sexy spoofs of popular entertainment. The sketches featured comics interacting with scantily clothed young women.[11] That is essentially what one gets from the Miss Torso parody sequences, as she is constantly surrounded by gladhanding men at her parties, and on a multiple male date night. One half expects to hear a particular *His Girl Friday* (1940) portion of a screwball comedy dialogue between its stars:

ROSALIND RUSSELL: I have a lunch date.
CARY GRANT: Break it.
ROSALIND RUSSELL: I cannot break it. Get your hands off me. What are you playing? Osteopath?
CARY GRANT: Temper, temper.

However, Hitchcock does film some provocative Miss Torso ballet-like solos involving a minimally clothed Darcy, with one ever so fleeting flirting with a strip tease. Such situations are periodically played for humor by visitors to Stewart's apartment. Naturally, if Darcy received any review space, these racier scenes received the credit. For example, *Variety* stated, "Miss Torso ... is a Peeping Tom's delight, particularly when she loses her strapless bra."[12]

Yet another neighborhood couple meriting comic attention are the newlyweds. The growing joke is the young man seems to have married a nymphomaniac. Though the sex is off-camera (we are talking 1954), the increasingly exhausted husband is periodically seen in the window attempting to get air. Naturally, however, there are a few sad tales, too. These include the ever so moving Miss Lonely Hearts (Judith Evelyn), a blocked songwriter, and what becomes the focus couple—Burr's traveling salesman and his soon-to-be-missing invalid wife. The viewer does not meet everyone at once. Yet, they represent the Peeping Tom gang that has thus far become such an obvious obsession during Stewart's already lengthy convalescence. Consequently, Ritter has abundant evidence to call him on his voyeurism during her daily nursing visits.

Eventually Stewart's lovely fashion model girlfriend Lisa (Grace Kelly) will come sweeping into his apartment. But for now it is just he and company nurse Ritter (provided by the magazine for which he works) there to give him a daily rubdown and just generally monitor his recovery. Meanwhile, Ritter, of America's crackerbarrel school of humor, offers blue-collar insights beyond the world of Peeping Toms. Indeed, she even provides metaphorical verbal résumé examples of her common sense. From seemingly left field her character comically interjects an earthy example of how she anticipated the 1929 stock market crash which caused the not-so-great Depression. Ritter had been nursing the president of General Motors for an alleged kidney problem. But she thought it was nerves, figuring:

> What does General Motors got to be nervous about? "Over production," I said. "Collapse." When General Motors has got to go to the bathroom 10 times a day the country is ready to let go.

Just prior to this suggestion that the Wall Street wise guys should have seen the crash coming, Stewart's teasing editor had called to chat and suggested his star photographer consider getting married. Jeff's less than friendly reply was he had no need for "a nagging wife." This is the catalyst for Stella to interject Grace Kelly into the story and how she is just waiting to marry him. A disgruntled Stewart says he's "not ready to get married," plus Kelly's Lisa is "too perfect."

Ritter's answer to this is pure "school of hard knocks" crackerbarrel populism: "Nothing has given the human race so much trouble as intelligence." It ties in perfectly with her stock market put-downs of the tony Ivy League types, and the celebration of horse sense. For instance, populist Will Rogers' greatest comic print rival was the still (in the 1950s) widely syndicated humorist Kin Hubbard's alter ego, Abe Martin, who was full of comments like, "Lester Mopps has been out o' school fer nigh on two years an' he can't even play the saxophone," or "Miss Tawney Apple's cousin says he's never been able t' find as good a job as he had before he went thru' college."[13] The common sense success of such a perspective coming from Ritter is that she is a bona fide physical embodiment of the people, a personality comedy supporting star whose persona's fathomless tiredness always made her Brooklyn-accented comments amusing. Even the often acid-tongued critic David Thomson was moved to write of her:

> In a flower-print dress and flat shoes, her hair screwed up in a home perm, and her face like a used newspaper, she might have had a full day washing and cooking before she came to the studio, and a few hours' office cleaning ahead of her as soon as she finished. It is a tribute to her sour inventiveness that ... [she] never seemed boring.[14]

To cast her was to have comedy in mind, and the knowledge that she would enhance that trait in others. In an earlier era she might have been paired with a contrasting beauty in comic short subjects, like Zasu Pitts to the lovely Thelma Todd. Be that as it may, Ritter amusingly steals every *Rear Window* scene she is in.

However, Ritter's mantra with Stewart seems to be that he and Lisa get married and stop overthinking it. Again, she could be quoting Hubbard's Martin, "Experience is a dear teacher but delivers th'goods."[15] The subject of marriage is belabored here because *Rear Window* is about marriage ... and with apologies to Ritter, how it just does not work. Indeed, one could argue that the film's murder case is Hitchcock's MacGuffin.

Whenever the subject of marriage comes up, whether from Ritter or on Lisa's first screen appearance, Jeff gets angry and uses the easy insignificant distraction of his voyeurism to change the subject. And that, in a nutshell, is a minimalist demarcation between the crackerbarrel world and that of the comic antihero. That is, the former is anchored in a rational world in which one solves a directly addressed problem. In contrast, the now dominant domain of funny is antiheroic comedy chaos. Instead of facing the issue, one immerses oneself in whatever minutiae are handy.[16]

This humor transition had been slowly taking place since the beginning of the 20th century. Yet, it really began to escalate during the British

Depression years of Hitchcock's career. While one could start piling on everything from "the bomb" to global warming, the initial reason to stick one's head in the sand was the battle of the sexes, especially in the inspired writing of James Thurber and S.J. Perelman. And as already noted in the text, this is a theme at the heart of Hitchcock's humor, be it dark comedy or farce—the inherent incompatibility of the sexes. This is *Rear Window*'s comic core. Moreover, the man/woman divide remains one of life's major complications, or as Woody Allen's premier antiheroic poster child later stated, "Relationships are like the Middle East; there is no solution."

This people predicament is telegraphed from the beginning of *Rear Window*—there is no Jeff- Lisa romantic scenario in the short story upon which the movie is based, Cornell Woolrich's "It Had to Be Murder." Then add on Hitchcock's own complicated relationship in his own marriage, compartmentalized around the movies. Next, review his body of work, especially the movies highlighted in this text, and the relationship dilemma looms ever larger. Finally, with Chris Greenhalgh's 2012 non-fiction book, *Seducing Ingrid Bergman*, which explores the real doomed-to-failure affair between Bergman and the most celebrated of World War II photographers, Robert Capa, one knows this would have been in Hitchcock's mind when making *Rear Window*.

The director had a close friendship with Bergman, arguably his favorite actress after Grace Kelly. And while there are key differences between the *Rear Window* couple and the Bergman-Capa relationship, such as that the actress was married at the time (though this seldom stopped her affairs), the main thrust of the movie star appearance of Kelly's character and Stewart being a celebrated action photographer are not to be denied. Yet, even the Bergman-Capa affair could not be sustained. Bergman had countless lovers throughout her career, and Capa could not escape the adrenaline high that produced such haunting photographs as the Spanish Civil War image of a soldier still running forward at the precise moment he was fatally shot. (This photo was undoubtedly the stimulus for the unforgettable freeze frame conclusion to Peter Weir's anti-war film *Gallipoli*, 1981).

I have periodically suggested throughout the text that the dark comedy perspective on the MacGuffin could make it interchangeable with Samuel Beckett's *Waiting for Godot*. That is, just as something at the beginning of a Hitchcock film sucks the viewers into the story, only to have little or no meaning at the close, Beckett's entertaining duo keep us entertained throughout this play of life—in which God never comes. Whatever one's perspective on this idea, Hitchcock MacGuffins constantly pull once battling couples together throughout some adventure ... but will they stay together? As I now further begin to unreel *Rear Window*'s story, it will be up to the viewer to personally apply that important D.H. Lawrence piece of advice, "Never trust the teller, trust the tale"—the meaning is in the viewer's hands. However, it would be unfair to not add that most of the boxed-in couples in Stewart's menagerie of marriages are unhappy.

Regardless, one might now want to ask has not the forthcoming chaos of *Rear Window* sandbagged Ritter's crackerbarrel character? The simple answer is "no" on two counts. First, she correctly said ugly things would come of his voyeurism, which will soon be mapped out. Second, I purposely linked her with crackerbarrel humorist Kin Hubbard, because just as Ritter gets pulled into Stewart's Peeping Tom diversion, Hubbard was a transitional figure from the populist to the antihero—which also explains why he was syndicated so long.[17] Plus, his pioneering use of the antihero was fittingly fueled by a challenging late-in-life marriage. Along these lines, what follows is one of his classic and most stolen (including by W.C. Fields) antiheroic axioms, "Two can live as cheaply as one, just not as long."[18]

Moreover, Ritter's joining of Stewart's voyeuristic pastime has the feel of the farcical, seemingly harmless parlor games on murder practices by *Rope*'s (1948) Jimmy Stewart character and Robert Walker's Bruno in *Strangers*. That is, until Jeff pulls out his telephoto lens and metaphorically enters those squared dark comedy cages which pass for *Rear Window* apartments, one can convince oneself that it is merely harmless fun, playing upon the innocent snoopy nature in many of us. Plus, with Ritter's comic populist patter, and Stewart as a curmudgeonly straight man, there is a great deal of humor. And laughter is arguably the most effective manner in which to bend societal norms. In fact, that is a pivotal point in the *Hollywood Reporter*'s review of *Rear Window*, which also more than accents the *comic* thriller nature of the film:

> Throughout the film, Hitchcock maintains a half-comic mood of spying and eavesdropping that makes the audience feel it is indulging in one of the most persistent of human fables. The laughs are almost continuous.[19]

The earlier references to farce also make for a perfect transition here to Grace Kelly's entrance early that evening, as well as being a spoof of German Expressionism—a shadow starts to fall over a Stewart asleep in his wheelchair—and then becomes arguably Hitchcock's most bewitching image of beauty in his complete oeuvre. This close-up of Kelly is not only beautiful but frustrating—how could this actress soon give up movies for Monaco, a "kingdom" smaller than Central Park? Regardless, *frustrating* is a legitimate feeling here. She is so much in love with Stewart, and the now awake patient treats her poorly as they argue about a life together.

Still, the world of farce and social parties, nightclubs, and high society walks in the door with her arrival. If his condition keeps him cloistered, she is capable of bringing the world of the Fortune 500 to his door. She arrives in an $1,100 dress ($11,000 when adjusted for today), with a caterer from the posh "21 Club" and an elaborate lobster dinner for two. She directs her assistant in culinary arts to place the meal in Stewart's oven on low, and then politely dismisses him so she can engage her reluctant boyfriend in discussion.

Kelly's immediate small talk continues along the lines of a miniaturized soirée that one has seen in earlier Hitchcock films, such as the intermittent blather to be heard in *Rope* (1948). For example, Lisa has generously planted stories about Jeff in all the right newspapers, and encouragingly suggests how easy it would be for him to open a portrait salon. And what soon follows is a series of events which touch upon several comedy genres all wrapped in a black humor blanket.

First, Stewart tells her, "Let's stop talking nonsense" (about a shared life)—which is precisely how so many screwball comedies begin, such as the stalking socialite Katharine Hepburn of *Bringing Up Baby* (1938), attempting romance with a definitely disinclined opposite—Cary Grant's professorial zoologist. Second, almost simultaneously in *Rear Window* one hears a recording of Bing Crosby singing, "To See You Is to Love You." Dark comedy slithers in here, since the genre's use of music often does not match the image, such as *A Clockwork Orange*'s (1971) Malcolm McDowell beating someone while warbling "Singin' in the Rain." Now nothing so drastic as that is occurring in *Rear Window* yet, but Crosby's song certainly does not match Stewart's anger with Kelly at that particular moment. Indeed, a better musical match here would have been something like the later blues song, "I Pity the Fool (That Falls in Love with You)." To him, Lisa is out to castrate him by separating him from the work that defines his seemingly macho life. And as Hitchcock's surrogate in the film, one cannot help remembering variations of the director's favorite introduction, "It's just 'Hitch,' no cock."

Moreover, as a flashforward look at such a union, one need only view the unhappy image of Stewart's marriage at the beginning of Hitchcock's later remake of his own *The Man Who Knew Too Much* (1956). Stewart has married another beautiful blonde, Doris Day, who, like Grace Kelly, had also been used to the high life, having been a popular professional singer. Yet, despite having quit her job for him, Stewart is still a bully.... And the couple are even on *vacation*. As in the original *Too Much* film, only the kidnapping of their child brings them together ... but for how long?

Third, an early 1950s film audience would also associate Crosby's "To See You Is to Love You" with personality comedy, since it had been used in the popular Hope & Crosby *Road to Bali* (1953), helping make it a hit. Moreover, despite the romantic song, for any of the legion of "Road Picture" fans, this movie franchise inevitably brings to mind two oversexed guys pursuing "Miss Torso" types around the globe. Romance is M.I.A. here.

10. Rear Window (1954)

Fourth, playing upon dark comedy's theme of absurdity, such as the mismatching of music and image, *Rear Window* next has Stewart toast Miss Lonely hearts across the courtyard. Here is where the dark comedy and absurdity became multifaceted. However, a brief set-up is necessitated. Judith Evelyn's friendless figure gets dressed up and prepares a meal for an imaginary date, all of which Peeping Tom Stewart has been following. And Jeff toasts Judith just as she pours wine for her phantom boyfriend ... with Lisa beside him! Castration comes to mind again.

Fifth, it gets better and/or worse along absurdity lines. "To See You Is to Love You" is all ironically imaginary for Miss Lonely Hearts—lost in her solo play. Moreover, while Jeff can see Judith, he might as well be a ghost, both in her world *and* his own—since he seems to like women only at *distance*. In that way, women cannot bother him, and while he can feel pity for Judith, there is also a degree of dark comedy superiority—a bored God looking down at His puzzled humanity. At the very least he is a Robert Browning figure, whose "interests [are] on the dangerous edge of things."

Sixth, the absurdity continues, because the next neighbor Stewart focuses on is Miss Torso, surrounded by *real* men who lust after her (the dark comedy theme of man as beast) but about whom she could care less. In another Hitchcock film she might have been a victim, given that Jeff is such an extension of the director. And the Catholic Church had warned Hitchcock the child about these temptresses. Moreover, both his shyness and bulk had negated any hope for contact with them, even if he could get past the papal brainwashing.

Seventh, dark comedy absurdity continues to be in a *Rear Window* full-court press. Stewart next glances to the apartment of Raymond Burr's Thorwald and his invalid wife. Keep in mind, Lisa has just brought Jeff supper—since his broken leg keeps him housebound. Along similar lines, Thorwald has prepared an evening meal for his bedridden wife and brought it to her. As with Jeff and Lisa, there is an almost immediate argument. The Thorwalds rate two windows, and Burr immediately retreats from the bedroom to the living room and makes a call. It is implied he possibly has a woman on the side. Yet, since this is a Hitchcock film, why could it not be to his mommy? Regardless, the blonde Mrs. Thorwald, who, at a distance, looks somewhat like Lisa, laughs derisively at poor Lars—a name which seems to give him even more childlike sympathy. One realizes amidst all this absurdity pinballing about in Jeff's head that the film's Bing Crosby song is even more of a dark comedy joke. Dark comedy also squares here, because it connects Stewart and Burr through nagging women.

Hitchcock, despite being an artist of almost always pending chaos, does bring his brief tour of the neighborhood windows full circle, back to the screwball comedy-like party of two setting of Stewart and Kelly. Thus, one must have a little repartee, as biting as it may be. The substance for this is provided by the final window visited—the blocked songwriter. Stewart meanly quips to Lisa that the man's problem is "he probably had a very unhappy marriage." The ever upbeat Kelly romantically counters, "It's like he's writing it [the song] for us." Stewart quickly counters with, "No wonder he's having so much trouble." (Hitchcock's cameo is here, which arguably could be called dark comedy—since for the director, the art of his cinema centered on the writing, consequently to be blocked....)

The fact that Hitchcock has given the viewer another trip around Stewart's Peeping Tom domain is important for three potentially comic reasons. First, one could argue it represents a tie-in with the director's beloved author Edgar Allan Poe. The poet/short story writer's most voyeuristic tale is "The Man of the Crowd." Poe's central character sits in a London coffee-house and watches people pass. He too, like Jeff, has been recovering from a medical condition. And the evolution of his Peeping Tom tendencies anticipates Jeff's experiences:

> At first my observations took an abstract and generalizing turn. I looked at the passengers in masses, and thought of them in their aggregate relations. Soon, however, I descended into details.[20]

Thus, while Stewart will never lose count of all his neighbors, Lars and his soon to be missing wife are about to become his focus.

A second Hitchcock lesson drawn from the Poe story is more complex. Like the short story from which *Rear Window* is adapted, Poe also did *not* have a possible romantic figure with a vested interest to join the voyeuristic adventure—a comic co-detective of sorts with whom to draw in and/or fool a larger audience. Hitchcock comically tops the master here. Third, Poe's essay close about the ephemeral nature of "knowing" anyone reveals Hitchcock's misdirection happy ending. That is, Poe states, "It will be in vain to follow [spy on someone], for I shall learn no more of him, nor of his deeds."[21]

As noted earlier in the text, when a dark comedy like *Rear Window* ends upon an overly upbeat note, it is to be questioned as yet more black humor. Consequently, *Rear Window*'s last view of most Stewart neighbors as happy is comic suspension of disbelief, like the finally happy W.C. Fields who closes *It's a Gift* (1934). Ironically, such a smoke screen is just another way of avoiding Ritter's chapter opening advice to be introspective. And remember Hitchcock's disdain for logic—always a wonderful philosophy for the sleight of hand that often bolsters dark comedy.

In addition, Hitchcock's comic manipulation is that of confidence man, grafter, diddler ... whatever the name for a character which has been around as long as there have been people. In Poe's sardonic essay on the phenomenon, "Diddling Considered as One of the Exact Sciences," he observes, "To diddle is his [man's] destiny.... This is his aim—his object—his end. Perhaps the first diddler was Adam."[22] Thus, in one of the rare *Rear Window* moments when Hitchcock does *not* restrict the viewer to Stewart's view of his neighbors (Jeff has fallen asleep in the wheelchair), Lars leaves the apartment with a woman resembling his wife. Agreed, at the film's near end, one hears a cop say Lars is "ready to take us on a tour of the East River [for presumed body parts]." But this comic murder movie still closes upon circumstantial evidence. One is reminded of the *Monkey Business* (1931) conversation between Hollywood's greatest grafter of absurdity, Groucho Marx, and the neglected blonde comedian, Thelma Todd, just after he has slipped out of her bedroom closet:

> THELMA: Don't try to hide, I know you're in that closet.
> GROUCHO: Did you see me go in the closet?
> THELMA: No.
> GROUCHO: Am I in the closet now?
> THELMA: Well, no.
> GROUCHO: Then how do you know I was in the closet [lying on her bed].... Your Honor, I rest my case!

Rear Window's Jeff is like Thelma Todd. Groucho had been in the closet, and Burr probably killed his wife, but like Todd, Jeff never saw a thing. Diddling Hitchcock is playing with us, and spoofing the easy mob mentality of the national film movement that so helped shape him—German Expressionism.

However, like Truffaut's *400 Blows'* (1959) alter ego boy in the amusement park's spinning centrifuge ride, one must return to how *Rear Window* whirls us to its upbeat unlikely close. After Stewart's argumentative evening with Kelly, he sleeps on and off in his wheelchair. At one point there is a scream, "Don't!" Later he is awakened by a storm, which ends the comedy of the neighbors trying to sleep on the fire escape. On and off he sees Burr leave with a suitcase, only to return, then repeat the action.

Indeed, his neighbors seem more active at night. It is, of course, Greenwich Village. The frustrated songwriter is drunk and knocks over his sheet music stand. Stewart is again asleep, only to be awakened by Miss Torso successfully fighting off a date at her door. Burr returns yet again with his suitcase. Like a dream sequence in a Buster Keaton world, one could question what is real. At the very least, Stewart's nodding off and on in a seated position is comically reminiscent of anyone trying to reconstruct a movie s/he has seen only intermittently while snoozing. Obviously, one's narrative of the events is full of holes. Unlike Keaton's title character in *Sherlock, Jr.* (1923), Jeff has not been able to enter the dream, if that is what it is. Thus, his scorecard is full of missing innings.

Naturally, Jeff attempts to engage his small circle of friends in a growing theory that Burr has murdered his wife—chopped her up, and removed her piece by piece via a suitcase. At first it is a comic hard sell. For example, he asks his resident stand-up comic crackerbarrel character, Ritter's Stella, why any husband would leave his apartment three times in one night. Without missing a beat, she replies, "He likes the way his wife welcomes him home?" He also receives amusing comebacks from Lisa and an old war buddy, now working as a detective, Wendell Corey as Doyle.

Of course, during Doyle's initial visit he is first distracted by Miss Torso doing her daily minimally attired dancing. Paradoxically, this even inspires a comic quip from Stewart, "How's your wife?" Though just a passing joke, it also allows Hitchcock to yet again sideswipe marriage. Indeed, Hitchcock disciple Truffaut recycles the same line and situation in his Oscar-winning film on filming, *Day for Night* (1973), which also comically showcases monogamy as a train wreck. Moreover, Doyle's embarrassment at being voyeuristically caught then also allows Hitchcock to briefly feed his catalyst for periodically using art for comic effect. As one is prone to do when discovered gawking, Doyle quickly turns away, and finds himself briefly staring at a painting on Jeff's wall. Said artwork elicits a double take that passes as comic surprise to the viewer. A framed action photo by Jeff had appeared early in *Rear Window*, representing classic Hitchcock visual shorthand for Jeff's broken leg and dangerous career. However, the painting that surprises Doyle is only fleetingly showcased. It is some sort of still life or pastoral setting which is completely alien to his friend's apartment. The painting has undoubtedly been hung by Lisa, and is, at face value, another comic example of her ongoing attempt to domesticate/change Jeff.

Be that as it may, in time Lisa, Stella, and a comically reluctant Doyle are on board for this murder. As noted before, the killing is the MacGuffin which will create a dangerous adventure and put Jeff and Lisa on the same page, instead of society versus the outback. Stewart's evidence at this point is close to a whole lot of nothing. However, like voyeurism, a murder mystery has a way of also eventually drawing in a crowd. The *Chicago Tribune*'s review even opens by saying most people would like to show "the homicide squad a thing or two."[23] However, interest in murder merits a more earthy description. A winning example occurs in the Hitchcock-like *Gaslight* (1944), a title synonymous with films in which the heroine feels threatened and frightened (whether the danger is real or imagined) by the man she loves. Hitchcock had already gone there with *Rebecca* (1940) and *Suspicion* (1942). However, my point in noting *Gaslight* is to entertainingly document the broad demographic of the public which has a murder fascination in even a Hitchcock-like film. One *Gaslight* sequence is so like the director's work it could nearly serve as an outtake from *The Lady Vanishes* (1938). A young Ingrid Bergman finds herself on a train seated beside a British stranger—an older, pleasantly matronly Dame May Whitty (*Vanishes*' Miss Froy):

10. Rear Window (1954)

WHITTY: Oh, oh, oh. Oh my goodness. Good gracious.
BERGMAN: Your book?
WHITTY: It's all about a girl who marries a man and what do you think? He's got six wives buried in the cellar.
BERGMAN: Seems a lot.
Whitty: Yes, and I'm only on page 200. So I'm sure there's still more to come. It's a wonderful book.
BERGMAN: It sounds a little gruesome.
WHITTY: Well, I'm afraid I enjoy a good murder now and then. My brother always calls me Blood Thirsty Bessie. Have a biscuit [cookie, offered to Bergman]?

The key phrase here is most people "enjoy a good murder now and then." Though both *Rear Window* women believe in Stewart's story before his detective friend, the situation plays better to the earthy crackerbarrel Thelma Ritter. Examining the logistics of the crime fits her worldly wise methodical type. For example, with a furrowed brow she suddenly blurts out that Burr must have cut up his misses in the bathtub, for an easier clean-up detail. The sequence is funny on several levels. First, as one review noted, the observation is "hilarious" because it is so suitable to the "blunt and talkative nurse."[24]

Second, she suddenly divulges this graphic detail just as Stewart has started to eat the breakfast she has prepared for him. For Hitchcock, the man with the gargantuan appetite, food and funny are frequent components in his work. In this comic case, poor Stewart will definitely not be eating until lunch. Ironically, Hitchcock's most famous example of food and dark comedy comes from his TV series—an episode he directed, "Lamb to the Slaughter" (1958), in which a woman kills her husband with a frozen leg of lamb and then "thoughtfully" feeds the investigating police the murder weapon for supper. One of the cops, fixated on finding the weapon, says, "For all we know, it could be right under our very noses." The episode was written by the multi-talented author Roald Dahl, whose many works include the dark novel which was the basis for *Willy Wonka & the Chocolate Factory* (1971).

Regardless, the third explanation for the brusque mixing of where Mrs. Thorwald was dismembered and the delivering of Stewart's meal is that black humor is an extension of reason two—with the focus on Ritter. The juxtaposing of two such opposites (meals and murder) and not being bothered is disturbingly funny. Moreover, one could broaden it by tacking on Hitchcock's belief that anyone was capable of killing. Moreover, if Ritter can talk about these things while handling kitchen chores, even with Stella being one of the "good guys," this is yet more evidence for Hitchcock that killing is not that far out of the realm of possibility for anyone.

As an addendum to the earlier mix of death and eating—a popular variation on the theme was a staple of Hitchcock's beloved silent comedy. One assumes the director would have been a fan of *The Circus* (1928) sequence in which Chaplin's Tramp is constantly near death during his attempt at a high wire act, while one of the tubby audience members far below is stuffing popcorn in his mouth as fast as possible.

Be that as it may, while *Rear Window* is one of Hitchcock's funniest *comic* thrillers, one particular scene is a dark comedy throwback to the aforementioned Nietzschean trilogy. The cute dog that periodically has been lowered in a basket as a substitute for a walk is found killed in the middle of the movie. The couple who own the dog have used it as a surrogate child to maintain their union (another Hitchcock hamstringing of marriage). Regardless, the wife's outburst upon finding her dead pooch could be considered the signature scene of the picture, even more than Stewart's ultimate confrontation with Burr.

Like the Nietzschean trilogy, the woman's screaming attack on her neighbors once again expresses Hitchcock's extreme black humor view of humanity in the most passionate manner, especially because up until this point *Rear Window* has played more as a comedy than a thriller:

> Which one of you did it? Which one of you killed my dog? You don't know the meaning of the word neighbor. Neighbors like each other, speak to each other, care if anybody lives or dies but none of you do. But I couldn't imagine any of you bein' so low that you'd kill a helpless friendly dog.

Hitchcock ratchets up the emotion further by breaking his normal visual norm of being limited to Stewart's perspective. For example, the brief concerned look of Miss Torso is from an angle Peeping Tom Stewart would not have had. But still, no one says or does anything to comfort the grieving woman. The pet owner's "show" is just a brief interruption to her neighbors' lives, and they soon return to whatever they were doing—dark comedy at its blackest.

That is, while Jeff and company can casually and frequently discuss dicing a person up, the picture's only real emotional scene involving death, until the near conclusion, concerns a mere dog. And even then, it only comes from the owner. Hitchcock literature makes much of the point that everyone rushes to their windows when the screaming starts, save Burr. In his darkened apartment only the periodic pinpoint light of a cigarette can be seen, meaning he must have done it. But so what? Reinforcing Hitchcock's dark comedy view of humanity, all the people drawn to their windows by the pet owner's eruption soon nonchalantly return to whatever they were doing, probably thinking (and I use the expression loosely) no further than the popular period utterance, "Tomorrow's pay day and bath night."

Be that as it may, as Ritter and Kelly do the detective leg work for wheelchair bound Stewart, Ritter's dark comedy one-liners continue to fly. Indeed, not noted today, period reviewers sometimes highlighted Ritter's comic role *more* than Kelly's romantic one. In fact, the *Chicago Tribune*, after heavily praising Ritter, said of Kelly, "[She] is mighty pretty, even though she seems to have affected a stilted form of speech for her role."[25] And returning to

10. Rear Window (1954)

Ritter, the *Los Angeles Times* review added, "Miss Ritter provides a great commentary on all occasions. She enlivens the whole film."[26] Nevertheless, the amateur detective work continues, with Stewart having penned Burr a note when he was out, which Kelly slides under his door, "What have you done with her?" However, it is Ritter's assignment to report on Burr's response— "It wasn't the kind of expression that would get him a quick loan at the bank." However, now inspired as much by Ritter as by Stewart, Kelly fully joins this mini-homicide squad with a casual dark comedy observation, when the two women decide to dig up Burr's flower garden. The catalyst is that the dog turned up dead after having pawed about the grounds.... Did the patch include buried body parts? Kelly observes, in the most offhand manner, which increases its potentially grisly outcome to further dark comedy effect, "I've always wanted to meet Mrs. Thorwald."

While nothing is found here, Kelly next pushes the envelope by entering the Thorwald apartment when Burr is gone. However, he returns before she can escape, and as things prepare to get ugly, a distraught Stewart calls the police to report a disturbance in that apartment. The cops arrive quickly, and Kelly's arrest actually equals a rescue. However, another signature moment occurs just before Kelly's Lisa is taken to jail. She has found the wedding band of Burr's missing wife. Placing it on her finger, with her back to the window, Lisa signals the discovery to Peeping Tom Stewart. The action puts into motion several things, both real and hypothetical. First, Burr has seen her gesture to someone. Lenses tend to make camera people feel invisible, and Jeff has not gotten back quickly enough.

Second, the ring is more evidence that Mrs. Thorwald has been murdered. But with dark comedy perversity, Lisa beams with successful detective glee, as if she has won at a game of "Risk." Third, by gambling everything, she now feels, if only subliminally, she has proven herself as brave enough to share Jeff's dangerous world. Fourth, to get the ring out, it is only natural for her to hide it in plain sight by wearing it.

Yet, a ring on her finger can also represent something else to marriage-damning Hitchcock. With dark comedy symbolism, does it not imply that Jeff and Lisa will soon marry? This is reminiscent of the comically ominous threat of marriage which closes *The 39 Steps* (1935). Robert Donat and Madeline Carroll secretly hold hands behind their backs. However, hanging down beside their hands are the handcuffs still strapped to Donat's wrist, courtesy of their recent adventure. This too, does not bode well for their implied future marriage.

Despite all these pockets of expression, Hitchcock leaves it to his resident comic commentator, Ritter, to put a dark humor spin on the story thus far. After Stewart's detectives friend bails out Kelly, and Stella return to Jeff's apartment, the following exchange occurs:

JEFF: How long will he [Burr] stay there [in that apartment]?
STELLA: Unless he's dumber than I think he is, he won't stay until his lease is up.

Stewart makes a call to detective friend Tom. Time passes and Jeff finds himself alone when the phone rings. Thinking it is Tom with more information about Burr, Stewart's excitable character starts talking first and then realizes it is probably Burr on the line, before the phone clicks dead. From this point on things move quickly. Anticipating he will soon be attacked, wheelchair-bound Stewart devises the best holding action a photographer can devise—in his darkened apartment, he will use powerful flashbulbs to temporarily blind Burr.

Stewart's hunch is correct, and Burr soon reverses the Buster Keaton/ *Sherlock, Jr.*, analogy to metaphorically come off the screen and enter Jeff's seemingly once removed space. Moreover, any thriller trappings to the sequence are mitigated by the pitifully, almost darkly comic personification of the monster one expects. (Hitchcock is working his way towards 1960's *Psycho* and Norman Bates.) What follows are questions from Burr in essentially a pause-ridden monologue, with the first one something Stewart might have asked of the nagging Kelly at the film's beginning:

What do you want from me? [pause]
Your friend, the girl, could have turned me in, why didn't she? [pause]
What is it you want, a lot of money? I don't have any money. [pause]
Say something! Say something. Tell me what you want. Can you get me that ring back?

Ultimately Stewart tells him the police have it by now. The Burr one sees brings to mind writer Hannah Arendt's comments about Adolf Eichmann's trial in Jerusalem, which she described as "the banality of evil." However, Burr does come for Stewart, and though the flash bulbs (each time Jeff covers his eyes) do slow him down, eventually our hero is tossed out the window—with his fall partially mitigated by the last minute arrival of the police.

However, Hitchcock soon even turns this attempted murder into dark comedy—the next day Stewart is back in his wheelchair with casts on *two* broken legs. Moreover, he and Lisa are apparently fated to marry, with each of them seemingly compromising. Jeff's wheelchair is turned away from the window, and Lisa is sitting on the couch in jeans more befitting Stewart's former action lifestyle ... but can one assume it will be *forever*? Those are designer jeans, and while she is reading something fittingly manly for him, a book entitled *Beyond the High Himalayas*, as soon as this man old enough to be her father nods off, she pulls out a fashion magazine to read.

The same "beautiful day in the neighborhood" has also descended on the apartment complex. The composer's song has been completed and recorded—with Miss Lonely Hearts visiting as a potential romantic interest. The couple who lost their dog now have a new one. The chubby sculptor has finished her chubby piece called "Hunger." Miss Torso is so happy that her serviceman *husband* is back, despite having surrounded herself by an army of men while he was gone. (Some texts call him Miss Torso's "boyfriend," but if you listen closely, the way he enthusiastically says, "It's good to be home" suggests otherwise.) The Thorwald apartment is being repainted, and even the weather has chipped in. Oh, it was not third grader bundle-up time but the temperature gauge was considerably cooler.

The only blip on the radar screen is the single couple that was formerly happy. It turns out the bride was probably not a nympho, since she has found out her groom does not have the job she thought he had. Plus, one has to question the long term happiness of a Hitchcock character named Miss Lonely Hearts, if one knows Nathanael West's classic 1933 novel *Miss Lonelyhearts*. The book was conceived in Greenwich Village, and its title character is a messed-up Catholic male who dies trying to help someone. It even includes a mantra Hitchcock attempted his whole life, "Forget the crucifixion, remember the Renaissance.... *Art Is a Way Out*."[27] Plus, though uncredited, an original West script was the starting point for Hitchcock's *Suspicion* (1941), a title which also could easily have been substituted for *Rear Window*.[28] How appropriate that a novel, *Miss Lonelyhearts*, now compared to the theatre of the absurd *Waiting for Godot*, can legitimately rub shoulders with *Rear Window*. Hitchcock's comic thriller is so much more, even with Paramount's overly cute close—a shade is pulled down over the screen. Oh, and with Hitchcock's dark comic "suspicion" of marriage, I give the duration of any Jeff-Lisa relationship the time it takes two broken legs to heal.

11

The Trouble with Harry (1955)

> "Mother always said I'd come to a bad end"—Captain (Edmund Gwenn), after he thinks he has killed the title character of *The Trouble with Harry*

"Understatement is important to me," Hitchcock said. "*Harry* is an approach to a strictly British genre, the humor of the macabre. I made that picture to prove that the American public could appreciate British humor."[1] But the picture did not quite prove that statement correct, initially. It opened to mixed American reviews and lost money. Moreover, Hitchcock had been peppering most of his sound films with macabre humor from the beginning, and *Harry* has a fair share of American dark comedy, from Edgar Allan Poe, to Charles Addams' *New Yorker* cartoons and their "horrification of American bourgeois living"—two artists Hitchcock dearly loved."[2]

The director later observed, "It lost, I suppose, half a million dollars. So that's an expensive self-indulgence. I didn't think enough about the audience."[3] That perspective was often found in period reviews, too. For example, the *Los Angeles Examiner*'s critique comically observed, "There are those ... who think it should have been called 'The Private Joke of Producer Hitchcock,' or 'A Pixie Has Himself a Ball!'"[4] And thirty-odd years later Andrew Sarris' revisionist *Village Voice* critique basically summarized that view—"...at the time it was seen as self-indulgent."[5]

However, like an old Jerry Lewis joke, the French immediately loved *Harry*. (This might also have been fueled by young auteur critics like François Truffaut and Jean-Luc Godard, who were already pioneering Hitchcock-as-artist advocates.) Regardless, a Paris theatre even played *Harry* continuously for a year and a half. Moreover, while some American critics hated the film, such as the *New York Post* describing it as "hitting bottom," the *New York Journal-American* called it an "exercise in whimsy."[6] However, flashforward

11. The Trouble with Harry (1955)

to 1984 and *Harry* received the full comic credit it had long deserved. For example *Los Angeles Weekly* called it a "little gem of a black comedy—alive with the sort of wry, sparkling wit we associate with *Punch* or *The New Yorker*."[7]

Be that as it may, after setting up the opening for this multifaceted comedy, the "self-indulgent" factor needs to be rebooted. Because while *Harry* is finally getting at least some of the attention it deserves, the phrase "self-indulgent" is still, for some odd reason, being used as a negative. Thus, in Charlotte Chandler's Hitchcock biography, with a cover blurb by his daughter calling it "the best book ever written about my father," there is the general suggestion the film was still flawed because Hitchcock's collaborating spouse had not monitored the picture enough:

> In Alma's [his wife's] presence, Hitchcock had told me [Chandler] that one of the few things they didn't share was a similar sense of humor. "I had to curb his sense of humor," she told me but in *Harry* she had let her husband go his own way, without her usual restraint.[8]

As the film opens, a freshly dead body of an outsider has suddenly appeared on the hillside above a small Vermont village. Given the film's exquisite Technicolor, on the most ravishing of New England autumn days, it is the most unrepresentative of places to find a dead body ... thus adding to the dark comedy. Regardless, a series of individuals, one by one, will come by the corpse as if it were the most natural of things to discover—dark comedy absurdity. The first is a little boy (Jerry Mathers of later *Leave It to Beaver* TV fame), the screen son of Jennifer Rogers (Shirley MacLaine, in her first film role). Carrying his toy space gun (the Soviets launched Sputnik two years later), the child runs off to tell his mother. (Herein lies more absurdity; the youngest passerby will be the only one to show a modicum of awareness that something is not normal.)

The next passerby is the Captain. Since he has just gotten three shots off hunting rabbits, he is afraid that he has killed Harry. One should add at this point that Hitchcock often films the corpse in the most amusing perspectives, such as a low angle shot with the bottom of his big shoes dominating the frame of reference. Regardless, just as the dispassionate Captain grabs Harry's feet in an attempt to hide him, the hamlet's spinster lady with the paradoxically appropriate name Ivy Gravely (Mildred Natwick) happens by.

She ever so calmly asks the Captain, "What seems to be the trouble?" He briefly explains the situation and begs her not to say anything. Touching his hand, Gravely promises not to tell, and casually adds, "I'm sure you've seen worse things." Ironically, a flirtation suddenly begins over the dead body, and she invites him to her cottage later for muffins and wine. Keep in mind

The morgue brigade, from left to right: Mildred Natwick, Edmund Gwenn, Jerry Mathers, Shirley MacLaine, and John Forsythe—with horizontal Harry.

that dark comedy often links death and sexuality. If that seems a stretch for this senior couple, Gwenn's character will later say of Gravely, "[She's a] well preserved woman and preserves have to be opened someday." (It also later comes out that she is feeling guilty, because Harry had attempted to pull her into the bushes and she struck him on the head with the heel of her shoe. This incident was represented by never explained noises at the story's beginning.)

Once Gravely leaves but before the Captain can drag Harry off into the woods, he hears more noise coming up the path and is forced to hide himself. Rogers' son has brought her back to view the body. She makes the blasé comment, "Thank Providence that's the last of Harry." Eventually it is revealed that he was her estranged husband, and that Harry had also recently made unwarranted advances upon her and she had hit him on the head with a milk bottle. Thus, Harry's attack on Gravely had probably occurred with Harry in a dazed state, thinking it was Rogers.

Once the mother and her boy casually leave for lemonade but before the captain can come out of hiding, the village doctor/intellectual comes by immersed in a book. He trips over the corpse and falls, losing his glasses. After finding his spectacles, he gets up and goes back to walking and read-

11. The Trouble with Harry (1955)

ing—never even noticing dead Harry. Almost immediately a tramp (Barry Macollum) happens by, and with no concern for the deceased, he fixates on Harry's bright shiny new shoes. Checking sizes, the tramp is soon walking away wearing both a big smile and footwear comically incongruous to his shabby attire. However, more amusing now are the exposed socks Harry is wearing, which Hitchcock showcases in that same low angle feet-first perspective—but now with the brightest two-tone blue and red tipped stockings. Like a precursor to Rodney Dangerfield, even in death Harry gets "no respect." All this uncaring sets the table for dark comedy's "man as beast." Moreover, when the story eventually factors in the gun, the boot heel, and the milk bottle factor, everyone save the boy might actually have killed Harry. This matches Hitchcock's perspective that anyone is capable of killing. Moreover, with even the child toting a toy *gun*, one might suggest with dark comedy irony that the training to kill starts early. In fact, when the Captain's rabbit directed shots are fired, the boy immediately hits the ground like a combat veteran.

There will be one more person randomly passing the corpse, but first Hitchcock will include some scenic cutaways to again suggest the peculiar presence of death in such bright and lovely surroundings, as well as the passage of time. Hitchcock then couples the paradox of death in such an appealing location by returning to a close-up of Harry's feet and the equally comic paradox of such dazzling socks being on dead feet. Next, in the distance, another ironic mismatch is occurring. One hears a male singing the most upbeat, funny tune, "Flaggin' the Train to Tuscaloosa." The soloist turns out to be the village artist San Marlowe (John Forsythe). Again, one has a dark comedy component perfectly tied-up—merry music which does *not* match the dead visual. (And Hitchcock even manages to get in a reference to his love of trains.)

However, before Sam gets to the Captain's "trouble with Harry," Hitchcock takes the viewer through part of the hamlet. One sees a stand with Sam's unsold paintings and various food related items. Mrs. Wiggs (Mildred Dunnock) is in charge of the booth and her nearby general store. There is also an ever so fleeting moment with her surly grown son, Deputy Sheriff Calvin Wiggs (Royal Dano). Finally, Forythe's Sam is in the woods and spots horizontal Harry, and is taken with those bright socks and legs and begins to sketch them. He does not realize Harry is dead at first. Briefly, he starts to leave, then he nonchalantly returns to sketching Harry, as lackadaisical as looking at road kill. Yet, the Christ-like face he draws will later have dark comedy implications.

Now that the *Harry* story set-up is established, deeply ingrained in the dark comedy fundamentals already noted (and which will shortly be expanded upon), it is time to get at the many other kinds of comedy looking to be recognized. First, the phrase "self-indulgence" needs to be dusted off and reframed as a positive key catalyst for calling the Captain a Hitchcock personality comedy alter ego, complete with biographical overtones. One might start with the Captain's chapter opening quote, "Mother always said I'd come to a bad end." Nothing is more Hitchcockian than linking one's mother to something threatening. Indeed, the director always said his epitaph should be, "This is what happens to bad little boys."

In fact, one could hazard a guess that Hitchcock was immediately taken with the novel from which *Harry* is adapted by Gwen's observation being ever so close to an even more amusing observation by the book's narrator, "His mother had always said he would hang sooner or later, and it was later."[9] (The film follows the book and Hitchcock extremely closely, including having a chubby Captain.)

Second, Hitchcock himself (through Edmund Gwenn) had all the best lines, something that was just now beginning to happen to him in real life as the host of the long-running TV show, *Alfred Hitchcock Presents*, which premiered the same year as *Harry*. His macabre dry wit opening and closing segments entertainingly anchored the program, and made it a hit, unimaginable without these "bookends." With regard to his sardonic *Harry* observations, there was a clever mix of Hitchcock foreboding and the unflappable elderly directions of a comic New England Yankee. For example, soon after the Captain finds dead Harry, he observes, "The first thing I seen when I rolled out [got up] this morning was a double-breasted robin drunk as a hoot owl from eating fermented choke cherries. Right away I knew someone was in trouble. What I didn't know was it was me."

Third, as this text has already well documented, Hitchcock had the greatest of fears with regard to the police. This anxiety is liberally sprinkled throughout the Captain's dialogue. For instance, early in the film he discusses his apparent killing of Harry with Forsythe's artist. The Captain confesses he is not really that bothered by the shooting, especially given that he neither has a conscience, nor believes in heaven. But the problem is he has an immense fear of the police. Later in the story, when the Captain realizes he was not responsible for Harry's death, the old sailor still is afraid the killing will be pinned upon him unless something is done—"[Then] I'll get shakier whenever I see a policeman." And later still in the film the paranoid Hitchcock-like Captain expands upon why the law gives him such horrible apprehensiveness: "They just wear you down and wear you down and wear you down and you're almost grateful when they [the authorities] give you the gas chamber!"

Fourth, as already suggested with the Gwenn-Forsythe conversation, like Hitchcock, the Captain has little regard for humanity. Yes, he is troubled when he thinks he has killed Harry; however, it is all about what will happen

11. The Trouble with Harry (1955)

to *him* (the Captain). Moreover, Gwenn is also upset when he does not recognize the corpse, as if knowing the victim would somehow make the shooting acceptable—more dark humor absurdity.

The Captain next doubles down on this nonsensical attitude by lecturing dead Harry: "If you're going to get yourself shot, do it where you're known." Then, when Gwenn checks Harry's pockets for some sort of ID, or place of residence, he discovers a letter noting the corpse is from Boston. This triggers the most couldn't-care-less bit of nihilism from the Captain: "From the looks of it you won't get back for Christmas." While the *New York Daily News* review describes a cast in which "nothing is held sacred," the phrase best fits the Captain.[10] As if to establish that fact early, when one first meets the Captain, he says out loud, "Fewer things in life give man more pleasure than hunting." He then further clarifies that statement—seemingly more for the audience, à la a director's note, than for himself—because hunting satisfies man's "primitive nature." And Hitchcock was all about man's thin veneer of civilization, and the necessity in a sedate world for "controlled thrills."

Fifth, the Captain parallels a comic personality twist on Hitchcock by way of being the only person in this Vermont outpost whose sardonic comments touch upon the entertainment world. For example, as people keep coming by Harry before he can be buried, the concealed, exasperated Captain says, "I couldn't have had more people here than if I'd sold tickets." Yet, the modest one-at-a-time parade continues and the Captain is moved to observe, "The next thing you know they'll be televising the whole thing." Beyond the plot, one could "read" the reference as either a simple plug for Hitchcock's TV show or a bit of self-referential spoofing, since he and his small screen program were already a hit that year.

Even late in *Harry*, when Forsythe's painter begins to sell his work, his prices reflect on Gwenn/Hitchcock as media related. That is, a passing chauffeur-driven millionaire (Parker Fennelly) wants to buy all of the Forsythe/Sam paintings. The artist's thoughtfully eccentric price is having each of his village friends make a simple wish. The Captain's request essentially boils down to a frontier outfit, which the note-taking millionaire reduces to the shorthand phrase "Davy Crockett—the works."

Though this parody-related joke is now lost on most audiences, it invariably receives an immense laugh from aging Baby Boomers. *Davy Crockett* was an enormously popular 1954–1955 miniseries on the *Disneyland* TV show. Shot in color with Fess Parker as the title character and Buddy Ebsen as his sidekick, the hourlong segments were so in demand, the first three episodes were edited into the hit 1955 feature film, *Davy Crockett, King of the Wild Frontier*, a few months before *Harry* was released. The miniseries was so well-liked that it spawned a cottage industry, with children everywhere (including this author) essentially begging for a "Davy Crockett—the Works" outfit. (As an addendum to the millionaire buyer, millionaire art collector Hitchcock fittingly has his cameo walking by this rich individual.)

Another link between the media and Gwenn-Hitchcock also involves Forsythe. When the Captain and the artist first meet over the corpse, Forsythe innocently says something that further spooks Gwenn's character. The Captain's reply again reveals his insecurity about the police, but more to the point here, it reveals the old sailor's awareness that people in the arts/media are known for being more flexible towards establishment norms (the target of dark comedy). Thus, when the Captain incorrectly thinks Forsythe's figure has some questions about Harry's death, Gwenn becomes radioactive with concern: "If you, an artist, suspect the worst, what are they, the police, going to think?"

However, one might ask, if Gwenn is Hitchcock's alter ego, does not the director most associate with his villains? Yet neither the Captain nor any of the other *Harry* principals are traditional villains (all characters lose some compassion points for not caring a rat's ass about dead Harry), yet Gwenn is the most morally flexible. Indeed, in American print humor, his Captain is also often like figures from our Old Southwestern humor, too. For example, in Johnson J. Hooper's 1867 book, *Simon Suggs' Adventure*, his famous title character shares a fundamental axiom also ever so fitting for Gwenn's character, "It is good to be shifty in a new country."[11]

Indeed, given Hitchcock's cinematic perspective on mothers, whether the director had even heard of Hopper's celebrated Suggs, it seems the two artists shared a dark comedy viewpoint on mothers, too. When Suggs rode away from home for the final time he had "...stolen into his mother's room, and nicely loaded the old lady's pipe with a thimble full of gunpowder; neatly covering the villainous saltpeter [potassium nitrate] with tobacco."[12]

Moreover, with Hitchcock's coming out of the shadow of his cameos, and the subtextual association with his movies' slick scoundrels, in order to create his more mainstream TV persona that same year, conceivably he was feeling more "whimsical" himself, concerning Gwenn's Captain. Yet, there had been previous casual small screen talks, and the director had guest hosted the radio show *Murder by Experts* (1949–1951), as well as having been an occasional 1940s radio guest on *Information, Please* (1938–1951). Thus, maybe PR obsessed Hitchcock felt further saturation of the media marked via TV had him feeling what *New Yorker* critic Hilton Als has so insightfully described as "the rub of life." That is, "...we exist somewhere between who we really are and how we'd like to be perceived."[13]

Ironically, the quintessential word critics used in their attempts to define *Harry* was some variation of "whimsical." Reviewers could not decide on a genre for the film but it almost seemed required that some form of "whimsical" be attached to each critique. In fact, it often even headlined the review,

11. The Trouble with Harry (1955)

from the *New York Journal-American*'s "Hitchcock Tries Hand at Whimsey," to the *Los Angeles Mirror-News*' "Hitchcock Enters Realm of Whimsey."[14] However, if ever a word was misused, *Harry* is an "A" answer for your blue book final, unless the term is applied paradoxically.

Harry takes one past the black humor post–Nietzschean trilogy world of *Shadow of a Doubt* (1943), *Rope* (1948), and *Strangers on a Train* (1951). In those films an individual could sever his emotion to kill. In the world of *Harry*, the characters *already* have a simultaneous disconnect with the recently dead. Nietzsche felt that a joke must be "no better than an epitaph on the death of feelings."[15] For example, a dark comedy joke about Lincoln's assassination now, over 150 years past his death, would offend few people. But *Harry*'s inherent black humor shock is that a recent death results in an indifferent new norm. In fact, one period review suggested "the cast acted as if they'd just undergone half a lobotomy...."[16] In a sense, this could say *Harry* has reached the black humor maximum—no one cares, despite the death's immediacy.

One is seeing a close variation upon that theme in the more recent dark comedy work of David Lynch, the Coen Brothers, and Hiro Murai (*Atlanta*, on FX). Murai likens it to "a soup of ambiguity."[17] Yet, these artists and Hitchcock usually allow(ed) one old school normal character to exist. For example, one of the more insightful period *Harry* reviews, from the *Hollywood Reporter*, opined:

> All the scenes are funny but they risk monotony by being funny in the same way ... few of the laughs are played against any straight character and that, from start to the last ... creates no real dramatic development.[18]

Paradoxically, even this perceptive review was entitled "Hitchcock Film *Whimsical* [my italics] Treat." Regardless, the *Hollywood Reporter* comment about dark comedy playing against a "straight character" anticipates Yossarian in *Catch-22* (1970). He seems to be the only figure aware that the world has jumped the tracks.

There is, however, a precedent for this single note character in other humor genres. For example, Howard Hawks' *Bringing Up Baby* (1938) is one of the seminal screwball comedies. However, it was a critical and commercial failure when it was released. Hawks blamed himself, feeling that he should not have made *everyone* screwball.[19] Now the public's embrace of total eccentric saturation comedy has all but turned *Bringing Up Baby* into the template for screwball comedy. Consequently, Hitchcock's steeping of *Harry* in emotionless characters, at least toward death, was simply ahead of its time. Yes, Samuel Beckett's *Waiting for Godot* (1953) had also preceded it, but *Godot* was hardly geared for a mainstream audience. Moreover, there is still something to be said for dark comedy including a straight character, or two barometers, such as Edward Albee's *The Goat, or Who Is Sylvia?* (2001).

Be that as it may, there is an additional chilling element in *Harry*'s ho-hum attitude towards death. In trying to minimize the Captain's fear of the police, with regard to his seemingly having produced a corpse, Forsythe's artist tells Gwenn an interesting bit of philosophy. And while couched in a heavenly reference or two, it still comes off sounding like Nietzsche 101:

> Suppose it was written in the book of Heaven that this man [Harry] was to die at this particular time at this particular place. [If the Captain had not shot him]. Why, then, a thunderbolt or something would have knocked him off! [You have done a good thing.]

This reads rather like an open invitation to be able to kill anyone, anywhere, since everyone has to check out sometime ... though writer William Saroyan always hoped an exception would be made in his case.

So how does all that whimsical talk get attached to the film? Well, the quasi-second act of the picture is that dear old Harry keeps getting buried and then dug up again. How's that? First, after the Captain and Forsythe talk awhile, the painter agrees to help plant Harry, given Gwenn's fear of the police. But as the two dig and continue to discuss the situation, the Captain comes to realize that he could not have shot Harry. That is, he realizes that none of his rabbit directed bullets could have hit Harry.

Sadly, the reasoning takes the length of time required to bury the body. But now the Captain ponders, an individual does not bury a corpse if s/he is innocent. So Harry must come out of the ground. However, soon the Captain and the artist start second guessing who might have killed Harry. Given that it could involve either of their potential romantic interests, Mildred Natwick's spinster, or Shirley MacLaine's lovely Jennifer, it is back in the ground for Harry, the budding MacGuffin.

Harry's resting place remains as such for a while, and this yo-yo body can get some peace. However, in time the spinster feels she was responsible for the killing. And since it was self-defense, she wants to bring up Harry for air. When she has this epiphany, Mildred is alone with the Captain. Given that he has been doing a lot of the spade work on the misadventures of Harry, Hitchcock milks additional dark humor out of the situation by having Mildred essentially doing all the digging.

More time passes and as these industrious New Englanders later gather for further discussion, the artist convinces the spinster that while she is innocent, the police and press could make it a rather messy situation for her and/or Jennifer, since the deceased is her estranged husband. By now this eclectic bond has become sort of a traveling mortuary ... for one. The novel summarizes it best when Jennifer says, "Let's all go up there [in the woods]. I've never witnessed an unofficial funeral."[20] Certainly, this will be the last one! Not so much. More time passes, and the artist Forsythe surprises himself by proposing. One is back to "fearful farce." With Jennifer's MIA husband, at

11. The Trouble with Harry (1955)   219

least to the outside world, the wannabe couple would have to wait seven years before Harry could officially be declared dead ... and any marriage could take place. Consequently, the man with the bright socks has to be dug up one final time.

Of course, once a body is in and out of the ground several times, it takes a bit of the luster from the recently dead, not to mention the corpse's wardrobe, including those dazzling socks. Consequently, *Harry* provides additional dark humor by way of this "grave gang" needing to tidy him up before leaving him where he was originally found. Oh, and by now, there is no fear of a murder charge, because the aforementioned book-reading doctor that originally tripped over Harry, without even noting him, has declared the deceased died of natural causes. Though this verdict is important, the absent-minded professor-like Dr. Greenbow fits New England Yankee humor perfectly—education is overrated. (Please see previous chapter.)

Accordingly, like so much that passes for dark comedy, the movie ends as it began—with dead Harry back above ground in the woods to be discovered once again by Jennifer's little boy. Again, it is like Buster Keaton's career-defining treadmill of life image in *Day Dreams* (1923). The *Los Angeles Times'* take on the sequence is probably the most ironically amusing—the engine starts up while he happens to be in the ship's side-wheel—reducing him to "a squirrel in a wheel."[21] As Marxist philosopher Antonio Gramsci wrote of humanity, "History teaches, but has no pupils."[22] Welcome to dark comedy.

One can, of course, take the black humor to an even more murky place. It could be argued that Hitchcock's twisted connection to Catholicism has the director having satirical fun with the resurrection of Christ. Donald Spoto's *The Art of Hitchcock* notes that the sketch of Harry's face by Forsythe's artist resembles painter Georges Rouault's (1871–1958) *Christus*/Christ.[23] And while Spoto adds some unnamed European critics would like to take the link further, he brushes this off as not "very persuasive."[24]

Spoto, however, does not address this topic along dark comedy lines, especially given that *Christus* is also used as an epithet for Catholic priests—not especially pleasant figures from Hitchcock's childhood. Moreover, Spoto also seems unfamiliar with Story's *Harry* novel. However, before quoting, in part, a lengthy description of the sketch from that book, I am compelled to state that in nearly a half-century of film scholarship, I have *never* encountered such a close adaptation of a text:

> The dead face of this man held the millions and millions of dead faces of all the centuries. In that dead face lay all dead humanity; all cold history; and the odd attitudes and mistakes ... all the staring eyes ... dull with misunderstanding and ignorance. The faces of the Jews and the Gentiles ... [and] the people who watched across the years and the centuries; the children at scriptures; the teachers; the monks ... all standing looking and not knowing.[25]

John Forsythe stares down Royal Dano who's holding his Christ-like portrait in *The Trouble with Harry*.

No dark comedy? Even some period reviews, including the *New York Times*, had stated, "So amiable is their [the villagers'] indifference and so flexible is their handling of the deceased that you'd not be amazed if he [Harry] should rise up and baffle them utterly."[26]

This provocative use of Christ for dark comedy in mainstream movie anticipates Hal Ashby's 1979 adaptation of Jerzy Kosinski's novel *Being There*. The story is about a cipher of a man, Chauncey Gardiner (Peter Sellers), who has been forced into the real world from his work as a gardener, thus the name. But his limited mentality, expressed in simple comments about gardening, satirizes a public that accepts the Biblical-sounding comments as insightful truths. However, Ashby's improvised sendup of a close has brainless Chauncey walking on water and mocking mankind.

Be that as it may, in moving beyond examining *Harry* along personality comedian and dark comedy lines, or what Hitchcock had called his "black pastoral comedy," there is simply the broad parody perspective of a murder mystery body which will just not stay buried.[27] However, the next best *Harry* humor analysis direction to explore is screwball comedy. *Variety*'s review

11. The Trouble with Harry (1955)

even credited it with being something of a matchmaking film, with Gwenn and Natwick, as well as Forsythe and MacLaine, becoming couples.[28] Plus, the *Los Angeles Examiner*'s description of *Harry*, though it, like many period publications, struggled to pigeonhole the film's genre, reads like accounts once made of *My Man Godfrey* (1936), "...all in all [it is] just about the goldurndest, cockeyedest, most pixilated concoction you ever did see!"[29] ("Pixilated," meaning mentally unbalanced or whimsical, was sometimes used to describe screwball comedy in the 1930s, possibly because it was a pivotal word in an entertaining scene in *Godfrey*—one of the first films given that genre label.)

Keying upon Forsythe and MacLaine, they fit many of the screwball markers. For example, as noted previously, this is a genre famous for actors playing variations of themselves. Given this was impish MacLaine's first film, Hitchcock was taken with the fact, "I shall have fewer bad [acting] knots to untie."[30] Moreover, plucked from a Broadway musical at only twenty-two, she still saw herself as more of a dancer. And with little direction from Hitchcock, she later observed, "I didn't know how to act. I could hardly read the script.... I sort of played myself, or whatever."[31]

Moreover, unlike romantic comedy, screwball comedy has an instant kismet component which often plays out as almost a stalker mentality, such as Katharine Hepburn towards Cary Grant in *Bringing Up Baby*, or Carole Lombard concerning William Powell in *Godfrey*. Such is the case in *Harry*, except it is Forsythe who is instantly smitten with MacLaine. The object of the sudden affection is often rather childlike, such as in screwball comedy characters like Henry Fonda in *The Lady Eve* (1941), or Renée Zellweger in the *Bridget Jones's Diary* films (2001, 2016). The extent of capturing that natural elixir quality in MacLaine has normally been limited to just stating the sudden Broadway to film transition previously reported. Yet, the full story of this natural "pixilation" is tied to a seldom noted screen test of this actress named for Shirley Temple:

> MacLaine, wearing almost no make-up sat on a stool, dressed in a short sweater, shorts, and long black stockings. As [director Daniel] Mann asked her questions about herself, the camera moved in close on Shirley's expressive face while she answered with disarming candor. The screen test ended in full view of MacLaine dancing, without music, to a few short bits from *The Pajama Game* [the Broadway play in which she had been performing]... Mann called the screen test "animal-like" in its naturalness. One journalist wrote, "Old hands at Paramount could not recall a performer since Audrey Hepburn who displayed such virtuosity and casual charm in a first test."[32]

Besides making his dark comedy, Hitchcock recognized, at least intuitively, what he needed in a screwball couple.

Consistent to this childlike world, there is little romantic foreplay in screwball comedy. Things are said with few filters. For example, on Forsythe's first meeting with MacLaine, the adolescent-like painter, with little small talk, matter-of-factly says, "I'd like to paint you nude." This was rather racy stuff for the time. Indeed, like Charlie Chaplin's Tramp using his cane to pull up a woman's skirt, the impulsive painter slightly turns up MacLaine's dress.

With the kookiness which would soon become part of MacLaine's screen persona, she takes it all in stride, like a latter day Lombard. Later, when Forsythe proposes, she matter-of-factly tells him, "I just got my freedom" (her estranged husband Harry is dead). She tells him that she will have to think about it. However, with little or no time having elapsed MacLaine's Jennifer accepts. Then, in a childlike screwball tit for tat, or another case of the genre's absentminded professor (à la the film's Dr. Greenbow), Forsythe says, "I'd almost forgotten that proposal." Fittingly for Hitchcock's view of relationships, one can see with such a response, similar to so many childlike screwball couples, this duo will no doubt have a short shelf life.

Indeed, one can already see cracks in their relationship almost immediately. That is, the proposal had occurred near the picture's ending. However, for the close, as noted, Harry had to first be spic and span, before being placed back in his original forest resting spot by morning. MacLaine's son had been left out of the preceding adventures of New England's most active corpse. But to come full circle, the child had to now once again discover him in the woods. Thus, while the mortuary squad looks on, the youngster finds Harry anew but does not immediately run off to tell someone. Forsythe then says under his breath, "Beat it you little creep!" However, with an instant glare from MacLaine, he quickly corrects himself with, "I mean, hurry home, son, to tell someone." This is hardly a promising stepfather beginning.

Regardless, for a genre born of the escapist Depression era, screwball comedy has to have big money as a given, especially at the end. For example, Preston Sturges' classic *The Palm Beach Story* (1942) probably does it in the most interesting triple threat manner. First, there is an inspired cameo by a Wienie King (Robert Dudley), who provides Claudette Colbert with some getaway cash. Next her travel plans are augmented by a train car full of Ale and Quail Club hunting millionaires. And finally she meets John D. Hackensacker III (Rudy Vallee), a John D. Rockefeller type, and finishes her trip to Palm Springs aboard his yacht. For *Harry*, there are the periodic appearances of the chauffeured millionaire art connoisseur, who by story's end buys everything Forsythe's painter has done, or will ever do. But in a rare departure from the novel, Hitchcock makes things even a little more screwball, by having the painter grant wishes to each member of the shovel brigade. In the novel the artist simply takes cash.

Before closing the examination of *Harry* humor, one needs to briefly address the comedy of Mildred Natwick's spinster, Miss Gravely, and her interest in the Captain. Some of her best lines are not found in the original novel. And yes, while the book and film are a delightful spoof of dark comedy, combined with the screwball elements already delineated, there is still Miss Gravely. Now, as with most of the Hitchcock humor already dissected, I am not necessarily making a claim for any direct historical links from other sources to the script. This study simply continues to be an attempt to provide a methodical on point link to specific comedy genres that Hitchcock and his collaborators could have intuitively tapped into. Why all the fuss? Because one simply tires of everything being lumped unceremoniously together into something minimized as mere "Hitchcock comic relief."

Along related lines, print humor by American women in the 19th century needs a great deal more research. However, shortly before the Civil War a few New England writers, such as Frances Whitcher, particularly in her book *The Widow Bedott Papers* (1856), provided title characters who periodically took on rustic narrow-mindedness in a robust manner while, as a critic put it, being "obsessed with finding a new husband."[33] She can also be self-deprecating in her forever pivoting humor. The dialogue sample between *Harry*'s spinster Gravely and the Captain seems reminiscent of Widow Bedott:

> GRAVELY: Why Captain Wiles, what a surprise.
> CAPTAIN: But you invited me Miss Gravely. At least that's how I remember it.
> GRAVELY: Of course I did Captain, but somehow it's still a surprise.... Won't you come in Captain?
> CAPTAIN: Thank you. I ... I've looked forward to it. Takes a good cook to make a blueberry muffin....
> GRAVELY: I pick'em up near where you shot that unfortunate man.
> CAPTAIN: [Wanting to change the subject] A real handsome man's cup [he remarks of the mug].
> GRAVELY: It's been in the family for years. [Actually, she just bought it at the general store.] My father always used it until he died.
> CAPTAIN: I trust he died peacefully, slipped away in the night.
> GRAVELY: He was caught in a threshing machine. I hope I haven't distressed you Captain.
> CAPTAIN: Not at all. Not at all.... I am a man who's faced death many times [not really].
> GRAVELY: Rather recently, too [Harry]...

Later she will casually tell the Captain, "After we've dug him up, we'll go back to my place and make you some hot chocolate." Pioneer American print humor historian Walter Blair would place Frances Whitcher among the country's "Down East Humorists," a category in which Gravely also could be included.[34]

Regardless, one of the great *Harry* ironies of Hitchcock's career was that when he totally devoted himself to a dark comedy, or essentially a parody of reaffirmation black humor, it would initially be an American critical and commercial failure. Paradoxically, while many reviewers could not find the appropriate genre, or felt there were too many from which to choose (including the *New York Times*' even referencing "dry Yankee types"[35]), there is often a sense the critics were not listening to their own comments. For instance, here are two quotes from different mainstream Los Angeles reviews, "[It's a] comedy about a corpse," and "[They] can't seem to keep him buried for any length of time."[36] Now how does either of those comments not scream dark comedy? The next focus film of the text will receive an entirely different response from the public and critics. And more than a little of that success will be owed to its blend of comedy genres.

12

North by Northwest (1959)

> I made *North by Northwest* with tongue-in-cheek; to me it was one big joke. When Cary Grant was on Mount Rushmore, I would have liked to put him inside Lincoln's nostril and let him have a sneezing fit.[1]—Alfred Hitchcock (MGM print ads even included the director as one of the monument heads)

The question before the house is why close this focused examination of Hitchcock and humor here? The answer is that after the director's bloated *The Man Who Knew Too Much* remake (1956), *The Wrong Man* (1956), and *Vertigo* (1958), which followed *The Trouble with Harry* (1955), *Northwest* had him coming full circle back to his classic British "fearful farces." These were best represented by *The 39 Steps* (1935) and *The Lady Vanishes* (1938), the movies which brought him to America. However, *Northwest* is not only an American *39 Steps*, it is a spoofing send-up of the farcical *39 Steps*. And when a genre seems played out, either independently, or late in an auteur's oeuvre, as *Northwest*'s comic thriller/screwball comedy was, parody is often the result. Moreover, with *Northwest* Hitchcock had now reached the point of making a "wrong man" *comedy*. Though he spoofed up *Northwest*, Cary Grant biographer Geoffrey Wansell also noted, "Hitchcock wanted it to be the American version of his acclaimed *The Thirty-Nine Steps*."[2] And as will be examined shortly, without even trying, Grant brought an added comic touch to any role, especially in screwball comedy.

As with the previously discussed films, Hitchcock employs various genres of comedy, beyond his perennial role as a front man for black humor. However, as the director's chapter opening comments about *Northwest* being "one big joke" suggest, parody of a farcical nature is the overriding comedy in use here. As one follows its convoluted story, the film becomes a textbook guide to spoofing.[3] Indeed, another phrase, "tongue-in-cheek," the most blatantly burlesque of expressions, had occurred in numerous period reviews.[4] However, one could just resist any reading between the period lines, and flash forward to a revisionist *London Times* Walter Mitty–like critique. Coyly linking *Northwest* to the past, the review baldly opines:

> This time he [Hitchcock] pushed through into parody by asking what would happen if you woke up one morning and found your life turning into a Hitchcock film? You'd have to laugh, of course. And so you do, right from the first scene.[5]

Fittingly, however, for Hitchcock tradition, the film's title is anchored in the basic dark comedy theme of absurdity. Drawn from *Hamlet*, the title signifies both a non-direction and Hamlet becoming unhinged, "I am but mad north-north-west...."[6] Nevertheless, what follows is a *Northwest* plot peppered with parody. Starting with Hitchcock's cameo rush to catch a bus during the opening credits, the director sets in motion varied hurried movements of transportation, harking back to an affectionate spoofing of silent cinema— often noted by period critics.[7] While parody rules in *Northwest*, forever changing backdrops provides Roger O. Thornhill (Cary Grant) with an ever-changing personality comedian range of places and persons with whom to amusingly interact. Spoofing the most witty of Madison Avenue executives, Grant dictates to his secretary Maggie (unbilled Doreen Lang) as he steals a cab from a man and makes it seem like a thoughtful gesture:

> ROGER: I beg your pardon. I have a very sick woman. You don't mind [if we take your cab]?
> MAGGIE: Poor man.
> ROGER: I made him a happy man. I made him feel like a Good Samaritan.

In Grant's rush to meet some business associates at New York's signature hotel, the Plaza, 1950s film fans would enjoy the in-joke that the actor had maintained an apartment at the hotel for years. Comically, though probably a hyperbolic story, since Hitchcock provided little direction to his actors, someone once asked him about why there was little orchestration of Grant's striding through the Plaza as the film begins. To paraphrase Hitchcock, "Grant's been walking across the lobby for years. Why would I need to tell him how?"

Moreover, while any genre can and does utilize the true characteristics of its players, both parody and screwball comedy/American farce, for which *Northwest* is a dual poster child, do this the most. For example, Leo McCarey had his performers (including Grant) wear their own clothing in *The Awful Truth* (1937), and Howard Hawks had Grant describing a *His Girl Friday* (1940) character as looking like Ralph Bellamy—who was actually the actor playing the part. Interestingly, Grant was so emblematic of screwball comedy that an in-joke reference to Grant occurred in John Cleese's later British reboot of the genre in 1988's *A Fish Called Wanda*. That is, Cleese's screen name was actually Grant's real name, Archie Leach. Regardless, at this early point in *Northwest*, Hitchcock and Grant find time to spoof many of the director's basic screen components. For example, even before rushing with Maggie to the cab stand, Roger had acknowledged a lobby staffer at his business and told him to "say hello to the missus." He received the quick reply, "We're not talking." Bingo—relationships are hamstrung in the opening seconds of yet another Hitchcock picture.

While Roger and Maggie are on their short cab ride, when he is not the most witty businessman in Gotham, he is obsessed with making sure his mother remembers their dinner plans at the ritzy 21 Club. When he dictates a note to said parent (Jessie Royce Landis), he suggests she need not "sniff his breath," since he will already have had a couple drinks. Maggie cannot believe the story. Roger quickly replies, "Sure she does, like a bloodhound."

Grant has just performed a Hitchcock parody double. First, he has established in record time yet another of the director's screen fundamentals—the love/hate relationships between a mother and son. Second, Roger has also spoofed Hitchcock's well-known ardor for food and liquor. Indeed, the director had made headlines on his first trip to America (1938) by eating a gargantuan meal at the same 21 Club, including three steaks, massive amounts of liquid fun and loads of vanilla ice cream—the latter of which he told reporters had now become a breakfast staple, too. In fact, Hitchcock's famed *Lifeboat* (1943) photo cameo as a newspaper picture in a weight loss ad was inspired by those fat facts. During his early American years he had put on well over a hundred pounds. Fittingly, he later named a pet dog Philip of Magnesia.

Appropriately for Hitchcock, who abhorred exercise, of all Roger's witticisms while he was with Maggie, the one most cited in period reviews could be added to the list of Hitchcock self-deprecating parody.[8] Roger thinks he has put on weight and instructs his secretary to place a note on his desk the following morning to "Think thin." It is pure Hitchcock. Regardless, after Grant is dropped off at the Plaza, his spoofingly droll lines soon become even more amusing merely by the situation in which he finds himself. That is, when he seems to answer to the name George Kaplan (an American spy whom the CIA has merely made up), after Roger attempts to hail a Plaza page calling Kaplan's name, two foreign spies kidnap him at gunpoint. Acting as if this is the most normal thing in the world, Grant tosses off quips with the same farcical coolness of Sean Connery's soon-to-follow James Bond films, which also double as reaffirmation parodies of meandering spy pictures, à la *Northwest*. (Grant was the model for Ian Fleming's Bond character.) Thus, as Roger eventually ends up in a library of a Long Island mansion, his casual catalog of one-liners includes:

> Don't tell me where we're going, surprise me.
> [Ushered into the stately home he observed]: By the way, what are we having for dessert? [More food].
> [Locked into the library and told "You will wait here," he answers]: "Don't hurry, I'll catch up on my reading."

As Grant looks out the library window, he observes more spy story spoofing—one of the enemy (Martin Landau) is playing croquet (also a game which had once been an obsession with many of the American humorists who seem to have influenced Hitchcock, such as Robert Benchley and James Thurber). Presently the spy mastermind Phillip Vandamm (James Mason) enters the library, with the *New York Herald Tribune* describing Mason spot on as having a "habitual air of pained politeness"—almost a burlesque description of a Hitchcock suave villain.⁹ The two begin to circle each other for a laughably long time. It anticipates in a modest way the longer drawn out Mexican stand-off parody which closes Sergio Leone's *The Good, the Bad and the Ugly* (1967).

Finally, *Northwest's* Mason compliments Grant for being more polished than he had expected of the phantom George Kaplan. Again, Grant's kidnapped businessman is ever so sardonically lackadaisical in his reply: "Not that I mind a game of abduction now and then but I had tickets to the theatre this evening." The cat and mouse two-step equals thriller parody dripping from every word. The response of Mason's Vandamm, "With such expert play acting you make this very room a theatre," sets up a situation multiple Oscar-winning Leo McCarey had to address when directing Grant two years earlier in the critical and commercial hit *An Affair to Remember* (1957), a remake of McCarey's *Love Affair* (1939).

That is, by this point in Grant's career, he was such a star that McCarey worked said celebrity status into the actor's international playboy *Affair* part. Thus, Grant's beloved *Affair* grandmother (Cathleen Nesbitt) describes him in a manner mirroring Grant's screen persona, "He's always attracted by the art he isn't practicing, the place he hasn't been, the girl he hasn't met." Throughout *Affair* people just recognize him.

Hitchcock's *Northwest* was in the same position and pushed the envelope further by periodically linking Grant to acting itself. This is like breaking the "fourth wall" and acknowledge the parody going on. In spoofing scholarship this is sometimes referenced as "genre genre." However, before going deeper down this acting rabbit hole, further understanding of *Northwest's* farcical parody element can be reached by pausing briefly on the recently noted Leo McCarey. Like Hitchcock, Grant had frequently worked with McCarey, and generously attributed much of his acting success to the skill of several directors he chose to work with:

> I [Grant] gravitated to men such as Hitchcock, George Stevens, George Cukor, Howard Hawks, Stanley Donen, and Leo McCarey. They understood me. They permitted me the release of improvisation during the rehearsing of each scene. They let me discover how far out I could go with confidence. I got accustomed to being with certain people, and I am deeply indebted to each of them.¹⁰

This point is belabored for several reasons. First, arguably the best work Grant did with each of these directors, save Hitchcock, was in screwball comedies, a genre in which improvisation is pivotal. And *Northwest* often spoofs itself into being a quasi-screwball comedy. Indeed, many of its signature scenes are critically described in that matter. For example, in Richard Schickel's *Cary Grant: A Celebration*, he observes:

> ... the auction house sequence, where he [Grant] deliberately calls attention to himself with crazy overbidding (it's really a screwball scene) so that so much attention is focused on him that the spies cannot murder him....[11]

And there are so many other classic screwball sequences, starting with the sexually provocative train scenes between Grant and Eva Marie Saint—with "Saint" hardly being a fitting moniker.

Second, despite *Northwest's* witty script, and all the stories about Hitchcock being bored during a shoot, given everything had been blocked and written, Grant was allowed to tweak his dialogue. Thus, just as the film was a revisionist *39 Steps*, it also harked back to the screwball heyday of that picture, and an improvisational genre Grant helped to create, especially with McCarey productions like *The Awful Truth* (for which the director won his first Oscar) and *My Favorite Wife* (1940).

Third, arguably the most quintessential screwball title is *Nothing Is Sacred* (1937)... including love. Though of a more gentle nature, it is the closest of all the comedy genres to black humor.[12] Thus, throughout screwball comedies marriages are showcased as something to be avoided. And while ultimately the films end with a couple in love, story components suggest the unions will be over in twenty minutes. This is pure Hitchcock, and yet another reason his out-and-out screwball comedy, *Mr. and Mrs. Smith* (1941), has been so wrongly neglected.

Fourth, one cannot touch on Grant and humor without footnoting McCarey's inadvertent makeover of the actor during *The Awful Truth* as mirroring the lady's man director's personality. McCarey's demonstrative storytelling on the set was often "infectious" for actors.[13] Consequently, Grant's penchant for everything from flirtatiously self-deprecating humor to the amusingly expressive use of his hands and eyes were all signature trademarks of McCarey long before they became synonymous with the actor. And these traits are all amusingly on display in *Northwest*. For example, when a very hammered Grant makes it to court, after the spies had set him up for a drunken car crash death, to be addressed shortly, the court doctor asks him how much bourbon he has had. Grant visually "replies" by stretching his arms about a yard apart.

No less an artist than writer/director Garson Kanin, who worked with Grant on *My Favorite Wife*, later baldly stated, "How much of that [Grant] personality was directed into him by Leo McCarey, I'm not prepared to say ... [but] he polished that [*Awful Truth*] personality, and he played it over and over

230 Hitchcock and Humor

again—each time more skillfully."[14] A fascinating footnote to McCarey's influence on Grant is that period critics even saw the two men as looking alike. For instance, here is one description of the director from 1939—"the handsome McCarey, with the twinkling Irish eyes and his resemblance to Cary Grant."[15] (When I did my McCarey biography I managed to use an on-set still of the director and actor for the cover in which Grant seems to be mirroring every aspect of his mentor.[16])

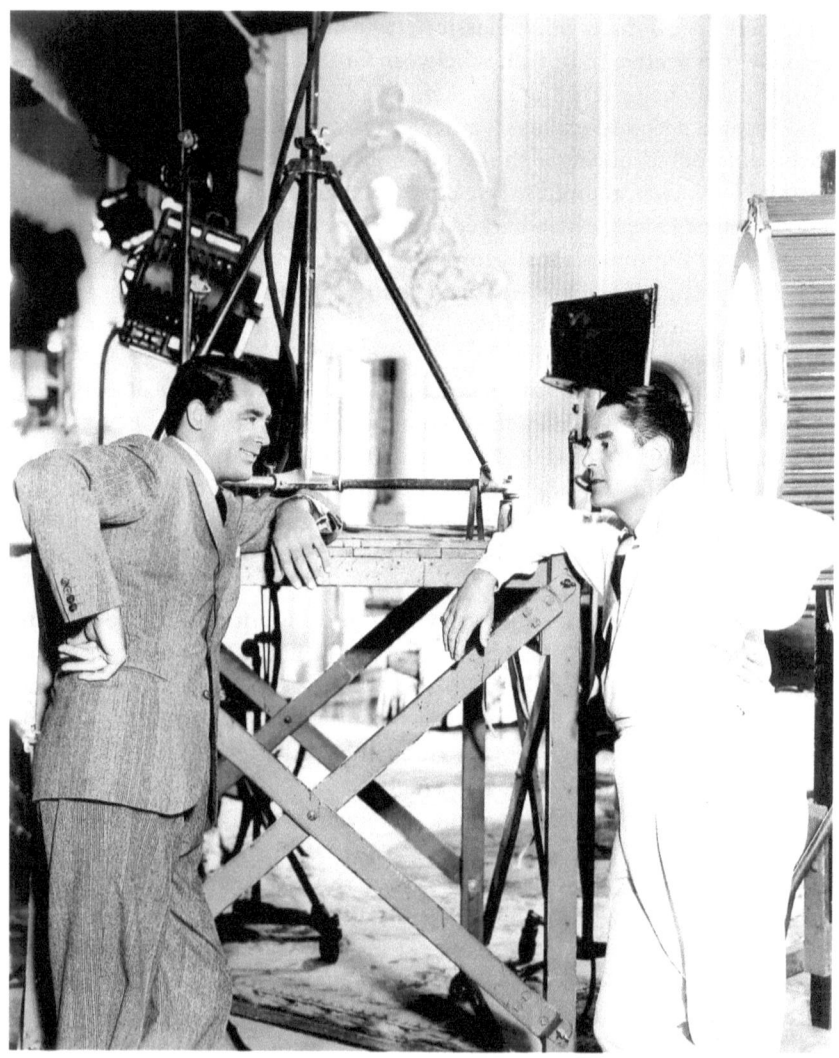

Cary Grant mirroring Leo McCarey. This photo graces the cover of my biography of McCarey.

12. North by Northwest (1959)   231

Fifth and finally, *The Awful Truth* anticipates two additional things about *Northwest*. The first seems to be an unintentional joke that grows throughout Hitchcock's film. Grant has been kidnapped and soon has a murder pinned upon him, which is the catalyst for him to pinball all over the country to prove his innocence. All this happens without Grant even having a chance to get a change of clothes, yet he seems to have a limitless supply of cash for meals, tips, cabs, and so on. Where is it coming from?

Grant had found himself in the same situation on *The Awful Truth* and confronted McCarey about it. Given the high society escapist nature of the genre, the director told him to just not worry about it. Thus, it represents a slowly building component of overall absurd escapist comedy in both films. Ironically, such concerns, despite Grant's excellent choice of directors, gave him such misgivings about whether *The Awful Truth* and *Northwest* would be successful that he attempted to get out of each picture. Both directors essentially ignored his worries, and the films went on to be major critical and commercial successes.

These successes provide a segue back to addressing the major fame Grant had achieved by the 1950s, and how directors like McCarey and Hitchcock had to incorporate this into his screen roles. McCarey's *Affair* had gone a route which feels rather contemporary—Grant was a celebrity for some sort of ephemeral reason, famous for being famous. In contrast, Hitchcock had taken the parody route and played upon Grant the actor. Variations of the phenomenon are played throughout *Northwest*. But one example is particularly nuanced in its presentation.

This occurs at the aforementioned gallery auction, which tops all previous Hitchcock uses of art for comedy. However, just prior to Grant's creatively screwball disruption, he and Mason have another more complex self-referential conversation on "acting." It embraces such an elaborate realm of reaffirmation parody that there is much to be missed—most fitting for Hitchcock's love of in-jokes:

> MASON: Has anyone ever told you [Grant] you overplay your various roles severely Mr. Kaplan? First you're the mistaken Madison Avenue man, who claims he's been mistaken for someone else [This comes close to Grant's 1958 *Indiscreet* part], then you play the fugitive from a crime he knows he did not commit [This is the perfect capsulation of Grant's character in 1942's *The Talk of the Town*], and now you play the peevish lover, stung by jealousy and betrayal [exactly Grant's situation in Hitchcock's own *Notorious*, 1946]. It seems to me you fellows could use ... a little training from the Actor's Studio.
> GRANT: Apparently the only performance that will satisfy you is when I play dead.
> MASON: Your very next role. You'll be quite convincing.

While this subject will be further addressed later, it seems time to return to an analysis of an often parodic twisted farce ... with spies. Thus, this critique comes back to the circling men in the library, with Mason's mistaken belief he has captured an American spy. Suddenly his screen "wife" (later revealed to be his sister), opens the door and casually observes, "Excuse me dear, the guests are here." It is a scene straight out of *The 39 Steps*, when the spouse of the villain with the partially missing finger makes the same sort of ever so civilized interruption into the world of soirées, spies, and mistaken identity. The incongruity of Hitchcock juxtaposing dinner parties and death reminds the viewer that while *Northwest* has gone parody on us, there is still the director's dark comedy core.

Even Vandamm's order to have Grant's Thornhill killed, however, has an urbane air to it—"Give him a drink." However, this is shorthand for pour a bottle of bourbon down Thornhill's throat, with parody soon to meet personality comedy. That is, as the *New York Journal-American* review spoofingly observed, "Grant is taken to a Long Island estate where he's forced to get drunk (this is torture?) and given a ... car to drive himself to death."[17] This parody of an attempted killing is given increased humor by both the blitzed Grant's dialogue and Hitchcock's standard rear screen projection. Thus, as Roger is placed in the car he first sings a well lubricated, "I've grown accustomed to my bourbon," before politely telling his captors, "Don't worry about me fellows, I'll take the bus." And the winding cliff-hanging ocean road the thugs have chosen would necessitate an audience also be hammered to believe this is Long Island. But Hitchcock's always distracting rear view projection seems to have been ratcheted up for *Northwest*'s broad parody. Thus, it seems most appropriate here.

Luckily for Roger, the henchman (Adam Williams) in the car with him is more brawn than brains, the type whose "business meetings" would most likely take place on a park bench. He underestimates our hero. Sloshed Grant manages to push him from the auto and somehow muddles through driving down this twisted zigzagging road. Along the way he avoids crashing countless times while providing a visual treat of funny expressions not unlike those of the equally surprised and plastered Charlie Chaplin when he enters the most surreal of houses in *One A.M.* (1916).

As Hitchcock mixes parody and personality comedy here and elsewhere in *Northwest*, the film feels like a blend of the director kidding his comic thrillers and an homage to silent comedy. Consequently, the close to Grant's adventure in sauced driving involves a three-vehicle crash, including a police car, à la the Keystone Kops. Near the film's conclusion, when the action includes dangling for dear life from Mount Rushmore, again critics are reminded of more silent comedy—this time involving the thrill comedy of a Harold Lloyd or Douglas Fairbanks, Sr.[18] And specifically, when a hanging Eva Marie Saint almost takes a plunge caused by a clothing lifeline rip, one sees Hitchcock spoofing another bit of torn cloth leading to a fatal Statue of

Liberty fall in his own *Saboteur* (1942). Fittingly, one reviewer even suggests this lady in distress situation as an entertaining reference to the silent film Pearl White short subject series, with each episode ending with yesteryear's heroine in great danger.

When the drunken Grant has been arrested and is safely, for the time being, about to be jailed for a court hearing the next day, he gets the standard one phone call. This being a Hitchcock film, Roger naturally calls his mother Clara (Jessie Royce Landis). For another Hitchcock in-joke, Landis is actually the same real life age as Grant. The following slightly condensed version of Roger's call will be examined along three basic comic lines:

> Mother, this is your son Roger Thornhill. Wait a minute, where am I? [His mother seems to have asked Grant's whereabouts, and he asks the policeman assisting him with the call. Once informed he shares:] Glenn Cove Police Station. No Mother; I have not been drinking. These two men poured a whole bottle of bourbon in me. No, they didn't give me a chaser.

First, his funny drunken description of this murder attempt helps to further spoof Hitchcock's alleged thriller. Second, Grant's comic difficulty in telling an account of a real event brings to mind several similar situations from his screwball comedy filmography, even when sober. For instance, at the close of *My Favorite Wife*, Grant's nonsense attempt to explain why he is so indecisive to co-star Irene Dunne makes Hamlet sound like an articulate man of quick resolve. And there is Grant's effort to tell Katharine Hepburn's screen aunt, in Hawks' *Bringing Up Baby* (1938), why he is wearing a woman's nightgown. The bit ends with a frustrated Grant jumping up in the air and shouting, "I just went gay all of a sudden!"

Third, the fact that Grant's drunken single call after being arrested is to his mother, and that her only surprised response to his gibberish is that he did not even receive a chaser, suggests both are pure screwball material. Moreover, given the mother-son world of most Hitchcock films, one sees Clara as a nutty early version of Bruno's joined-at-the-hip mommy in *Strangers on a Train* (1951).

The following day in court is equally funny, and directly related to screwball comedy. The genre frequently has courtroom scenes, given that couples are often splitting up. Again, a fitting link to the world of Hitchcock. Such sequences could be referenced as the "McCarey factor," given that the director had briefly practiced law, and both *The Awful Truth* and *My Favorite Wife* feature hilarious courtroom scenes. Indeed, McCarey was a gifted raconteur, and his tale of his only case is no doubt largely hyperbole. But it is a must tell when screwball comedy is discussed.

McCarey had taken a case of an allegedly abused absurd husband whose wife was unfairly pushing for too much alimony. However, once in court the allegedly shrewish wife turned out to be a frightened little thing with blackened eyes—"I wish I could speak louder, your honor [she explained to the judge], but my husband kicked me in the ribs and I've got them taped up." Add to this two screaming children who cowered at the sight of their father, and McCarey saw his whole case disappearing.

Leo immediately asked the court for a postponement. When the judge requested an explanation, the young McCarey responded, "So this rat [his client] can get himself another lawyer!" With this, the one-time track star enjoyed relating that he literally ran from the courtroom, with his now former client hot on his tail. But as amusing as this slapstick comedy exit is, master storyteller McCarey topped it by adding an addendum about encountering an old newspaper friend during his impromptu track event. When the journalist asked what he was doing, a still running Leo panted, "I'm practicing law!" Peter Bogdanovich would later recycle this and other colorful elements of McCarey's life into his underrated film *Nickelodeon* (1976), an affectionate look at the early days of Hollywood. Moreover, when Bogdanovich did his loose remake of *Bringing Up Baby*, *What's Up, Doc?* (1972), he consciously included this McCarey screwball signature component to the film. In this very funny movie, *Doc*'s courtroom sequence is arguably its best.

Regardless, Grant sticks to his story in court, and soon leads two detectives and his mother to the Townsend mansion to which he had been kidnapped. But he is made to look foolish. The Townsend character Mason had claimed to be is a United Nations ambassador currently at work in the city, while the world body is in session. Moreover, even the library liquor cabinet, from which bourbon, without a chaser, had been poured down Roger, is merely full of books.

All of this turns Roger and mother Clara into a sort of Hitchcock Nick and Nora Charles, from the screwball comedy-like *Thin Man* franchise. And Landis' Clara has the dry comic delivery of Nora Charles (Myrna Loy). For instance, when there are only books in the cabinet previously full of alcohol, she quips, "I remember when it came in bottles." Moreover, she keeps the reflexive mood of "acting" alive, which Mason had introduced in that very library, by sarcastically reviewing her son's claims as, "What a performance!" Ultimately, she ends the court's involvement, via the detectives, by pronouncing the ultimate antiheroic axiom of failure, "Roger, pay the two dollars."

Not to be denied, Roger takes his mother, sans the detectives, back to the Plaza to see if he can meet this pretend George Kaplan, for whom he has been mistaken. Briefly, Clara reverts to being an eccentric Hitchcock style mother when Grant has to bribe her to get Kaplan's key from the front desk. However, once in Kaplan's hotel room, she reverts to the direct wisecracking Nora Charles.

McCarey's guiding principle, like most directors who started in the silent era, was to "Do it visually." This was certainly a truism he shared with Hitchcock. Indeed, most of the aforementioned directors Grant had singled out had begun in silent comedy. For instance, McCarey had teamed and molded Laurel & Hardy, with George Stevens being one of the team's early cameramen.[19] Thus, screwball comedy was usually a mix of visual comedy, personality comedy style, and witty dialogue.

This is a fitting comic set-up for the remaining time Roger and Clara spend in the hotel. For example, the CIA has gone to the trouble of providing the fictitious Kaplan with both a wardrobe and an itinerary, booking him into various hotels around the country. The reason is to divert attention from a real agent who has infiltrated Vandamm's small band.

With all this in mind, Hitchcock has the perfect opportunity to play with the visual and verbal wit of screwball comedy. Thus, Grant tries on a comically much too small "Kaplan" sports jacket. Clara then milks the bit further: "I don't think that does anything for you." Next, Grant puts on a pair of equally too small pants, and Clara sardonically comments, "Now, that's much better."

While they are in the room the phone rings, and against Clara's advice, Grant answers. It is Vandamm's henchmen, and they are calling from the lobby. Roger and Clara must exit quickly. But now that her son's spy story appears real, Clara would like to linger, which is again Nora-like. That is, while *The Thin Man* films of the 1930s and '40s were progressive for the period, with regard to the couple's egalitarian relationship, Nick still inevitably would take charge by the close. Thus, when Clara dallies and says, "I think I'd like to meet these killers," it rather sounds like Nora wanting to get more involved. However, the greater takeaway is comic incongruity of *who wants to meet killers?* Why, a typical Hitchcock mother reverting to crazy town.

Roger and Clara are not fast enough, and they end up in a crowded down elevator with the Vandamm thugs. This provides the setting for one last Clara salvo from the Looney Tunes environs of most Hitchcock mothers. She asks the heavies, "Gentlemen, you really aren't trying to kill my son, are you?" This creates an awkward moment in the packed elevator, before the two goons atypically/spoofingly begin to laugh nervously as a cover, which proves infectious, and everyone joins in—again, another out-of-left-field spoof of spy films.

Roger manages to escape when the elevator stops, and heads to the U.N. to meet the real Lester Townsend (Philip Ober). But he has been followed by Vandamm's men, and just as he meets Townsend, the poor man is murdered at a distance by a thrown knife. Since Roger was speaking to the ambassador at the moment, and the dying Townsend falls into his arms, Grant's character is immediately implicated in the murder. For nearly the remainder of the film he will be that wrong "comic" man on the run. Yet, much of the comedy to follow satirizes the basic Hitchcock premise of an ordinary man placed in an extraordinary situation. However, there is nothing ordinary about Grant. Any man should be so lucky ... just not in this movie.

Since Kaplan's next destination was to have been Chicago, Roger's now fugitive from justice target is the same. But how to get on a train is a poser, since his face is everywhere, from the front pages of New York's once numerous newspapers, to the inside of all Grand Central Station ticket booths. (Would a Hitchcock character take any other means of transportation?) Though *Northwest* plays as one long parody of Hitchcock's past, one is about to enter the film's most prolonged provocative embrace of farce. This occurs when Grant meets a most attractive modern day Mata Hari, Eva Marie Saint's Eve Kendall—though neither he nor the audience is initially aware of that fact. (The train is the *Twentieth Century*, the same famous sophisticated locomotive which was the setting for the pioneering 1934 screwball comedy of the same name.)

Regardless, the overly wise viewer might have anticipated increased danger by the overhead shot of Grant escaping the U.N. Given that the height resembles a view from the moon, and overhead shots are never a good sign in Hitchcock anyway, the extreme elevation qualifies as spoofingly bad news for Grant. This metaphor then becomes firmly anchored in the dark comedy of which Hitchcock always wants one to be aware. Suddenly the audience meets a CIA group in conference, headed by The Professor (Leo G. Carroll).

The gathering then provides a quick litany of black humor's three themes. *Absurdity* comes by way of one agent saying, "How can he [Grant] be mistaken for George Kaplan when George Kaplan doesn't even exist?" *Man as Beast* is next, when another operative adds, "It's so horribly sad, [yet] how is it that I feel like laughing?" The *presence of death* follows a question by a third agent, "How long will he stay alive?" The Professor answers, "That's his problem."

Once these puppeteers, not unlike uncaring gods, or a dark comedy-enamored director, make their pronouncements, it is back to marionette Grant about to meet a sexy lady named Eva. What could be dangerous about that? With this framework in mind, the audience is now prepared to witness such an amped up example of steamy farce, or is that "seamy," that one is now prepared for a broad parody of the situation.

Roger and Eva meet comic cute visually. While she is a passenger on the train, Roger has slipped on board and is busy playing hide-and-seek with authorities. As the two approach each other from opposite ends of a narrow train corridor, in their polite attempts to make way for the other, the duo inadvertently keep taking the same side. In comedy theory it would fall under the "theatre of the real" scenario—who has not done some variation of that two-step with a stranger? However, with unseen-to-the-viewer police approaching, he ducks into an empty compartment, and Eva directs the mini-posse elsewhere.

Grant then casually explains to her the police are after him because of "seven parking tickets." The train begins to move and now he is dodging ticket checking conductors. Hitchcock follows this sophisticated understatement by a regression to adolescent bathroom humor. Though Grant has disappeared, one soon gets the idea he is hiding in a restroom, because the director holds a camera shot for a lengthy period of time on the "toilet" sign near the dining car. Sure enough, Grant soon emerges. *Northwest* will feature an inordinate number of excuses to place him in a toilet during the course of the movie.

However, the film immediately returns to farce when Grant enters the dining car and is seated at Saint's table. Before their dialogue turns to the aforementioned overblown take on the genre which passes for affectionate spoofing, Hitchcock manages a sort of comedy trifecta. In quick succession there is an in-joke, followed by a variation on the self-referential humor practiced earlier by Mason, concerning the actor, and then Hitchcock self-parody. First, Grant sits down, and after small talk, orders a Gibson—a cocktail made with gin and dry vermouth, often garnished with a silverskin onion. But the name is the comic payoff. Given that Hitchcock was a liquor connoisseur, this is no doubt another "Where's Waldo?" moment. Thus, just after being seated with a lovely lady, Grant orders this particular cocktail. And while there are various stories concerning the origins of the drink's name, the most probable is its association with the artist Charles Dana Gibson, famous for his Gibson Girl illustrations (starting in the 1890s), which are considered the first widespread visual standard for a beautiful American woman.

Second, now able to focus on Saint, Grant obligingly tells her, "[I know,] I look vaguely familiar. You feel you've met me somewhere before." (A cult audience would now respond by shouting, "At the movies!") Third, the *not quite certain* identity suggestion then dovetails into burlesquing the *Rope* (1948) sequence in which several guests faintly remember given films and/or actors, but cannot come up with their names. Moreover, the *Northwest* link to this *Rope* sequence also repeats the purpose of the original movie—satirizing a medium as less than important, since these screenings do not seem to fully register. This doubles back to Hitchcock in two ways. First, because one of his favorite self-deprecating lines was, "It's only a movie." And second, Grant's face being "vaguely familiar" was partially because of the director, since *Northwest* was Grant's fourth Hitchcock picture.

Indeed, one might even make a case for a self-referential parody on Grant's fame in a Hitchcock movie as early as *To Catch a Thief* (1955). Granted, it is given more regional range than McCarey's use in *Affair*, or Hitchcock's *Northwest*. Still, in *Thief* Grant is a lionized cat-burglar on the French Riviera. Regardless, Saint continues the self-referential path a bit further by dwelling on what a "nice face" Grant has—move star fodder to be sure. In fact, by the end of the 20th century, the American Film Institute (AFI) would select Grant as second to only Humphrey Bogart as the country's greatest male movie star.

Soon, however, the scene moves on to the provocative sexual patter, which should not be unexpected, given that Saint has tipped the waiter five dollars to have Grant seated at her table should he enter the dining car. The degree of that "friendly" gesture is often lost on contemporary audiences. In today's currency, Saint's layout would be over $40. Thus, an expectation of the sensual dialogue to follow would have been telegraphed to a 1959 audience more quickly. Regardless, what follows is a sampling of Grant angling for her angle after discovering she knows he is wanted:

> SAINT: I told you, it's a nice face.
> GRANT: Is that the only reason?
> SAINT: It's going to be a long night.
> GRANT: True.
> SAINT: And I don't particularly like the book I've started.
> GRANT: Ahhh.
> SAINT: You know what I mean?
> GRANT: Uh, let me think. [pause] Yes, I know exactly what you mean.
> SAINT: I'm a big girl.
> GRANT: Yeah, and in all the right places too....

Without quoting in total this witty, broad romantic comedy dialogue (the opposite situation of what the French call "staircase wit"—the predicament most people have of thinking of the perfect line on the staircase, *after* a missed opportunity), Hitchcock includes another piece of dialogue which further suggests *Northwest* as being a collection of his greatest hits. At this point neither Grant nor the viewer knows that Saint's real plans for him involve death. Consequently, only a second screening will allow a viewer to appreciate the irony of Grant's question, "Tell me. What do you do besides lure men to their doom on the Twentieth Century Limited?"

The notion of *Northwest* being a collection of Hitchcock's "greatest hits" is easily supported and is expressed in various sources. In Peter Fitzgerald's 2000 documentary *Destination Hitchcock: The Making of North by Northwest*, screenwriter Ernest Lehman is on record as wanting to make "...the Hitchcock picture to end all Hitchcock pictures."[20] And this was also apparent to the performers at the time. For instance, Fitzgerald's film quotes later Oscar winner Martin Landau, Vandamm's first lieutenant, as saying *Northwest* was "... a quintessential Hitchcock film because it has a lot of pieces from a lot ... [of the director's earlier work, including] *39 Steps*"....[21]

Be that as it may, before the sexual dining car sequence must end, given Grant now needs to run from authorities unexpectedly stopping the train,

One of many farcical moments between Cary Grant and Eva Marie Saint, yet now he distrusts her.

Hitchcock is again back to amusing himself with Grant as a personality comedian. A sexy cigarette lighting moment (the director is playing the farce card fully) reveals that Grant's screen initials are monogrammed on his cigarette match packet—R.O.T. (for Roger O. Thornhill). Later a plot point, here it is played for broad antiheroic humor.

Eve asks what the letter O stands for and Roger says "nothing"—rather appropriate for a non-introspective man chasing someone (Kaplan) who does not exist. Moreover, it gets better. As previously noted, Hitchcock was a fan of the train-loving, dark comedy–driven silent comedian Buster Keaton. His nickname in Europe was "Zero" ("nothing"), interchangeable with the letter "O." All Hitchcock comedy roads seem to lead back to black humor, especially since decomposition/death, or *rot*, is also a central theme of the genre. Moreover, one could push the genre link further by saying that for most of the *Northwest* populace, Grant as Kaplan is a figure which simply does not exist … more theatre of the absurd.

Be that as it may, Eva makes sure Roger knows her train car cabin number before he must make like Jesse Owens to escape the latest set of authorities. However, the cipher or invisible man analogy continues in the next scene. One is now inside Eva's compartment and Grant is nowhere to be seen, but the clown shtick continues, as she seems to be talking to no one. (This also replicates the later 1930s *Topper* screwball comedies, the first of which starred Grant as a ghost, with sometimes the same seemingly one-way conversations.):

> GRANT: Got any olive oil?
> SAINT: Olive oil?
> GRANT: Might as well be packed in olive oil if I'm going to be a sardine [He is somehow squeezed into her closed upper bunk.]

One's personality comedy thoughts might run back to Laurel & Hardy, since this sort of train travel dilemma was periodically in their wheelhouse. Yet, 1959 was a unique year for clown comedy train berths, which could suddenly pinball effortlessly into dark comedy and farce and back again. Billy Wilder's *Some Like It Hot* had been a critical and commercial hit earlier in the year, with Tony Curtis even imitating Grant in the screwball sequences of the film. Regardless, the exchange between Eva and an invisible Grant (crushed into a compartment berth) suddenly turns farcical again when he is sprung:

> GRANT: Cops gone?
> SAINT: Still breathing?
> GRANT: Hurry up, or get me a snorkel.
> SAINT: I'm looking for the can opener [a device that locks the bunk] I stole from the porter.

Finally, she springs him and the sudden opening breaks some funny-looking sunglasses he had worn earlier for the world's worst disguise. And then it is back to screwball comedy:

> GRANT: Why are you so good to me?
> SAINT: Shall I climb up to tell you why?

But then Hitchcock brilliantly reaches back into his greatest hits bag and spoofs the memorably long, physically moving kissing scene between Grant and Ingrid Bergman in *Notorious*.

12. North by Northwest (1959)

Though this revisionist *Northwest* parody version is not without sex appeal, the limited space of the compartment makes the motion more like a twisted pretzel comedy smooch, peppered with funny lines, such as, "The train's a little unstable," followed by "Who isn't." (The illusion to a twisted pretzel also brings to mind Sandra Bullock's about-to-pass-out description of pretzel types in 2002's screwball comedy *Two Weeks Notice*, with an updated Cary—Hugh Grant.) Regardless, the best moment in *Northwest*'s spoof of the earlier Hitchcock sequence has Saint rambling on about all the things Grant can probably make a woman do, and he responds with Bond-like understatement, "I'm beginning to think that I'm underpaid."

Just in time to avoid censorship issues, though "M" (For Mature Audiences) had already been applied to *Hot*, the porter rings to ironically make up the bed and Grant must hide yet again in a toilet ... with its smallness adding to the comedy. Once the porter leaves, Eva accents the child-like nature of men in both screwball and personality comedy by repeating the hide and seek game jingle, "Come out, come out, wherever you are." Again, as a potentially sexy scene begins to unfold *Northwest* skirts potential problems by having Eva tell Grant, though not that convincingly, that he is "going to sleep on the floor." (All this is not to say *Northwest* did not have any post-production censorship. For example, back in the sexy dining car sequence, Saint's original line, "I never make love on an empty stomach" is redubbed, "I never discuss love on an empty stomach." (Next time, watch her lips closely.)

Given the period, the bending to the censor is not surprising. However, what throws viewers a curve is that Eva has secretly given the porter a note which is delivered to a compartment down the corridor. Vandamm's special assistant Leonard (Landau) then gives it to his napping boss. Upon opening it a seemingly bemused Mason reads, "What do I do with him in the morning?" Any astonishment that Eva is a spy is matched by the casualness with which Mason's mistress will be bedding down with such a handsome target. But then dark comedy is always about lust over love, so it is fitting. And appropriately enough, it is Hitchcock's black humor stance on the subject, too.

The next scene is the following morning, and it delivers several more comic personality sight gags. Grant is dressed in a rail station redcap's (porter) uniform carrying Eva's bags off the train. It is a funny visual, like Don Juan as a bell hop. This is topped by next seeing a redcap in his underwear, the source of Grant's uniform. Hitchcock then goes to comedy's rule of three, with another topper—after the police leave the undressed redcap, the viewer sees him counting a wad of money. This was no forced job; Grant, with his seemingly unlimited supply of money, has bribed him to tell the cops he was forcibly stripped. It is such an old gag—Hitchcock had even had Robert Donat change clothes with the milkman in *The 39 Steps*—that the director expects us not to notice that Cary Grant's redcap uniform seems hand tailored, yet the unclothed source is a little old man. Hitchcock's comic greatest hits continue.

This comic visual is quickly followed by another—Grant is once again in a toilet, partially changed back into his old clothes, but seemingly still invisible to the cops who race through. Why? His face is fully lathered up, like a pie to the face silent comedian, attempting to shave with Eva's small razor. But Hitchcock again ups the visual humor by a comic doppelganger effect, a modest version of McCarey's *Duck Soup* (1933) mirror sequence. That is, the man right next to Grant in the station toilet is Grant's height and build and also has a lathered face. He too is attempting to shave in the bathroom's large mirror. In turning to look at Grant, he does a double-take, as if looking at himself. Despite the significance of Bernard Herrmann's score for the picture, for several minutes Hitchcock has again effectively transported us back to silent comedy.

The shaving sketch is interspersed with still another old but effective visual sight gag. Though Grant is no longer redcap attired, the authorities still think he is. Consequently, suddenly an army of cops are dashing about grabbing every redcap in sight to see if he is Grant. This action, just as it was so easy for Roger to get off the train as a redcap, also speaks to the dark comedy of most people being zeroes—often going unnoticed, especially if they work in what society would deem lesser blue-collar professions.

Regardless, while Hitchcock has had comic fun returning us to the silent cinema of his youth, Eva has volunteered to call the non-existent Kaplan. However, she is really receiving an unheard Vandamm directive for Roger to be sent to the flat farmland of northern Indiana (actually shot near Bakersfield, California), which storywise would place him just outside of Chicago, to meet Kaplan. Like a John Ford Western, the large expanse of empty space and a high skyline make Grant seem minimal, vulnerable, and crushed by the enormous blue firmament. So it plays well to the former zero significance of Roger.

In addition, there is the personality humor fundamental of the character being completely outside his element, like Chaplin's Tramp sliding around a glacier in *The Gold Rush* (1925). That is, Grant, the iconic image of urban sophistication with his good looks and tailored suit, is eventually hiding in a Hoosier cornfield. Moreover, as Grant waits, after the Greyhound bus has dropped him in the middle of nowhere, Hitchcock subjects Roger to more clown comedy situations, such as speeding vehicles going by, covering him with dust. Also, like a classic screwball comedy, which celebrated the open spaces but satirized the rural population (such as a dog-like child that bites Fredric March in *Nothing Sacred*), the farmer (an unbilled Andy Albin) Roger encounters is less than friendly.

12. North by Northwest (1959)   243

Thinking the farmer might be Kaplan, Roger approaches the closed-mouthed man. But Albin is just waiting for the next bus. However, the farmer does serve as an introduction to one of cinema's signature scenes—telling Roger that a crop dusting plane, suddenly close at hand, is spraying a field devoid of crops. Once the bus and Albin leave, the crop dusting biplane, like a scene from a World War I movie (more of Hitchcock looking to the past), begins swooping down, attempting to kill Roger.

The aircraft forces Grant to go sprawling several times. He next dashes to a nearby cornfield for cover. However, the biplane soon flushes him out by making a pass and crop dusting his hideaway. Now more than desperate, Grant darts to the highway and stands in the middle of the road in an attempt to flag down a gasoline tanker. A semi-truck is barely able to stop in time. Roger ends up safely on his back just under the vehicle's hood. But the biplane crashes into the tanker, causing first a small and then a major, fiery explosion. Roger does, however, manage to get away from the blaze.

Now, there is nothing intrinsically funny about the attack, beyond possibly a Brooks Brothers suit-attired Grant hiding in a cornfield, or maybe vicariously enjoying the possible Hitchcock prankster catalyst of putting someone he would wish to be (this handsome movie star) through a grueling sequence. Yet, keep in mind the over-the-top greatest hit parody nature of *Northwest*, and one looks at the extended sequence differently. Hitchcock is always about throwing logic out the window.

While this is one of film history's most deservedly pre-eminent scenes, it is arguably (with the exception of running about on Mount Rushmore—which is coming shortly) also asking the viewer to choke down more logical breaches than an Indiana cornfield could hold. Hitchcock has outdone himself here in tap dancing on reason. Why send Roger out of Chicago to be killed in a Hoosier cornfield? With all due respect for Chicago being Carl Sandburg's "city of broad shoulders," it is also famous for cement boots in Lake Michigan. Indeed, it is such a template for all-American murder, South Chicago's Al Capone once killed a man with a baseball bat. Consequently, even in this exciting crop-dusting sequence, Hitchcock has truly outdone himself in getting the viewer to swallow a sense of dark comedy absurdity. Moreover, he fittingly closes it with broad humor. As people stop to watch a horrific accident (more black humor commentary on humanity), suave Grant escapes by stealing one of the gawkers' old battered pickups, complete with a broken-down refrigerator strapped down in back.

Knowing Eva's hotel, and that she has set him up, Roger naturally goes to her like a pissed (how an upset dark comedy moth is described) comic moth to a flame. Yet, while seeming to express genuine joy that he is okay, she warns him to stay away—that whatever they briefly had is over. Roger goes into stall mode and holds out for at least some dinner. When Eva finally concurs, farce returns with her demand that his dirty suit be cleaned. Roger immediately asks, "Now what could a man do with his clothes off for twenty minutes?" Yet, once again he heads to a bathroom for an alleged shower, and as we hear the water running, Hitchcock cannot resist some more beloved movie parody as we hear Grant whistling "Singin' in the Rain."

Yet, as if anticipating what Hitchcock is capable of with a shower, Grant is really keeping an eye on Saint, correctly anticipating she will slip out on him. Once she is gone, he figures out her destination by the pen indentations left behind on a hotel note pad. The address leads him to a tony auction house. Prior to his aforementioned screwball safety antics of crazy bidding and mocking the artwork, he makes a satirically biting attack on Eva to Vandamm, cracking that she really puts "her full body into her work." One half expects to hear the Dorothy Parker line, "You can lead a horticulture, but you can't make her think." His outburst makes Mason question Saint's loyalty, while the audience enjoys the lampooning to which farce sometimes leads.

Grant, however, is in the most immediate danger, given his *Notorious*-like jealousy, only to escape death from Vandamm's thugs via his screwball hijinks and a police escort from the auction house. But Hitchcock's dark comedy core immediately pivots to a broadly smiling arrested Grant taunting Vandamm's more brutish heavy (Adam Williams), "Sorry old man, keep trying [to kill me]." Regardless, when Grant is safely in the squad car, instead of going to the sanctuary of a jail, he is *mystified* (a word which describes his *Northwest* character as much as R.O.T.) to be taken to the Chicago airport.

Randomly, another appropriate term for his life since the Plaza, or dark comedy in general, he has forced the CIA not so much to save him as to have him assist them. Saint is actually a CIA agent, and his auction house outburst has put her cover in question. In other words, as Mark Twain would say, "It ain't what you don't know that gets you in trouble. It's what you know for sure that just ain't so." Regardless, as is consistent with the dark comedy norm, any establishment institution, even if it is our own red, white, and blue CIA, does not care about the average individual. And until he realizes Saint's life is in danger, Grant wants nothing to do with them. However, Hitchcock immediately turns Roger's close-up guilt acquiescence into more dark comedy, by then cutting to a close-up of Mount Rushmore—a sardonic tweaking of his imposed patriotism. Already having arrived on the site, Roger's comment about the monument is equally ironic, suggesting at least one of the stone presidents is suspicious of his loyalty, "I don't like the way Teddy Roosevelt is looking at me."

Northwest then makes one of its final references to play acting. Grant asks, "What little drama are we here for today?" However, the difference this time is that there actually will be a mini-drama, or at least an acted-out scene, within this play of a movie. Grant and Mason are to meet at a restaurant/tourist shop near the monument, which will feature a climactic confrontation between Roger and Eva—with her seemingly shooting him to death. This will bolster her cover, and the Cold War can continue along its merry way.

Of course, the shooting of Grant is a surprise befitting *Northwest*'s scatter gun parody format, maybe best summarized in another context by novelist/critic Jeff Giles as "...a riddle wrapped in an enigma and cloaked in crazy"—screwball crazy.[22] What is more, when Grant and Saint are able to meet briefly after the fake shooting, once again the subject of acting comes up. Indeed,

Between shooting, a tourist moment for Cary Grant and Eva Marie Saint.

the two even briefly critique his performance! Roger tells her he thought his fall was "quite graceful." And she agrees by way of saying "... considering it's not your kind of work." But while Grant thinks Saint will now be soon out of it, the CIA's Professor has not played straight with him. Another reason for dark comedy to distrust all establishment institutions. A spying Saint is to continue as Mason's mistress. Grant attempts to stop this action but is knocked out by one of the Professor's men.

When the unharmed Grant comes to in the hospital, which was doubling as his cover from supposedly being shot by Saint, he and the Professor play nice. But when Leo G. Carroll's character goes to get some liquid fun for them, Grant breaks out of his locked room. Climbing out the window, he carefully walks along the ledge and enters the next window. What follows is one of the film's biggest laughs, and another indirect reference to his handsome star persona. The woman patient in the room he has entered frightfully says, "Stop." However, upon putting on her glasses, after he has stopped, she repeats the term in a most friendly manner, and Grant merely gives her an affectionate wagging "no" of his finger, coupled with "Ahh," and moves on.

Roger to the rescue turns out to be a good thing, since Landau's Leonard has figured out the fake shooting, and Eva is to be done away with. As this discovery is being made, Roger is climbing the exterior of Vandamm's Frank Lloyd Wright–like house in the woods, near Mount Rushmore. Both actions affectionately spoof earlier Hitchcock, from Grant's physical actions being reminiscent of his cat burglar role in the director's *To Catch a Thief* (1955) to the sexual persuasion of Leonard. That is, as noted earlier in the text, Hitchcock often hired gay actors, feeling they were more talented, given a closeted era's necessity for them to act 24/7. Moreover, some Hitchcock projects played upon actual gay characters, such as the *Rope* duo. Thus, in Fitzgerald's documentary on *Northwest*, screenwriter Lehman acknowledges taking conscious credit for a tongue-in-cheek footnoting of that tendency in this Hitchcock film.[23] Consequently, at one point Leonard has the line, "Call it my woman's intuition," and at another moment Vandamm tells Leonard he is flattered that Landau's character seems jealous of Eva. (In later years Landis would sometimes take credit for playing the character as gay, with screenwriter Lehman adding the "intuition" line, and Hitchcock being okay with it.[24])

The climax of the film, dashing about and hanging from Mount Rushmore, is yet another Hitchcock given—a film culmination in a famous place. And just that idea was the original catalyst for the film. However, only some *Northwest* shooting was done on site (somehow the National Park Service thought it was all going to be done there) instead of on the mock-ups back in Hollywood. This misunderstanding resulted in *Northwest* receiving some angry yet funny production PR. For example, one critic suggested they should "...go back to England and film pictures of people scampering around on the Queen's face."[25]

That distrusting Teddy Roosevelt on the Hollywood monument facsimile, with Cary Grant and Eva Marie Saint.

Every Harold Lloyd–like piece of Rushmore "thrill comedy" is made that way by coupling danger with quips. For instance, at one point as Grant and Saint are barely hanging on, she asks why his two wives had divorced him. His response, "I led too dull of a life." Plus, the last apparent moment of danger, after Vandamm has been arrested and both his henchmen are dead, is turned into a comic bit of sexual innuendo. That is, Grant pulling Saint up from a Rushmore ledge turns into a form cut of him hoisting her into a train compartment bunk, followed by a quick cut of the engine and cars going into a tunnel. As George Carlin said in a famous bit from an early comedy set, "You don't have to be Fellini to know what that means."

With all the activity on the face of Rushmore, Roger also managed to add a marriage proposal, too. Consequently, one has the perfect censors' setup for the final words of the film starting with "Mrs." And if one ever wanted a "happy ever after" for a couple, it would be Grant and Saint. But since Hitchcock films do not promote happy unions and everything has been done here to make this picture a greatest hits package—tradition makes it a thumbs down future for the duo. Moreover, when the couple spoke briefly before the

The sexy finish, with Cary Grant and Eva Marie Saint.

misadventures on Rushmore, Grant asked her how she became involved with Mason. Her answer would give pause to most potential husbands, "I guess I had nothing to do that weekend; so I decided to fall in love."

Add to this a twice-divorced Roger Thornhill eventually pondering her *patriotic* act of continuing to sleep with Vandamm, after becoming a spy (patriotism/nationalism does not score high on the dark comedy meter). Finally, add the thought of how many Roger Thornhills had preceded him ... and the odds here are not very good for a long skip down lovers' lane, especially when one also throws in the questionable projected success rate of screwball comedy couples.

Regardless, *Northwest* proved to be a major critical and commercial success, with the reviews, as suggested at the chapter's opening, possibly best summarized by the *New York Times* encapsulation—a film with "a breezy sense of humor," or the ongoing mantra for the movie as "tongue-in-check."[26] And as periodically noted, *Variety* was said to say, "At times it seems Hitchcock is kidding his own penchant for the bizarre but his sardonic attitude is so deftly handled it only enhances...."[27]

Epilogue, and Thoughts on *Psycho*

> Short, plump, his [Hitchcock] is the most famous profile in film. He bobs when he walks, like a sea-tossed buoy, and his bowling ball figure is, like his movies, at once scary and comic.—Biographer Patrick McGilligan[1]

With *North by Northwest* (1959) Alfred Hitchcock had come full circle back to his British comic thrillers, à la *39 Steps* (1935) and *The Lady Vanishes* (1938), which had brought him to America. Thus, it seemed a good stopping point for examining the various comedy genres he had so elaborately intertwined around his filmography's black comedy core. However, one cannot close without some passing thoughts on *Psycho* (1960), though it has periodically been referenced in the text.

Psycho has now reached a cult dark comedy status not unlike that of *The Rocky Horror Picture Show*. Indeed, it now sometimes even turns up on the midnight movie circuit that made *Rocky Horror*. Regardless, however, *Psycho* is also something of a British Hitchcock reboot to the picture that put the director on the cinema map—1927's Jack the Ripper inspired *The Lodger*. Be that as it may, *Psycho* has spawned a cottage industry of products, from tomes to toys, including Norman Bates dolls and Hitchcock shower turtles. Plus, countless comics have mined jokes from the movie. For example, "There is a hidden bird motif in *Psycho*—but if it's hidden, what good is it?"

There is also the fact that so many darkly comic thrillers since *Psycho* seem to necessitate a Hitchcock footnote for validation, such as Danny Boyle's first picture, *Shallow Grave* (1994). Of course, in this case parallels do pile up: comic thriller, voyeurism, a cold blonde, disposing of a body, sinking a car in water, and the still shock effect of losing a star quickly. Boyle himself observed of killing British name actor Keith Allen:

Obviously, it's like Hitchcock and *Psycho*, [The audience thinks] ... if you cast a celebrity like Keith Allen there's no way you're killing him off early.... It throws everyone about [confuses the audience]. What's coming next? ... It gives the death ... a kind of significance, which triggers everything else in the film.²

Fittingly, *Shallow Grave* won the "Golden Hitchcock" award at the British Dinard Film Festival, and went on to win BAFTA's Best Picture prize, England's version of an Oscar.

Psycho, therefore, so oozes dark comedy that a chapter on the film seemed too obvious. However, three universal Hitchcock comedy components merit noting. First, because so many of his characters have a comic mother fixation, especially Bates' "first cousin" Bruno, from *Strangers on a Train* (1951), it seems therefore devilishly comic that Norman ultimately *becomes* his mother. Second, art often has a pivotal comic part in Hitchcock's films, especially the various shades of dark comedy allocated to *Blackmail*'s (1929) painting of a jester. However, Hitchcock's darkly comic attention to art specifics in *Psycho* is off the charts. That is, when Janet Leigh undresses for a shower, Anthony Perkin peeks at her through a tiny hole in the wall.

A lighter moment on the *Psycho* (1960) set, with Janet Leigh and Anthony Perkins.

The painting which normally covers said hole is of Susanna and the Elders—the *Biblical* story of a woman overtaken in her bath by voyeurs whose passions were aroused as they spied on her.

You can say what you want about Hitchcock—especially now that he is dead—but the man was a stickler for detail. Moreover, with dark comedy being his métier, the Susan and the Elders painting plays to the genre in additional ways particular to Hitchcock. First, dark comedy is anti-establishment. And after his ongoing skewering of the law, the Catholic church (given his strict religious upbringing) was a fun target for Hitchcock. Thus, getting a dig in at the *Bible* would have pleased him. Second, Hitchcock enjoyed inside jokes, especially dark ones which the audience would not get, if ever, without multiple screenings. Therefore, here was a peephole Biblical gag all to himself. Third, Hitchcock was *the* West Coast distributor of voyeurism, and to have his in-film voyeur use a picture of voyeurs to cover Bates' peephole would be comically hard to top.

The last Hitchcock component so obvious in Psycho is the red herring—making something insignificant initially seem important. In *Hitchcock land* it is referred to as a "MacGuffin," and a prime example is the $40,000 Leigh steals at the start of *Psycho*, which drives the movie's first half. Yet, this "MacGuffin" has two levels of dark comedy attached to it. One, Hitchcock audiences are not usually meant to be shown how easily they were fooled by directly buying into the trick. That is, in *Psycho*, after Leigh has been murdered, Perkins just tosses her and the newspaper in which the money has been hidden into her car and drives it into the ever-handy swamp on the Bates back forty.

Next, one joins Norman to watch the car sink away. However, suddenly it stops and the viewer gets his second degree of MacGuffin-related dark comedy. That is, the car is not submerging. Consequently, Norman and viewers panic (like you do); it is never good to have murder evidence sticking out of your neighborhood bog. Then the car resumes its descent and we, like Norman, can breathe easily again. Of course, one feels perverse about having rooted for the sinking car but time passes and you continue to eat your popcorn. Yet, it is classic Hitchcock dark comedy—being implicated to a negative act, such as this action, or cheering on *Strangers'* Bruno squeezing his arm through the sewer grating bars in order to retrieve a cigarette lighter with which to frame the hero. Yet, sad to say, we have caught up with Hitchcock. One feels less connected to any shared guilt produced by the artist—such is the evolution of dark comedy, and cinema itself since the French New Wave.

The MacGuffin reference, however, is an excellent transition from the comic particulars of *Psycho* to the Hitchcock filmography in general. The director constantly stated all his movies were dark comedies, despite how this book has hopefully demonstrated he was a master at wrapping his films in an assortment of other comedy genres, too. Yet, who would have guessed that his most famous yet seemingly innocuous signature filmmaking device, the MacGuffin, was a direct link to dark comedy—a sort of Hitchcock Rosetta Stone.

That is, in the theatre of the absurd black humor of Samuel Beckett's *Waiting for Godot* (1953), or Tom Stoppard's *Rosencrantz and Guildenstern Are Dead* (1966), one is entertainingly diverted by the frivolous, sometimes funny, but always seemingly important antics of two *dumb* representatives (another Hitchcock given) of the human comedy. Yet, at the tale's end, are their actions not like MacGuffins—distractions from life's main storyline—reflecting Kafka's comment that "the meaning of life is we die."

Now one might say, where is the humor in that? The dark comedy lies in how effectively humanity blocks the subject. Rosencrantz is spot on when he observes:

> Whatever became of the moment when one first knew about death? There must have been one, a moment, in childhood when it first occurred to you that you don't go on forever. It must have been shattering—stamped into one's memory. And yet I can't remember. It never occurred to me at all. What does one make of that?....[3]

Maybe Rosencrantz best summed up humanity's Teflon relationship with death best when he, like the proverbial "wise fool," sardonically describes the subject as too depressing—"Eternity is a terrible thought. I mean, where's it going to end?"[4] Put another way, Nietzsche would say we need lies to live. Most forms of humor are the benevolent lies. However, dark comedy lets one peek behind the curtain. At best we are *briefly* ping pong balls in a wind chamber, which no doubt also concentrated to Hitchcock's cinematic view of matrimony.

Be that as it may, what of the rest of this text? For many writers, myself included, there is a tendency to regurgitate a condensed form of the preceding pages—bad idea. I am reminded of an expletive ridden "theatre of the real" comment by Richard Pryor addressed to his audience one night that I would direct back on a recycling author. A very young Robin Williams recalled Pryor appearing on stage in a Los Angeles comedy club:

> Everyone would come and watch. It was like an audience for the pope. I saw him do stuff [on stage] that he would never do again. People would yell out "Do Mudbone! [one of Pryor's characters—a rambling street smart old man]" and he'd [Pryor] say, "You do Mudbone, motherfucker. You know it better than me." It was a kind of a transformative thing....[5]

If you have embraced any of the preceding pages, hopefully I have done a modestly transformative thing—exposed what has always seemed so obvious to me, that Hitchcock was just as methodically attuned to comedy as he was to the thriller—and it is your turn to further widen and appreciate this

Though Keaton was strictly for hire on his first feature, *The Saphead* (1920), the title might have doubled for his idea of cinema matrimony, a view Hitchcock, a Keaton fan, often emulated on screen.

crack in the door. One might liken it to the ability of any great artist to take a subject and through some alchemy make it all his own. The examples are many. Fatty Arbuckle first filmed "the dance of the dinner rolls," which Charlie Chaplin inspiringly made all his own in *The Gold Rush* (1925). And the Beatles song "A Little Help from My Friends," from rock 'n roll's universally acclaimed greatest album, *Sgt. Pepper's Lonely Heart's Club Band* (1967), suddenly became a Joe Cocker song after his Ray Charles tinged, angst ridden rendition at 1969's Woodstock—which the Beatles were the first to admit. In each case a pleasantly nonchalant work was enriched with a shadow of darkness—a grieving Tramp, and a vocalist exposed behind his own self-proclaimed curtain of "Mad Dogs and Englishmen."

Hitchcock was not so unlike the neglected scholarly humorist Richard Armour, who was fond of saying he "...wore two outfits—cap and gown and cap and bells."[6] Thus, look beyond the Hitchcock thrills ... and his English undertaker's garb. The cap and bells are there, too.

Filmography

June 30, 1929 (UK)

Blackmail
(British International Pictures, BIP, 84 minutes) Director: Alfred Hitchcock. Screenplay: Hitchcock and Benn W. Levy, adapted from the Charles Bennett play. Music: Jimmy Campbell, Reg Connelly, Hubert Bath; Billy Mayerl song: "Miss Up-to-Date." Stars: Anny Ondra, voiced by Joan Barry (Alice White), John Longden (Detective Frank Webber), Donald Calthrop (Tracy), Cyril Ritchard (the artist), Charles Paton (Mr. White), Sara Allgood (Mrs. White), Hannah Jones (landlady), Harvey Braban (Chief inspector), Phyllis Monkman (neighbor).

December 1934 (UK)

The Man Who Knew Too Much
(Gaumont-British Picture Corporation, 75 minutes) Director: Alfred Hitchcock. Screenplay: Edwin Greenwood and A.R. Rawlinson, from a Charles Bennett and a D.B. Wyndham-Lewis story. Music: Arthur Benjamin. Stars: Leslie Banks (Bob Lawrence), Edna Best (Jill Lawrence), Peter Lorre (Abbott), Nova Pilbeam (Betty Lawrence), Frank Vosper (Ramon Levine), Hugh Wakefield (Clive), Pierre Fresnay (Louis Bernard), Cicely Oates (Nurse Agnes).

June 6, 1935 (UK)

The 39 Steps
(Gaumont British Distributors, 86 minutes) Director: Alfred Hitchcock. Screenplay: Charles Bennett and Ian Hay, adapted from John Buchan's novel *The Thirty-Nine Steps*. Music: Jack Beaver and Louis Levy (uncredited). Stars: Robert Donat (Richard Hannay), Madeleine Carroll (Pamela), Lucie Mannheim (Annabella Smith), Godfrey Tearle (Professor Jordan), John Laurie (Crofter), Peggy Ashcroft (his wife), Helen Haye (Mrs. Jordan), Frank Cellier (the sheriff), Wylie Watson (Mr. Memory).

May 1936 (UK)

Secret Agent
(Gaumont-British Picture, 86 minutes) Director: Alfred Hitchcock. Screenplay: Charles Bennett, Alma Reville and Ian Hay, from a W. Somerset Maugham story. Music: no credit. Stars: John Gielgud (Richard Ashenden), Madeleine Carroll (Elsa), Peter Lorre (The General), Robert Young (Marvin), Percy Marmont (Caypor), Florence Kahn (Mrs. Caypor).

October 7, 1938 (UK)

The Lady Vanishes
(Gainsborough Pictures Gaumont British, 97 minutes) Director: Alfred Hitchcock. Screenplay: Sidney Gilliat and Frank Launder, adapted from the Ethel Lina White novel *The Wheel Spins*. Music: Louis Levy and Charles Williams (uncredited). Stars: Margaret Lockwood (Iris Henderson), Michael Redgrave (Gilbert), Dame May Whitty (Miss Froy), Paul Lukas (Dr. Hartz), Cecil Parker (Mr. Todhunter), Linden Travers (the mistress), Naunton Wayne (Caldicott), Basil Radford (Charters), Mary Clare (Baroness), Catherine Lacey (the "nun").

January 31, 1941 (USA)

Mr. & Mrs. Smith
(RKO Radio Pictures, 94 minutes) Director: Alfred Hitchcock. Screenplay: Norman Krasna. Music: Edward Ward. Stars: Carole Lombard (Ann Smith), Robert Montgomery (David Smith), Gene Raymond (Jeff Custer), Philip Merivale and Lucile Watson (Custer's parents), Jack Carson (Chuck Benson).

January 12, 1943 (USA)

Shadow of a Doubt
(Universal, 108 minutes) Director: Alfred Hitchcock. Screenplay: Thornton Wilder, Alma Reville, and Sally Benson, adapted from a Gordon McDonnel story. Music: Dimitri Tiomkin (original score). Stars: Joseph Cotten (Uncle Charlie), Teresa Wright (Charlie Newton), Patricia Collinge (Emma Newton), Henry Travers (Joseph Newton) Hume Cronyn (Herbie Hawkins), Edna May Wonacott (Ann Newton), Charles Bates (Roger Newton) Wallace Ford (Fred Saunders).

August 26, 1948 (USA)

Rope
(A Transatlantic Picture, 80 minutes) Director: Alfred Hitchcock. Screenplay: Arthur Laurents, from a Hume Cronyn story, adapted from a Patrick Hamilton play. Music: David Buttolph and Francis Poulenc (uncredited). Stars: James Stew-

art (Rupert Cadell), John Dall (Brandon), Farley Granger (Phillip), Sir Cedric Hardwicke (Mr. Kentley), Constance Collier (Mrs. Atwater), Douglas Dick (Kenneth), Edith Evanson (Mrs. Wilson), Joan Chandler (Janet), Dick Hogan (David Kentley).

June 30, 1951 (USA)

Strangers on a Train

(A Transatlantic Picture, 101 minutes) Director: Alfred Hitchcock. Screenplay: Raymond Chandler, Whitfield Cook, and Czenzi Ormonde, adapted from Patricia Highsmith's novel. Music: Dimitri Tiomkin. Stars: Robert Walker (Bruno Antony), Farley Granger (Guy Haines), Laura Elliott *also known as Kasey Rogers* (Miriam Haines), Ruth Roman (Anne Morton), Patricia Hitchcock (Barbara Morton), Leo G. Carroll (Senator Morton), Marion Lorne (Mrs. Antony).

September 1, 1954 (USA)

Rear Window

(A Warner Bros—First National Picture, 112 minutes) Director: Alfred Hitchcock. Screenplay: John Michael Hayes, adapted from a Cornell Woolrich short story. Music: Franz Waxman. Stars: James Stewart (L.B. Jefferies), Grace Kelly (Lisa), Thelma Ritter (Stella), Wendell Corey (Tom Doyle), Raymond Burr (Lars Thorwald), Irene Winston (Mrs. Thorwald), Judith Evelyn (Miss Lonelyhearts), Ross Bagdasarian (the composer), Georgine Darcy (Miss Torso).

October 3, 1955 (USA)

The Trouble with Harry

(Paramount Pictures, 99 minutes) Director: Alfred Hitchcock. Screenplay: John Michael Hayes, adapted from the Jack Trevor Story novel. Music: Bernard Herrmann. Stars: Edmund Gwenn (Captain Albert Wiles), John Forsythe (Sam Marlowe), Shirley MacLaine (Jennifer), Mildred Natwick (Miss Graveley), Mildred Dunnock (Mrs. Wiggs), Jerry Mathers (Arnie Rogers), Royal Dano (Calvin Wiggs), Parker Fennelly (millionaire), Philip Truex (Harry).

July 28, 1959 (USA)

North by Northwest

(MGM, 136 minutes) Director: Alfred Hitchcock. Screenplay: Ernest Lehman. Music: Bernard Herrmann. Stars: Cary Grant (Roger O. Thornhill), Eva Marie Saint (Eve Kendall), James Mason (Phillip Vandamm), Jessie Royce Landis (Clara Thornhill), Leo G. Carroll (the professor), Philip Ober (Lester Townsend), Martin Landau (Leonard), Adam Williams (Valerian), Robert Ellenstein (Licht).

Chapter Notes

Prologue

1. Jim Leach, "The Screwball Comedy," in *Film Genres and Criticism*, ed. Barry K. Grant (Metuchen, New Jersey: Scarecrow Press, 1977), 75.
2. *Alfred Hitchcock's Mystery Magazine* (North Palm Beach, Florida: H.S.D. Publications, Inc., August 1960).
3. François Truffaut, *Hitchcock/Truffaut* (1967; rpt. New York: Simon & Schuster, 1983, with bonus material).
4. "The *Sight & Sound* Top 50 Greatest Films of All Time," *Sight & Sound* (British Film Institute), September 2012, cover page article.
5. Robert A. Harris and Michael S. Lasky, *The Films of Alfred Hitchcock* (1976; rpt. Secaucus, New Jersey: Citadel Press, 1979), 5.
6. Charlotte Chandler, *It's Only a Movie: Alfred Hitchcock: A Personal Biography* (Montclair, New Jersey: Applause Theatre & Cinema Books, 2006), 91.
7. Charles Chaplain cover blurb for the Alma Reville biography by Hitchcock's daughter: Pat Hitchcock O'Connell and Laurent Bouzereau, *Alma Hitchcock: The Woman Behind the Man* (2003; rpt. New York: Berkley Books, 2004).
8. John Russell Taylor, *Hitch: The Life and Times of Alfred Hitchcock* (1978; rpt. New York: Random House, 1980), 11.
9. Donald Spoto, *The Dark Side of Genius: The Life of Alfred Hitchcock* (Boston: Little, Brown and Co., 1983), 148.
10. Anthony Slide, "The 39 Steps," in *Magill's Survey of Cinema*, English Language Films, First Series, volume 4, ed. Frank N. Magill (Englewood Cliffs, New Jersey: Salem Press, 1980), 1723.
11. Chandler, *It's Only a Movie: Alfred Hitchcock: A Personal Biography*, 104.
12. Spoto, *The Dark Side of Genius: The Life of Alfred Hitchcock*, 304–305.
13. Truffaut, *Hitchcock/Truffaut*, 334.
14. *Ibid.*, 346.
15. See the author's *Will Cuppy, American Satirist: A Biography* (Jefferson, NC: McFarland, 2013); and his *American Dark Comedy: Beyond Satire* (Westport, Connecticut: Greenwood Press, 1996).
16. Edgar Allan Poe, "The Murders in the Rue Morgue," in *The Complete Tales and Poems of Edgar Allan POE* (New York: Barnes & Noble, Inc., 2007), 375.
17. *Ibid.*
18. See the author's *Will Cuppy, American Satirist: A Biography*.
19. Will Cuppy, *How to Tell Your Friends from the Apes* (1931; rpt. Boston: Nonpareil Books, 2005), 31.
20. Anthony Lane, "The Current Cinema: Desperadoes," *The New Yorker*, August 21, 2017, 82.
21. A.M. Sperber, *Murrow: His Life and Times* (New York: Freundlich Books, 1986), 470.
22. Mark Twain, "The Stolen White Elephant," in *World's Great Detective Stories*, ed. Will Cuppy (New York: World Publishing Co., 1943), 314, 315.
23. The quote occurs in Harris and Lasky's *The Films of Alfred Hitchcock*, 115; and of his many references to seeing murderers as heroes occurs in Spoto's *The Dark Side of Genius: The Life of Alfred Hitchcock*, 33.
24. Truffaut, *Hitchcock/Truffaut*, 346.
25. James Atlas, *The Shadow in the Garden: A Biographer's Tale* (New York: Panthean Books, 2017), 9.
26. *Ibid.*
27. See the author's *Charlie Chaplin: A Bio-Bibliography* (Westport, Connecticut: Greenwood Press, 1983); and his *Chaplin's War Trilogy: An Evolving Lens in Three Dark Comedies, 1918-1947* (Jefferson, NC: McFarland, 2014).
28. See the author's *Buster Keaton in His*

Own Time: What the Responses of 1920s Critics Reveal (Jefferson, NC: McFarland, 2014).

29. Robert E. Sherwood, "Silent Drama: Young Mr. Keaton," *LIFE* (humor magazine, not the later pictorial magazine), November 16, 1922, 24.

30. See the author's *American Dark Comedy: Beyond Satire* (Westport, Connecticut: Greenwood Press, 1996); and his *Personality Comedians as Genre: Selected Players* (Westport, CT: Greenwood Press, 1997).

31. "The Hitchcock Formula," *New York Times*, February 13, 1938, Section 10:4.

32. *Ibid.*

33. Again, see the author's *American Dark Comedy: Beyond Satire.*

34. "The Hitchcock Formula."

35. Roger Pippet, *PM* dust jacket quote on H. Allen Smith's *Lost in the Horse Latitudes* (1941; rpt. Philadelpha: The Blakiston Company, 1946).

36. H. Allen Smith, "Hitchcock Likes to Smash Cups," *New York World-Telegram,* August 28, 1937, 7.

37. *Ibid.*

38. Truffaut, *Hitchcock/Truffaut,* 158–159.

39. Robert Benchley, "Johnny-on-the-Spot," in *From Bed to Worse or Comforting Thoughts About the Bison* (New York: Harper & Brothers, 1934), 255–259; also see the author's *"Mr. B" or Comforting Thoughts About the Bison: A Critical Biography of Robert Benchley* (Westport, Connecticut: Greenwood Press, 1992).

40. Gehring, *"Mr. B" or Comforting Thoughts About the Bison: A Critical Biography of Robert Benchley.*

41. Robert Benchley, letter to his wife, March 25, 1940, in "The Robert Benchley Collection," Special Collections. Boston University Mugar Library, Boston, Massachusetts.

42. "Dialogue on Film No. 5: Alfred Hitchcock," Los Angeles, California: American Film Institute, 1972.

43. See the author's *Screwball Comedy: A Genre of Madcap Romance* (Westport, Connecticut: Greenwood Press, 1986); and his *Romantic Versus Screwball Comedy: Charting a Difference* (Lanham, Maryland: Scarecrow Press, 2002).

44. Michael Chabon, *Wonder Boys* (New York: Picador, 1995), 251.

45. Dashiell Hammett, *The Thin Man* (1933; rpt. New York: Vintage Books, 1992), 71–75.

46. C.A. Lejeune, "Meet Alfred Hitchcock," *New York Times,* December 15, 1935, Section 2:7.

47. Truffaut, *Hitchcock/Truffaut,* 114.

48. See the author's *Parody as Film Genre: "Never Give a Saga an Even Break"* (Westport, Connecticut: Greenwood Press, 1999).

49. *Ibid.*; Other observations on reaffirmation parody are drawn from the author's text.

50. Patrick Hamilton, *Rope* (1929; rpt. United Kingdom: Samuel French, 1988), 33.

51. Truffaut, *Hitchcock/Truffaut,* 111.

52. "Blackmail: Selwyn," *New York Herald Tribune,* October 7, 1929, 17.

53. "Alfred Hitchcock, Under Thirty, Rated Leading English Director," *New York American,* October 6, 1929, 6-D.

54. See the author's humor book *Film Classics Reclassified: A Shocking Spoof of Cinema.* (Davenport, Iowa: Robin Vincent Publishing, 2001).

55. Peter Ackroyd, *Alfred Hitchcock: A Brief Life* (2016; rpt. New York: Anchor Books, 2017), 60.

Chapter 1

1. Of the author's various books on the subject, especially see his *American Dark Comedy: Beyond Satire* (Westport, Connecticut: Greenwood Press, 1996).

2. "At the Selwyn [*Blackmail*]," *New York Evening World,* October 7, 1929, 15.

3. Broad *Blackmail* ad campaign, such as it appeared in the *New York American,* October 7, 1929.

4. Charles Bennett, *Blackmail: A Play in Three Acts* (London: Rich & Cowan LTD, 1928).

5. "'Blackmail': A British International Production," *New York World,* October 7, 1929, 15.

6. "'Blackmail': British Made," *Variety,* October 9, 1929.

7. Bennet, *Blackmail: A Play in Three Acts,* 26.

8. *Ibid.,* 27.

9. Eileen Creelman, "First English Talkie: 'Blackmail,'" *New York Sun,* October 5, 1929, 5.

10. "'Blackmail': British Made," *Variety.*

11. Especially see the author's *Chaplin's War Trilogy: An Evolving Lens in Three Dark Comedies, 1918–1947* (Jefferson, NC: McFarland, 2014); *Genre-Busting Dark Comedies of the 1970s: Twelve American Films* (Jefferson, NC: McFarland, 2016); *Film Clowns of the Depression: Twelve Defining Comic Performances* (Jefferson, NC: McFarland, 2007); *Forties Film Funnymen: The Decade's Great Comedians at Work in the Shadow of War* (Jefferson, NC: McFarland, 2010); *Charlie Chaplin: A Bio-Bibliography* (Westport, Connecticut: Greenwood Press, 1983); the aforementioned *American Dark Comedies: Beyond Satire*; and *Buster Keaton in His Own Time: What the Responses of 1920s Critics Reveal* (Jefferson, NC: McFarland, 2018).

12. Anita Gates, "Harry Dean Stanton, Scene-Stealing Actor, Dies at 91," *New York Times,* September 16, 2017, B-13.

13. François Truffaut, *Hitchcock/Truffaut*

(1967; rpt. New York: Simon & Schuster, 1983, with bonus material),
14. Donald Spoto, *The Dark Side of Genius: The Life of Alfred Hitchcock* (Boston: Little, Brown and Company, 1983).
15. Davie Sterritt, *The Films of Alfred Hitchcock* (New York: Cambridge University Press, 1993), 29.
16. Bennett, *Blackmail: A Play in Three Acts*, 96–97.
17. Ibid., 98.
18. See the author's *Personality Comedians as Genre: Selected Players* (Westport, Connecticut: Greenwood Press, 1997).
19. Edgar Allan Poe, "The Premature Burial," in *The Complete Tales and Poems of Edgar Allan Poe* (New York: Barnes & Noble, 2006), 587–597.
20. Charlotte Chandler, *It's Only a Movie: Alfred Hitchcock: A Personal Biography* (2005; rpt. Montclair, New Jersey: Applause, 2006), 37–38.
21. George Perry, *The Films of Alfred Hitchcock* (1965; rpt. London: Blue Star House, 1970), 30.
22. Ernest Marshall, "London Film Notes," *New York Times*, July 14, 1929, Section 9:4.
23. "What the Critics Think of *Blackmail*," *New York Telegram*, October 9, 1929, 10; "'Blackmail' [Review]," *New York Herald Tribune*, October 7, 1929, 17.
24. "At the Selwyn [*Blackmail*]," *New York Evening World*.
25. "'Blackmail': A British International Production," *New York World*.
26. "'Blackmail': British Made," *Variety*.
27. Creelman, "First English Talkie: 'Blackmail,'" *New York Sun*.
28. "'Blackmail': British Made," *Variety*.

Chapter 2

1. Film historian Philip Kemp, Bonus Features, 2013 DVD of 1934's *The Man Who Knew Too Much*, Criterion Collection.
2. Farran Smith Nehme, "Wish You Were You," in *The Man Who Knew Too Much* (New York: Criterion Collection monograph, 2013), n.p. [4].
3. Anthony Lane, "The 39 Steps," *Magill's Survey of Cinema: English Language Films, First Series*, ed., Frank N. Magill (Englewood Cliffs, New Jersey: Salem Press, 1980), 1723.
4. Anthony Lane, "In Love with Fear," *The New Yorker*, August 16, 1999, 80.
5. See the author's *Screwball Comedy: A Genre of Madcap Romance* (Westport, Connecticut: Greenwood Press, 1986; and *Romantic vs. Screwball Comedy: Charting the Difference* (Lanham, Maryland: Scarecrow Press 2002).

6. Dashiell Hammett, *The Thin Man* (1933; rpt. New York: Vintage Books, 1992), 5.
7. Herb Stone, *I Married a Witch* review, *Rob Wagner's Script* (December 19, 1942), in *Selected Film Criticism, 1914–1950*, ed. Anthony Slide (Metuchen, New Jersey: Scarecrow Press, 1983), 85.
8. See the author's *Carole Lombard: The Hoosier Tornado* (Indianapolis: Indiana Historical Society Press, 2003).
9. Charles Washburn, "The Nassau Sweepstakes," *New York Times*, February 7, 1937, Section 10:5.
10. David Thomson, *The New Biographical Dictionary of Film* (New York: Alfred A. Knopf, 2003), 532.
11. "The Hitchcock Formula," *New York Times*, February 13, 1938, Section 10:14.
12. See the author's humor book *Film Classics Reclassified: A Shocking Spoof of Cinema* (Davenport, Iowa: Robin Vincent Publishing, 2001).
13. See the author's *Laurel & Hardy: A Bio-Bibliography* (Westport, Connecticut: Greenwood Press, 1990).
14. That is, one would be contrasting Hollywood's quasi-realist "invisible editing" with the formalistically self-conscious transitions for the French New Wave.
15. See film historian Philip Kemp's commentary track on the 2013 DVD of 1934's *The Man Who Knew Too Much*, Criterion Collection.
16. François Truffaut, *Hitchcock/Truffaut* (1967; rpt. New York: Simon & Schuster, 1983, with bonus material.), 91.
17. Ibid.
18. See the author's *Movie Comedians of the 1950s: Defining a New Era of Big Screen Comedy* (Jefferson, NC: McFarland, 2016).
19. See the author's *Red Skelton: The Mask Behind the Mask* (Indianapolis: Indiana State Historical Society Press, 2008).
20. Truffaut, *Hitchcock/Truffaut*, 94.
21. Kemp, Bonus Features, 2013 DVD of 1934's *The Man Who Knew Too Much*.
22. Stephen D. Youngkin, *The Lost One: A Life of Peter Lorre* (Lexington: University Press of Kentucky, 2012), 19.
23. Andre Sennwald, "The Screen: Peter Lorre in His First American Photoplay," *New York Times*, August 5, 1935, Section 20:2.
24. Youngkin, *The Lost One: A Life of Peter Lorre*, 99–100.
25. Ibid., 100–101.
26. Youngkin, *The Lost One: A Life of Peter Lorre*, 94; also see the author's *"Mr. B" Or Comforting Thoughts About the Bison: A Critical Biography of Robert Benchley* (Westport, Connecticut: Greenwood Press., 1992).
27. "[Review of the] 'Man Who Knew Too

Much,'" *Variety*, April 3, 1935; "Mayfair Presents Exciting Melodrama," *New York Daily News*, March 23, 1935, 28; Richard Watts, Jr., "'The Man Who Knew Too Much' [Review] Mayfair," *New York Herald Tribune*, March 25, 1935, 10; Eileen Creelman, "The New Talkies: 'The Man Who Knew Too Much,'" *New York Sun*, March 23, 1935, 7.

28. Robin Wood, *Howard Hawks* (1968; rpt. London: British Film Institute, 1981), 58, 60–61.

29. "'Man Who Knew Too Much' Dull, Slow-Paced Picture," *Hollywood Reporter*, March 29, 1935, 7.

30. William Boehnel, "First Rate Schocker at the Mayfair," *New York World-Telegram*, March 23, 1935, 22.

31. Wood, *Howard Hawks*, 58, 60.

32. Michael Wood, *Alfred Hitchcock: The Man Who Knew Too Much* (Boston: New Harvest, 2015), 111.

33. "[Review of the] 'Man Who Knew Too Much,'" *Variety*.

34. For example, see the pioneering example: H.C. McNeile's *Bulldog Drummond* (1920; rpt. Lexington, KY: First Rate Publishers, 2017).

35. Alexandra Alter and Dan Bilefsky, "Genre-Spanning Author of 'Remains of the Day' Wins Nobel," *New York Times*, October 6, 2017, 1.

Chapter 3

1. William Boehnel, "The New Movie," *New York World-Telegram*, September 14, 1935, 19.

2. See the author's books on screwball listed in the bibliography.

3. "Donat Highlight; Carroll-Tearle Good," *Hollywood Reporter*, June 29, 1935, 7.

4. "New Gallery: 'The Thirty-Nine Steps,'" *London Times*, June 6, 1935.

5. "'The Thirty-Nine Steps' [Review]," *London Cinema Quarterly*, Summer 1935, Vol. 3, Issue 4, P. 241.

6. "'The 39 Steps' [Review]," *BFI Monthly Bulletin*, June 1935, Vol. 2, No. 17.

7. Thornton Delehanty, "'The 39 Steps' at the Roxy Is Best of All Spy Movies," *New York Post*, September 14, 1935, 11.

8. *Ibid*.

9. "A Genius of the Films: Alfred Hitchcock and His Work," *London Observer*, November 17, 1935.

10. "'The 39 Steps' [Review]," *BFI Monthly Bulletin*.

11. Eileen Creelman, "The New Talkie: 'The 39 Steps,'" *New York Sun*, September 16, 1935, 17.

12. "Donat Highlight; Carroll-Tearle Good," *Hollywood Reporter*.

13. *The Art of Film: Vintage Hitchcock*, DVD Bonus Feature on 1934's *The Man Who Knew Too Much* (USA: Janus Films: Criterion Collection, 1999).

14. See Stanley Cavell's *Pursuits of Happiness: The Hollywood Comedy of Remarriage*. (Cambridge, Mass: Harvard University Press, 1991).

15. Ben Kenigsberg, "A Watershed Moment of Cinematic Terror," *New York Times*, October 13, 2017, C-9.

16. Andre Sennwald, "'The 39 Steps' [Review]," *New York Times*, September 14, 1935, 8.

17. John Buchan, *The Thirty-Nine Steps* (1915), in *The Complete Richard Hannay Stories* (Hertfordshire, England: Wordsworth Classics, 1987), 42.

18. *Ibid.*, 42–43.

19. *Ibid.*, 71.

20. *The Borders of the Possible*, DVD Bonus Feature on 1935's *The 39 Steps* (USA: Criterion Global Entertainment, 2012).

21. Boehnel, "The New Movie," *New York World-Telegram*.

22. Sennwald, "'The 39 Steps' [Review]," *New York Times*.

23. "'The 39 Steps' [Review]," *Variety*, June 19, 1935.

24. "A Genius of the Films: Alfred Hitchcock and His Work," *London Observer*.

25. "Entertainment Best 100 Pictures," BBC, broadcast September 23, 1999.

Chapter 4

1. Thorton Delehanty, "'Secret Agent' At the Roxy," *New York Post*, June 13, 1936, 9.

2. Regina Crewe, "'Secret Agent' Gives Thrills As British Film Spy Story with Romance and Comedy," *New York American*, June 15, 1936, 9.

3. *Ibid*.

4. See the bibliography for the author's book on personality comedians as genre, as well as additional biographies on various screen clowns.

5. Michael Newton, "Master of the Macabre," *London Guardian*, September 12, 2014.

6. *Ibid*.

7. Philip French, "Peter Lorre: A Great Screen Actor Remembered," *London Guardian*, August 30, 2014.

8. Newton, "Master of the Macabre."

9. Check the bibliography for the author's books on the Marx Brothers.

10. W. Somerset Maugham, "The Hairless Mexican," in *Ashenden: or The British Agent* (Garden City, New York: Doubleday, Doran & Company, Inc., 1928), 59.

11. *Ibid.*, 56.
12. W. Somerset Maugham, "The Dark Woman," in *Ashenden: or the British Agent* (Garden City, New York: Doubleday, Doran & Company, Inc., 1928), 79–80.
13. Maugham, "The Hairless Mexican," 69.
14. W. Somerset Maugham, "The Traitor," in *Ashenden: or The British Agent* (Garden City, New York: Doubleday, Doran & Company, Inc., 1928), 158.
15. *Ibid.*
16. "'Secret Agent' [Review]," *Variety*, June 17, 1936.
17. "'Secret Agent' [Review]," *New York Times*, June 13, 1936, 13.
18. "Gaumont 'Secret Agent' Will Repeat Success of '39 Steps,'" *Hollywood Reporter*, May 18, 1936, 6.
19. Martin Riker, "Rescued from Memory," *New York Times*, November 5, 2017, Book Review section: 22.
20. "'Secret Agent' [Review]," *New York Times*.
21. "Gaumont 'Secret Agent' Will Repeat Success of '39 Steps,'" *Hollywood Reporter*.
22. Otis Ferguson, "'Secret Agent' [Review]," *New Republic*, June 24, 1936.
23. Howard Barnes, "On the Screen: 'Secret Agent,'" *New York Tribune*, June 13, 1936, 10.
24. William Boehnel, "'Secret Agent' at the Roxy New Thriller by Hitchcock," *New York Daily News*, June 13, 1936, 26; "Gaumont 'Secret Agent' Will Repeat Success of '39 Steps,'" *Hollywood Reporter*.
25. Jonathon Lethem, "A Labyrinth and a Mirror," *New York Times*, October 29, 2017, Book Review section: 10.
26. Eric Rohmer and Claude Chabrol, trans., Stanley Hochman, *Hitchcock* (New York: Frederick Ungar Publishing, 1979), 46.

Chapter 5

1. Otis Ferguson, "'The Lady Vanishes' [Review]," *New Republic*, October 19, 1938.
2. Frank Nugent, "'The Lady Vanishes' [Review]," *New York Times*, December 26, 1938, 29.
3. Archer Winston, "'The Lady Vanishes' Seen at the Globe Theatre," *New York Post*, December 24, 1938, 9.
4. Howard Barnes, "On the Screen: 'The Lady Vanishes,'" *New York Herald Tribune*, December 26, 1938, 17.
5. *Mystery Train: Hitchcock and the Lady Vanishes*, DVD Bonus Feature by Leonard Leff with 1938's *The Lady Vanishes* (USA: Criterion Collections, 2007).
6. Thomas F-R, "My Favorite Hitchcock," *London Guardian*, July 24, 2012.

7. "'Night Train' [Review]," *Variety*, October 30, 1940.
8. "'Night Train' [Review]," *New York Times*, December 30, 1940, 21.
9. See the author's *Carole Lombard: The Hoosier Tornado* (Indianapolis: Indiana Historical Society Press, 2003); Also see the Bibliography for books on screwball comedy by the author.
10. Ethel Lina White, *The Wheel Spins* (New York: Popular Library, 1936), 41.
11. See the author's *Laurel & Hardy: A Bio-Bibliography* (Westport, Connecticut: Greenwood Press, 1990).
12. *Ibid.*
13. See the author's *Leo McCarey: From Marx to McCarthy* (Lanham, Maryland: Scarecrow Press, Inc., 2005); also see his biography of the co-star of *The Awful Truth, Irene Dunne: First Lady of Hollywood* (Lanham, Maryland: Scarecrow Press, Inc., 2003).
14. Stanley Cavell, *Pursuits of Happiness: The Hollywood Comedy of Remarriage* (Cambridge, Mass.: Harvard University Press, 1981).
15. For example, John Russell Taylor's text is one such example: *Hitch: The Life and Times of Alfred Hitchcock* (1978 rpt. New York: Berkley Publishing, 1980), 138.
16. George O'Brien, "All Aboard" (monograph) included as a DVD Bonus Feature with 1938's *The Lady Vanishes* (USA: Criterion Collection, 2007), 5.
17. White, *The Wheel Spins*, 6.
18. *Ibid.*, 26.
19. *Ibid.*, 8, 32, 35.
20. Please see the Bibliography. The author has written one or more books on each of these subgenres, not to mention many biographies and critical studies of personality comedians.
21. "Chamberlain on Pan For Censoring Clips," *Hollywood Reporter*, December 6, 1938, 6.
22. White, *The Wheel Spins*, front cover.
23. Kurt Vonnegut, *Slapstick* (New York: Delacore Press/Semour Lawrence, 1976), 1.
24. George Perry, *The Films of Alfred Hitchcock* (1965 rpt; New York: E.P. Dutton and Co., 1970), 64.
25. Otto D. Tolischus, "Nazis Now Drive to Complete Their Program," *New York Times*, November 20, 1938, Section 4:3.
26. White, *The Wheel Spins*, 125, 53.
27. *Ibid.*, 124.
28. *Ibid.*, 125.
29. *Ibid.*, 9, 53, 23.
30. Michael Chabon, *Wonder Boys* (New York: Picador, 1995).
31. White, *The Wheel Spins*, 49.
32. Frank S. Nugent, "Chips Off the Yule Log: The Season Ends on a Merry Note," *New York Times*, December 25, 1938, Section 9:7.

33. *Ibid.*
34. "Cinema Sights In London," *New York Times*, November 20, 1938, Section 9:4.
35. Eileen Creelman, "The New Talkies: 'The Lady Vanishes,'" *New York Sun*, December 27, 1938, 12.
36. William Boehnel, "Excellent Spy Stuff at the Globe," *New York World-Telegram*, December 24, 1938, 8.
37. Rudy Behlmer, ed., *Memo from David O. Selznick* (New York: Viking Press, 1972), 260.
38. Nugent, "'The Lady Vanishes' [Review]," *New York Times*.
39. Thomas F-R, "My Favorite Hitchcock."
40. Julia Johnson, *The Lady Vanishes*, in *Magill's Survey of Cinema: English Language Films*, First Series, Volume 2, Frank N. Magill, ed. (Englewood Cliffs, NJ: Salem Press, 1980), 933.

Chapter 6

1. Frank Nugent, "'The Lady Vanishes' [Review]," *New York Times*, December 26, 1938, 29.
2. Archer Winsten, "'The Lady Vanishes' Seen At the Globe Theatre," *New York Post*, December 24, 1938, 9.
3. William Boehnel, "'Mr. and Mrs. Smith' Gleeful Comedy," *New York World-Telegram*, February 21, 1941, 7.
4. François Truffaut, *Hitchcock/Truffaut* (1967; rpt. New York: Simon & Schuster, 1983—with bonus material), 139.
5. Donaldo Spoto, *The Dark Side of Genius: The Life of Alfred Hitchcock* (Boston: Little, Brown and Company, 1983), 237.
6. Larry Swindell, *Screwball: The Life of Carole Lombard* (New York: William Morrow and Company, 1975), 279.
7. See the author's award-winning *Carole Lombard: The Hoosier Tornado* (Indianapolis: Indiana Historical Society Press, 2003).
8. See the author's award-winning *Chaplin's War Trilogy: An Evolving Lens in Three Dark Comedies, 1918-1947* (Jefferson, NC: McFarland, 2014).
9. "Films: 'The Lady Vanishes,'" *London Mercury*, November 1938, 64.
10. Much of Carole Lombard material in the chapter is drawn from the research done for the author's biography of the actress, see footnote 7. Also, see the Bibliography for the author's books on screwball comedy.
11. Todd McCarthy, *Howard Hawks: The Grey Fox of Hollywood* (New York: Grove Press, 1997), 201.
12. Gerald Mast, *Howard Hawks, Storyteller* (New York: Oxford University Press, 1982), 194.
13. McCarthy, *Howard Hawks: The Grey Fox of Hollywood*, 202.
14. Noel F. Busch, "A Loud Cheer for the Screwball Girl" (cover article), *LIFE* (not to be confused with the earlier satirical magazine with the same name), October 17, 1938, 48-50, 62-64.
15. *Ibid.*, 48.
16. Charlotte Chandler, *It's Only a Movie: Alfred Hitchcock* (Montclair, NJ: Applause: Theatre & Cinema Books, 2005), 133.
17. Warren G. Harris, *Gable and Lombard* (New York: Simon and Schuster, 1974), 112.
18. Regina Crewe, "'The Princess Comes Across' Is Delightful Film Offering with Its Humor and Thrills," *New York American*, June 4, 1936.
19. Kate Cameron, "'True Confession' a Mad, Merry Farce," *New York Daily News*, December 16, 1937.
20. "'True Confession' [Review]," *Time*, December 27, 1937.
21. See the author's *Irene Dunne: First Lady of Hollywood* (Lanham, Maryland: Scarecrow Press, Inc., 2003).
22. John McCarty and Brian Kelleher, *Alfred Hitchcock Presents* (New York: St. Martin's Press, 1985), 294.
23. Paul Murray Kendall, *The Art of Biography* (1965; rpt. New York: W.W. Norton & Company, 1985), 130.
24. Tobi Haslett, "Acts of Attention," *The New Yorker*, December 11, 2017, 75.
25. "'Mr. and Mrs. Smith' [Review]," *New York Times*, February 21, 1941, 16.
26. Dee Wedemeyer, "William H. Gass, Author Known for His Inventive Use of Words, Dies at 93," *New York Times*, December 8, 2017, A-24.
27. "Director Brilliant; von Hernreid Great," *Hollywood Reporter*, January 16, 1941, 3.
28. Lewis Jacobs, "Film Directors at Work: Alfred Hitchcock," *Theatre Arts*, January 1941, 41-42.
29. Wes D. Gehring, "Interview with Pandro S. Berman" (unpublished), Hillcrest Country Club, Los Angeles, June 1975. Article on the interview, with key quotes: "Dancing to Screwball," *USA TODAY Magazine*, May 2018, 77.
30. See the author's *Carole Lombard: The Hoosier Tornado*.
31. See the author's *Leo McCarey: From Marx to McCarthy* (Lanham, Maryland: Scarecrow Press, 2005).
32. Kate Cameron, "New Hitchcock Film at the Music Hall," *New York Daily News*, February 21, 1941, 42.
33. Howard Barnes, "On the Screen: 'Mr. and Mrs. Smith,'" *New York Herald Tribune*, February 21, 1941, 10.
34. Irene Thirer, "'Mr. and Mrs. Smith' Gay Comedy at Music Hall," *New York Post*, February 21, 1941, 13.

35. "'Mr. and Mrs. Smith' [Review]," *New York Sun*, February 21, 1941, 7.
36. "At the Music Hall: 'Mr. and Mrs. Smith,'" *New York Times*, February 21, 1941, 16.
37. "Noted Comic Is Slightly Irked by Film Awards," *Washington Post*, March 12, 1937; also see the author's books on Fields, especially *Groucho & W.C. Fields: Huckster Comedians* (Jackson: University Press of Mississippi, 1994).
38. Frederick Othman, "Carole Lombard Gets Revenge By Directing Alfred Hitchcock," incomplete citation, Carole Lombard File, Margaret Herrick Library, Academy of Motion Picture Arts and Sciences, Beverly Hills, CA.
39. *Ibid.*

Chapter 7

1. *Beyond Doubt: The Making of Hitchcock's Favorite Film*, DVD Bonus Feature on 1943's the *Shadow of a Doubt* (Universal City, CA: Universal/Skirball Productions, 2000).
2. *Ibid.*
3. Jason Zinoman, "Highlights in a Year of Parodoxes," *New York Times*, December 26, 2017, C-1.
4. Thornton Wilder, *Our Town* (1938 rpt. New York: Harper & Row, 1985), 100, 101.
5. *Ibid.*, 101.
6. Mel Gussow, "A Theatrical Vision Endures," *New York Times*, December 20, 1987, Section 2:36.
7. David Thomson, *The New Biographical Dictionary of Film* (New York: Alfred A Knopf, 2003), 133.
8. David Freeman, *The Last Days of Alfred Hitchcock* (Woodstock, New York: Overlook Press, 1999), 34.
9. Mark Twain, *The Man That Corrupted Hadleyburg and Other Essays and Stories, Vol. 23* (New York: Harper & Brothers, 1903), 14.
10. Lewis Jacobs, "Film Directors at Work," *Theatre Arts*, March 1941, 228.
11. See the author's books on Red Skelton, especially *Red Skelton: The Mask Behind the Mask* (Indianapolis: Indiana Historical Society, 2008).
12. Anthony Lane, "Bespoke," *The New Yorker*, January 8, 2018, 68.
13. Joseph Heller, *Catch-22* (1961; rpt. New York: Dell, 1968), 47.
14. See the author's chapter on *Chinatown* in his *Genre-Busting Dark Comedies of the 1970s* (Jefferson, NC: McFarland, 2016).
15. "Chaplin Spouting 'Landru Spinach [Beard],'" *Hollywood Reporter*, December 8, 1941, 1.
16. See the author's *Buster Keaton in His Own Time: What the Responses of 1920s Critics Reveal* (Jefferson, NC: McFarland, 2018).

17. William, Rothman, *Hitchcock: The Murderous Gaze* (1982; rpt. Albany: State University of New York Press, 2012), 189.
18. Geoffrey Nowell-Smith, Visiting Professor of Film, Graduate Seminar on American Film Melodrama Notes, Iowa City: University of Iowa, Summer Session, 1976.
19. Bosley Crowther, "'Shadow of a Doubt'... Is at the Astor," *New York Times*, January 13, 1943, 18.
20. Pat Hitchcock O'Connell and Laurent Bouzereau, *Alma Hitchcock: The Woman Behind the Man* (New York: Berkley Books, 2003), n.p.
21. "Romans: 15–17," *The Living Bible: Paraphrased* (Wheaton, Illinois: Tynsdale House Publishers, 1971.), 903.
22. "$5,000 Production; Hitchcock Makes Thriller Under WPB [War Production Board] Order On New Sets," *LIFE*, January 25, 1943, 70–73, 75.
23. *Ibid.*, 70.
24. Archer Winsten, "'Shadow of a Doubt' Opens at the Rivoli Theatre," *New York Post*, January 13, 1942, 46.
25. Thomson, quoting John Boorman on the dark side of Lee Marvin, 568.
26. Kate Cameron, "'Shadow of a Doubt' Gripping Film Drama," *New York Daily News*, January 13, 1943, 48.

Chapter 8

1. Rose Pelswick, "New Horror Film Full of Suspense," *New York Journal-American*, August 27, 1948, 11.
2. Alton Cook, "Hitchcock' 'Rope' Hangs Up Bravos," *New York World-Telegram*, August 26, 1948, 18.
3. See the author's "Leopold & Loeb: The Movies' Favorite 'Crime of the Century,'" *USA TODAY MAGAZINE*, September 2012.
4. François Truffaut, *Hitchcock/Truffaut* (1967; rpt. New York: Simon & Schuster, 1983, with bonus material), 184.
5. Jorge Luis Borges, "Two Films," from *Home Magazine* (1936–1939), in *Selected Nonfictions*, ed. Eliot Weinberger (New York: Viking, 1999), 149.
6. For the Monroe stories see James Thurber's *The Owl in the Attic and Other Perplexities* (1931; rpt. New York: Harper & Row, 1959); James Thurber, "The Secret Life of Walter Mitty," in *My World—And Welcome to It* (New York: Harcourt, Brace and Company, 1942).
7. Thurber, "The Secret Life of Walter Mitty," in *My World—And Welcome to It.*
8. Kim Newman, "'Scream' [Review]," *Sight and Sound*, May 1997, 53. Also see the author's

Parody as Film Genre (Westport, Connecticut: Greenwood Press, 1999).
  9. James Thurber, "The Unicorn in the Garden," in *The Thurber Carnival* (New York: Harper & Brothers, 1945).
  10. Bosley Crowther, "'Rope' [Review]," *New York Times*, August 27, 1948, 12; "Rope" [Review], *Variety*, September 1, 1948.
  11. See the author's *Laurel & Hardy: A Bio-Bibliography* (Westport, Connecticut: Greenwood Press, 1990).
  12. Robert Benchley, "Matinées—Wednesdays and Saturday," in *No Poems, or Around the World Backwards and Sideways* (New York: Harper & Brothers, 1932), 329; Also see the author's "*Mr. B*" or Comforting Thoughts About the Bison: A Critical Biography of Robert Benchley* (Westport, Connecticut: Greenwood Press, 1992).
  13. *Ibid.*
  14. Henry James, "The Romance of Certain Old Clothes," in *The Best Ghost Stories Ever*, ed. Christopher Krovatin (New York: Scholastic Inc., 2003), 149.
  15. *Ibid.*, 150–151.
  16. Susan Elston Wallace, [and related material] *Ginèvra or the Old Chest* (1984; rpt. USA: Brebook Publishing, no date).
  17. Alton Cook, "Hitchcock's 'Rope' Hangs Up Bravos," *New York World-Telegram*, August 26, 1948, 18.
  18. Bosley Crowther, "'Rope' [Review]," *New York Times*, August 28, 1948, p. 8.
  19. "'Rope' [Review]," *Variety*, September 1, 1948.
  20. Eileen Creelman, "The New Movie: 'Rope,'" *New York Sun*, August 27, 1948, 17.
  21. *Ibid.*
  22. Howard Barnes, "On the Screen: New York Herald Tribune*, August 27, 1948, 10.
  23. See some of the author's dark comedy texts, such as *American Dark Comedy: Beyond Satire* (Westport, Connecticut: Greenwood Press, 1996), or *Genre-Busting Dark Comedies of the 1970s: Twelve American Films* (Jefferson, NC: McFarland, 2016).
  24. Anthony Lane, "Shallow Grave," in *Nobody's Perfect: Writings from The New Yorker* (New York: Alfred A Knopf, 2002), 107.

Chapter 9

  1. Patricia Highsmith, *Strangers on a Train* (1950; rpt. New York: Harper & Brothers, 1993), 29–30.
  2. Donaldo Spoto, *The Art of Hitchcock: Fifty Years of His Motion Pictures* (1976; rpt. New York: Doubleday, 1992), 188–189.
  3. Frank Eng, "'Rope' [Review]," *Los Angeles Daily News*, September 25, 1948, 16.
  4. Vincent Canby, "Hitchcock's 'Rope': A Stunt to Behold," *New York Times*, June 3, 1984, Film section: 1.
  5. "Hitchcock Without Camera," *Los Angeles Times*, August 19, 2001, 42–43.
  6. Andre Bazin, "The Myth of Monsieur Verdoux," in *What Is Cinema? Volume II* (1971; rpt. Los Angeles: University of California Press, 1972), 105.
  7. See the author's *Chaplin War Trilogy: An Evolving Lens in Three Dark Comedies, 1918–1947* (Jefferson, NC: McFarland, 2014).
  8. Highsmith, *Strangers on a Train*, 11.
  9. David Thomson, "Robert Walker," in *The New Biographical Dictionary of Film* (New York: Alfred A. Knopf, 2003), 910.
  10. Charlotte Chandler, *It's Only a Movie: Alfred Hitchcock: A Personal Biography* (2005; rpt. Montclair, NJ: Applause Theatre & Cinema Books, 2006), 193.
  11. Archer Winsten, "Hitchcock Thriller at Warner Theatre," *New York Post*, July 8, 1951, 32.
  12. "'Strangers on a Train' [Review]," *Variety*, June 20, 1951.
  13. Marilyn Fabe, quoted Robin Wood in her "Strangers on a Train" profile in the *Pacific Film Archive*, January 28, 2011.
  14. Kate Cameron, "'Strangers on a Train' a Hitchcock Thriller," *New York Daily News*, July 4, 1951, 34.
  15. Thomson, "Robert Walker," 910.
  16. See the author's *American Dark Comedy: Beyond Satire* (Westport, Connecticut: Greenwood Press, 1996).
  17. Louis Buñuel, *My Last Sigh*, trans. Abigail Israel (1982; rpt. New York: Random House, 1984), 14.
  18. Anthony Lane, "Second Time as Farce," *The New Yorker*, March 19, 2018, 93.
  19. Cobbett Steinberg, *Reel Facts: The Movie Book of Records* (New York: Random House, 1978), 405.
  20. James Ursini, *Preston Sturges: An American Dreamer* (New York: Curtis Books, 1973), 133–134.

Chapter 10

  1. François Truffaut, *Hitchcock/Truffaut* (1967; rpt. New York: Simon & Schuster, 1983, with bonus material), 200.
  2. Charlotte Chandler, *It's Only a Movie: Alfred Hitchcock: A Personal Biography* (2005; rpt. Montclair, NJ: Applause Theatre & Cinema Books, 2006) 212–213.
  3. Archer Winsten, "'Rear Window' at Rivoli," *New York Post*, August 5, 1954, 12.
  4. Kate Cameron, "Laughs and Shudders Mark 'Rear Window,'" *New York Daily News*, August 5, 1954, 60.

5. Otis L. Guernsey, "Screen: 'Rear Window,'" *New York Herald-Tribune*, August 5, 1954, 12.
6. "'Rear Window' [Review]," *Variety*, July 14, 1954.
7. John Beauf, "'Rear Window' on the Screen in Color," *Christian Science Monitor*, August 27, 1954, 5.
8. For example, see the reviews in the *New York Herald Tribune*, "Screen: 'Rear Window,'" or *Variety*, "'Rear Window' [Review]."
9. Alton Cook, "Hitchcock's 'Rear Window' Opens on Terror," *New York Telegram*, August 5, 1954, 12.
10. *Rear Window Ethics: An Original Documentary*, a Bonus Feature on Digital Hd: Ultraviolet's 1954 *Rear Window*, 1982.
11. See the author's *Red Skelton: The Mask Behind the Mask* (Indianapolis: Indiana Historical Society Press, 2008).
12. *Variety*, "'Rear Window' [Review]."
13. Kin Hubbard, *Fifty-Two Weeks of Abe Martin* (Indianapolis: privately published, 1924), 25, 86.
14. David Thomson, *The New Biographical Dictionary of Film* (New York: Alfred A. Knopf, 2003), 684.
15. Kin Hubbard, *Abe Martin's Brown County Almanack* (Indianapolis: privately published, 1909), [111].
16. See any of the author's many books exploring the subject. For example: *Leo McCarey and the Comic Antihero in American Film* (New York: Arno Press, A New York Times Company, 1980), or *Mr. "B" or Comforting Thoughts About the Bison: A Critical Biography of Robert Benchley* (Westport, Connecticut: Greenwood Press, 1992).
17. See the author's "Kin Hubbard's Abe Martin: A Figure of Transition in American Humor," *Indiana Magazine of History*, March 1982, 26–37.
18. See the author's *W.C. Fields: A Bio-Bibliography* (Westport, Connecticut: Greenwood Press, 1984).
19. Jack Meffitt, "'Rear Window' Sure B.O.," *Hollywood Reporter*, July 13, 1954, 3.
20. Edgar Allan Poe, "The Man of the Crowd," in *The Complete Tales and Poems of Edgar Allan Poe* (New York: Barnes & Noble, 2006), 357–358.
21. *Ibid.*, 363.
22. Edgar Allan Poe, "Diddling," in *The Complete Tales and Poems of Edgar Allan Poe* (New York: Random House, 1938, an earlier variation on the 2006 Barnes & Noble Poe collection), 367, 369; also see the author's *Groucho & W.C. Fields: Huckster Comedians* (Jackson: University Press of Mississippi, 1994).
23. Mae Tinee, "'Rear Window' Like Peeking: Fascinating!," *Chicago Tribune*, September 6, 1954, Part 3:16.
24. *Ibid.*
25. *Ibid.*
26. Edwin Schallert, "Hitchcock Razzle-Dazzles at Brilliant Premiere," *Los Angeles Times*, August 12, 1954, Part 3:9.
27. Nathanael West, *Miss Lonelyhearts & The Day of the Locust* (1933 rpt. New York: New Directions Books, 1950), 4–5.
28. Jay Martin, *Nathanael West: The Art of His Life* (New York: Carroll & Graf Publications, 1970), 366.

Chapter 11

1. Donald Spoto, *The Art of Alfred Hitchcock* (1976; rpt. New York: Doubleday, 1992), 233.
2. Iain Topliss, *The Comic Worlds of Peter Arno, William Steig, Charles Addams and Saul Steinberg* (Baltimore: Johns Hopkins University Press, 2005), 156.
3. Charlotte Chandler, *It's Only a Movie: Alfred Hitchcock: A Personal Biography* (Montclair, NJ.: Applause Theatre & Cinema Books, 2005), 225.
4. Kay Proctor, "It's Trouble in 'Trouble with Harry,'" *Los Angeles Examiner*, February 9, 1956, Section 2:8.
5. Andrew Sarris, "'The Trouble with Harry' [Revisionist Review]," April 10, 1984, 41, in *The Trouble with Harry* clipping file," Margaret Herrick Library, Motion Picture Academy of Arts and Sciences, Beverly Hills, CA.
6. Archer Winston, "Hitchcock's 'Trouble with Harry,'" *New York Post*, October 11, 1955, 46; Rose Pelswick, "Hitchcock Tries Hard at Whimsey," *New York Journal-American*, October 18, 1955, 13.
7. Mike Wilmington, "'The Trouble with Harry' [Revisionist Review]," *Los Angeles Weekly*, March 16, 1984.
8. Chandler, *It's Only a Movie: Alfred Hitchcock: A Personal Biography*, 226.
9. Jack Trevor Story, *The Trouble with Harry* (1949; rpt. London: Allison & Busby Limited, 1949), 30.
10. Wanda Hale, "A Brand New Hitchcock on Paris' [theatre] Screen," *New York Daily News*, December 18, 1955, 57.
11. Johnson J. Hooper, *Simon Suggs' Adventures* (1867; rpt. Americus, Georgia: American Book Co., 1928), 12.
12. *Ibid.*, 26.
13. Hilton Als, "The Theatre: Frozen: Hiding from Life in 'The Iceman Cometh,'" *The New Yorker*, May 7, 2018, 76.
14. Pelswick, "Hitchcock Tries Hand at Whimsey"; and Dick Williams, "Hitchcock Enters Realm of Whimsey," *Los Angeles Mirror-News*, February 9, 1956.

15. Topliss, *The Comic Worlds of Peter Arno, William Steig, Charles Addams and Saul Steinberg*, 135.
16. Winsten, Archer, "Hitchcock's 'Trouble with Harry.'"
17. Leigh-Ann Jackson, "Anxiety Adds Spice to 'Atlanta,'" *New York Times*, May 10, 2018, C-6.
18. "Hitchcock Film Whimsical Treat," *Hollywood Reporter*, October 7, 1955.
19. See the Bibliography for the author's works on screwball comedy.
20. Story, *The Trouble with Harry*, 164.
21. "Buster Keaton," *Los Angeles Times*, April 22, 1923, Part 3:27.
22. Alex Ross, "The Hitler Vortex," *The New Yorker*, April 30, 2018, 66.
23. Spoto, *The Art of Alfred Hitchcock*, 238–239.
24. *Ibid.*, 234.
25. Story, *The Trouble with Harry*, 84–85.
26. Bosley Crowther, "'The Trouble with Harry' [Review]," *New York Times*, October 18, 1955, 46.
27. Peter Ackroyd, *Alfred Hitchcock: A Brief Life* (New York: Anchor Books, 2015), 163.
28. *Variety*, "'The Trouble with Harry' [Review]," October 12, 1955.
29. Proctor, "It's Trouble in 'Trouble with Harry.'"
30. Ackroyd, *Alfred Hitchcock: A Brief Life*, 163.
31. *Ibid.*, 164.
32. Suzanne Finstad, *Warren Beatty: A Private Man* (New York: Harmony Books, 2005), 111.
33. Zita Dresner, "Women's Humor," in *Humor in America*, ed. Lawrence E. Mintz (Westport, Connecticut: Greenwood Press, 1988), 144.
34. Walter Blair, *Native American Humor* (1937; rpt. Scranton Publishing Company, 1960), 49–50.
35. Crowther, "'The Trouble with Harry' [Review]."
36. Williams, "Hitchcock Enters Realm of Whimsey"; and Edwin Schallert, *Los Angeles Times*, "Film Lacks Hitchcock Entertainment." (undated) in *The Trouble with Harry* clipping file," Margaret Herrick Library.

Chapter 12

1. François Truffaut, *Hitchcock/Truffaut* (1967; rpt. New York: Simon & Schuster, 1983, with Bonus Material), 102.
2. Geoffrey Wansell, *Haunted Idol: The Story of the Real Cary Grant* (New York: William Morrow and Company, 1984), 240.
3. See the author's *Parody as Film Genre: "Never Give a Saga an Even Break"* (Westport, Connecticut: Greenwood Press, 1999).
4. For example, see A.H. Weiler, "'North by Northwest' [Review]," *New York Times*, August 7, 1959, 28.
5. "Fear and Laughter in the Wild," *London Times*, April 7, 1996.
6. William Shakespeare, *Hamlet*, Act 2 Scene 2: 1142, *The Works of William Shakespeare* (1937 rpt; Roslyn, New York: Black's Reader Service Company, 1965.
7. For example, see Gene Gleason's "The New Movies," *New York Herald Tribune*, April 7, 1959, 9.
8. For example, see Archer Winsten's "Reviewing Stand," *New York Post*, August 7, 1959, 32.
9. Gleason, "The New Movies."
10. Nancy Nelson, *Evenings with Cary Grant* (New York: William Morrow and Company, 1991), 217.
11. Richard Schickel, *Cary Grant: A Celebration* (New York: Applause Book, 1999), 110.
12. See the bibliography for some of the author's books on screwball and dark comedy.
13. Joe Adamson, *Groucho, Harpo Chico, and Sometimes Zeppo* (New York: Simon & Schuster, 1973), 209.
14. Nelson, *Evenings with Cary Grant*, 98.
15. Incomplete McCarey interview, no publication cited, March 23, 1939, in the Leo McCarey File, Performing Arts Library, New York Public Library at Lincoln Center.
16. Wes D. Gehring, Cover of *Leo McCarey: From Marx to McCarthy* (See the Bibliography).
17. Jim O'Connor, "A Thriller-Diller In Hitchcock Style," *New York Journal-American*, August, 7, 1959, n.p.
18. For example, see Gleason, "The New Movies," and O'Connor, "A Thriller-Diller In Hitchcock style."
19. See the author's *Laurel & Hardy: A Bio-Bibliography* (Westport, Connecticut: Greenwood Press, 1990).
20. Peter Fitzgerald 2000 documentary, *Destination Hitchcock: The Making of North by Northwest*, a Bonus Feature on Turner Entertainment Blue Ray DVD of 1959's *North by Northwest*, 2015.
21. *Ibid.*
22. Jeff Giles, "Poison Pen," *New York Times* April 29, 2018, Book Review section: 19.
23. Fitzgerald, *Destination Hitchcock: The Making of North by Northwest*.
24. Devin Faraci, "Martin Landau on Playing Gay for Hitchcock," *Badass Digest*, October 1, 2012.
25. Fitzgerald, *Destination Hitchcock: The Making of North by Northwest*.
26. Weiler, "'North by Northwest' [Review]."
27. "'North by Northwest' [Review]," *Variety*, July 1, 1959.

Epilogue

1. Patrick McGilligan. ed., *Film Crazy: Interviews with Hollywood Legends* (New York: St. Martin's Press, 2000), 258.
2. Danny Boyle VO commentary on 1994's *Shallow Grave*. Criterion's Channel Four TV Corporation/Glasgow Film Fund DVD, 2012.
3. Tom Stoppard, *Rosencrantz & Guildenstern Are Dead* (New York: Grove Weidenfeld, 1967), 71–72.
4. *Ibid.*, 71.
5. David Itzkoff, *Robin* (New York: Henry Holt and Company, 2018), 75–76.
6. Wes D. Gehring conversation with Richard Armour at the first International Humor Conference (Los Angeles, 1979). See the author's discussion of the meeting in *Film Classics Reclassified: A Shocking Spoof of Cinema* (Davenport Iowa: Robin Vincent Publishing, 2001), xv.

Bibliography

Books

Ackroyd, Peter. *Alfred Hitchcock: A Brief Life*. 2016; rpt. New York: Anchor Books, 2017, 60.
Adamson, Joe. *Groucho, Harpo, Chico, and Sometimes Zeppo*. New York: Simon & Schuster, 1973, 209.
Allen, Richard, and S. Ishii-Gonzalés. *Alfred Hitchcock: Centenary Essays*. London: British Film Institute, 1999.
Atlas, James. *The Shadow in the Garden: A Biographer's Tale*. New York: Pantheon Books, 2017, 219.
Behlmer, Rudy. *Memo from David O. Selznick*. New York: Viking Press, 1972.
Bennett, Charles. *Blackmail: A Play in Three Acts*. London: Rich & Cowan LTD, 1928.
Blair, Walter. *Native American Humor*. 1937; rpt. Scranton: Scranton Publishing Company, 1960.
Buñuel, Luis. *My Last Sigh*, trans. Abigail Israil. 1982; rpt. New York: Random House, 1984, 14.
Cavell, Stanley. *Pursuits of Happiness: The Hollywood Comedy of Remarriage*. Cambridge, Mass.: Harvard University Press, 1991.
Chabon, Michael. *Wonder Boys*. New York: Picador, 1995, 251.
Chandler, Charlotte. *It's Only a Movie: Alfred Hitchcock: A Personal Biography*. Montclair, New Jersey: Applause Theatre & Cinema Books, 2006, 91.
Cohen, Paula Marantz. *Alfred Hitchcock: The Legacy of Victorianism*. Lexington: The University Press of Kentucky, 1995.
Cuppy, Will. *How to Tell Your Friends from the Apes*. 1931; rpt. Boston: Nonpareil Books, 2005, 31.
Finstad, Suzanne. *Warren Beatty: A Private Man*. New York: Harmony Books, 2005, 111.
Freeman, David. *The Last Days of Alfred Hitchcock*. Woodstock: Overlook Press, 1999, 34.
Gehring, Wes D. *American Dark Comedy: Beyond Satire*. Westport, Connecticut: Greenwood Press, 1996.
Gehring, Wes D. *Buster Keaton in His Own Time: What the Responses of 1920s Critics Reveal*. Jefferson, North Carolina: McFarland Press, 2018.
Gehring, Wes D. *Carole Lombard: The Hoosier Tornado*. Indianapolis: Indiana Historical Society Press, 2003.
Gehring, Wes D. *Chaplin's War Trilogy: An Evolving Lens in Three Dark Comedies, 1918–1947*. Jefferson, North Carolina: McFarland Press, 2014.
Gehring, Wes D. *Charlie Chaplin: A Bio-Bibliography*. Westport, Connecticut: Greenwood Press, 1983.
Gehring, Wes D. *Film Classics Reclassified: A Shocking Spoof of Cinema*. Davenport, Iowa: Robert Vincent Publishing, 2001.
Gehring, Wes D. *Film Clowns of the Depression: Twelve Defining Comic Performances*. Jefferson, North Carolina: McFarland, 2007.
Gehring, Wes D. *Forties Film Funnymen: The Decade's Great Comedians at Work in the Shadow of the War*. Jefferson, North Carolina: McFarland, 2010.

Gehring, Wes D. *Genre-Busting Dark Comedies of the 1970s: Twelve American Films*. Jefferson, North Carolina: McFarland, 2016.
Gehring, Wes D. *Groucho & W.C. Fields: Huckster Comedians*. Jackson: University Press of Mississippi, 1994.
Gehring, Wes D. *Irene Dunne: First Lady of Hollywood*. Lanham, Maryland: Scarecrow Press, Inc., 2003.
Gehring, Wes D. *Laurel & Hardy: A Bio-Bibliography*. Westport, Connecticut: Greenwood Press, 1990.
Gehring, Wes D. *Leo McCarey and the Comic Antihero in American Film*. New York: Arno Press, A New York Times Company, 1980.
Gehring, Wes D. *Leo McCarey: From Marx to McCarthy*. Lanham, Maryland: Scarecrow Press, Inc., 2005.
Gehring, Wes D. *Movie Comedians of the 1950s: Defining a New Era of Big Screen Comedy*. Jefferson, North Carolina: McFarland, 2016.
Gehring, Wes D. *"Mr. B" or Comforting Thoughts About the Bison: A Critical Biography of Robert Benchley*. Westport, Connecticut: Greenwood Press, 1992.
Gehring, Wes D. *Parody as Film Genre: "Never Give a Saga an Even Break."* Westport, Connecticut: Greenwood Press, 1999.
Gehring, Wes D. *Personality Comedians as Genre: Selected Players*. Westport, Connecticut: Greenwood Press, 1997.
Gehring, Wes D. *Red Skelton: The Mask Behind the Mask*. Indianapolis: Indiana State Historic Society Press, 2008.
Gehring, Wes D. *Romantic Versus Screwball Comedy: Charting a Difference*. Lanham, Maryland: Scarecrow Press, 2002.
Gehring, Wes D. *Screwball Comedy: A Genre of Madcap Romance*. Westport, Connecticut: Greenwood Press, 1986.
Gehring, Wes D. *W.C. Fields: A Bio-Bibliography*. Westport, Connecticut: Greenwood Press, 1984.
Gehring, Wes D. *Will Cuppy, American Satirist: A Biography*. Jefferson, North Carolina: McFarland, 2013.
Hamilton, Patrick. *Rope*. 1929; rpt. United Kingdom: Samuel French, 1988, 33.
Hammett, Dashiell. *The Thin Man*. 1933; rpt. New York: Vintage Books, 1992, 71–75.
Harris, Robert A., and Michael S. Lasky. *The Films of Alfred Hitchcock*. 1976; rpt. Secaucus, New Jersey: Citadel Press, 1979, 5.
Harris, Warren G. *Gable and Lombard*. New York: Simon & Schuster, 1974, 112.
Heller, Joseph. *Catch-22*. 1961; rpt. New York: Dell, 1968, 47.
Highsmith, Patricia. *Strangers on a Train*. 1950; rpt. New York: Harper & Brothers, 1998, 29–30.
Hooper, Johnson J. *Simon Suggs' Adventures*. 1867; rpt. Americus, Georgia: American Book Co., 1928, 12.
Hubbard, Kin. *Abe Martin's Brown County Almanack*. Indianapolis: Privately published, 1909, [111].
Hubbard, Kin. *Fifty-Two Weeks of Abe Martin*. Indianapolis: Privately published, 1924, 25, 86.
Itzkoff, David. *Robin* New York: Henry Holt and Company, 2018, 75–76.
Kendall, Paul Murray. *The Art of Biography*. 1965; rpt. New York: W.W. Norton & Company, 1985, 130.
Martin, Jay. *Nathanael West: The Art of His Life*. New York: Carroll & Graf Publications, 1970. 366.
Mast, Gerald. *Howard Hawks, Storyteller*. New York: Oxford University Press, 1982.
McCarthy, Todd. *Howard Hawks: The Grey Fox of Hollywood*. New York: Grove Press, 1997, 201.
McCarty, John, and Brian Kelleher. *Alfred Hitchcock Presents*. New York: St. Martin's Press, 1985, 294.
McGilligan, Patrick. *Film Crazy: Interview with Hollywood Legends*. New York: St. Martin's Press, 2000.
McNeile, H.C. *Bulldog Drummond*. 1920; rpt. Lexington, Kentucky: First Rate Publishers, 2017.
Nelson, Nancy. *Evenings with Cary Grant*. New York: William Morrow and Company, 1991.

O'Connell, Pat, and Laurent Bouzereau. *Alma Hitchcock: The Woman Behind the Man*. New York: Berkley Books, 2003. n.p.
Perry, Dennis R. *Hitchcock and Poe*. Lanham, Maryland: Scarecrow Press, 2003.
Perry, George. *The Films of Alfred Hitchcock*. 1965; rpt. London: Blue Star House, 1970.
Phillips, Gene D. *Alfred Hitchcock*. Boston: Twayne Publishers, 1984.
Rohmer, Eric, and Claude Chabrol. *Hitchcock: The First Forty-Four Films*, trans. Stanley Hochman. New York: Frederick Ungar Publishing, 1979, 46.
Rothman, William. *Hitchcock: The Murderous Gaze*. 1982; rpt. New York: State University of New York, 2012.
Schickel, Richard. *Cary Grant: A Celebration*. New York: Applause Books, 1999, 110.
Shakespeare, William. *Hamlet*. Act 2, Scene 2: 1142. *The Works of William Shakespeare*. 1937; rpt. Roslyn, New York: Black's Reader Service Company, 1965.
Sperber, A.M. *Murrow: His Life and Times*. New York: Freundlich Books, 1986.
Spoto, Donald. *The Art of Hitchcock: Fifty Years of His Motion Pictures*. 1976; rpt. New York: Doubleday, 1992, 188–189.
Spoto, Donald. *The Dark Side of Genius: The Life of Alfred Hitchcock*. Boston: Little, Brown, and Co., 1983, 148.
Steinberg, Cobbett. *Reel Facts: The Movie Book of Records*. New York: Random House, 1978, 405
Sterritt, David. *The Films of Alfred Hitchcock*. New York: Cambridge University Press, 1993, 29.
Stoppard, Tom. *Rosencrantz & Guildenstern Are Dead*. New York: Grove Weidenfeld, 1967, 71–72.
Story, Jack Trevor. *The Trouble with Harry*. 1949; rpt. London: Allison & Busby Limited, 1949, 30.
Swindell, Larry. *Screwball: The Life of Carole Lombard*. New York: William Morrow and Company, 1975, 279.
Taylor, John Russell. *Hitch: The Life and Times of Alfred Hitchcock*. 1978; rpt. New York: Random House, 1980.
Thomson, Charles. *The New Biographical Dictionary of Film*. New York: Alfred A. Knopf, 2003, 532.
Thurber, James. *The Owl in the Attic and Other Perplexities*. 1931; rpt. New York: Harper & Row, 1959.
Topliss, Iain. *The Comic Worlds of Peter Arno, William Steig, Charles Addams and Saul Steinberg*. Baltimore: Johns Hopkins University Press, 2005, 156.
Truffaut, Francois. *Hitchcock/Truffaut*. 1967; rpt. New York: Simon & Schuster, 1983—with bonus material.
Twain, Mark. *The Man That Corrupted Hadleyburg and Other Essays*. Vol. 23. New York: Harper & Brothers, 1903, 14.
Ursini, James. *Preston Sturges: An American Dreamer*. New York: Curtis Books, 1973, 133–134.
Wansell, Geoffrey. *The Haunted Idol: The Story of the Real Cary Grant*. New York: William Morrow and Company, 1984, 240.
West, Nathanael. *Miss Lonelyhearts & The Day of the Locust*. 1933; rpt. New York: New Directions Books, 1950, 4–5.
White, Ethel Lina. *The Wheel Spins*. New York: Popular Library, 1936, 41.
Wilder, Thornton. *Our Town*. 1938 rpt; New York: Harper & Row, 1985, 100, 101.
Wood, Michael. *Alfred Hitchcock: The Man Who Knew Too Much*. Boston: New Harvest, 2015, 111.
Wood, Robin. *Hitchcock's Films Revisited*. New York: Columbia University Press, 2002.
Wood, Robin. *Howard Hawks*. 1968; rpt. London: British Film Institute, 1981, 58, 60–61.
Youngkin, Stephen D. *The Lost One: A Life Portrait of Peter Lorrie*. Lexington: University Press of Kentucky, 2012, 19.

Shorter Works

"Alfred Hitchcock, Under Thirty, Rated Leading English Director." *New York American*. October 6, 1929, 6-D.

Bibliography 273

Alfred Hitchcock's Mystery Magazine. North Palm Beach, Florida: H.S.D. Publications, Inc. August 1960.
Als, Hilton, The Theatre: FROZEN: Hiding from Life in 'The Iceman Cometh.'" *The New Yorker.* May 7, 2018, 76.
Alter, Alexandra and Dan Bilefsky. "Genre-Spanning Author of 'Remains of the Day' Wins Nobel." *New York Times.* October 6, 2017, 1.
"At the Music Hall: 'Mr. and Mrs. Smith.'" *New York Times.* February 21, 1941, 16.
"At the Selwyn [*Blackmail*]." *New York Evening World.* October 7, 1929, 15.
Barnes, Howard. "On the Screen: 'The Lady Vanishes.'" *New York Herold Tribune.* December 26, 1938, 17.
Barnes, Howard. "On the Screen: Mr. and Mrs. Smith.'" *New York Harold Tribune.* February 21, 1941, 10.
Barnes, Howard. "On the Screen: 'Rope.'" *New York Harold Tribune.* August 27, 1948, 10.
Barnes, Howard. "On the Screen: 'Secret Agent.'" *New York Tribune.* June 13, 1936, 10.
Bazin, Andre. "The Myth of Monsieur." In *What Is Cinema? Volume II.* 1971; rpt. Los Angeles: University of California Press, 1972, 105.
Beauf, John. "'Rear Window' on the Screen in Color." *Christian Science Monitor.* August 27, 1954, 5.
Benchley, Robert. "Johnny-on-the-Spot." In *From Bed to Worse or Comforting Thoughts About the Bison* (New York: Harper & Brothers, 1934) 255–259.
Benchley, Robert. Letter to his wife. In "The Robert Benchley Collection." Special Collections. Boston University Mugar Library. Boston, Massachusetts.
Benchley, Robert. "Matinées—Wednesdays and Saturday." In *No Poems, or Around the World Backwards and Sideways.* New York: Harper & Brothers, 1932.
Blackmail ad campaign. In *New York American.* October 7, 1929.
"'Blackmail': British Made." *Variety.* October 9, 1929.
"'Blackmail'—a British International Production." *New York World.* October 7, 1929, 15.
"'Blackmail'—Selwyn." *New York Herold Tribune.* October 7, 1929, 17.
Boehnel, William. "Excellent Spy Stuff at the Globe." *New York World-Telegram.* December 24, 1938, 8.
Boehnel, William. "'Mr. and Mrs. Smith' Gleeful Comedy." *New York World-Telegram.* February 21, 1941, 7.
Boehnel, William. "The New Movie." *New York World-Telegram.* September 14, 1935, 19.
Boehnel, William. "'Secret Agent' at the Roxy New Thriller by Hitchcock." *New York Daily News.* June 13, 1936, 26.
Borges, Jorge Luis. "Two Films," from *Home Magazine* (1936–1939). In *Selected Non-Fiction,* ed. Eliot Weinberger. New York: Viking, 1999, 149.
Buchan, John. The *Thirty-Nine Steps* (1935). In *The Complete Richard Hannay Stories.* Hertfordshire, England: Wordsworth Classics, 1987, 42.
Busch, Noel F. "A Loud Cheer for the Screwball Girl" (cover article). *LIFE* (not to be confused with the earlier satirical magazine with the same name). October 17, 1938, 48–50, 62–64.
"Buster Keaton," *Los Angeles Times.* April 22, 1923, Part 3:27.
Cameron, Kate. "Laughs and Shudders Mark 'Rear Window,'" *New York Daily News.* August 5, 1954, 60.
Cameron, Kate. "New Hitchcock Film at the Music Hall." *New York Daily News.* February 21, 1941, 42.
Cameron, Kate. "'Shadow of a Doubt' Gripping Film Drama." *New York Daily News.* January 13, 1943, 48.
Cameron. Kate. "Strangers on a Train: A Hitchcock Thriller." *New York Daily News.* July 4, 1951, 34.
Cameron, Kate. "'True Confession' a Mad, Merry Farce." *New York Daily News.* December 16, 1937.
Canby, Vincent. "Hitchcock's 'Rope': A Stunt to Behold." *New York Times.* June 3, 1984, Film section: 1.
"Chamberlain on Pan for Censoring Clips." *Hollywood Reporter.* December 6, 1938, 6.
Champlin, Charles, Cover blurb for the Alma Reville biography by Hitchcock's daughter: Pat

Hitchcock O'Connell and Laurent Bouzereau. *Alma Hitchcock: The Woman Behind the Man*. 2003; rpt. New York: Berkely Books, 2004.
"Chaplin Spouting 'Landru Spinach [Beard].'" *Hollywood Reporter*. December 8, 1941, 1.
"Cinema Sights in London." *New York Times*. November 20, 1938. Section 9:4.
Cook, Alton. "Hitchcock's 'Rear Window' Opens on Terror." *New York Telegram*. August 5, 1954, 12.
Creelman, Eileen. "First English Talkie: 'Blackmail.'" *New York Sun*. October 5, 1929, 5.
Creelman, Eileen. "The New Movie: 'Rope.'" *New York Sun*. August 27, 1948, 17.
Creelman, Eileen. "The New Talkies: 'The Lady Vanishes.'" *New York Sun*. December 1938, 12.
Creelman, Eileen. "The New Talkies: 'The 39 Steps.'" *New York Sun*. September 16, 1935, 17.
Creelman, Eileen. "The New Talkies: 'The Man Who Knew Too Much.'" *New York Sun*. March 23, 1935, 7.
Crewe, Regina. "'The Princess Comes Across' Is Delightful Film Offering with Its Humor and Thrills." *New York American*. June 4, 1936.
Crewe, Regina. "'Secret Agent' Gives Thrills as British Film Spy Story with Romance and Comedy." *New York American*. June 15, 1936, 9.
Crowther, Bosley. "'Rope' [Review]." *New York Times*. August 27, 1948, 12.
Crowther, Bosley. "'Shadow of a Doubt'... Is at the Astor." *New York Times*. January 13, 1943, 18.
Crowther, Bosley. "'The Trouble with Harry' [Review]." *New York Times*. October 18, 1955, 46.
Delehanty, Thorton. "'Secret Agent' at the Roxy." *New York Post*. June 13, 1936, 9.
"Dialogue on Film No. 5: Alfred Hitchcock." American Film Institute, 1972. Los Angeles, California.
"Director Brilliant; von Hernreid Great." *Hollywood Reporter*. January 16, 1941, 3.
"Donat Highlight; Carroll-Teare Good." *Hollywood Reporter*. June 29, 1935, 7.
Dresner, Zita. "Woman's Humor." In *Humor in America*, ed. Lawrence E. Mintz. Westport, Connecticut: Greenwood Press, 1988, 144.
Eng, Frank. "'Rope' [Review]" *Los Angeles Daily News*. September 25, 1948, 16.
"Entertainment Best 100 Pictures." BBC. Broadcast September 23, 1999.
Fabe, Marilyn. Quoted in "Strangers on a Train" profile. In *Pacific Film Archive*. January 28, 2011.
Faraci, Devin. "Martin Landau on Playing Gay for Hitchcock." *Badass Digest*. October 1, 2012.
Ferguson, Otis. "'The Lady Vanishes' [Review]." *New Republic*. October 19, 1938.
Ferguson, Otis. "'Secret Agent' [Review]." *New Republic*. June 24, 1936.
"$5,000 PRODUCTION; Hitchcock Makes Thriller Under WPB [War Production Board] Order On New Sets." *LIFE*. January 25, 1943, 70–73, 75.
French, Philip. "Peter Lorre: A Great Screen Actor Remembered." *London Guardian*. August 30, 2014.
Gates, Anita. "Harry Dean Stanton, Scene-Stealing Actor, Dies at 91." *New York Times*. September 16, 2017, B-13.
"Gaumont 'Secret Agent' Will Repeat Success." *Hollywood Reporter*. May 18, 1936, 6.
Gehring, Wes D. "Dancing to Screwball." *USA Today Magazine*. May 2018, 77.
Gehring, Wes D. "Hitch Had His 'Doubts.'" *USA Today Magazine*. March 2018, 33.
Gehring, Wes D. "Interview with Pandro S. Berman" (unpublished). Hillcrest Country Club, Los Angeles, June 1975.
Gehring, Wes D. "Kin Hubbard's Abe Martin: A Figure of Transition in American Humor." *Indiana Magazine of History*. March 1982, 26–37.
"A Genius of the Films: Alfred Hitchcock and His Work." *London Observer*. November 17, 1935.
Giles, Jeff. "Poison Pen." *New York Times*. April 29, 2018, Book Review section: 19.
Gleason, Gene. "The New Movies." *New York Herald Tribune*. April 7, 1959, 9.
Guernsey, Otis L. "Screen: 'Rear Window.'" *New York Herald Tribune*. August 5, 1954, 12.
Gussow, Mel. "A Theatrical Vision Endures." *New York Times*. December 20, 1987, Section 2: 36.
Hale, Wanda. "A Brand New Hitchcock on Paris [theatre] Screen." *New York Daily News*. December 18, 1955, 57.
Haslett, Tobi. "Acts of Attention." *The New Yorker*. December 11, 2017, 75.

"Hitchcock Film Whimsical Treat." *Hollywood Reporter.* October 7, 1955.
"The Hitchcock Formula." *New York Times.* February 13, 1938, Section 10:4.
"Hitchcock Without Camera." *Los Angeles Times.* August 19, 2001, 42–43.
Jackson, Leigh-Ann. "Anxiety Adds Spice to 'Atlanta.'" *New York Times.* May 10, 2018, C-6.
Jacobs, Lewis. "Film Directors at Work: Alfred Hitchcock." *Theatre Arts.* January 1941.
James, Henry. "The Romance of Certain Old Clothes." In *The Best Ghost Stories Ever*, ed. Christopher Krovatin. New York: Scholastic, Inc., 2003, 149.
Johnson, Julia. *The Lady Vanishes.* In *Magill's Survey of Cinema: English Language Films.* First Series, Volume 2, Frank N. Magill, ed. Englewood Cliffs, New Jersey: Salem Press, 1980, 933.
Kenigsberg, Ben. "A Watershed Moment of Cinematic Terror." *New York Times.* October 13, 2017, C-9.
Lane, Anthony. "Bespoke." *The New Yorker.* January 8, 2018, 68.
Lane, Anthony. "The Current Cinema: Desperadoes." *The New Yorker.* August 21, 2017, 82.
Lane, Anthony. "In Love with Fear." *The New Yorker.* August 16, 1988, 80.
Lane, Anthony. "Second Time as Farce." *The New Yorker.* March 19, 2018, 93.
Leach, Jim. "The Screwball Comedy." In *Film Genres and Criticism*, ed. Barry K. Grant. Metuchen, New Jersey: Scarecrow Express, 1977.
Lejeune, C.A. "Meet Alfred Hitchcock." *New York Times.* December 15, 1935, Section 2:7.
Lethem, Jonathon. "A Labyrinth and a Mirror." *New York Times.* October 29, 2017. Book Review section: 10.
"'Man Knew Too Much' [Review]." *Variety.* April 3, 1935.
"Man Who Knew Too Much: Slow-Paced Picture." *Hollywood Reporter.* March 29, 1935, 7.
Marshall, Ernest. "London Film Notes." *New York Times.* July 14, 1929. Section 9:4.
Maugham, W. Somerset. "The Hairless Mexican." In *Ashenden: or The British Agent.* Garden City, New York: Doubleday, Doran & Company, Inc., 1928, 59.
Maugham, W. Somerset. "The Traitor." In *Ashenden: or The British Agent.* Garden City, New York: Doubleday, Doran & Company, Inc., 1928, 158.
"Mayfair Presents Exciting Melodrama." *New York Daily News.* March 23, 1935, 28.
McCarey interview. Incomplete, without full citation. March 23, 1939. In Leo McCarey file. Performing Arts Library, New York Public Library at Lincoln Center.
Meffitt, Jack. "'Rear Window' Sure B.O." *Hollywood Reporter.* July 13, 1954, 3.
"Mr. and Mrs. Smith' [Review]." *New York Sun.* February 21, 1941, 7.
"Mr. and Mrs. Smith' [Review]." *New York Times.* February 21, 1941, 16.
Nehme, Farran Smith. "Wish You Were You." In *The Man Who Knew Too Much.* New York: Criterion Collection monograph. 2013. n.p. [4].
"New Gallery: 'The Thirty-Nine Steps,'" *London Times.* June 6, 1935.
Newman, Kim. "'Scream' [Review]." *Sight & Sound.* May 1997, 53.
Newton, Michael. "Master of the Macabre." *London Guardian.* September 12, 2014.
"'Night Train' [Review]." *New York Times.* December 30, 1940, 21.
"'Night Train' [Review]." *Variety.* December 30, 1940.
"'North by Northwest' [Review]." *Variety.* July 1, 1959.
"Noted Comic Is Slightly Irked by Film Awards." *Washington Post.* March 12, 1937.
Nowell-Smith, Geoffrey. Visiting Professor of Film. Graduate Seminar on American Film Melodrama Notes. Iowa City: University of Iowa, Summer Session, 1976.
Nugent, Frank. "'The Lady Vanishes' Review." *The New York Times.* December 26, 1938, 29.
Nugent, Frank S. "Chips off the Yule Log: The Season Ends on a Merry Note." *New York Times.* December 25, 1938. Section 9:7.
O'Brien, George. *All Aboard* (monograph). Included as a DVD Bonus Feature with 1938's *The Lady Vanishes.* USA: Criterion Collection, 2007, 5.
O'Connor, Jim. "A Thriller-Diller in Hitchcock Style." *New York Journal-American.* August 7, 1959, n.p.
Othman, Frederick. "Carole Lombard Gets Revenge by Directing Alfred Hitchcock." Incomplete citation. Carole Lombard file. Margaret Herrick Library. Academy of Motion Picture Arts and Sciences. Beverly Hills, California.
Pelswick, Rose. "Hitchcock Tries Hand at Whimsey." *New York Journal-American.* October 18, 1955, 13.

Pelswick, Rose. "New Horror Film Full of Suspense." *New York Journal-American.* August 27, 1948.
Pippete, Roger. "Hitchcock Likes to Smash Cups." *New York World-Telegram.* August 28, 1937, 7.
Poe, Edgar Allan. "Diddling." In *The Complete Tales and Poems of Edgar Allan Poe.* New York: Random House, 1938, 367, 369.
Poe, Edgar Allan. "The Man of the Crowd." In *The Complete Tales and Poems of Edgar Allan Poe.* New York: Barnes & Noble, 2006. 357–358.
Poe, Edgar Allan. "The Murders in the Rue Morgue." In *The Complete Tales and Poems of Edgar Allan Poe.* New York: Barnes & Noble, Inc., 2007, 375.
Poe, Edgar Allan. "The Premature Burial." In *The Complete Tales and Poems of Edgar Allan Poe.* New York: Barnes & Noble, 2006, 587–597.
Proctor, Kay. "It's Trouble in 'Trouble with Harry.'" *Los Angeles Examiner.* February 9, 1956. Section 2:8.
"'Rear Window' [Review]." *Variety.* July 14, 1954.
Riker, Martin. "Reserved from Memory." *New York Times.* November 5. 2017. Book Review section: 22.
"Romans: 15–17" In *The Living Bible: Paraphrased.* Wheaton, Illinois: Tynsdale House Publishers, 1971, 903.
"'Rope' [Review]." *Variety.* September 1, 1948.
Ross, Alex. "The Hitler Vortex." *The New Yorker.* April 30, 2018, 66.
Sarris, Andrew. "The Trouble with Harry [Revisionist Review]." April 10, 1984, 41. In *The Trouble with Harry* clipping file. Margaret Herrick Library. Motion Picture Academy of Arts and Sciences. Beverly Hills, California.
Schallert, Edwin. "Hitchcock Razzle-Dazzles at Brilliant Premiere." *Los Angeles Times.* August 11, 1954, Part 3:9.
"'Secret Agent' [Review]." *New York Times.* June 13, 1936, 13.
"'Secret Agent' [Review]." *Variety.* June 13, 1936.
Sennwald, Andre. "The Screen: Peter Lorre in His First American Photoplay." *New York Times.* August 5, 1935, Section 20:2.
Sennwald, Andre. "'The 39 Steps' [Review]." *New York Times.* September 14, 1935, 8.
Sherwood, Robert E. "Silent Drama: Young Mr. Keaton." *LIFE* (humor magazine, not the later pictorial publication). November 16, 1922, 24.
"The Sight & Sound Top 50 Greatest Films of All Time." *Sight & Sound.* British Film Institute, September 2012. Cover article.
Slide, Anthony. "The 39 Steps." In *Magill's Survey of Cinema—English Language Films.* First Series, Volume 4, ed Frank N. Magill. Englewood Cliffs, New Jersey: Salem Press, 1980, 1723.
Smith, H. Allen. "Hitchcock Likes to Smash Cups." *New York World-Telegram.* August 28, 1937, 7.
Stone, Herb. "I Married a Witch" review. *Robert Wagner's Script.* December 19, 1942. In *Selected Film Criticism,* 1914–1950, ed Anthony Slide. Metuchen, New Jersey: Scarecrow Press, 1983, 85.
"'Strangers on a Train' [Review]." *Variety.* June 20, 1951.
Thirer, Irene. "'Mr. and Mrs. Smith' Gay Comedy at Music Hall." *New York Post.* February 21, 1941, 13.
"'The 39 Steps' [Review]." *BFI Monthly Bulletin.* June 1935, Vol 2, No. 7.
"'The 39 Steps' [Review]." *Variety.* June 19, 1935.
Thomas, David. "Robert Walker." In *The New Biographical Dictionary of Film.* New York: Alfred A. Knopf, 2003, 910.
Thomas, F-R. "My Favorite Hitchcock." *London Guardian.* July 24, 2012.
Thurber, James. "The Secret Life of Walter Mitty." In *My World—And Welcome to It.* New York: Harcourt, Brace, and Company, 1942.
Thurber, James. "The Unicorn in the Garden." In *The Thurber Carnival.* New York: Harper & Brothers. 1945.
Tinee, Mae. "'Rear Window' Like Peeking: Fascinating!" *Chicago Tribune.* September 6, 1954, Part 3:16.

Tolischus, Otto D. "Nazi Now Drive to Complete Their Program." *New York Times.* November 20, 1938. Section 4:3.
"'The Trouble with Harry' [Review]." *Variety,* October 12, 1955.
"'True Confession' [Review]." *Time.* December 27, 1937.
Twain, Mark. "The Stolen White Elephant." In *World's Great Detective Stories,* ed. Will Cuppy. New York: World Publishing Co., 1943, 314, 315.
Vonnegut, Kurt. *Slapstick.* New York: Delacorte Press/Semour Lawrence, 1976, 1.
Wallace, Susan Elston. *Ginèvra or the Old Chest [and related material].* 1894; rpt. USA: Brebook Publishing. no date.
Washburn, Charles. "The Nassan Sweepstakes." *New York Times.* February 7, 1937, Section 10:5.
Watts, Richard, Jr. "'The Man Who Knew Too Much' [Review]."—Mayfair. *New York Herald Tribune.* March 25, 1935, 10.
Wedemeyer, Dee. "William H. Gass, Author Known for His Inventive Use of Words, Dies at 93." *New York Times.* December 8, 2017, A-24.
Weiler, A.H. "North by Northwest' [Review]." *New York Times.* August 7, 1959, 28.
"What the Critics Think of Blackmail." *New York Telegram.* October 9, 1929, 10.
Williams, Dick. "Hitchcock Enters Realm of Whimsey." *Los Angeles Mirror-News.* February 9, 1956.
Wilmington, Mike. "'The Trouble with Harry [Revisionist Review]." *Los Angeles Weekly.* March 16, 1984.
Winsten, Archer. "Hitchcock Thriller at Warner Theatre." *New York Post.* July 8, 1951, 32.
Winsten, Archer. "Hitchcock's 'Trouble with Harry.'" *New York Post.* October 11, 1955, 46.
Winsten, Archer. "'The Lady Vanishes' [Review]." *New York Post.* December 24, 1938, 9.
Winsten, Archer. "'Rear Window' at Rivoli." *New York Post.* August 5, 1954, 12.
Winsten, Archer. "Reviewing Stand." *New York Post.* August 7, 1959, 32.
Winsten, Archer. "'Shadow of a Doubt' at the Rivoli Theatre." *New York Post.* January 13, 1942, 46.
Zinoman, Jason. "Highlights in a Year of Paradoxes." *New York Times.* December 26, 2017, C-1.

Documentaries

Affair to Remember: Cary Grant, Directed by Leo McCarey. A Bonus Feature (including the author). On Twentieth Century Fox's DVD 50th Anniversary Edition of 1957's *An Affair to Remember,* 2007.
The Art of Film: Vintage Hitchcock. DVD Bonus Feature. On 1935's *The Man Who Knew Too Much.* USA: Janus Films: Criterion Collection, 1999.
Beyond Doubt: The Making of Hitchcock's Favorite Film. DVD Bonus Feature on 1943's the *Shadow of a Doubt.* Universal City, California: Universal/Skirball Productions, 2000.
The Borders of the Possible. DVD Bonus Feature. On 1935's *The 39 Steps.* USA: Criterion Global Entertainment, 2012.
Danny Boyle VO commentary on 1994's *Shallow Grave.* Criterion's Channel Four TV Corporation/Glasgow Film Fund DVD, 2012.
Fitzgerald, Peter. *Destination Hitchcock: The Making of North by Northwest,* 2000. A Bonus Feature on Turner Entertainment Blue Ray DVD of 1959's *North by Northwest,* 2015.
Kemp, Philip. Bonus Features. 2013 DVD of 1935's *The Man Who Knew Too Much.* Criterion Collection.
Mystery Train: Hitchcock and The Lady Vanishes. DVD Bonus Feature with 1938's *The Lady Vanishes.* USA: Criterion Collection, 2007.
Rear Window Ethics: An Original Documentary. A Bonus Feature. On Digital Hd: Ultraviolet's 1954 *Rear Window.* 1982.

Index

Numbers in **_bold italics_** indicate pages with illustrations

Abe Martin 197, 199
Addams, Charles 167, 210
An Affair to Remember 228, 237
Albee, Edward 217
Alfred Hitchcock's Mystery Magazine 4
Allen, Woody 1, 7, 34, 148, 159
All of Me 87
An American Werewolf in London 188
Arsenic and Old Lace 176–177
Arthur 130
Ashby, Hal 220
Ashenden: or The British Agent 81–85
The Awful Truth 70, 101, 126, 161, 226, 229, 230–231, 233

Barrymore, John 118, ***119***, 121
"The Battle of Sidney Street" 57
Bazin, Andre 176
Beatles 15
Beckett, Samuel 26, 137, 198, 217, 252
Being There 220
Benchley, Robert 18–19, 55, 116, 166, ***167***, 228; drawing by ***18***
Bennett, Charles 8, 31–32, 33, 40–41, 45–46
Bergman, Ingmar 108, 164, 198, 204–205, 240
Berman, Pandro S. 130
The Birds 5
Blackmail **_Frontispiece_**, 29–44, ***30***, ***31***, ***40***, 158; uses of sound and 34, 35, 43
Blair, Walter 223
Blue Velvet 145–146
Bogart, Humphrey 185, 190, 238
Bogdanovich, Peter 135, 234
Bonnie and Clyde 16, 94
Bracken, Eddie 189
Brazil 171
Bringing Up Baby 66, 71, 85–86, 97, 98, 200, 217, 221, 234

Buchan, John 2, 73–74
Bunny, John 195
Buñuel, Luis 14, 183

Camus, Albert 83, 156
Capa, Frank 198
Capra, Frank 20–21, 97, 101
Carlin, George 247
Carrey, Jim 189
Carroll, Leo G. 179, ***184***
Carroll, Madeleine **_Frontispiece_**, 7–8, 61–77, ***76***, 81, 85, ***86***–92, ***93***, ***100***, 207
Catch-22 144, 171, 183, 217
Chabon, Michael 20, 110
Chamberlain, Neville 101, 105, 106, 109
Chaplin, Charlie 13, 16, 17–18, 19, 20, 30, 37; *The Circus* 107, 205; *City Lights* 46, 57; *The Gold Rush* 13, 242, 253; "In the end everything is a joke" 54, 116, 222; *Monsieur Verdoux* 120, 124, 144, 172, 176–177; *One A.M.* 232; *The Pilgrim* ***20***; *A Woman of Paris* 108, 145
Charters & Caldicott 95–96, 99, 100–102, 104–109, 111, 140, 148
Chinatown 144
Churchill, Winston 149
The Clock 178
A Clockwork Orange 139
Cohen Brothers 217
Cotten, Joseph 134–138, ***139***, 140–152, 175, 185
Cronyn, Hume 140–141, 146, 147–148, 162
Cuppy, Will 11–12, 251

Dali, Salvador 14, 62
Dall, John 154, ***155***, 156–163, ***164***, 165–168, 170–172, 185, 188
"The Dark Woman" 81, 82

Index

The Decline and Fall of Practically Everything 11
The Disaster Artist 8
Dr. Strangelove: Or, How I Learned to Stop Worrying and Love the Bomb 183
Donat, Richard **Frontispiece**, 7–8, 59, 61–77, **76**, 121, 135, 162, 207, 241
Duck Soup 97, 126, 157, 242

Ferguson, Otis 93, 95
Fields, W.C. 41, 48, 86, 133, 140, 150, 186, 189, 199, 202
A Fish Called Wanda 226
Foreign Correspondent 19, 55, 115, 116–117
Forsythe, John **212**, 213–216, 218, **220**, 221–222
French New Wave 189, 210, 251
Frenzy 5
Fuller, Sam 186

Gable, Clark 119, **120**
Gaslight 204–205
Gielgud 78, 79, **80**, 81–92, **93**
The Goat or Who Is Sylvia 217
Gogal, Nikolay 88
The Good Soldier Schweik 54
Goodbye to Berlin 81
Granger, Farley 154, **155**–163, **164**, 165–168, 170–172, 176, 177, **178**, 179–183, 188, 189–191
Grant, Cary 225, 234–238, **239**, 240–244, **245**, **247**, 248; Chaplin and 232; the example of self-referential parody 231; in-joke reference to real name 226; McCarey personality basis of persona 229, **230**; model for James Bond 227, 228; thrill comedy and 232–233; see also *The Awful Truth*; *Bringing Up Baby*; *His Girl Friday*; *My Favorite Wife*
"The Greek" 81, 83, 84
Guinness, Alex 177
Gwenn, Edmund 210–211, **212**, 213–218, 221–223

"The Hairless Mexican" 81
Hamlet 226, 233
Hammett, Dashiell 20–21, 46, 62
Harold and Maude 171, 183
Hawks, Howard 55–57, 71, 74, 85–86, 97, 98, 117, 119, 217, 226, 228; see also *Bringing Up Baby*; *His Girl Friday*; *Twentieth Century*
Heathers 184
Hedren, Tippi 125
Highsmith, Patricia 174, 177
His Girl Friday 195–196, 226
Hitchcock, Alfred **3**, **80**, **155**; actors as cattle 24, 58, 133; cameos **Frontispiece**, 4, 17, 41, 133; Catholicism 6–8, 58, 68, 71, 83, 108, 119, 143, 150, 157, 163, 168, 170, 181, 183, 201, 209, 219; cops 6, 38, 39, 71, 89, 190, 214; experiments 17, 155; famous locations 31, 41, 53, 69, 129, 225; favorite film 182; filmic use of art 31, 32–34, 38–39, 69, 73, 92, 105, 165, 180–181, 195, 204, 216, 229, 250–251; fundamental fears 6, 7, 8, 15, 24; German Expressionism 32, 33, 38, 49, 60, 61, 72, 73, 103, 111, 146, 199, 203; misanthropy 12, 25, 26, 43, 64, 103, 125, 134–135, 148, 156, 158, 175, 206, 214, 218; misogyny 12, 15, 29, 33, 158; mothers 7, 56, 126, 149–150, 159, 160, 181, 214, 216, 227; Poe and 9–13, 38, 42, 94; relationships and 35, 39–40, 41, 58, 64, 66, 67, 70, 97, 127, 128–129, 144, 148, 151, 163, 170, 196, 197, 198, 199, 200, 202, 207, 227
Hitchcock, Alma (wife) see Revilla, Alma
Hitchcock, Patricia (daughter) 182, 185, 186
Hooper, Johnson J. 216
Hope, Bob 52, 76–77, 79, 92, 107, 164, 187
How to Tell Your Friends from the Apes 11, 12
Hubbard, Kin 197, 199

I Am a Fugitive from a Chain Gang 52, 55
In a Lonely Place 185, 190
Isherwood, Christopher 81
It Happened One Night 20–21, 46, 63, 97, 101, 111, 117
It's a Gift 189, 202
It's a Wonderful Life 137, 142, 146

Kafka, Franz 94, 184, 187, 252
Kanin, Garsin 229; see also *My Favorite Wife*
Kaye, Danny 189
Keaton, Buster 15, 37, **41**, 66, 128, 157, 203, 208, 219; *Day Dream* 187; *Zero* 240, **253**
Kelly, Grace 194, 196–202, 204, 206–209
Kennedy, John F. 105
Keystone Kops 15, 16, 22, 70, 89, 232
Kind Hearts and Coronets 176–177
"Krazy Kat" 15

LaCava, Gregory 130
The Lady Eve 221
The Lady Vanishes 75, 95–113, 204–205; full circle and 225
Lake, Veronica 159
Lane, Anthony 11, 143, 173, 183
Laurel & Hardy **14**, 15, 21, 50, 51, 95, 101, 106, 195; *Leave 'Em Laughing* 52; Leo McCarey and 235; "Two Minds Without a Single Thought" 53
Laurents, Arthur 8–9
Leach, Jim 3, 4
Leigh, Janet **250**; see also *Psycho*
Leopold and Loeb 153–154, 156, 161, 167, 176, 188
Lewis, Jerry 189, 210
Lewton, Val 5
Lifeboat 17, 155, 172
Little Caesar 55
Lockwood, Margaret 97–99, **100**–105, 107, **110**–111
Lombard, Carole 66, 70, 76, 78, 85, 87, 92, 98, 105, 114–133, **120**, 221, 222

Index

Lorre, Peter 53–57, **56**, 59, 61, 78–93, **79**, **80**, **93**, 127, 165; Chaplin friendship 54, 79; "the disturbing likable villain" 49; Harpo Marx and 19, 78, 81–82, 89, 90, 92, 189; *Waiting for Godot* 54; "the walking overcoat" 53, 54, 88; see also *The Man Who Knew Too Much*; *Secret Agent*
Lubitsch, Ernest 37, 88, 122, 127, 131
Lynch, David 145–146, 217

M 49, 61, 72, 92, 127
"MacGuffin" 26, 73, 98, 99, 209, 217, 251; linking *Waiting for Godot* 26, 198, 209, 217, 252
MacLaine, Shirley 211, **212**, 218, 221
Mad Love 54, 56, 165
The Man That Corrupted Hadleyburg 137–138, 151
The Man Who Knew Too Much 45–60; see also Lorre, Peter
Martin, Dean 130
Marx, Groucho 206; *Duck Soup* 97, 126, 157
Marx, Harpo 19, 78, 81–82, 89, 90, 92, 189; see also Lorre, Peter
Mason, James 228, 231–232, 234, 241, 244, 245, 246
Maugham, W. Somerset 81–85
McCarey, Leo 101, 126, 131, 161, 226, 228, **230**, 231, 233–234, 237; see also *The Awful Truth*; Grant, Cary; Laurel & Hardy; *My Favorite Wife*
McCarthyism 139
Merry Widow 135, 142, 147, 152
The Miracle of Morgan's Creek 127, 140
Miss Lonely Hearts 209
Mr. and Mrs. Smith 66, 76, 78, 92, 114–133, 229
Montgomery, Robert 114, 122–133
Muni, Paul 52, 73
"Murders in the Rue Morgue" 10–13
My Favorite Blonde 76–77; see also Hope, Bob
My Man Godfrey 85, 87, 117, 130, 221; see also Lombard, Carole
The Mysterious Stranger 138, 147

Nelson, Willie 186
Nietzsche, Friedrich 134, 153–154, 158, 163, 167, 171, 172, 174, 182, 185, 206, 217, 252
Night Train 96–97
North by Northwest 225–248; coming full circle 249; *Notorious*' kissing scene spoof 240–241
Nothing Sacred 70, 87, 105, 120, 121, 229
Notorious 9, 158, 240–241, 244; see also *North by Northwest*
Nowell-Smith, Geoffrey 146

Our Town 134, 136–137

The Palm Beach Story 87, 222
Patinkin, Mandy 80–81

Peeping Tom 5
Perelman, S.J. 198
Perkins, Anthony **250**; see also *Psycho*
The Pilgrim 19–20
Poe, Edgar Allan 9–13, 94, 124, 202, 203, 210
Powell, Michael 5
Princess Comes Across 98, 121
Psycho 119, 138, 143–144, 148, 161, 180, 183, 208, 249–252, **250**
Public Enemy 55

Ray, Nicholas 185
Raye, Martha 177
Rear Window 192–209, **192**
Rebecca 115–116, 119
Redgrave, Michael 97–99, **100**–101, 102, 104–105, 107, **110**, 111
Renoir, Jean 105–106
Reville [Hitchcock], Alma (wife) 119, 130, 182; influence on 6–7, 16, 25, 211
Ritter, Thelma 192–194, 196–199, 202, 204–207
Roman, Ruth 179, 189
Rope 153–173, **164**, 185; "The Mistletoe Bough" and 167–171; modern audiences and 175
Rosencrantz and Guildenstern Are Dead 252
Rules of the Game 105–106

Saint, Eva Marie 229, 232, 236–238, **239**–244, **245**, 246, **247**, 248
The Saphead **253**
Scarface 52, 53, 55–57, 60, 73
Secret Agent 78–93; use of sound 84, 156; see also Lorre, Peter
See Here, Private Hargrove 177, 189
Seldes, Gilbert 166
Sennett, Mack 15, 16, 22, 43, 48, 89, 117, 129
Shadow of a Doubt 7, 12, 134–152, **139**; favorite film 148; *forced* to go on location 151; more Hitchcock darkness 175
Shallow Grave 249–250
Sherwood, Robert 15
Shoulder Arms 54; see Chaplin, Charlie
Simon Suggs' Adventure 216
Slide, Anthony 2, 8, 45
Smith, H. Allen 16–17
Stewart, Jimmy **155**, 157–158, 160, 163, **164**, 166–167, 171, 185, 192, **193**, 194, 196, 199–209
Stoppard, Tom 252
The Stranger 83, 156
Stranger on a Train 174–191, **178**, **184**; see also Walker, Robert
Sturges, Preston 51, 127, 140, 161, 189, 222
Suspicion 209

The Thin Man 20–21, 46, **47**, 59, 61, 87, 93, 117, 130, 234
The Third Man 58–59
39 Steps **Frontispiece**, 7–8, 59, 61–77, **65**, 225

Thomson, David 178, 183
Throw Momma from the Train 174–175
Thurber, James 160, 161, 166, 198, 228
To Be or Not to Be 37, 122, 131
To Catch a Thief 9, 36
Top Hat 98
Topper 240
Torn Curtain 162
"The Traitor" 81, 83, 84
Travers, Henry 140–141, 146, 147–148, 151, 160, 162
Travers, Linden 97, 109, **110**
The Trouble with Harry 92, 210–224, **212**; Christ-like painting and 213, 219, **220**
True Confession 98, 121–122
Truffaut, Francois 6, 170, 189, 203, 204; Hitchcock book collaboration 4, 9, 12, 25, 39, 52, 115, 143, 154
The Truman Show 137
Twain, Mark 12, 100, 137–138, 148, 150, 151, 244
Twentieth Century 20, 117, 121, 236
Two Week's Notice 241

Un Chien Andalou 14
Unfaithfully Yours 127, 161
The Unforgiven 157

Vertigo 125, 130
Vonnegut, Kurt 73, 83, 106, 124, 150

Waiting for Godot 38, 54, 124, 137; the "McGuffin" and 26, 198, 209, 217, 252
Walker, Robert 176, 177, **178**, 179–183, **184**, 185–192, 199
Welles, Orson 58–59, 76, 183
West, Nathanael 209
The Wheel Spins 99, 102, 103, 106, 109, 110, 111
Whitcher, Frances 223
White, Ethel Lina 99, 102, 109, 110
White Heat 188
Whitty, Dame May 98–99, **100**–109, 111, 204–205
The Widow Bedott Papers 223
Wilder, Thornton 134, 136–137, 151
Wonder Boys 20, 110
Wood, Grant 69, 70
Wood, Robin 55–57, 182
Wright, Teresa 135–138, **139**, 140–149, 151–152, 175

You Can't Take It with You 99–100
Young, Robert 85, **86**, 88–92, **93**

www.ingramcontent.com/pod-product-compliance
Lightning Source LLC
Chambersburg PA
CBHW051212300426
44116CB00006B/531